THE
Triumph &
Tragedy of
Lyndon Johnson

THE WHITE HOUSE YEARS

Joseph A. Califano, Jr.

SIMON & SCHUSTER
New York • London • Toronto
Sydney • Tokyo • Singapore

SIMON & SCHUSTER
Simon & Schuster Building
Rockefeller Center
1230 Avenue of the Americas
New York, New York 10020

10 9 8 7 6 5 4 3 2 1

Library of Congress Cataloging-in-Publication Data

Califano, Joseph A., date.
   The triumph and tragedy of Lyndon Johnson : the
White House years / Joseph A. Califano, Jr.
      p.   cm.
   Includes bibliographical references and index.
   1. Johnson, Lyndon B. (Lyndon Baines), 1908–1973.
2. Presidents—United States—Biography.   3. United
States—Politics and government—1963–1969.
4. Califano, Joseph A., date.
I. Title.
E847.C32   1991
973.923'092—dc20
[B]   91-24439
                                                          CIP

ISBN: 0-671-66489-1

To Mark, Brooke, Joe III, Frick, and Claudia

May your children give you the same
pride and joy you have given me
and
May each of you experience
the exhilaration and exhaustion
of spending yourself in a worthy cause

Contents

NIGHTMARE YEAR   251

genuine and consuming. It stemmed in part from a Texas youth in which he witnessed the effects of poverty and bigotry and in part from his southern populist's political gut. Equal opportunity became, for him, a constitutional obligation, and he pursued it with messianic conviction. His quest for racial equality generated as much resistance as his policy in Vietnam. For both he risked his presidency, and I believe that his dark moments after he left office were spent less in self-pity than in self-examination, wondering what he could have done differently to get the American people to understand his conduct of the war and to achieve greater racial equality.

Lyndon Johnson saw himself in a desperate race against time as he fought to remedy the damage generations of prejudice had inflicted on black Americans. He was always in a hurry because he feared that, once black Americans sensed the prospect of a better life, their acceptance of discrimination would turn to impatience and dissatisfaction with progress however real, and they would subvert their own cause.

He was in a race against time with Congress and the affluent majority of Americans. LBJ knew that the sympathy generated by John Kennedy's assassination and the huge margin of his own presidential victory in 1964 gave him a unique opportunity to change America, if he could move fast enough. He was always conscious that his days were numbered and that his political capital, however enormous as he began his presidency, was limited.

He felt entitled to every available lever, to help from every person, every branch of government, every business and labor leader. After all, as he often reminded us, he was the only President we had. He had no inhibitions in reaching out for advice, ideas, talent, power, support. He often saw traditions of separation of powers, or an independent press, or a profit-minded corporate executive, as obstacles, to be put aside in deference to the greater national interest as *he* defined it.

He wanted to control everything. His greatest outbursts of anger were triggered by people or situations that escaped his control—whether it was the Senate Foreign Relations Committee on the Vietnam War, southern Democrats on a civil rights measure, a union leader holding out for an inflationary wage settlement, the North Vietnamese refusing to negotiate, his daughter Luci deciding to get married before her parents thought she was ready, some anonymous leak that made it harder to pass a bill, or not being able to find me because I had forgotten to leave a phone number at the White House.

Johnson was haunted by the Kennedys, caught between the glorious memories of an assassinated President and the evident ambition of the brother who considered himself the heir apparent. Lyndon

Johnson set out to do what John Kennedy had said he hoped to do, and when he had done it all, and more, he couldn't understand why Robert Kennedy continued to despise him.

Johnson changed the country more than most of us realize. By the time he left office, he had pushed through Congress Medicare and Medicaid to provide health care for the aged and most of the poor; funds for preschool, elementary, secondary, and higher education; air, water, and noise pollution laws; measures to preserve land; civil rights legislation; food stamps for the needy; a massive housing bill, and a score of consumer-protection laws. He had articulated the concept of affirmative action, dramatized the blight of poverty amid unprecedented wealth, signed the Freedom of Information Act, and created the National Endowments for the Arts and Humanities, the John F. Kennedy Center for the Performing Arts, the Corporation for Public Broadcasting, several cabinet departments and agencies, and he had changed the role of the federal government in American life.

What Lyndon Johnson was about during his presidency was social and economic revolution, nothing less. To what extent he succeeded and how beneficial his successes were I leave to each reader to assess, and to the judgment of history.

What kind of a person was Lyndon Baines Johnson? What impact did his volcanic personality, his emotional highs and lows, his relentless drive, enormous energy, and thundering ambition for his country and himself have on those tumultuous years? What kind of complicated man led the nation through some of its most exhilarating and searing experiences? I hope here to provide an intimate portrait of the man and his presidency—his happy days as he sought to outdo Franklin Roosevelt, his hero whose likeness he hung over the fireplace mantel in the Oval Office, and his sleepless nights and nightmare year.

At the moment John F. Kennedy was shot on November 22, 1963, I was inspecting a dam in West Virginia as General Counsel of the Army. I dashed back to the Pentagon. By the time I landed in Washington, I was dazed.

Kennedy's New Frontier had given me special purpose and inspiration. Born and raised in Brooklyn, educated in Jesuit schools and at Harvard Law, I had signed on as a raw recruit in the political trenches after reading James MacGregor Burns's book *John F. Kennedy: A Political Profile*, in February 1960. I rang thousands of doorbells on Manhattan's Lower East Side and debated on behalf of Kennedy's candidacy for the presidential nomination before Democratic reform clubs. The other contenders were Minnesota Senator

Hubert Humphrey, Senate Majority Leader Lyndon Johnson, Missouri Senator Stuart Symington, and two-time Democratic presidential candidate Adlai Stevenson. In the ballots after these debates before liberal audiences, Stevenson invariably won big; Humphrey often got several votes; and, despite my impassioned oratory, Kennedy (like Johnson and Symington) rarely got any.

But Kennedy won the nomination, and I worked every night and through the weekends until November stuffing envelopes, making phone calls, selling buttons, and walking up apartment-house stairs distributing campaign literature. I stood in the rain to catch a glimpse of Kennedy during his stop in New York on the Saturday before the election, helped old people get to the polls on election day, and stayed up all night and through the next morning until Kennedy claimed his cliffhanger victory around noon.

As I went to bed exhausted that evening, I knew I had to be part of the Kennedy administration. On advice of a law-school roommate, John McGillicuddy (who in later years became chairman of Manufacturers Hanover Corporation), I wrote to Cyrus Vance, the newly designated General Counsel of the Defense Department, and eventually became one of Defense Secretary Robert McNamara's whiz kids. I quickly came to believe that no achievement was beyond the New Frontiersmen, as Kennedy and McNamara created the Green Berets to fight guerrilla wars, stood up to Soviet boss Nikita Khrushchev in Berlin and during the Cuban missile crisis, began to conquer space, and desegregated the universities of Mississippi and Alabama. In 1963, McNamara and Vance named me the Defense Department's representative to work with Martin Luther King's "I-Have-a-Dream" March on Washington that August. It was then I knew for sure that on that sparkling, crisp Inaugural Day, in a capital glistening with fresh snow, when Kennedy had spoken of handing the torch to a new generation of Americans, he was talking to me.

So, after the assassination, as I drove from the airport to the Pentagon, I ached not just with grief but with a sense that this bullet had snatched the promise of the best years of life from my country and from my generation.

I went straight to Vance, who was by then Secretary of the Army. I told him I intended to leave government. I didn't think a Johnson presidency was much to stay around for.

Vance's quiet smile did not hide his own sadness. "I thought that's why you wanted to see me," he said. "You're wrong." He had worked for Johnson when Johnson had conducted a Senate investigation of the "missile gap" between the U.S. and the U.S.S.R. "This town has never seen a President like Lyndon Johnson," Vance told

me. "Stay around for a while. You're going to see things move."
I didn't believe it.[1]

"I've got some work for you," Vance said. "Jacqueline Kennedy
wants the President buried in Arlington Cemetery. You should meet
the Attorney General over there tomorrow."

On Saturday I met a shattered Robert Kennedy. In pouring rain,
we walked the perimeter of a 3.2-acre site on the rolling hill above
Memorial Bridge and below the Lee Mansion, as I outlined it on a
cemetery map. The Attorney General then got in his car and I returned to the Pentagon. A call from McNamara was waiting for me.

"Joe, I want to tie up that land for President Kennedy so that no
one can ever take any of it away for any other purpose," McNamara
said. "And I want to be damn sure we own it."

"It's in the middle of Arlington Cemetery," I said.

"I don't give a damn. Get a title search made. Write a legal
opinion nailing down the title to the land. I want to sign the deed that
sets this land aside forever."

On Sunday I signed a legal opinion describing the results of the
title search, and prepared an order setting the 3.2 acres aside forever,
which Vance signed. Though it wasn't necessary, McNamara wanted
to sign the order as well. He was so distraught that he had to do
something to relieve his sense of helplessness. I took the order over to
Arlington Cemetery, where he was making certain the gravesite was
right in the center of the view from the bridge. Sitting in his car,
McNamara signed the order and handed it back to me.[2] "Thanks," he
said, and added, "We're counting on people like you more than ever."

I wasn't convinced by McNamara any more than by Vance, but
I respected them both and decided to stay for a while.

Happy Days

ONE

The Beginning

THE FIRST CALL came on November 4, 1964. I was working as Special Assistant to Robert McNamara. My office at the Pentagon was directly across the hall from his. That morning *The Washington Post* and *New York Times* were on my desk, their headlines proclaiming Lyndon Johnson's landslide over Barry Goldwater, 61 to 39 percent.

McGeorge Bundy, the President's National Security Adviser, rasped cheerily over the phone: "Califano! Can you get over here and meet with Bill Moyers [a Special Assistant to the President] and me at eleven o'clock?"[1]

"Sure," I said. "About what?"

"We want to talk to you about joining the White House staff."

Moyers and Bundy were waiting in Moyers's office. They said the President (whose only previous contact with me was a handshake in August 1964)[2] wanted me to take on two tasks: administration headhunter and White House expert on Latin American affairs. Moyers said my experience with McNamara gave me good lines to top talent, and Bundy thought work I had done on Cuba, Panama, and the Dominican Republic gave me a grounding in Latin America. I told them I would have to talk to McNamara. They urged me to wait until the President had spoken to him. I said I couldn't.

As soon as I returned to the Pentagon, I joined McNamara at lunch.[3] His response was almost brusque. "Out of the question. First, they should never have talked to you without talking to me. Second, the work you're doing here is far more important. There are only two jobs over there that would be more important: Bundy's and Moyers's. Moyers's job only if the President made it a domestic adviser, in charge of the legislative program, coordinating economic policy and domestic matters generally. Forget about it. I'll talk to the President."

Less than a week later, returning from a meeting at the LBJ Ranch in Texas,[4] McNamara told me I would not be going to the White House. "At least for now," he added. "But I fear we've whetted the President's appetite. So you may just have a six-month reprieve."

The second call came eight months later, on July 8, 1965, from Jack Valenti, another of the President's special assistants. "The President wants you on his staff," he said. "George Reedy [the presidential press secretary] is resigning today. Moyers is replacing him. The President wants you to pick up his old job."

"I'll have to talk to McNamara," I responded, excited but nervous and unsure about my boss's reaction.

"The President already has," Valenti chortled. "He doesn't make the same mistake twice. Get on over here."

At the White House Moyers and Valenti said that my new job would be to prepare legislative programs, manage domestic crises, and act as a general-utility infielder on the domestic scene.

When I got back to the Pentagon, McNamara told me to come right to his office.

"It's also important that you work on matters relating to the economy," he said. "The economic problems are bound to be severe as Great Society programs need more and more funds, since the cost of the war in Vietnam is likely to rise."

An hour later, McNamara called me in to tell me that he had convinced the President he should let me coordinate economic policy.

"What a job!" I gasped.

"It's not a job. With this President, it's not even a job description. It's an opportunity. You'll have to prove yourself to him to turn it into a job," McNamara said.

"What do you want me to do?"

"Take it. He needs someone to pull the domestic side together. It won't be easy. I assure you of this: you will never work for a more complicated man as long as you live. But you're also not likely to work for a more intelligent one. Anyway, you've been in the Defense Department four years. The change will be good for you. No one should stay in a job for more than four or five years."

Late that afternoon, Moyers called to say the President wanted me at the White House mess for dinner. "He's having a small dinner for the chairmen of the 1964 Great Society task forces and he wants you to have an opportunity to meet them."

I said I was planning to have dinner with a friend from Panama who was already on his way to the restaurant. I thought I'd best skip the White House dinner. Moyers understood.

Five minutes later, he called again. "The President told me to send a car out for your friend and take him home and for you to come here, period."

So went my first lesson: this President did not like people to say no to him.

At dinner,[5] Johnson listened intently as each academic spent a few minutes outlining the most serious problems and opportunities facing America and the President. Remarkably, at least in retrospect, the Vietnam War was scarcely mentioned. Everyone was confident we could solve our domestic problems. In only nineteen months after assuming the presidency, Johnson had made enormous progress on the Democratic party's progressive agenda.

The President, with whom I had not yet spoken, introduced me as a member of his staff. On my way out, he said he expected to see me at the LBJ Ranch for the weekend. As I drove home, I thought about my only direct experience of Lyndon Johnson in action.

On October 14, 1964, it was reported that Walter Jenkins, a long-time Johnson aide (as close to a White House chief-of-staff as the President ever tolerated), had been arrested a week earlier for making advances to a sixty-one-year-old man at the downtown Washington YMCA. The story broke less than three weeks before the presidential election and promised to fuel Goldwater's charges of corruption and improprieties in Johnson's past.

Around seven that evening, McNamara called me into his office. "Walter Jenkins was a member of an Air Force Reserve unit on Capitol Hill," he said, speaking sharply. "The President wants a copy of his Reserve personnel file immediately. Get it. Make damn sure that everything is Xeroxed and nothing is removed. Have one of your guys do the Xeroxing himself or watch it being done."

I called Air Force Deputy Chief of Staff for Personnel, Lieutenant General William Stone. "The Secretary of Defense wants a complete copy of Walter Jenkins's Air Force Reserve personnel record," I explained. "This is so sensitive I'm asking you to Xerox it yourself. One of my staff will come down immediately to help you. After it's copied, I suggest you keep the original in a safe in your own office."

Two military officers on my staff were still around, Army Lieutenant Colonel Alexander Haig and an Air Force lieutenant colonel. Rather than put a young Air Force officer in the impossible position of standing over a general in his own service, I sent Al Haig to monitor the Xeroxing.

As soon as we had a copy, McNamara and I rushed to Moyers's White House office. As Bundy, McNamara, and I gathered around a speaker phone, Moyers called Valenti at the Waldorf-Astoria Hotel in New York City, where the President was speaking to the Alfred E. Smith Memorial Dinner. Lady Bird Johnson was preparing a sympathetic statement supporting Walter Jenkins and his family.[6] When the President got on the phone, he expressed his suspicion that Jenkins had been framed or set up by the Republicans. He asked McNamara to read him texts of Jenkins's Air Force Reserve fitness reports signed by the commanding officer of the Capitol Hill Air Force Reserve unit. One was more glowing than the next.

"Well," said the President, "I'd better call Walter's commanding officer. He'll be shaken by what's happened to Walter. And, in any case, I know he wouldn't want to embarrass himself by making any damned-fool statements."

Moyers and Bundy smiled. McNamara and I exchanged glances. The commanding officer who had signed Jenkins's glowing reports was Air Force Reserve Major General Barry Goldwater.

I got up at 3 A.M. on Saturday, July 10, 1965, to shower, pack, dress, and drive to Andrews Air Force Base outside Washington to catch a presidential Lear Jet. Valenti, his wife Mary Margaret, and speechwriter Richard Goodwin were also on board. We arrived at the ranch just after 9 A.M. Johnson met us at the airplane and sent us off to our rooms. Then Mrs. Johnson offered us scrambled eggs and spicy deer sausage. When I demurred, she said, "I suggest you eat something now, young fellow. You never know with Lyndon what time the next meal will be." After breakfast we changed into bathing suits and joined the President at the pool, where he was swimming. His secretary, Victoria (Vicky) McCammon, sat on the side with her feet in the water.

The pool, directly southeast of the ranch house, was surrounded by a red-brick border, a concrete sidewalk, and Bermuda grass. The President was still in the water when I dove in. He was talking about the Senate's passage of the bill to create Medicare the day before. From the shallow end of the pool he shouted to me, "Are you ready to come help your President?"

"It would be an honor and a privilege," I called back.

In the early afternoon, the President, with me next to him in the front seat, took his white Lincoln convertible, top down, for a drive around the ranch. Johnson had changed to dry trunks and a clean shirt, but I was still in my one pair of wet trunks and a knit shirt.

It was incredibly hot; the dust clouds made it hard to breathe. But there was relief. As we drove around, we were followed by a car and a station wagon with Secret Service agents. The President drank Cutty Sark scotch and soda out of a large white plastic foam cup; I had a Coca-Cola. Periodically, Johnson would slow down, sometimes stop for a moment, and hold his left arm outside the car, shaking the cup and ice. A Secret Service agent would run up to the car, take the cup and go back to the station wagon. There another agent would refill it with ice, scotch, and soda as the first agent trotted behind the wagon. Then the first agent would run the refilled cup up to LBJ's out-stretched arm and waiting hand, as the President's car moved slowly along.

As he drove, the President would call his ranch foreman, Dale Malechek, on the car's Motorola radiophone.

"Dale, the Hereford in East Barley Field, I think it's number 481 [many Herefords were numbered on a horn], get on over and look at him. He doesn't seem to be eating properly and looks a little under-weight."

"Dale, on the feeding tree in the Fish Tank, get some more salt for the deer."

"Dale. This Goddamn fence at Dales Trap needs to be fixed. Get it done in the morning."

As we passed from one section of the ranch to another, Secret Servicemen would jump out of the car in front and rush to open gates so we could drive through without stopping.

We stopped at LBJ's birthplace, a small two-room building with a tiny barn behind, drove back for a fast ride on the airstrip and again around the ranch, ending at the ranch house around 2 P.M. Shortly afterward, we boarded a helicopter for the Haywood Ranch, another of Johnson's properties, and Coca-Cola Cove at Lake LBJ, part of a chain of artificial lakes set in central Texas, thanks to the persistence of Congressman Lyndon B. Johnson. We lunched and spent the af-ternoon and early evening on a thirty-seven-foot yacht. From lake-front properties and in small motorboats, wire-service photographers constantly sought to take pictures. Secret Service agents in black speedboats tried to keep the photographers away. Johnson took care to drink out of an opaque plastic cup, usually below deck, whether it was filled with scotch or Fresca.

We went ashore briefly at a house on the lake that the President called "Jack and Mary Margaret's," after the Valentis. As we walked through the house, the President stopped in a bright shaft of sunlight in the living room. He unbuckled his belt and twisted toward his right side as he lowered his pants and pushed down his undershorts, trying to look at his increasingly bare right buttock.

"Something hurts back there," he said, now exploring the surface with his right hand. "Is that a boil?" he asked me as I stood to his right. Astonished, I looked—"peeked" would be a better word—and gulped, "Yes." "I'll have to get Dr. [presidential physician George] Burkley to look at it," the President said matter-of-factly as he tucked in his shirt, pulled up his pants, and buckled his belt.

In the late afternoon, the President took me waterskiing. He drove his twenty-foot gold-colored speedboat up and down the lake and under a bridge with concrete supports about every ten yards. He drove faster and faster, zigging and zagging around the lake and between the concrete pillars. The faster he drove and twisted, the more I was determined to stay up. He threw me once. He was going so fast that I thought I'd split apart when I flew off the skis and hit the water. Determined to prove myself, I got back up and managed not to fall off again.

We returned to shore around 8 P.M. The President, with Vicky McCammon in the seat alongside him and me in the back, was now driving around in a small blue car with the top down. We reached a steep incline at the edge of the lake and the car started rolling rapidly toward the water. The President shouted, "The brakes don't work! The brakes won't hold! We're going in! We're going under!"

The car splashed into the water. I started to get out. Just then the car leveled and I realized we were in an Amphicar. The President laughed. As we putted along the lake then (and throughout that evening), he teased me. "Vicky, did you see what Joe did? He didn't give a damn about his President. He just wanted to save his own skin and get out of the car." Then he'd roar.

Around 9 P.M. we went to the Haywood ranch house for dinner. I was still in my wet bathing suit. The others, more experienced in LBJ's ways, had brought along a change of clothing. Near midnight we returned by chopper to the main ranch house, and the President asked me to come to his office. For half an hour, he handed me one paper after another, directing me to give them, along with his instructions, to various White House aides or cabinet members. When he finally retired, White House aide Jake Jacobsen gently took the papers from me and said he would carry out the President's instructions. I went to bed, almost twenty-four hours after I'd gotten up in Washington.

Life at the ranch would always be unpredictable. We never knew when we would work or play. In the pool, on the boat, during a meal, the President might give us an order to do something or to get an agency or department head to take some action. Breakfast was always early and on our own, but lunch could be anywhere from one to four o'clock; it might be at the LBJ Ranch, on the boat, or at one of the Johnsons' other ranches. The President usually took a nap, which could last anywhere from thirty minutes to a couple of hours. Dinner might be at eight or midnight and its location was just as uncertain. On Sundays we had no idea whether we would return that evening or Monday morning, afternoon, or evening, and we often departed on less than an hour's notice. Mrs. Johnson displayed ceaseless patience in accommodating her husband's spur-of-the-moment style.

That first Sunday, Johnson and I attended separate services, he at the First Christian Church in Johnson City and I at St. Mary's Catholic Church in Fredericksburg. Back at the ranch, Johnson held a press conference to name Major Hugh Robinson as his new Army aide. I had interviewed several black Army officers for the job only a month before and had recommended Robinson.[7] He became the first black military aide to a U.S. President.

We lunched at 3 P.M., the President napped until 6 P.M., and then decided to spend the night in Texas, so we spent the early evening driving around the LBJ and Lewis ranches.

After dinner, the President took me on a walk to see his third cousin, Oreale Ruth Keele Bailey. Cousin Oreale lived in a small frame house on the LBJ Ranch. The President took care of her. She was about seventy-seven years old and suffered mild dementia and hearing loss. Outside the house, Johnson shouted to her and then went in and sat on her bed. He talked to her loudly, teased her gently, laughed with her, hugged her, and lifted her off her feet. Cousin Oreale loved it.

On Monday morning, I met Johnson at his boyhood home in Johnson City, which had been opened to the public the previous May. He took me on a tour, describing everything with zest, insisting, as he stood over me, that I read two letters from his mother, which were framed and hanging on the wall. The first was written on November 30, 1934, to her son and Lady Bird, his new bride:

> Often I have felt the utter futility of words; never more than now when I would wish my boy and his bride the highest and truest happiness together. That I love you and that my fondest hopes are centered in you, I do not need to assure you, my own dear children. . . .
>
> My darling boy, I rejoice in. . . . the happiness you so richly deserve, the fruition of the hopes of early manhood, the foundation of a completely rounded life. I have always desired the best in life for you. Now that you have the love

and companionship of the one and only girl, I am sure you will go far.[8]

The second was written in April 1937 on his election to Congress:

> My darling Boy:
> Beyond "Congratulations, Congressman" what can I say to my dear son in this hour of triumphant success? . . . I love you; I believe in you, I expect great things of you.
> To me your election not alone gratifies my pride as a mother in a splendid and satisfying son and delights me with the realization of the joy you must feel in your success, but it [sic] in a measure it compensates for the heartache and disappointment I experienced as a child when my dear father lost the race you have just won. The confidence in the good judgment of the people was sadly shattered then by their choice of another man. Today my faith is restored. How happy it would have made my precious noble father to know that the first born of his first born would achieve the position he desired! It makes me happy to have you carry on the ideals and principles so cherished by that great and good man. I gave you his name. I commend to you his example. You have always justified my expectations, my hopes, my dreams.[9]

Afterward we drove around Johnson City, and the President talked about his hopes for America and for its poor people. A man was stumbling along the road, unshaven, dirty, and red-eyed. He looked like a drunk. Johnson turned to me and held his right thumb and forefinger within a hair of each other. "Don't ever forget," he said, "that the difference between him and me and him and you is that much."

We returned to Washington that night, arriving on the White House south grounds at one in the morning.[10] As the President said good-bye, he smiled at me. "They tell me you're pretty smart, way up in your class at Harvard. Well, let me tell you something. What you learned on the streets of Brooklyn will be a damn sight more helpful to your President than anything you learned at Harvard."

As he seemed to have concluded, I said goodnight and turned to walk away. I'd taken a few steps when Johnson called after me, "Now, you get on over here as fast as you can finish up your work for Bob McNamara. And I don't want any Goddamn leaks about your appointment until we announce it.!"[11]

As a White House car took me home, I pondered the impossibility of preventing a leak. Thirty or more White House correspondents had seen me with the President on Lake LBJ, at his Sunday press conference, at his boyhood home, and in Johnson City.

When I reported to McNamara in the morning, he told me to finish up my work in the Pentagon and take the next week off. "The President expects you to report to the White House on Monday, July 26," McNamara said. "I told him I needed you for two more weeks because I want you to have a week off. Enjoy it." He smiled. "It will be the last week you'll have off until you stop working for him."

McNamara's advice was on the mark. It didn't take long in Lyndon Johnson's White House to realize that for the President a minute was well spent, an encounter enjoyable, a day good, an evening memorable, only if it contributed to his goals. He wanted that same intensity from his staff. They had to be reachable and under his control at all times.

The telephone was Johnson's chosen instrument.* He installed direct lines to his top assistants from the Oval Office (both desk and coffee table) and his bedroom. This line was easily distinguishable from the clear buttons on our phone consoles not only by its red color, but by the letters POTUS (President of the United States) and by the fact that when the button lit up our phones emitted a constant single ring until they were answered. These POTUS lines easily earned the term "hot." If there was a slight delay in picking up, the President conveyed the impression that the phone hadn't been answered promptly enough. He was invariably annoyed if any of us were not at the other end to answer.

Soon after I arrived at the White House, around eight o'clock one morning, Johnson called on my POTUS line. Down the hall from the Oval Office, my office had its own adjoining bathroom, which is where I was when he called. My secretary, Peggy Hoxie, picked up. "He's not here, Mr. President," she answered a little nervously.

"Where the hell is he?" the President asked.

"He's in the bathroom, Mr. President," Peggy responded.

"Isn't there a phone in there?" Johnson asked incredulously.

"No, Mr. President," she responded, just as incredulously.

"Then have a phone put in there right away."

"Yes, sir."

When I emerged from the bathroom, Peggy told me to call the

---

* The sculptor Jimilou Mason had such a hard time getting Johnson to stay off the phone and sit still that she finally did a piece of the President running, holding the base of a phone in one hand and the receiver up to his ear in the other.

President immediately. Then she repeated what he had said about the phone. "Like hell," I responded. "Just forget about it."

The following morning, at almost exactly the same time, the President called me on the hotline. I was, unfortunately, again in the bathroom. "I told you to put a phone in that toilet," Johnson shouted at my secretary. "I want that phone installed this morning. Do you hear me?"

"Yes, Mr. President."

Within minutes, as I came out of the bathroom, Peggy was standing in my office, a little shaky, with two Army Signal Corps technicians from the White House Communications Agency. "The President wants a phone installed in your john immediately, sir," one of them said. I shrugged my shoulders, smiled, and surrendered. The phone, complete with POTUS line, was installed and functioning in less than an hour.

On one Sunday morning the President called while I was at mass at Holy Trinity Church in Georgetown. When I arrived home and got the message, I returned the call. After asking me if I had prayed for him (I had, but not as hard as I prayed for myself), the President told me I should never be out of telephone touch with the White House. I said I understood that, but it was only for an hour. Then he said, "The reason they have those Motorola radiophones in White House cars is so that I can get you at any time." From now on, he instructed me, when you go to church on Sunday, go in a White House car, and sit in the back of the church. Then, "if your President ever needs you," the driver can go in and quietly get you out so you can talk on the phone. So from then on, a White House limousine waited for me when I went to mass. The President, however, never called me out of church.

Johnson could not stand for anyone to be beyond his reach or not working. He didn't like his cabinet members to leave Washington at all, even for short vacations or personal trips. He summarily summoned people back from vacations or from home. He even ordered Secretary of Commerce John Connor off the Washington area Chevy Chase and Burning Tree golf courses on weekends. He said he didn't want an "Ike golf image" for his administration.[12]

The President's desire to control his staff extended to the way we dressed. He never hesitated to tell secretaries what colors or styles most became them, and sometimes he even selected dresses for them. On at least one occasion, he told Juanita Roberts, his senior secretary, that "all the girls in [her office] needed more hair spray."[13] He loved selecting designer dresses for his daughters, Lynda and Luci, and for his wife.

I had my own dress-code experiences with LBJ. The President called me into his office as he was autographing pictures. He showed me one of a group of us in his office. I was in a light poplin suit, standing out from the other aides and business and labor leaders, in their dark suits. "You look like an ice-cream salesman," Johnson said, "not like a presidential aide."

At the ranch one morning, the President was chatting with me in his dressing room. He stared at my tie, and said, "Let me have it." I looked at him, surprised. "Take the tie off," he said. "That four-in-hand knot looks like a limp prick. Let me show you how to tie a knot."

He loosened the tie around my neck, took it off, and tied it into a Windsor knot, in the process tearing the Brooks Brothers label off the tie. "I always tear the labels off so you can expand the noose easily and never have to untie a good knot," he said. He then took the tied tie, put it around my neck, under my collar, and tightened it. "There. That's a good-looking knot."

At this point Lady Bird walked in. "Look at Joe's tie," Johnson said, beaming. "He's got a man's knot now, not a limp one."

Mrs. Johnson looked at me and then at her husband, and said, "Maybe Joe likes his tie the other way, darling." With that, she had made it clear, nicely but quite firmly, that the President had over-stepped.

I learned fast that Johnson used every waking minute of every day. He'd start around 6:30 or 7, going through several newspapers, watching the morning television shows, reading overnight cables and the *Congressional Record*, with paper clips attached to passages that referred to his programs and to speeches he'd had us plant with members of Congress in support of his policies. He ate breakfast in bed, drinking several cups of tea and giving orders to one of his aides, in the early years Jack Valenti, then Jake Jacobsen or Marvin Watson, and in the last year, Larry Temple or Jim Jones. One of them would arrive each morning to be available from the moment the President awoke. He spent much of this early-morning time on the phone with cabinet officers, especially Secretary of State Dean Rusk and McNamara, and any others of us who were working on problems of the moment.

After 8 A.M., other aides would gather at the President's bedside when they had matters of pressing importance. If Mrs. Johnson had not gotten out of the couple's big fourposter before aides began arriving, she would patiently lie there next to him, bed jacket on, covers modestly pulled up to her chin. Extraordinarily for a man with such a large ego and intense sense of mission, LBJ deeply loved his wife. He liked to have her close by and, always accommodating, she made herself appear as comfortable as she could, though we all sensed how awkward she must sometimes have felt. Eventually, Mrs. Johnson would say, "Now you boys look the other way," or "Now you gentlemen get out of here just for a minute," so that she could exit to the privacy of her dressing room next door.

Johnson would continue working with one or two aides throughout his morning toilet. He'd get out of bed, disrobe, get into his high-pressure shower, bringing the aide into the bathroom outside the shower as he continued to discuss whatever was at hand. He would be talking as he emerged drying himself and continue, standing naked as he shaved, brushed his teeth with an electric toothbrush, and combed his hair. Each morning, he'd take a small plastic container filled with pills, mostly for his heart (he'd suffered a massive heart attack in 1955), toss the contents into his mouth, and go on speaking with them still there, making his point before washing them down with water.

Johnson worked in the Oval Office and presided at various White House ceremonies from late morning until lunch, which could be anywhere from 1 P.M. to late afternoon. After lunch, he would take a nap, usually lasting about forty-five minutes to an hour, for which he would undress and put on fresh pajamas. "The only way to relax is to peel off all your clothes and make believe you're going to bed for the evening," he told me.

He'd awake from his nap refreshed. Sometimes he would call to ask, "What's going on? Who'd you have lunch with? What're you doing?" Or to see if I had done what he'd asked earlier that day, or to issue new instructions. Then he'd shower and return to the White House offices, where he worked until late in the evening. Dinner, frequently shared by the aides he was working with when he got hungry, could be anywhere from 8:30 until after midnight.

Dinner would of course be earlier if there was a White House social event, which he sometimes turned into a working session.[14] At a stag affair for top executives of Fortune 500 companies, with a sprinkling of celebrities, including actors Gregory Peck and Hugh O'Brian (TV's Wyatt Earp), Treasury Secretary Henry (Joe) Fowler explained the President's "speaker-writer" exercise to the guests. A basket with slips of paper would be passed around each table. Each guest was to draw a slip; one would be marked "Speaker," the others would be marked "Writer." The President would call on each table's "speaker," who was to rise and tell LBJ what was on his mind. The others at the table were to write the President later. Johnson promised to read all the letters (and he did).

After dinner, the President called on the speaker from each table.

Some urged action on the economy, others supported the President on Vietnam, others offered help with education or the unemployed. When each had finished, the President led the applause.

Then one executive rose. "Mr. President, we've heard these briefings and we've seen these people in your cabinet. They are very talented, very bright, very wise people. But they all look very tired. Mr. President, in business at our company we require that our top executives each go away and take at least a month of vacation each year. I suggest you insist on that for your top people." We all turned to Johnson. His face clouded with a dark look familiar to those of us who worked closely with him. The President did not applaud and so commanding was his presence that no one else did either. He simply motioned for the next table's speaker.[15]

Shortly after midnight, the President took Peck, O'Brian, and me up to his bedroom. We were served drinks, then the President stripped naked for his evening massage. As he lay on his massage table, he read memos from his night reading* aloud, talked, and joked, sometimes raucously, in high spirits. At 1 A.M. Lady Bird appeared in her nightgown. Seeing us there, she started to back out, but Johnson waved her in to "Say hello" to Peck and O'Brian, which she did with remarkable grace, and then left. As he became drowsy from the late hour and the massage, Johnson finally motioned us out and called Lady Bird in.[16] He relished his wife's pillow talk and was lonely when she was not there during the night.

In fact, Lyndon Johnson hated to be alone, especially at night. As he confided to me over a late-afternoon lunch, "I don't like to sleep alone ever since my heart attack."[17] He would almost always have an aide or friend with him until he fell asleep at night, either on his massage table or in his bed, going through his night reading. If Lady Bird was away, the President would often call friends, like Vicky McCammon and her husband, and ask them to stay at the White House in the room next to his. Sometimes, on the spur of the moment after dining with them, he would outfit Vicky's husband in presiden-

---

* Each night, Johnson would have on his bed night reading often exceeding one hundred pages, neatly wrapped in big folders usually tied with ribbon. The night reading included messages to Congress and speeches to edit, and scores of memos from aides with decisions to be made by checking lines (Approve—, Disapprove—") or writing, "See me," "Call me," or some question, order, or epithet. He insisted that each memo bear the time as well as the date of writing. Because he went through his night reading with highly sharpened soft lead pencils, we could measure the level of his anger or impatience by the number of broken points apparent on any notes he sent back. Over the years I worked in the White House all but a handful of the hundreds of memos I sent him for night reading were acted on and returned to me the following morning.

tial pajamas (several sizes too large for him) and insist that they stay in Lady Bird's dressing room. "The only deal is," he would say, "you've got to leave your door open a crack so that if I holler someone will hear me." His severe heart attack had left him terrified of having another when he was alone some night on the second floor of the White House living quarters.[18]

TWO

The Decision

DURING MY FIRST WEEK in the White House Lyndon Johnson made the decision that would shape his presidency.

He had been under pressure to expand American involvement in Vietnam from his earliest days in the Oval Office. For many years the United States had supported South Vietnam's non-Communist government, led by President Ngo Dinh Diem, with economic and military aid and U.S. forces on the ground as military advisers. When Diem proved corrupt and out of touch, President Kennedy endorsed a South Vietnamese military coup, in which Diem was assassinated. That was on November 2, 1963. South Vietnam began a slide into political chaos. Its army was increasingly ineffective against the Vietcong, the Communist rebels supported by the North Vietnamese. After Kennedy's assassination on November 22, 1963, the Joint Chiefs of Staff pressed Johnson to bomb North Vietnam, but he turned them down, trying to keep our commitment limited. He did, however, approve covert operations against the North and he sent more advisers to South Vietnam to join the sixteen thousand Americans there when he took office.

In August 1964, a few months before the presidential election, North Vietnamese gunboats attacked an American destroyer on an intelligence mission off the North Vietnamese coast in the Gulf of Tonkin. The U.S. did not respond. Two days later, that destroyer, and a second one, which had come to its aid, reported that they were under attack from North Vietnamese gunboats. There was some uncertainty, but McNamara personally checked the report with the military commander in charge of U.S. forces in the Pacific, and at the Pentagon we were convinced that the attack had occurred.[1] This time Johnson ordered retaliatory air strikes against North Vietnam and asked Congress for a joint resolution granting him broad authority to conduct military operations in Vietnam. The Tonkin Gulf resolution received near unanimous approval from Congress (only Democratic Senators Wayne Morse of Oregon and Ernest Gruening of Alaska voted against it). But Johnson did not escalate further. He vetoed military requests for a bombing campaign against North Vietnam and refused to authorize any big buildup of American forces there.

In those days I was McNamara's assistant. I had listened as the Defense Secretary attributed Johnson's resistance to his desire not to make crucial decisions (such as military buildups) during the heat of a presidential campaign. "We don't want our American boys to do the fighting for Asian boys," the President had declared on the campaign stump.

The prospect of a Johnson landslide over Goldwater became more likely in the days leading up to the election, and we in the Defense Department expected the President to make a decision about Vietnam immediately after the election. We were poised to increase military activities there and bomb North Vietnam. But Johnson just kept asking more and more questions. In the eyes of the Pentagon he was a querulous wallflower, disappointingly reluctant to join the war dance in Southeast Asia.

Johnson was insisting that the shaky South Vietnamese government get more solid footing before he would approve any bombing of North Vietnam; otherwise, he feared that Vietcong reprisals for the American raids would topple the government in the South. He sent McGeorge Bundy to South Vietnam for a personal assessment. By early 1965, after the Vietcong attacked U.S. military barracks at Pleiku, killing nine Americans and wounding more than one hundred, Johnson concluded that the time had come to bomb the North.

In late February 1965, General William Westmoreland, the commander of American forces in Vietnam, requested two battalions of Marines to protect the U.S. air base at Danang. Johnson okayed the troops, limiting their mission to protecting the airfield. In March, Westmoreland asked for more men, and an expanded mission to conduct offensive search-and-destroy operations against the Vietcong. In early April, Johnson approved a secret and ambiguously worded National Security Action Memorandum, which permitted such operations within fifty miles of Danang air base.

At least one of Johnson's advisers saw the danger in this escalation. On May 17, Washington lawyer Clark Clifford, who had been an aide to President Harry Truman, wrote the President: "Our ground forces in South Vietnam should be kept to a minimum, consistent with the protection of our installations and property in that country." Otherwise, Clifford warned, "This could be a quagmire . . . an open end commitment on our part that would take more and more ground troops, without a realistic hope of ultimate victory."[2]

As Clifford had feared, the situation in South Vietnam continued to deteriorate. In early June the U.S. Ambassador in Saigon, Maxwell Taylor, cabled the President with a bleak report on the South Vietnamese government and army, which concluded, "It will probably be necessary to commit U.S. ground forces to action."

Taylor's cable could not have come at a worse time for Johnson. The House and Senate were passing his Great Society health, education, and poverty programs at a breathtaking pace, and the 89th Congress promised to be the most productive in the nation's history. Still hoping for some way to avoid a major war in Southeast Asia, LBJ began a lengthy, almost desperate search for alternatives. He read cables and memos, prowled the halls of the living quarters and office wing of the White House, and called Taylor back to face him down on the grim text of his cable. He popped in on a meeting of his key national security advisers, who were preparing for the Taylor visit. "Lady Bird is away," he said. "I was alone and I heard you fellows were getting together, so I thought I'd come over."

On June 7, the day before Taylor was to face his President, Westmoreland asked for a dramatic buildup of American forces in South Vietnam—up to 150,000 American troops immediately, perhaps more later—and an expanded combat mission for them. The Joint Chiefs seconded Westmoreland's recommendation.

Johnson plumbed his advisers for all the options. And to buy time to review them, he felt compelled to honor Westmoreland's request to send American troops on search-and-destroy operations throughout the South Vietnamese countryside, effectively lifting all restraints on their combat role.

By early July 1965, Johnson's advisers had given him three options:

1. Get out of Vietnam.

2. Continue with the 75,000 men there, and hope for some breaks.

3. Give Westmoreland what he wants: declare a national emergency, call up the reserves, expand bombing of North and South Vietnam, destroy rail and highway bridges from China to North

Vietnam, mine Haiphong harbor, and mount parallel diplomatic initiatives to negotiate a settlement.

Undersecretary of State George Ball wanted out. McNamara favored option 3. National Security Adviser McGeorge Bundy dismissed McNamara's program as "rash to the point of folly." Secretary of State Dean Rusk, who was prepared to support whatever decision the President made, tilted toward McNamara. But he wanted to go slow on heavy bombing of North Vietnam and hesitated to blockade Haiphong harbor.[3]

As the President brooded over his dismal choices, he asked Bundy for an analysis of the French experience in Vietnam. Why weren't we headed for the same traps? Was there any real difference? On June 30, Bundy gave LBJ a lengthy memo, which concluded that the situations were different: The French were colonials "seeking to reimpose . . . overseas rule"; by contrast the United States was "responding to the call of a people under Communist assault."[4]

Before he would decide, Johnson sent McNamara and Henry Cabot Lodge, his new Ambassador to South Vietnam, succeeding Taylor, who had resigned, to Saigon for one last on-the-ground look. On July 17, Deputy Secretary of Defense Cyrus Vance sent a back-channel, eyes-only message to McNamara in Saigon. It provided the first glimpse of the President's thinking.

Vance cabled that the "current intention" of "highest authority" was to approve Westmoreland's request, but not to submit to Congress, before January 1966, any request for "more than $300–400 million" to pay for the escalation because "[i]f a larger request is made to the Congress, he believes it will kill domestic legislative program." LBJ wanted McNamara "prepared to explain to the Congress that we have adequate authority and funds . . . to finance recommended operations until next January, when we will be able to come up with clear and precise figures as to what is required." According to Vance's cable, Johnson at this time thought legislation for a reserve call-up "would be acceptable."[5]

Johnson would have been infuriated had he seen Vance's cable, for it reflected decisions he had not made and revealed concerns he wanted to keep to himself. LBJ never made a decision until he absolutely had to, and he tried never to reveal his thinking until he had a place for every piece of the puzzle. He was anxious about maintaining the momentum of his Great Society at home, but he did not want anyone to know it. He feared political repercussions from his enemies on the right for not being aggressive enough in resisting communism and from his allies on the left for endangering the Great Society's progressive revolution by escalating the war. He would not have appreciated Vance's candor about the President's "intention" not to pay for any buildup in 1965.

On July 19, the day before McNamara's return from Saigon, Johnson had Bundy prepare a memo listing "The Reasons for Avoiding a Billion Dollar Appropriation in Vietnam":

> 1. It would be a belligerent challenge to the Soviets at a time when it is important to do only the things which we have to do (like calling reserves).
> 2. It would stir talk about controls over the economy and inflation—at a time when controls are not needed and inflation is not that kind of a problem.
> 3. It would create the false impression that we have to have guns, not butter—and would help the enemies of the President's domestic legislative program.
> 4. It would play into the hands of the Soviets at Geneva [the site of U.S.-Russian arms control negotiations], because they could argue that it was a flagrant breach of the policy of "mutual example" on defense budgets.
> 5. It is not needed—because there are other ways of financing our full effort in Vietnam for the rest of the calendar year, at least.

When he read Bundy's memo, Johnson ordered a rewrite to eliminate paragraph 3 and the parenthetical reference, "(like calling reserves)," in paragraph 1. Johnson wanted no paper trail disclosing his concern about the impact of a Vietnam buildup on his legislative program, and he was not as committed to calling up the reserves as Vance's cable had indicated.

In a somber July 20 report on his trip to Vietnam, McNamara pressed to escalate the war. He proposed sending an additional 100,000 to 125,000 men to South Vietnam. He wanted Johnson to declare a national emergency and ask Congress to call up 235,000 reserves and national guardsmen; increase the regular armed forces by 375,000 men; extend enlistments and increase recruitment and draft calls; and commit U.S. ground forces to all-out combat. McNamara favored stepped-up bombing of military targets and supply routes in North Vietnam; asking Congress for a supplemental appropriation of "$X"; and launching vigorous diplomatic initiatives to end the fighting. He laid out the risks of his recommendation—including the danger that an additional 100,000 men might be needed the following year. But he concluded that "the course of action recommended . . . stands a good chance of achieving an acceptable outcome within a reasonable time in Vietnam."[6]

Johnson met with McNamara and other key advisers the day after the Defense Secretary returned. Throughout the meeting a skeptical President quizzed McNamara and the others. What consequences follow from a reserve call-up? Why can't we get more of our allies to send troops? Are we heading for continuing stalemate? If we pull out now, will we have to fight with more troops and casualties at a later date? Have we tried everything else? What other alternatives are available to us? Why this number of troops? Why not more? Why not fewer? What will these troops really accomplish? LBJ kept insisting that "our mission should be as limited as we dare make it."

All the advisers, except Ball, supported McNamara's program. Nevertheless, the President kept asking Bundy and Ball "constantly to explore alternatives" to McNamara's proposals. As the meeting ended at one in the afternoon, Johnson asked Ball to come back later in the day with a full description of his proposal to pull out.

In the afternoon Cabinet Room session, Ball spelled out his alternative and summed it up this way: withdrawal will be less costly to the United States than trying to give "cobalt to a terminal cancer case." Johnson was troubled by the instability of the South Vietnamese government, and he shared Ball's doubts about Westerners' ability to fight a war in Vietnam. He regretted that we were embroiled in Vietnam, "But," he said ruefully, "we *are* there."

At this point, Bundy pressed hard for the McNamara proposals, which no longer included mining Haiphong harbor or bombing raids near the Chinese border. Much of what Bundy had earlier characterized as "rash to the point of folly" he now found necessary. Prior doubts about whether "we want to invest 200,000 men to cover an eventual retreat,"[7] he now dismissed, as a wary and worried LBJ repeatedly raised them.

For Rusk, the fundamental point was to stand by our word; that was far more important than the opinion or support of the non-Communist countries. But Rusk struck a responsive chord with Johnson by doubting "whether we should be too dramatic about the increase in U.S. forces."

"Calling up the reserves will require a certain amount of drama," Bundy countered.

As the three-hour meeting ended, Johnson seemed weary and frustrated as he wondered aloud "whether we could win without using nuclear weapons if China entered the war."[8]

Later that afternoon the President addressed the White House Conference on Education,[9] a subject, as he put it, "high among my own concerns . . . at the core of all our hopes for a Great Society." As the President spoke of his aspirations at home, Bundy was composing a memo urging him to announce the escalation as soon as possible, preferably by Monday, July 26. Bundy offered plenty of dramatic stage direction: "On Friday, or Saturday morning, we might announce that you are calling the [congressional] Leadership to a meeting Sunday afternoon or Monday morning, and expect to go [in person] to Congress Monday afternoon or Monday evening."

Bundy noted that McNamara was trying "to plan this whole job with only $300–$400 million in immediate new funds." But he reported the Secretary's belief that "our posture of candor and responsibility would be better if we ask for $2 billion to take us through the end of the calendar year, on the understanding that we will come back for more, if necessary." McNamara did not believe that the administration could get away with the "idea that a call up of the planned magnitude can be paid for by anything so small as another few hundred million." Costs for the following year would be "on the order of $8 billion."[10]

Nothing would trumpet the coming of war more loudly than a reserve call-up, and Johnson wished to avoid such a move in order to minimize the domestic impact of any escalation. He wanted his advisers to come to a consensus that matched his own inclination before he revealed his decision. When Johnson woke up on July 22, he asked McNamara for alternative ways to carry out the Secretary's third option.[11]

At noon, Johnson discussed Vietnam with the Joint Chiefs of Staff.[12] The meeting included this exchange:

THE PRESIDENT: But if we put in 100,000 men won't they put in an equal number, and then where will we be?
ADMIRAL [D. L.] MCDONALD [Chief of Naval Operations]: Not if we step up our bombing . . .
THE PRESIDENT: Is this a chance we want to take?
MCDONALD: Yes, sir, when I view the alternatives. Get out now or pour in more men.
THE PRESIDENT: Is that all?
MCDONALD: Well, I think our allies will lose faith in us [if we pull out].
THE PRESIDENT: We have few allies really helping us now.

Toward the end of the meeting, Johnson leaned hard on the Chiefs for restraint: "But remember they are going to write stories about this like they did in the Bay of Pigs. Stories about me and my advisers. That is why I want you to think carefully, very, very carefully about alternatives and plans."

Johnson then had lunch with McNamara; Rusk; Clifford; General Earle (Buzz) Wheeler, Chairman of the Joint Chiefs of Staff; Vance; and Valenti. Then he went with them to the Cabinet Room, where they were joined by the Army, Navy and Air Force secretaries, and two representatives from his Panel of Foreign Affairs Consultants, Arthur Dean, who had negotiated the Korean War settlement, and "Wise Man" John McCloy, former U.S. High Commissioner for Germany.[13] Again the President listened, probed, and played devil's advocate, trying to be certain that what virtually everyone was telling him to do was what he had to do.

In a Rose Garden talk to foreign correspondents early that evening,[14] Johnson returned to the battles he wanted most to wage and win, "the wars that we have declared on the ancient enemies of mankind: ignorance, illiteracy, poverty and disease," not just for "190 million people in this country . . . [but for] all the 3 billion people of the world." He was on the phone late into the night, however, still sifting every morsel of his Vietnam problem.[15]

The next day, McNamara suggested three ways to carry out his proposed escalation. One alternative did not require a declaration of national emergency or reserve call-up.[16] As he neared his decision, the President again huddled in the Cabinet Room with McNamara, Rusk, Ball, Wheeler, McGeorge Bundy, Bill Moyers, and long-time confidant-speechwriter Horace Busby, who would help draft the presidential announcement. Later that afternoon, Johnson met privately with Dean Rusk.*[17]

Early that evening, Johnson talked to John Chancellor, then NBC News White House correspondent, about becoming head of the Voice of America, and to Senate Foreign Relations Committee Chairman William Fulbright (D-Ark.) about the situation in Vietnam. Later he asked for all two thousand letters on Vietnam mentioned in the latest weekly mail summary, and helicoptered to Camp David for the

---

* After someone leaked views Rusk expressed early in the Kennedy administration, the Secretary of State rarely expressed his firm opinion in groups of any size. He would await an opportunity to talk to the President alone. Johnson valued Rusk's opinion and, rare for the President, he had almost complete trust in Rusk's loyalty. This was partly because Johnson knew Rusk was trustworthy and partly because Robert Kennedy had tried so aggressively to get Rusk fired. Johnson said that Kennedy began trying to have him fire Rusk in 1963, persisted throughout 1964, and, finally in the spring of 1965, as LBJ put it, "Bobby Kennedy came down to my little room [adjoining the Oval Office] and proposed . . . that I make Bill Moyers Secretary of State to succeed Dean Rusk." At the time (Moyers was thirty years old and inexperienced in foreign affairs), Johnson said, "I wondered if there were something wrong with his thinking processes." In any event, no testament to Rusk's loyalty could be more persuasive to Johnson than Kennedy's desire to see the Secretary fired.[18]

weekend.* Busby joined him there. The President spent much of Sunday morning walking and driving around Camp David alone, an unusual activity since he always liked people around. He attended services conducted by his minister, the Reverend Bill Baxter, shortly after noon.[20]

At five o'clock, he met with McNamara, Clifford, and Supreme Court Justice Arthur Goldberg, who had recently agreed to Johnson's request to step down in order to succeed Adlai Stevenson as Ambassador to the United Nations. They discussed whether to seek a UN resolution calling for unconditional negotiations to end the war in Vietnam. As the discussion turned to McNamara's recommendations, Clifford urged Johnson to "underplay Vietnam until [next] January." He spoke in cataclysmic terms: "If we send in 100,000 more, the North Vietnamese will meet us; if the North Vietnamese run out of men, the Chinese will send in volunteers. Russia and China don't intend for us to win the war. If we don't win, it is a catastrophe. If we lose 50,000 plus, it will ruin us. . . . [I] can't see anything but catastrophe for my country."[21] Johnson already knew Clifford's views, but he wanted McNamara exposed to them, because if the President did send troops to Vietnam, he intended to do so in a much less dramatic way than the Secretary of Defense preferred. Johnson returned to the White House late that night.[22]

It was the following day that I joined the White House staff. That morning in the Rose Garden, the President swore in Arthur Goldberg as UN Ambassador.[23] The President made much of Goldberg's sacrifice for his country and Goldberg made much of the vaunted LBJ arm twisting. Actually, it hadn't taken that much pressure to persuade Goldberg (John Kenneth Galbraith had tipped the President that Goldberg might be willing to leave the Court), but Johnson let the charade of tenacious arm twisting become a myth that took on its own reality. It nourished his stature as the Great Persuader, and enhanced Goldberg's status at the United Nations.

In his new UN Ambassador Johnson had a Jewish liberal who would serve as visible evidence of his commitment to Israel (which was increasingly isolated at the world organization) and perhaps muffle some of the left's rumblings about Vietnam. Goldberg was a world-class negotiator with deep roots in the labor movement, which he had represented for years. And his departure from the Supreme Court meant that Johnson could fill the vacancy with a trusted ally.

* Johnson had a weekly summary prepared of letters to him. Shortly after I came to the White House, and until the end of 1966, he had me send him a weekly summary of letters on Vietnam that McNamara received.[19]

After the ceremony, the President went once more to the Cabinet Room with Rusk, Ball, McNamara, Wheeler, Bundy, Central Intelligence Agency Director Admiral William Raborn and his deputy Richard Helms, Lodge, Goldberg, Clifford, several special assistants, and Vice President Hubert Humphrey. The long meeting centered on how to explain the escalation of the Vietnam War to the American public, Congress, and the world.[24] Only Johnson knew whether he would declare a national emergency and call up the reserves, and his reluctance was increasingly evident.

That night, Johnson did not sleep well. Three times he called the White House situation room, the nerve center for international crises, at 1:00, 3:30 and 7:35 A.M.[25] He wanted to check on bombing raids against a surface-to-air missile site near Hanoi and a power plant one hundred miles south of the North Vietnamese capital.

The President ended all doubts the next day, July 27. The morning began with a Democratic Leadership breakfast, at which he pressed to move his Great Society programs through Congress.*[26] At 10:30 A.M., he went to the Flower Garden to announce his nominations of departing Secretary of Health, Education, and Welfare Anthony Celebrezze to a federal judgeship and of John Gardner to Celebrezze's cabinet post. Celebrezze, the political pro, had done his work on the Hill well, helping push through the first major wave of Great Society legislation in health and education. Johnson expected Gardner, the Carnegie Foundation president, a prestigious thinker and liberal Republican, to attract a brilliant team to administer these programs.

Johnson took the opportunity to signal that, whatever his problems in Vietnam, the pursuit of the Great Society at home would continue: "Mr. Gardner will shortly . . . start administering the program that this good Congress has, or is enacting, and will also have a farsighted, 20th century plan for the Congress that is to come in January."

That afternoon, the President spent a couple of hours talking to Abe Fortas,[27] his lawyer and cherished adviser, about Vietnam, and

* When Congress was in session, LBJ held weekly breakfasts in the White House living quarters with the Democratic leaders and his legislative staff. They were sumptuous meals of perfectly poached or scrambled eggs, thick bacon, deer sausage, homemade bread toasted, freshly squeezed orange juice, and rich coffee. Near one end of the table around which we ate, a large posterboard hovered over the group from an easel. One part of the board was marked "House"; another, "Senate." Each major bill was named on a small card, which progressed from each side through committee, passage by each house, House-Senate conference, down into a bowl drawn on the board to signify final passage. Johnson used the posterboard as a prop while he encouraged, charmed, and cajoled the leaders to move each of his proposals through the legislative process.

pressing him to take the Supreme Court seat he'd urged Goldberg to relinquish. Fortas wasn't taking.

Shortly afterward, Johnson convened a National Security Council meeting to reveal his decision and cement a consensus behind it. After presentations by Rusk and McNamara on the overall situation in Vietnam and a brief discussion, Johnson took over the meeting to seek his advisers' approval for a more limited and restrained plan than most had recommended. He got it.[28]

He then called the bipartisan congressional leadership to a meeting at 6:45 that evening in the Cabinet Room. I was invited. It was my first closeup of him in action. Though he was tired and strained, I was struck by the theater, by the President's riveting performance, even when he wasn't speaking.

At the middle of the long cabinet table, leaning back in his highback black leather swivel chair, he noted somberly that "The situation in Vietnam is deteriorating." Then he sat straight up, and using his large weathered hands for punctuation, he set out five choices:

1. Use our massive power, including SAC [Strategic Air Command], to bring the enemy to his knees;

2. Get out on the grounds that we don't belong there;

3. Keep our forces at the present level;

4. Dramatically declare a state of emergency and request several billion dollars and everything else we might desire from Congress—authority to call up the reserves, acceptance of the deployment of more combat battalions; or

5. Do what is necessary to meet the present situation, but not be unnecessarily provocative to either the Russians or the Communist Chinese.

Option 5 would involve, the President added, doubling Army draft calls (from 17,000 to 35,000 monthly), extending Navy and Marine enlistments, requesting from Congress a supplemental appropriation of $1 to $2 billion, shifting already appropriated defense funds to the Vietnam effort and preparing carefully and quietly a sizable budget request for January.

For him, the President said, looking like a man choosing between being boiled in water or fried in oil, "the choice is between four and five." He called on Rusk and McNamara.

Rusk evaluated the chances for a negotiated settlement as slim. "Moscow has no real influence on the ground. Peking is adamant against negotiations; its remarks are bitter and harsh." While he thought Hanoi might be more inclined than Peking to negotiate, he added, that wasn't saying very much. McNamara described the worsening military and economic conditions in South Vietnam.

The President said he saw the disadvantage of option 4 this way: "If we're too dramatic about the buildup," the North Vietnamese would be able to ask the Chinese Communists and the Soviets to increase their aid and add to their existing commitments. "The advantage of 5 is that we give the military commanders what they need, get as much money as we need out of the budget pending in the Senate Appropriations Committee, and use our transfer authority* until January when we will go to the Congress with a full request." He added, "We will neither brag about what we are doing nor thunder at the Chinese Communists and Russians. Meanwhile we'll push with Goldberg and Lodge and all the other channels on the diplomatic side."[29]

Senator George Smathers (D-Fla.), Democratic Conference Secretary, said he had thought that U.S. policy was to deny the Vietcong victory and, at the same time, avoid World War III by not bringing in China and Russia. He asked, "Has our policy changed?"

The President, squinting (I learned later he resented the nasty campaign Smathers had run against Claude Pepper for his Senate seat in 1950), responded that our objective was "to support the South Vietnamese, not to take on the war ourselves," and that "there is no change in policy."

Senator Russell Long (D-La.), Majority Whip, said, "If we back out, they'd move somewhere else. Are we ready to concede all Asia to the Communists? I'm not ready to turn tail. If a nation with eighteen million people can make Uncle Sam run, what will China think?"

House Speaker John McCormack (D-Mass.) agreed: "I don't think we have any alternatives. Our military men tell us they need more and we should give it to them. The lesson of Hitler and Mussolini is clear. I can see five years from now a chain of events far more dangerous to our country if we don't fight."

House Minority Leader Gerald Ford (R-Mich.) wanted an explanation of the difference between options 4 and 5. Under 4, he thought that the administration would not be asking Congress for any money. The President corrected the Minority Leader: "We will ask Congress for money either way. Under 5, we ask for a reasonable amount now, see what happens during the monsoon season, and then come back in January. Under 5 we ask for no legislation, don't scare the Russians, and send in troops as we need them." (I thought the President was almost tart with Ford. I would learn that he viewed the House Minority Leader as one of the least thoughtful and most partisan Re-

* Presidential power to move funds from one defense account to another.

publicans in Congress, which prompted his now-famous crack, "Jerry Ford can't chew gum and walk at the same time.")

Ford pressed Johnson on increasing draft calls and extending enlistments. The President allowed that such moves were necessary "to use this period to show them they can't run us out."

Ford asked, "Under 4 you would—"

"Would call up the reserves now and send up a whole new appropriations bill," Johnson interrupted. "Under 5 we would simply put $1.8 billion or whatever into the appropriations [bill now under consideration] on the Senate side and then come back in January."

McNamara then said, "We don't know what the total cost of the war is going to be. Under 4 we'd have to ask Congress for a blank check. Under 5 we can be more specific, now and in January." McNamara knew that congressional Republicans would not want to provide a blank check for the administration.

Ford asked, "Under 5, no more money?"

McNamara responded, "Under 5 we would ask for one to two billion dollars now."

Senate Minority leader Everett M. Dirksen (R-Ill.) spoke. His voice was as deep and mellifluous as it sounded on television. He agreed "fully with your [LBJ's] premise." The first business, he said, was "to peel off the dramatics. When Woodrow Wilson sent divisions to Germany, he said, 'This is serious business, undramatic serious business.' But you must tell the people that this is serious business. The people are apathetic. We must stay in South Vietnam and keep Southeast Asia as our outside perimeter. The next line is Alaska and Hawaii. I'm in no position to make military decisions. The Commander-in-Chief has to make them."

Dirksen paused a moment as he and LBJ took each other's measure across the table. Johnson knew that Dirksen was saying: I support the Commander-in-Chief, whatever he decides, because it's his responsibility, not mine, to make the decision. But down the road, I'm free to assess how well the Commander-in-Chief fulfilled his responsibility. With that communicated through their eyes, Dirksen added, "I'm afraid that we are stripping our European components for Vietnam."

"Baloney on stripping," McNamara replied curtly, using one of his favorite words. "We are not stripping. It is not necessary."

"We shouldn't withhold information [from the American people]," Dirksen said.

The President responded, "We won't withhold. We'll announce as soon as troops arrive. Tomorrow I'll consult with Ike and get his views; I'll see the chairmen of Foreign Relations, Appropriations, and Armed Services. Then I'll announce my decision at a press conference."

It was going as the President had hoped. So well, in fact, that when Dirksen urged him not to wait on any request for money, Johnson was candid, "We'll ask for some right away. Then when you come back in January, you'll have a bill of several billion dollars."

Senate Majority Leader Mike Mansfield (D-Mont.) took his pipe out of his mouth. Referring to his notes, he began to speak. Johnson listened intently, sucking the stem of his eyeglasses, assessing the Majority Leader's views on the merits of the situation and attempting to prepare for the problems these views might signal in Congress.

Mansfield pledged his "support, as Senate leader, to the very best of my ability." He would not "be true to my conscience," however, if he passed up the opportunity to speak. Mansfield argued that the American pledge of which "Rusk so eloquently spoke" was to assist South Vietnam "in its own defense, not to take over that defense from the South Vietnamese." And "whatever that commitment," Mansfield added steadily, "it was abrogated with the assassination of Diem. Since then, there has been no government of legitimacy [in South Vietnam]." At this stage, Mansfield said, American policy in Vietnam should be made not on the basis of any commitment, but on the basis of what is in our national interest, which we should decide "afresh each day."

Mansfield's argument puzzled Johnson. He believed then, as he often told me later, that John Kennedy had authorized Diem's assassination under cover of "plausible deniability" (which left behind no record of presidential approval). To Johnson, the question was: Could the United States engineer the assassination of a nation's leader, and then walk away from its commitment to that nation on the ground that the legitimate leader of the people was no longer in power? But Mansfield could not then have known of Johnson's belief about Kennedy's role in Diem's assassination, so the question that was troubling Johnson could not occur to him. Johnson considered Mansfield an honorable man. On more than one occasion when some rough muscle was needed in the Senate, he would sigh in exasperation: "Why do I have to have a saint for Majority Leader? Why can't I have a politician?"

Mansfield argued that we were getting deeper into a war for which neither the survivors nor the rest of the world would thank us—"even if we win, which I doubt." He pointed out that we could "not depend on any nation of consequence fighting with us in this situation." He was deeply concerned about rifts that would arise among our own people over time, "particularly as racial issues, the use of draftees and partisan [politics become involved]." He glanced for just a second at Ford as he made the final point.

The Majority Leader's point about racial issues struck home with Johnson. Mansfield mentioned the possibility that civil rights leaders might merge with an anti-Vietnam peace movement. Johnson was sensitive to that danger, but he also believed that one of the reasons that some senators, including Senate Foreign Relations Committee Chairman Fulbright, were initially lukewarm, and eventually opposed to the Vietnam War, was that we were fighting for "brown people, Asians," rather than white Europeans.

Mansfield concluded by saying that he did "not believe we have any tangible national interest involved [in Vietnam]." He recognized "the decision is the President's," but he wanted "all of us to go into it with our eyes open."

Johnson was quiet as Mansfield finished.

Senator Bourke Hickenlooper (R-Iowa), Chairman of the Republican Policy Committee, broke the silence. He was convinced that "anything short of a result which will make" an effective buffer of South Vietnam against communism was "out of the question." He joined the chorus sung by many conservative Republicans and Democrats since World War II, Yalta, and Potsdam: "We win victories in war and lose in negotiations."

Mansfield and Hickenlooper represented the extremes: end the commitment now, or do everything possible to win right up to the brink of war with China or the Soviet Union. And both senators realized that the President wasn't going to pursue either course, so they offered "support," but not "approval."

"I'm in the same position," Johnson said as he bent forward, looking first at Hickenlooper, then Mansfield. "I supported the decisions in 1954 [which led to U.S. involvement after the French defeat], but did not approve of them. I opposed going in then, but we're there now," he said wearily.*

Hickenlooper returned to his doubts: "We're treating symptoms here. There's a danger we end up with a stalemate and lose again in options 4 or 5."

---

* LBJ was referring to a meeting of Secretary of State John Foster Dulles with the congressional leadership in 1954. Dulles discussed sending some American troops to Vietnam during the French crisis at Dien Bien Phu, but backed off in the face of objections from the members of Congress present. Then Senator Lyndon Johnson kept asking Dulles which nations would join the United States, and on receiving an answer that none would, expressed his opposition to sending American troops.[30]

"I've tried to negotiate," the President said. "We just can't get together with them."

"What are we trying to do?" asked Hickenlooper.

"To get the South Vietnamese where they can defend themselves. I've got to help Westmoreland," the President said.

"Let's get you united support," Speaker McCormack said like a cheerleading football coach through the cloud of cigar smoke around him.

Senator Long agreed. "They'll negotiate better if they know we won't cut and run."

At this point, the President embarked on a refrain I would hear often over the next three and a half years: "I've asked you to come here not as Democrats or Republicans but as Americans. I don't want any of you to talk about what is going on. Don't give the Communists in North Vietnam the opportunity to get huge relief. The press will be all over you. Let me appeal to you as Americans to show your patriotism by not talking to the press. I'm going to do everything I can with honor to keep Russia and China out."

The meeting ended about 8:30 P.M. Johnson had heard from his critics in both parties, but everyone had agreed to support him, whatever their misgivings, and now, grudgingly, he could proceed. After the congressmen left, Johnson ordered Busby to prepare a statement, "the essence of which should be that we are giving Westmoreland what he's asked for and needs."[31]

The President then went to his office to sign appointments, routine bills passed by Congress, and mail, ate dinner at about 10:30 P.M. with Mrs. Johnson and their close friends the Willard Deasons, and then worked on his night reading until after midnight.[32]

He began the next day, July 28, by reviewing a nineteen-point memorandum from Senator Mansfield, which had formed the basis for the Majority Leader's comments at the leadership meeting the evening before and which summarized results of a meeting Mansfield had held with key Democratic and Republican senators. Mansfield reported "a general sense of reassurance that your objective was not to get in deeply and that you intended to do only what was essential in the military line until January, while Rusk and Goldberg were concentrating on attempting to get us out. A general desire to support you in this course was expressed."[33]

The President asked me to have McNamara prepare a "brief and succinct" response to eighteen of the nineteen points to be sent to Mansfield that same day. In a cover note transmitting the McNamara memo to Mansfield and the other senators, the President responded to Mansfield's nineteenth point, that "McNamara has been a disappointment in his handling of this situation, probably because he is being used in a way in which he ought not to be used." In his note, the President wrote, "I consider Bob McNamara to be the best Secretary of Defense in the history of this country. Like myself, he is searching for the best solution to a very difficult situation."[34]

But privately Johnson was concerned about McNamara. In March of 1964, Senator Morse had begun calling Vietnam "McNamara's War." Over time, as the war dragged on, many in the press and on Capitol Hill had picked up Morse's term. The Defense Secretary had begun to show strain from the burdens of that charge. (In early 1966 the President said to me, "They'll destroy that man. This isn't his war. If it belongs to anybody, it's my war. Let's stop him from talking about it so much, and I'll defend it. Make it the President's War, not McNamara's War.")

Later that morning, the President, Rusk, and McNamara briefed members of the Senate Foreign Relations and House Foreign Affairs committees, and the Senate and House Armed Services and Appropriations committees.[35]

After the briefings, the President, accompanied by Bill Moyers and me, went to the Pentagon to hand out awards at the annual Defense Department Cost Reduction Ceremony.[36] On the way over in his car, Johnson complained that Rusk and McNamara were taking too long to give their Vietnam briefings. As he wondered what to do about it, his eyes lit up: "From now on I want you to have an alarm clock at those briefings. We'll set it for five minutes from the time they start. And when it goes off, they'll sit down!" (I thought the President was at best half joking until I went to the State Dining Room the following afternoon to the Vietnam briefing for the governors.[37] There, as Johnson introduced the Secretary of State, Marvin Watson put a large Westclox timer on the floor in front of him, set to go off after five minutes. He reset it for each of the remaining presentations, including those of McNamara and Wheeler.)

On the way back from the Pentagon, the President said that in addition to the Vietnam buildup he wanted to announce something newsworthy for evening television and morning papers that would please the White House Press Corps and those likely to be critical of the step-up in the war. "Let's announce the new head of the Voice of America and the new Supreme Court Justice," he exclaimed.

Moyers said he would put something together on the VOA appointment, whom we both knew to be White House correspondent John Chancellor. The President told me to give him a very brief statement for the Supreme Court appointment. But I didn't know whom Johnson had in mind. "Just write a statement that will fit any truly distinguished lawyer and scholar," Johnson said. "Someone like Clark Clifford. But make it general, leave the name blank."

It was my first presidential statement. It was after 11:30 A.M. and the press conference was scheduled to begin at 12:30 P.M. I raced back to my office and dictated at my secretary's desk as she typed it directly on her typewriter. I brought it into the Oval Office at 12:15. I found Johnson in his rocking chair and Fortas seated on a couch next to him. Johnson had called Fortas thirty minutes earlier and asked him to come to the White House.[38] I gave the President the statement. He didn't show it to Fortas, but read it to himself:

> . . . I will shortly send to the Senate my nomination of ——— ——— to be an Associate Justice of the Supreme Court.
>
> For many years, I have regarded ——— ——— as one of this nation's most able, most outstanding citizens—a scholar, a profound thinker, a lawyer of superior ability, and a man of humane and deeply compassionate feelings toward his fellow man. That opinion is shared by the legal profession, by members of Congress, and by leaders of business, labor and other sectors of our national life.

The President nodded at me. Mrs. Johnson came into the room, and we rose to walk over to the East Room for the press conference.[39] The President turned to Fortas, who had been stubbornly resisting his strenuous efforts to place him on the Court. Fortas had masterminded the legal battle that nailed down Johnson's election to the Senate by 87 votes in 1948. Since then, he'd been an LBJ intimate, and Johnson considered him the smartest lawyer in the country. "Abe, I'm sending fifty thousand boys to Vietnam today and I'm sending you to the Supreme Court. You can watch the announcement here on television or you can come over with me to the press conference." Johnson spoke firmly, not lightly, and the tone of his voice as well as the expression on his face made it clear that he would nominate Fortas, whatever his friend's wishes. Muttering about his responsibilities to his law firm, slouching his shoulders, and shaking his head, Fortas joined us as we went to the East Room without saying a word.[40]

As Johnson delivered his opening statement about sending fifty thousand young men to Vietnam, the need to send more later, and doubling draft calls, he revealed his own anguish:

> I do not find it easy to send the flower of our youth, our finest young men, into battle. . . . I have seen them in a thousand streets, of a hundred towns, in every State in this Union—working and laughing and building, and filled with

hope and life. I think I know, too, how their mothers weep and how their families sorrow.

This is the most agonizing and the most painful duty of your President.

Then LBJ spoke about the Great Society he was determined to build:

> . . . When I was young, poverty was so common that we didn't know it had a name. An education was something that you had to fight for, and water was really life itself. I have now been in public life 35 years . . . and in each of those 35 years I have seen good men, and wise leaders, struggle to bring the blessings of this land to all of our people.
>
> And now I am the President. It is now my opportunity to help every child get an education, to help every Negro and every American citizen have an equal opportunity, to have every family get a decent home, and to help bring healing to the sick and dignity to the old.
>
> As I have said before, that is what I have lived for, that is what I have wanted all my life since I was a little boy, and I do not want to see all those hopes and all those dreams of so many people for so many years now drowned in the wasteful ravages of cruel wars. I am going to do all I can to see that that never happens.

Despite the announcements of Fortas and Chancellor, the press of course concentrated its questions on Vietnam. One reporter asked about Oregon Governor Mark Hatfield's strong criticism that the United States had "no moral right to commit the world and especially our own people to World War III unilaterally or by the decision of a few experts." Johnson simply said he did not interpret the situation that way and hoped that Governor Hatfield and other governors would share his view after he counseled with them the following afternoon.*

---

* Hatfield's criticism persisted and sharpened when he moved to the Senate in 1967, and to Johnson it was as annoying as a fingernail scratching on a blackboard. I remember one Sunday in the White House living quarters, as Johnson and I watched an interview with Hatfield on a religious broadcast. Hatfield, a born-again Christian, told the interviewer that sometimes, as he drove along the vast empty stretches of Oregon, he was so moved by the beauty God had given us that he would pull his car over to the side of the road and get down on his knees to pray. The President slapped my knee and with a mischievous twinkle said, "Don't ever trust a sonuvabitch who pulls over to the side of the road to get down on his knees and pray!"[41]

After the press conference, Fortas lunched with the President[42] and we drove to his new house on R Street, across from Dumbarton Oaks in Georgetown. As we entered the hallway, Fortas pointed to a rectangular hole above the stairway. "That, my friend," he said, "was to have been our central air conditioning. Now we won't be able to afford it." It was the first of several complaints I heard Fortas make about the income he would forfeit from his private law practice. Nevertheless, Fortas, who on July 19 had written the President declining the Court nomination, would the next day write a graceful note of surrender, expressing his "profound gratitude for the confidence in me that you have shown by nominating me as Associate Justice—and for your generous remarks yesterday." Fortas recognized that "the adjustment will be difficult for me" and concluded his handwritten letter, "I can only hope that you will continue to see me and to call upon me for anything that I can do to help."[43]

The next day, when Johnson met with officials of the American Medical Association,[44] Vietnam was on his mind. The doctors had come to complain about Medicare, which they had opposed as "socialized medicine." The program was soon to go into effect amid administration doubts whether doctors would participate in sufficient numbers. But the President had another agenda.

Sitting around the cabinet table,[45] the AMA officials waited politely for Johnson to say something as he settled into his chair. The President took his time, gazing at their cold stares. Then he talked about his need for physicians in Vietnam to help serve the civilian population. Would the AMA help? Could it get doctors to rotate in and out of Vietnam for a few months? "Your country needs your help. Your President needs your help," he said. He got the reply he expected. Of course, the AMA would start a program immediately, the doctors responded, almost in unison.

"Get a couple of reporters in here," Johnson said.

The President described the AMA Vietnam medical program, heaping praise on the doctors present. But the reporters wanted to know about Medicare. Would the doctors support the Medicare program?

"These men are going to get doctors to go to Vietnam where they might be killed," Johnson said indignantly. "Medicare is the law of the land. Of course they'll support the law of the land."

LBJ turned to Dr. James Appel, the AMA president. "Tell him," he said. "You tell him."

"We are, after all, law-abiding citizens," the top AMA official responded, "and we have every intention of obeying the new law."

Johnson shook hands warmly with the delegation.

On Friday, July 30, on his way to the LBJ Ranch, the President stopped at the Harry S. Truman Library in Independence, Missouri, to sign the Medicare-Medicaid bill,[46] fulfilling a dream of Democrats ever since Franklin Roosevelt decided not to include health insurance as part of his original Social Security package. Touched by Truman's warm introduction and proud of his own achievement, Johnson said, "There just can be no satisfaction, nor any act of leadership, that gives greater satisfaction than this." Then turning to look at Truman, who had proposed a national health insurance program in 1948, he said: "And perhaps you alone, President Truman, perhaps you alone can fully know just how grateful I am for this day."

On Saturday morning, July 31, the President called from the ranch to tell me to come down that afternoon to discuss the legislative program.[47] Johnson was in the pool when I arrived and he signaled me to join him. We swam for a couple of minutes, then we stopped about two-thirds of the way toward the deep end of the pool. At six feet three, he could stand on the pool floor; at five feet ten I had to tread water because my feet could not quite touch the bottom.

His finger poking my shoulder as though it were punctuating a series of exclamation points, Johnson started talking. He saw America as a nation with many needs: "We'll put together lots of programs and we'll pass them. But there are three big ones I want to be damn sure you do. One, I want to straighten out the transportation mess in this country. We've got to start by getting our own house in order. There are too damn many agencies fiddling with transportation. I want to put them all together in one cabinet department."

I nodded, treading. He was so close to me, almost nose to nose, that I couldn't move around him so I could stand on the bottom of the pool.

"Next, I want to rebuild American cities."

I was breathing hard.

"Third, I want a fair-housing bill. We've got to end this God-damn discrimination against Negroes. Until people"—he started jabbing my shoulder as he recited each color—"whether they're purple, brown, black, yellow, red, green or whatever—live together, they'll never know they have the same hopes for their children, the same fears, troubles, woes, ambitions. I want a bill that makes it possible for anybody to buy a house anywhere they can afford to. Now, can you do that? Can you do all these things?"

"Yes, sir, Mr. President," I responded, not having the faintest idea how, but electrified by his energy and breathless from treading water as his finger against my shoulder kept pushing me down.[48] Not until months later, as I got to know him, did I realize that for this early exchange Lyndon Johnson had instinctively and intentionally picked a depth of the pool where he could stand and I had to tread water.

On Sunday, the President and I worked on a memorandum directing McNamara to get all the clerical and noncombat jobs he could out of the hands of men in uniform in order to keep draft calls as low as possible. The President had me call McNamara to give him the directive,[49] in part because he wanted both of us to recognize that our roles had changed, that now I worked for the President, not for Bob McNamara, and that as an arm and voice of the President I could pass orders to the Defense Secretary.

That evening, as I lay in bed at the LBJ Ranch, I realized that in our conversations in the pool and throughout the weekend, Johnson had not mentioned, or even alluded to, any limit to the push for Great Society programs, in spite of his decision to step up the war in Vietnam. Only once over the weekend, when we worked on the memo to McNamara, did Johnson touch upon anything related to Vietnam with me.

Events had forced Johnson to escalate the war in the middle of, as he described it, "the most productive and most historic legislative week in Washington during this century." He had completed the Democratic party's old agenda from the New and Fair Deals and settled Kennedy's New Frontier. And since sketching his vision of the Great Society, he had taken enormous strides toward fulfilling his own dreams.

Not surprisingly, then, Johnson joined the fight in South Vietnam with extreme reluctance. He feared the domestic repercussions either of a North Vietnamese victory or of putting the nation on a full wartime footing. For Roosevelt, World War II had stunted the New Deal; for Truman, the fall of China to the Communists and the Korean War had dashed any hope of progressive domestic legislation.

That night I began to realize what Johnson had truly decided: he had not simply decided to fight the war in Vietnam; he had made another big decision—to continue full-steam-ahead fighting for the Great Society. Unlike Roosevelt and Truman, Johnson was not going to let his war destroy his progressive vision.

While I could not fathom the consequences of the President's decision, I did realize as I dozed off that Johnson would pursue this course with all his legendary energy, commitment, and cunning, and that we were setting course on a daring and high-risk adventure.

THREE

Racing Against
High Expectations

FOR MOST AMERICANS in the early 1960s, racial tension had a southern accent. It had been southern legislators who had blocked civil rights bills; southern states that had posted WHITES ONLY at drinking fountains, movie theaters, lunch counters, and lavatories and relegated blacks to the back of the bus; a southern governor, George Wallace of Alabama, who had declared: "From this cradle of the Confederacy, this very heart of the great Anglo-Saxon Southland . . . I say, segregation now! Segregation tomorrow! Segregation forever!"

Lyndon Johnson's Texas roots gave him plenty of raw, firsthand experience with racial discrimination, but by the time he became Vice President he saw civil rights for black Americans as far more than a southern matter. He saw it as an overarching issue of his time. In the spring of 1963, when John Kennedy reported some advisers' concern about the political negatives of pushing for Negro rights, Johnson had argued that "civil rights for the Negro is a moral issue, not a political one." No issue had a greater call on the momentum he inherited after Kennedy's assassination and his own overwhelming election.

Johnson would often talk of the indignities that his black cook, Zephyr Wright, and his maid and her husband, Helen and Gene Williams, suffered during his Senate years, when they drove from Washington to the LBJ Ranch, forced to stay in Negro-only motels, not allowed to eat at decent roadside lunch counters. It made him angry, sometimes just about to tears. When his cousin Oreale Bailey attacked Earl Warren for his views on equal rights, Johnson told her that if he were to name "five of the finest men in the United States, the Chief Justice would be among the five."[1]

When civil rights legislation was pending, Johnson would make call after call, hold meetings into the night, and count congressional heads. He would press White House congressional liaison Larry O'Brien and other aides to repeat the exact words on which they based their conclusion about each member's vote. When his energies seemed drained, Johnson would turn again to the long, narrow tally sheet with each member's name printed on it and columns for "Yes," "No," and "Undecided." He would devour these tally sheets, thumb moving from line to line, like a baseball fanatic reviewing the box scores of his home team. It was never too late to make one more call or hold another meeting to nail down an uncertain vote.

LBJ would sit for hours in the evening with his friend Senate Minority Leader Dirksen, trading political tall tales and seeking the Illinois Republican's support. Dirksen enjoyed drinking Jack Daniel's bourbon, and the President would see that his glass was promptly refilled. Johnson preferred scotch, and he normally matched Dirksen drink for drink. But the President's drinks had only half an ounce of liquor in them; Dirksen's had an ounce-and-a-half.

In 1964, Lyndon Johnson (to borrow one of his favorite phrases) "shoved his stack of chips in the pot" to persuade the Senate for the first time in its history to impose cloture to end a civil rights filibuster. The move cleared the way for passage of the Civil Rights Act. Johnson had Democrat Clair Engle of California, who was dying of a brain tumor, wheeled in for the cloture vote. Since Engle was no longer able to speak, Johnson suggested that he signal his aye vote by pointing to his eye.

Hubert Humphrey, who was then Senate whip, told me later that he had reported to the President that he was finding it impossible to move one of his colleagues, who wouldn't even talk about his vote. The President asked him if his colleague's mistress knew of his position. "I didn't have the slightest suspicion that the guy had a mistress," Humphrey said. The President then snapped at him, "The reason that sonuvabitch won't talk about his vote is his mistress. He's been screwing a Negro woman for years!"

Johnson asked Humphrey where the Senator was.

"He's on the floor."

"Keep him there."

A few minutes later, the Senator got a call in the Democratic cloakroom. At Johnson's suggestion, Humphrey had positioned himself to overhear.

"Yes, dear," the Senator said. "But I can't. You have to understand. I just can't," he whispered. Then after listening for a couple of minutes, "Well, I didn't realize how important this was to you."

Humphrey said he knew he had one more precious vote. Whether the story is exaggerated or not, the conviction with which Humphrey told it reflected his awe at Johnson's vote-getting determination.*

LBJ understood how much of his and his party's political capital he was spending on civil rights. Scanning the banner headlines and glowing editorials on the night after he signed the 1964 act, Johnson remarked to Moyers, "I think we delivered the South to the Republican Party for your lifetime and mine."[3] And indeed he was defeated in five southern states in November 1964, four of them states the Democrats had not lost in eighty-four years. These losses didn't faze him. No sooner was he elected than, in January 1965, the Justice Department filed its first school-desegregation suits in Louisiana and Tennessee under the 1964 Civil Rights Act, and the President, now elected in his own right, turned his energies to voting rights for black Americans.

On February 9, 1965, the President met with Martin Luther King at the White House to hear a report on King's campaign to register blacks to vote in Selma, the capital of Dallas County, Alabama.[4] As a political leader preparing to persuade Congress to pass a voting rights bill, Johnson appreciated King's choice of Selma. Dallas County's population was almost 60 percent black; most of its 30,000 voting-age population was black, but only 335 out of the 10,000 registered voters were black. Voters could register only two days a month, after completing a form with more than fifty blanks, writing passages from the Constitution as officials read them aloud rapidly, and answering complex questions about the Constitution and American government. The county had effectively resisted a federal court injunction to end discrimination in voter registration since November 1963.

Johnson told King that he would soon send voting-rights legislation to Congress. He thought that the public pressure of Selma would help and hoped there would be no violence.

But there was violence. On February 26 a young Selma black was shot and clubbed to death; on March 7 Alabama state troopers used tear gas, clubs, and whips to halt a march from Selma to the state capital of Montgomery; and on March 9 a white minister from Boston

* Humphrey once described what he felt like being subjected to the Johnson persuasion treatment of argument, mimicry, humor, statistics, and analogy, with LBJ pulling one supportive clipping and memo after another out of his pocket. It was, Humphrey said, "an almost hypnotic experience. I came out of that session covered with blood, sweat, tears, spit—and sperm."[2]

was clubbed and died two days later. Johnson, appalled but not surprised, blamed George Wallace, whom he called a "runty little bastard" and "just about the most dangerous person around" with a "powerful constituency."[5] As television flashed pictures from Selma to horrified Americans, LBJ seized upon the awakening public sentiment to unveil his tough Voting Rights Act and press Congress to pass it.

On March 15, 1965, he went to Capitol Hill and outlined his proposed legislation in one of his most moving messages, "The American Promise." A number of senior senators had heard much of it in private conversations. Equal rights for American blacks presented a challenge "to the values and the purposes and the meaning of our beloved Nation." Assuring the right of everyone to vote was an act of obedience to the oath the President and the Congress take "before God to support and to defend . . . [the] Constitution." It was "not just Negroes, but really it is all of us, who must overcome the crippling legacy of bigotry and injustice."

> Somehow you never forget what poverty and hatred can do when you see its scars on the hopeful face of a young child.
>
> I never thought then, in 1928,* that I would be standing here in 1965. It never even occurred to me in my fondest dreams that I might have the chance to help the sons and daughters of those students and to help people like them all over this country.
>
> But now I do have that chance—and I'll let you in on a secret—I mean to use it. And I hope that you will use it with me.

Eyes steady and straight ahead, the President slowly intoned these words from the battle hymn of the civil rights movement, "And we shall overcome." For a fraction of a second the chamber was frozen in surprise. One southern congressman, seated next to White House counsel Harry McPherson, exclaimed in shocked surprise, "Goddamn!" Then almost everyone rose in a thunderous ovation.

Civil rights activity in the South accelerated throughout the spring. Johnson supported King's efforts to get a permit to march from Selma to Montgomery and called the Alabama Guard into federal service to protect the marchers. Not long after, as he delivered the commencement address at predominantly black Howard University in Washington, D.C., the President set the stage for affirmative action

---

* Johnson taught poor Mexican students in Cotulla, Texas, during the school year 1928–29.

with his analogy of two runners put at the same starting line: one who had been training for years while the other's legs had been locked in chains. He noted that fewer than half of black children lived to age eighteen with both their parents. For "the breakdown of Negro family structure," he charged, "most of all, white America must accept responsibility."

That summer, with the President hovering over them, the Congress agreed to a Voting Rights Act and sent it to the White House on August 4. That evening, a delighted Johnson visited Senate leaders Dirksen and Mansfield in Dirksen's hideaway Capitol Hill office to have a drink and thank them for acting so promptly on the bill. The next day, Johnson pressed King to devote his energy to registering black voters, a message he also delivered personally to several other black leaders.[6]

Johnson spent much of August 5 preparing for the moment of signing. He got ideas about the statement from everyone, including Horace Busby, Dick Goodwin, Moyers, Valenti, and me. He talked to Mansfield and McCormack. He wanted members of Congress and their families to be there and "a section for special people I can invite," like Rosa Parks (the forty-two-year-old black seamstress who had moved to the front of the bus in Montgomery) and Vivian Malone (the first black woman admitted to the University of Alabama in 1963). He told me to get "a table . . . so people can say, 'This is the table on which LBJ signed the Voting Rights Bill.'"[*] An exuberant President went to the Hill on August 6 to sign the Voting Rights Act in the Capitol's Rotunda. Military aide Hugh Robinson; Goodwin; Marvin Watson, the President's appointments secretary; and I crowded into the presidential limousine.[7] Johnson was beaming as he spoke of a new day, "If, if, if" he said, "the Negro leaders get their people to register and vote." I would rarely see him happier.

There was joyous pandemonium in the Rotunda. Live television covered it all as everyone shoved good-naturedly to get in the pictures. The nation seemed to cheer when LBJ said "to every Negro in this country: You must register. You must vote. . . . Your future, and your children's future, depend upon it." Johnson concluded, "If you do this, then you will find, as others have found before you, that the vote is the most powerful instrument ever devised by man for breaking down injustice and destroying the terrible walls which imprison men because they are different from other men."

Then Johnson walked, almost carried by the crowd, to the President's room, where, 104 years before to the day, Abraham Lincoln

* The table is now at the LBJ Library.

had signed a bill freeing slaves who had been pressed into any Confederate military or naval service. He gave the first pen to Humphrey and the second to Dirksen. There was such jostling for pens that the President used a different one not just for each letter of his name, but even for parts of letters. Then he signed his name a second time, as he kept gesturing for more pens. As he gave them to King and the other black leaders, he urged them to shift their energies "from protest to politics."*

Back at the White House, Johnson told me to make sure Attorney General Nicholas Katzenbach immediately mounted an all-fronts attack on poll taxes and literacy tests. Working around the clock, in less than a week the Justice Department filed suits in Mississippi, Alabama, Texas, and Virginia to have poll taxes voided, and suspended voter qualification tests in several states. Local federal employees were used as federal examiners to register black voters in cities and counties across Alabama, Mississippi, and Louisiana.

Buoyed by these triumphs, the President began planning a White House conference, To Fulfill These Rights, scheduled for June 1966. Well before, he met with Morris Abram, co-chairman of a November 1965 preliminary session, and Berl Bernhard, former staff director of the Civil Rights Commission. Abram and Bernhard asked the President what kind of a White House conference he wanted. The President paused for a moment. "In the hill country in the spring, the sun comes up earlier, and the ground gets warmer, and you can see the steam rising and the sap dripping. And in his pen, you can see my prize bull. He's the biggest, best-hung bull in the hill country. In the spring he gets a hankering for those cows, and he starts pawing the ground and getting restless. So I open the pen and he goes down the hill, looking for a cow, with his pecker hanging hard and swinging. Those cows get so Goddamn excited, they get more and more moist to receive him, and their asses just start quivering and then they start quivering all over, every one of them is quivering, as that bull struts into their pasture."

Abram's and Bernhard's jaws were ajar, just as the President wanted them. Clapping his hands together loudly, he said, "Well, I want a *quivering* conference. That's the kind of conference I want. I want every damn delegate quivering with excitement and anticipation

---

* Johnson gave out scores of pens at signing ceremonies. He needed so many at some of these extravaganzas that in the early years he gave out lots of fountain pens he hadn't used but which had previously been dipped in ink for authenticity. Then he started using felt-tip pens, which didn't have to be predipped in ink.

about the future of civil rights and their future opportunities in this country."[8]

On the evening of August 11, 1965, Lyndon Johnson had every reason to enjoy the satisfaction of monumental achievement. At least at home, things were under control: the Congress had passed his Voting Rights Act and major pieces of the Great Society were falling into place. He'd capped the day with a successful meeting, where he was at his persuasive, needling, good-humored best, getting wrangling governors and mayors to act together to battle the worst drought in the history of the Northeast.[9] He had demonstrated once again that LBJ could, when necessary, get all of us to "reason together" for the larger good, just as Isaiah, the prophet he quoted so often, taught.

That night, in the Watts area of Los Angeles, a highway patrolman arrested a twenty-one-year-old unemployed black man suspected of drunk driving. His mother rushed out on the street shouting at the police. Hundreds of residents gathered at the scene; many threw rocks, injuring some people. The event was unnoticed in the White House the next day, August 12, as the President soothed a Massachusetts congressional delegation led by Congressman Thomas (Tip) O'Neill trying to stop McNamara from closing an armory in Springfield, Massachusetts; swore in Henry Cabot Lodge as Ambassador to South Vietnam; hosted a stag party for foreign ambassadors on the presidential yacht *Sequoia*; and left after ten that evening for a relaxed weekend at the LBJ Ranch.[10]

That night, five thousand blacks rioted in Watts, burning and looting property and sniping at police. Los Angeles Police Chief William Parker, in a sideswipe at the President, stated publicly that violence must be expected, "When you keep telling people they are unfairly treated and teach them disrespect for the law."

By the morning of August 13, it appeared that more trouble lay ahead. I expected California's Lieutenant Governor, Glenn Anderson,* to ask the President to send federal troops. I assumed Johnson would want to avoid such involvement and keep responsibility to restore and maintain order firmly with state and local authorities. I wasn't to find out that Friday, however, because he didn't return my calls—the only time in the years I worked for Lyndon Johnson that this occurred.[11]

The rioting and looting in Watts intensified. Local police and sheriffs, now aided by hundreds of national guardsmen dispatched by

---

* The Governor, Edmund (Pat) Brown, was abroad, and Anderson was acting in his place.

Lieutenant Governor Anderson, were unable to stem it. Four people were dead, more than 100 police and civilians were injured and 250 rioters were arrested. Almost unnoticed, the black youth whose arrest had sparked the disturbances pleaded guilty to drunk driving in Los Angeles Municipal Court.

On Saturday morning the President authorized Bill Moyers to tell the press that he considered the Watts riots "tragic and shocking," and to warn rioters that their grievances could not be remedied through violence. Johnson continued to refuse to take my calls, withdrawing into the bosom of his family and intimate friends and aides— Lady Bird; Jesse Kellam, a close friend who ran the Johnsons' television station; Jack Valenti and Jake Jacobsen; his daughters, Lynda and Luci; his cousin Oreale Bailey; his business associate A. W. Moursund; and his secretary Vicky McCammon. He walked around the ranch with Mrs. Johnson and drove alone in his car and golf cart.[12]

In Watts, the police, Los Angeles Mayor Samuel Yorty, and state authorities were girding for a frightening Saturday night, and the State National Guard asked the U.S. Army for help. General Creighton Abrams, then Vice Chief of Staff of the Army, asked me for permission to "support" National Guard members with supplies and to use Air Force planes to transport them from northern California.[13]

Still unable to get the President on the phone, I told Jake Jacobsen the Guard was pressing the Pentagon for help. I also talked to McNamara and Katzenbach, who were on Martha's Vineyard off Cape Cod for the weekend. We agreed that we should provide whatever support the state needed and be prepared to send troops if the Guard couldn't control the situation. McNamara wanted a draft presidential order authorizing him to deploy troops, should that become necessary. Late that evening, McNamara asked for an okay to place troops at Fort Lewis, Washington, on full alert, and even send some to areas around Los Angeles.

I called the ranch again, but did not reach the President.

I got Deputy Attorney General Ramsey Clark to draft the order and proclamation, wired it to the ranch, and sent a Jet Star to Martha's Vineyard to stand by in case we needed to get McNamara and Katzenbach to Washington.[14]

California Lieutenant Governor Anderson called me several times demanding supplies for the national guardsmen. At one point, he charged, "If you don't provide support, the violence will rest on the White House's head." General Abrams called, echoing Anderson's pleas for Air Force planes and pilots to move guardsmen into Los

Angeles. He said the California Guard also needed food, trucks, tear gas, and ammunition from the Army.[15] Abrams wanted approval to help Anderson. Finally, I said very carefully to Abrams, "You've got White House approval."

"Do we have presidential approval?" he asked.

"You've got White House approval," I repeated, not wanting to reveal that I couldn't get the President to take a phone call.

I called the ranch and told Jack Valenti what I'd authorized. He was fearful that I'd done something the President wouldn't want. I complained to him that "I had more authority to deal with civil disturbances when I was in the Pentagon."

"The stakes were lower there," Valenti responded. "Here, when you act, you're acting for the President."

Valenti wrote Johnson a cautious note, protecting me:

> Secretary McNamara talked to Joe Califano and strongly recommended that the President send C-13_'s [sic] or comparable aircraft to transport California National Guardsmen from Northern California to LA. This, in response to a request made by General Hill, commander of the California National Guard. This request was also concurred in by General Abrams, Vice Chief of the Army. Request, on receipt of recommendation of McNamara, was given approval.

Valenti had not said that I'd given that approval, but the President called me from the ranch as soon as he'd read the note. It was 9:09 P.M. Eastern time, my first conversation with him since the disturbance had begun three nights earlier.[16] The President wanted no military personnel, no federal presence of any kind in Los Angeles. "Not one of our people sets foot there until you talk to me," he said. His voice was heavy with disappointment.

That night the rioting increased. Despite a curfew and the presence of 15,000 guardsmen and police, more than 20 people were dead by the next day, 600 more were injured and 1,400 had been arrested. But, as day dawned and Governor Pat Brown arrived in Los Angeles from Europe, the police and Guard were gaining control and restoring order.

The President called me early on Sunday morning. He said he had heard about the airlift, trucks, tear gas, ammunition, and supplies. He was deeply distressed, but he sounded more sorrowful than angry. He asked, On whose authority did the Army do this? I said I had authorized it, on the recommendation of McNamara, Katzenbach, and General Abrams, in response to the request of California authorities. The President reminded me who I worked for: "You work for the President. Not for McNamara. Not for Katzenbach. Not for Brown. And damn sure not for Yorty. Remember you work for your President."

Abruptly, he shifted gears and asked, "What's happening in Watts?" I reported on the violence and damage and said the situation was coming under control. He felt he had to issue a statement and he knew exactly what he wanted to say: "Congratulate Brown and city officials for restoring order; emphasize that law and order is a local responsibility; strike out against violence as a means of achieving progress in our society and against the denial of an equal chance to share in the blessings of our society."

The President was concerned that the riots not set back progress for blacks. He wanted Americans to understand the plight of Watts residents, "Out of work . . . living in filth . . . homes torn up." The President told me to call several black leaders—King; Whitney Young, head of the National Urban League; Roy Wilkins, executive director of the National Association for the Advancement of Colored People; A. Philip Randolph, head of the Brotherhood of Sleeping Car Porters—and ask them to condemn the violence.

Johnson talked about his concern that "Negroes will end up pissing in the aisles of the Senate," and making fools of themselves, the way, he told me, they had after the Civil War and during Reconstruction. He was worried that just as government was moving to help them, "the Negroes will once again take unwise actions out of frustration, impatience, and anger." He feared that the riots would make it more difficult to pass Great Society legislation and threaten the gains we'd already made.

What came through to me was how much Watts had depressed him. Johnson lived his presidency in a race against time. He could never get his programs to and through Congress fast enough; once they were passed, we could never get them in operation as rapidly as he ordered. On civil rights matters, he was at his most demanding. He knew it was essential to arouse the oppressed, and that, once aroused, their clock ticked impatiently. I began to grasp how acutely Johnson feared that the reforms to which he had dedicated his presidency were in mortal danger, not only from those who opposed, but from those he was trying to help.

Johnson told me to have Dick Goodwin write his statement. When the President called thirty minutes later to hear the draft, I told him the Coast Guard was searching for Goodwin, who was sailing in the waters off Martha's Vineyard. "We ought to blow up that Goddamned island," Johnson said.

Then the President talked about a wide variety of subjects, some related, some of no relevance to Watts, like his admonition to "remember one thing, always be good to Everett Dirksen, always. He's good to us." He wanted to be certain Governor Brown kept his eye on the rest of California and didn't let Ronald Reagan, the likely Republican gubernatorial candidate in 1966, make political hay out of the riots. He told me to ask Brown to name John Mc-Cone chairman of a state commission of inquiry into the riots: "An ex-CIA Director, conservative, if he says no communist conspiracy and describes the conditions in Watts, we'll be able to help those Negroes out there." He closed with words I heard at least once most every day I worked for him, "Do it now. Today. Not tomorrow. Not next week."[17]

A few days later, the President instructed me "in total secrecy, absolutely no leaks" (also words I heard from him almost daily), to assemble a package of federal programs to deal with the underlying causes of the riots in Watts. He wanted the Defense Department to train the National Guard in every state to handle civil disturbances and to issue standard orders restricting the use of live ammunition.[18]

White House counsel Lee White and I assembled a package of federal programs in remedial education, health care, jobs, small-business development, surplus food, housing, and pilot child-care centers, designed, as I put it in my memo to the President, to "provide care for children; thus freeing mothers for training and employment opportunities."[19]

LBJ worried about how the American public would react to putting any more social programs into Watts. He didn't want to do anything that might lay him open to charges of encouraging others to riot. On August 20, a few days before he announced his program, he compared the rioters to Ku Klux Klansmen: "A rioter with a Molotov cocktail in his hands is not fighting for civil rights any more than a Klansman with a sheet on his back and a mask on his face. They are both . . . lawbreakers, destroyers of constitutional rights and liberties, and ultimately destroyers of a free America." With this calculated prologue, less than a week later the President announced the program of social services for Watts.

But LBJ didn't heave any sigh of relief. He had sent Undersecretary of Commerce LeRoy Collins, a former Florida governor who had headed the Community Relations Service, to Los Angeles. Collins's confidential report to the President on Watts concluded with a grim warning that Johnson brooded over for weeks:

. . . the biggest and most dangerous ingredient is a feeling
on the part of the Negro community that they are "out of
it." They will continue to risk riots . . . until [they have] a
genuine example of participation in the affairs of the community at large.

And, what is even more sobering, this problem to one
degree or another is multiplied in every city in this country.[20]

Soon after Watts, I got a vivid example of the historical importance Lyndon Johnson attached to his own identification with the
cause of equal rights. He was not going to entrust this work to anyone, and that included his Vice President.

Relations between presidents and vice presidents are difficult,
particularly when the vice president has a politically independent base
and hopes for the future. No matter how much presidents gussy up
the status of their running mates, vice presidents are nagging remind-
ers of presidential mortality, cast into a post with few serious duties
and plenty of time to sulk in the shadows.

I knew how rude and demeaning some of Kennedy's staff had
been to LBJ. Kennedy's appointments secretary Kenneth O'Donnell
had insisted that the White House clear every request the Vice President made of the Pentagon, even the most routine. The Kennedy
staff rarely gave Johnson more than five minutes' notice of cabinet or
National Security Council meetings, and often invited Vice President
and Mrs. Johnson to social events at the last minute. On the few
occasions when Vice President Johnson was asked to speak near the
end of any meeting, he complained that Robert Kennedy would stand
up to leave, and interrupt, "Well, this meeting has run much too
long." LBJ made no bones about how miserable he'd been as Vice
President.[21]

Because of the way he'd been humiliated, I thought Johnson
would treat Hubert Humphrey differently. And he did, for a brief
time. But within weeks of Johnson's inauguration, Jack Valenti told
me that all vice presidential requests for support from the Pentagon,
even those for such routine items as transportation or mess aides to
serve meals, needed White House approval, an order that surely came
from LBJ. Even this did not prepare me for my experiences on
Johnson's staff.

On February 5, 1965, two weeks after his inauguration, LBJ had
created the President's Council on Equal Opportunity to coordinate all
of the administration's civil rights activities and had named Hum-

phrey its chairman, calling the Vice President his point man on civil rights. LBJ also had appointed Humphrey chairman of the President's Committee on Equal Employment Opportunity, which he himself had chaired in the Kennedy administration. This committee was charged with eliminating job discrimination by the government and its contractors. These appointments put the Vice President at the center of the administration's civil rights action.

In August 1965, the President asked me to "get with Nick Katzenbach" and recommend a more effective way to organize the government's civil rights efforts.*[22] Our work took on whirlwind momentum when Humphrey sent the President an ebullient memo on September 17, 1965. Humphrey described meetings he had set up with cabinet officers and agency heads, and directives he was giving them to end discrimination in education and employment, collect statistics on black participation in federal programs, and enforce the 1964 Civil Rights Act's mandate to wipe out discrimination in federally assisted programs, including schools, hospitals, and state and local welfare services.[23]

The next day the President and I had a one-hour, midafternoon lunch in the White House living quarters.[24] He was full of steam about the need to reorganize the government's civil rights effort. He complained about the inadequate effort of the civil rights leaders to register voters. He said we needed fair-housing legislation ("getting Congress to pass a law is a permanent national commitment; a presidential executive order can easily be changed"). But everything, he stressed, depended on reshuffling civil rights responsibilities. I got the message: Civil rights was a centerpiece of his administration; he had put his presidency on the line. He knew he had the guts, toughness, and ability to endure the pain that a civil rights revolution would inflict. But he wasn't sure that Humphrey did and, in any case, he had decided not to entrust this effort to anyone but himself.

The going was getting tougher on civil rights, the President cautioned. To make his point, he launched into a rambling conversation about his meeting the day before with Walter Reuther, the pas-

---

* Over the preceding few years an array of executive orders and new laws had vested the executive branch with a bewildering number of agencies with civil rights responsibilities, including: the Civil Rights Division in the Justice Department, U.S. Commission on Civil Rights, President's Committee on Equal Opportunity in Housing, President's Committee on Equal Employment Opportunity, Community Relations Service in the Commerce Department, Equal Employment Opportunity Commission, and President's Council on Equal Opportunity.

sionate liberal leader of the United Auto Workers, whom Johnson described affectionately as "a bomb thrower."[25]

Reuther had urged the President to mount a massive program to rebuild urban America,[26] and warned that without such an effort blacks would come out of the ghettos and burn the cities to the ground. After telling me this, Johnson said, "You know the difference between Hubert and me? When Hubert sits across from Reuther and Reuther's got that limp hand* stuck in his pocket and starts talking about burning down the cities if billions of federal dollars aren't poured into them, Hubert will sit there smiling away and thinking all the time, 'How can I get his hand out of his pocket so I can shake it?'

"Well, when Reuther is sitting in the Oval Office telling me that, I'm sitting in my rocker, smiling and thinking all the time, 'How can I get that hand out of his pocket—so I can cut his balls off!' " Johnson recounted the story with such zest that we both laughed. But I couldn't miss the point: Humphrey was just not tough enough to deal with upcoming civil rights tensions.

As we finished our Saturday lunch, Johnson said, "I want you and Nick to put together a plan and get the civil rights programs out from under the Vice President. He's got enough other things to do."

I talked to Katzenbach early Monday morning.[27] With White House counsel Lee White, we frantically assembled a reorganization plan, which I sent to the President that evening. The plan stripped the Vice President of all his civil rights responsibilities. It abolished the two commissions that Humphrey chaired, shifted coordinating responsibility to the Attorney General, and directed departments and agencies to handle civil rights for programs within their jurisdiction. The President liked most of the plan, and he scheduled a meeting with the Vice President, Katzenbach, White, and me for Wednesday, September 22, at 12:15 P.M.[28] Humphrey had no idea what the session was to be about.

Johnson sat in his rocker, holding a copy of the proposed plan in his right hand, using it as a set of talking points. He looked straight at the Vice President, who was sitting on the couch to his right. Johnson said he'd been thinking a lot about the need to strengthen our civil rights efforts and talking to people who were deeply interested in the area.

"*They say*, Hubert," Johnson continued, employing a technique ("they say") to which he often resorted in broaching ideas he antic-

---

* A would-be assassin shot Reuther in 1948 and the labor leader never regained full use of his right arm.

ipated would be unpalatable to his listener, "that the best way to strengthen these programs and speed up Negro rights would be to fold up a lot of the responsibilities you've got and put them on the Attorney General's shoulders."

There was an almost audible gasp from the Vice President.

"*They say*, Hubert," Johnson added, "that with the Vice President handling these programs they're one step removed from the departments where they need to be to become operational."

"But, Mr. President—" Humphrey tried to interject.

"*They say*, Hubert, that if we transfer these programs to the departments, then these people will know they're responsible to enforce these laws."

The Vice President blanched.

"*They say*, Hubert," the President continued, "that these programs will work better in the departments because these people will know they have to report directly to me then."

By this time, Humphrey was pale, as he realized that he was not there for consultation, but only to bless a decision the President had already made.

"Hubert, this is the kind of thing *they* have been recommending to me. But I didn't want to move on it without talking to you and getting your views. Do you think it's a good idea to strengthen our civil rights efforts this way?"

Humphrey, swallowing his pride as he had in the past and would so often in the future, responded, "Mr. President, I agreed to become your Vice President. I told you I would do whatever you wanted me to do. If you believe that's where these programs should go, then that's the way we'll do it."

"I thought you'd agree, Hubert," the President said, smiling.

There was small talk for just a few minutes, time for Humphrey to regain some color, perk up, and even say, "I'm with you on this, Mr. President. I'm sure we can do it in a way that will strengthen your administration's civil rights efforts." But, like all of us in the Oval Office at that moment, he knew he'd just been castrated.[29]

The next morning, the President called on the POTUS line.[30] He'd been thinking about the civil rights reorganization and the meeting with the Vice President. "You know, Joe, the Vice President said he's with me on these reorganization plans, that they'll strengthen our civil rights effort. I want him to get credit for them. If he wants to go forward with this reorganization, then he ought to get a memorandum over here recommending all these changes."

I wondered how the President intended to have the Vice President write such a memorandum. But not for long, as the President said to me, "You know exactly the details of this thing, and the Vice President's never been much of a detail man. Why don't you get yourself a piece of his stationery and type up these recommendations in a memo from him to me and bring it over to Hubert so he can sign it."

I was just weeks into the White House staff; I doubted I could pull something like that off. "Mr. President," I suggested, "maybe there's another way to do this. Suppose I go over and talk to the Vice President?"

"You go on over and talk to him. But when you do, you take a memorandum and tell him I want him to sign it."

At lunch that day[31] the President told me to get the memo signed "this afternoon, because tomorrow we ought to have a press conference announcing all these changes." At 5:30 P.M., I spoke with the Vice President and he agreed to meet with Katzenbach, White, and me at seven that evening.[32] When we arrived at his suite in the Executive Office Building, I suggested that we meet with him alone. He asked two members of his staff to leave.

"What is it now, Joe?" Humphrey sighed as he sat down and loosened his tie. The resilience he had displayed the day before seemed to slip away. I handed him a draft memo recommending the civil rights reorganization. "Mr. Vice President, I'm not sure how to tell you this," I began awkwardly.

"Go ahead, Joe. Tell me what he wants," Humphrey said as he got up to dress for a black-tie event he was going to that evening.

"Mr. Vice President, the President would like you to review this memorandum. If it's in accord with the discussion we had and your views, then he'd like you to sign it."

Humphrey looked at the memo and, almost audibly, lipread the sentence, "I believe the time has now come when operating functions can and should be performed by departments and agencies with clearly defined responsibility for the basic program, and that inter-agency committees and other inter-agency arrangements now only diffuse responsibility."[33]

Now what was left of Humphrey's resilience was gone along with the color from his face. "I'll have to talk to some of my people about this. They don't know anything about our meeting with the President."

"I'm afraid, Mr. Vice President, there won't be much time," I said.

"What does that mean?" the Vice President asked with a rare display of annoyance edging toward anger.

"The President would like you to sign this memo tonight."

"Well, I can't get it typed in time, not around here, because I need to talk to my staff first."

"Mr. Vice President, if you give me some of your stationery, I can have it typed tonight and delivered to your home whenever you get free of your engagement."

Humphrey was resigned. "Why don't you do that. Get it to me at my home tonight. I'll sign it. It'll give me a chance to talk to my people and you'll have it for the President first thing in the morning."[34]

I returned to the White House with some vice presidential stationery and reported to the President. At 1:20 A.M. Friday, I sent the President an unsigned version of the Vice President's reorganization memo, with a note that he would receive the signed version and all necessary papers by ten, in time for announcement at the press secretary's daily briefing, which usually took place around eleven.[35]

The President called me just as I arrived at my office that morning. "I've just read Hubert's memo. If the Vice President is so enthusiastic about this reorganization, why doesn't he come over here and announce it himself, instead of my announcing it?"

"I can certainly ask him," I said.

"Hell," said Johnson, "it's his recommendation. Get him over here with the others, and tell Hubert he can use the Cabinet Room if he wants to. This is an important announcement." The President hung up.

Humphrey rushed over and roused himself to join in announcing the reorganization. Only once did he allow himself a touch of irony. A reporter asked, "With . . . these [posts] being eliminated you no longer have an official title?" Humphrey responded, "That is correct, except Vice President."[36]

Lyndon Johnson was eager to jump into the civil rights enforcement effort. His Texas roots and more than thirty years of Washington experience made him keenly aware that laws passed by the Congress, especially civil rights laws, are not self-executing. In August 1965 he had ordered me to provide him with a state-by-state daily report, listing the number of school districts required to submit desegregation plans under the 1964 Civil Rights Act and the status of each district: Had a plan been submitted? Accepted? Was it being negotiated? If so, would negotiations be extensive?[37]

At the end of the month, the President announced that, of the more than 5,000 southern and border-state school districts involved, 4,463—88 percent—were "making preparations to comply." He was trying to put pressure on recalcitrant districts. At the same time, he directed Commissioner of Education Francis Keppel, a former Harvard School of Education dean, to work day and night to bring every school district into compliance with the law.

Johnson's carrot to encourage compliance, which also gave him a sizable stick, was to secure a one-billion-dollar congressional appropriation to fund the Elementary and Secondary Education Act he'd driven through Congress earlier in the year. This gave him lots of federal dollars to grant or withhold from virtually every school district in the nation. He wanted to make it financially, and therefore politically, costly for elected school officials to decline federal funds and thus ignore the 1964 Act. So LBJ pressed the Senate back into session to pass his appropriation bill on the day after Labor Day, an exceptionally prompt return and vote, even in a nonelection year.

Johnson's objective was to desegregate, not to cut off funds. He talked to me several times each day about ideas to spur compliance and gave me the names of politicians, educators, labor and business leaders across the South to call. He insisted that I meet frequently with Keppel and other government officials. Johnson even ordered a verbatim transcript made of one of my meetings to make sure I was pushing hard enough.[38]

Johnson particularly wanted all Texas school districts desegregated. When he noticed from my daily reports that twenty-nine Texas districts had not submitted plans, he mounted a special effort. He enlisted the aid of his friend Governor John Connally, phoned Texas Commissioner of Education Dr. J. W. Edgar, had Jake Jacobsen call each recalcitrant district, and pleaded with any Texan he thought could help, "Don't embarrass your President by having a Texas school district fail to submit a good plan."

The President sent handwritten notes to Jacobsen and me about Texas districts with unsatisfactory plans: "Please hurry and clear up once and for all." With Johnson pushing relentlessly, making strategic phone calls, and reminding everyone that "The eyes of the South and the North are fixed on what Texas does," we eventually pressed all Texas school districts that were receiving federal funds into compliance.[39]

Across the South as school began in the late summer of 1965, the number of blacks in desegregated southern schools tripled over the prior school year. In late September, however, as we were patting ourselves on the back, the first confrontation under the 1964 Civil Rights Act came unexpectedly from a city in the North.

•

On Sunday, October 3, the President traveled to New York City, to sign the first reform of the nation's immigration laws in more than a generation (eliminating discriminatory country-by-country quotas) under the Statue of Liberty and to have the first meeting on U.S. soil between an American president and a Roman Catholic pope.[40]

The decision to go forward with the meeting was not lightly taken. The President was at first reluctant. In getting Congress to pass and fund the Elementary and Secondary Education Act, Johnson had tapped all his persuasive and political skills. Republican opposition, bigotry, and concerns over separation of church and state had blocked federal aid to elementary and secondary schools for decades. Johnson had been forced to negotiate with three groups that had killed any such measure in the past: Catholics, who opposed aid to public schools unless parochial schools also received some assistance; Protestants, particularly southern fundamentalists, who would not support any aid to Catholic schools; many liberal Jews and Protestants, who opposed aid to parochial schools, including their own, on grounds of separation of church and state. It had been a bruising fight in which the President in the end dealt directly with the Reverend Billy Graham and Francis Cardinal Spellman, Archbishop of New York and the most powerful Catholic prelate in the United States. He also got some key assists from Jewish financial supporters. In the course of this battle, the President got a closeup sense of the intensity of anti-Catholic sentiment among fundamentalists in the South and many secular liberals in the North. In early September, as the fate of his request for the billion dollars for elementary and secondary education rested with Congress, Johnson did not want a meeting with the Pope to jeopardize funding for one of his legislative crown jewels. So word of the meeting was not released until funding was assured, and even then Johnson announced only a tentative session.

There was a lot of discussion of where and under what circumstances the American President might meet the Roman Pope. The location couldn't be at Cardinal Spellman's splendid quarters behind St. Patrick's Cathedral; that would be on Catholic turf and might offend southern fundamentalists. The White House was also out; the Pope's visit was not official—the United States did not then have diplomatic relations with the Vatican. Bigots might use pictures of the Pope at the White House against the President. Johnson also rejected the United Nations: too many East European, Irish, and Italian Catholics then viewed the United Nations as a Godless accomplice to the enslavement of Eastern Europe. Eventually Johnson settled on the Waldorf Towers, the luxurious wing of the hotel where UN Ambassador Goldberg had his apartment. That, Johnson thought, should take care of all angles: the Catholics would be pleased he was meeting with the Pope; the Protestants wouldn't get angry at his going on Catholic turf or inviting the Pope to the White House; liberal Jews couldn't complain if Arthur Goldberg provided the place and was at the center of the event.

With everything in place, the public pomp of the papal visit was suddenly overshadowed by an unanticipated political flap. Education Commissioner Keppel picked Chicago's elementary and secondary schools for the first cutoff of federal funds under the 1964 Civil Rights Act because of "evidence" of racial discrimination. Keppel announced the cutoff on October 1, two days before the President's trip to New York. Chicago Mayor Richard Daley, a key Johnson ally with tight control of the nation's most effective political machine, was outraged: why were his city's schools the first in the entire nation targeted to lose funds under a law that had been largely directed at the South? Daley was no ordinary mayor. Without his Chicago precincts in 1960, John Kennedy might never have carried Illinois or been elected President. More immediately important to Johnson, Daley was critical to the success of the Great Society. A call to Daley was all that was necessary to deliver the fourteen votes of the Illinois Democratic congressional delegation. Johnson and others of us had made many calls to the Mayor and Daley had always come through.

On the morning of the day he was to meet the Pope, Johnson sat down with a livid Richard Daley. He assured the Mayor he would look into the Chicago situation the moment he returned to Washington. Johnson told me to line up Health, Education, and Welfare Secretary Gardner, Keppel, Attorney General Katzenbach, White House Aide Doug Cater, and Wilbur Cohen, then Undersecretary of HEW, for an Oval Office meeting that evening. [41]

The President was still boiling over Keppel's precipitate action when he met the Pope, though he managed to disguise his agitation. The President and Pope greeted each other warmly, arms extended, and went into a room for a private discussion. Johnson and the Pope sat side by side, with a State Department interpreter on Johnson's side and Monsignor Paul Marcinkus, the Chicago priest long assigned to Rome who later became head of the Vatican bank, acting as the Pope's interpreter. The two leaders talked of peace and the role of the Pontiff and the United Nations in formal, head-of-state cadences. The Pope praised the President for his work in civil rights, the President extolled the Pope for "giving us a black bishop,"* Then the Pope lav-

---

* The Very Reverend Harold Robert Perry, Auxiliary Bishop of the New Orleans Archdiocese.

ished praise on the President's efforts in support of education for children, particularly poor children.

The President beamed. Then his face suddenly flushed. He turned to the Pope, his enormous hand reached out, stopping just short of the Pontiff's knee. The President blurted out agitatedly: "That's the work I want to do, your Holiness, educate poor children. But they're trying to stop me. One of my own cabinet members wants to shut off funds for poor children in one of our largest cities, Chicago, run by a fine Catholic mayor. Your Monsignor [Marcinkus] comes from Chicago; he'll tell you what a fine mayor Richard Daley is. But we'll help these children." The Pope was genuinely befuddled as Marcinkus translated. For his part, Marcinkus could hardly keep from laughing, but he held himself to a tightly controlled smile as his gray eyes twinkled with amusement. [42]

That afternoon, Johnson returned to Washington determined to resolve the Chicago situation. As Keppel explained his cutoff of funds, Katzenbach asked: Had Keppel advised Mayor Daley or the school superintendent of their failure to comply, given them a chance to desegregate, and, if they had refused, had Keppel notified the appropriate congressional committees thirty days before acting? All of this, Katzenbach noted, was required by law. Keppel sheepishly responded that he had not followed any such procedures. Keppel had jumped the gun. Now Johnson jumped Keppel. He sent Cohen to Chicago to work out a plan of voluntary compliance with the school board, and told me to let Daley know that funds would not be cut off and to urge the mayor to cooperate with Cohen. [43]

That meeting spelled the end of Keppel's role as Commissioner of Education; he had not only picked the most politically sensitive school district in the nation for the first fund cutoff, he had done it in a way that failed to comply with the clear terms of the law. Johnson soon moved him aside, leaving him with the title Assistant Secretary of Education, but replacing him as commissioner with Harold (Doc) Howe, who was as committed to desegregating schools North and South, but who was sensitive to the need to work out the politics as well as enforce the policy and who was endorsed by both senators from the state of North Carolina where he was working at the time Johnson tapped him for the post. *[44]

The political confrontation with Mayor Daley did not stay

---

* Postscript: When I became Secretary of Health, Education, and Welfare in 1977, the department and the city of Chicago were still at odds over the school-desegregation battle that began in 1965. No longer confronted by Daley or a monolithic political machine and bolstered by the increased number of black voters, we were able to work out a settlement.

Johnson's determination to attack school segregation throughout the country. A few weeks later, on November 17, the President asked the Civil Rights Commission to conduct a major study of de facto segregation in the North. "Although we have made substantial progress in ending formal segregation of schools," Johnson wrote, "racial isolation in the schools persists—both in the North and the South—because of housing patterns, school districting, economic stratification and population movements." Having grown up in a Brooklyn neighborhood, in which 90 percent of the population was equally divided between Italians and Jews, with blacks the other 10 percent and growing, I knew we had a difficult fight ahead. But none of us appreciated just how intractable de facto segregation would prove to be, or how the frustrations and resentments of blacks and whites would inflame the situation in the years ahead.

FOUR

The War Against Poverty and the Battle for Beauty

DIFFERENT FROM Roosevelt's New Deal, which had confronted vast unemployment and a national emergency among blue- and white-collar workers, Johnson's war on poverty targeted the hard-core poor. "The people I want to help," he would say, "are the ones who've never held real jobs and aren't equipped to handle them. Most never had enough money and don't know how to spend it. They were born to parents who gave up hoping long ago. They have no motivation to reach for something better because the sum total of their lives is losing."

The foundation of Johnson's strategy was a growing economy. If wages and profits increased, most Americans would prosper, job opportunities would expand sufficiently to make room for affirmative action for blacks without threatening whites, and higher federal revenues would finance Great Society programs without additional taxes. Johnson considered a robust, noninflationary economy so critical to his domestic program that he spent more time on economic matters than on any other subject during my years at the White House.

The war on poverty, as he saw it, was to help those who, on their own, had no chance of getting their fair share of economic growth. For poor people capable of helping themselves, the goal was to offer the kind of assistance most Americans receive from their parents. For the old or disabled, the objective was to make life more bearable. So viewed, the war on poverty encompassed a vast range of programs: those to offer a hand up (aid to education, child health and nutrition, adult literacy, and job training), and those to assist people who might never be able to help themselves (Medicare for the elderly and disabled, cash payments through Social Security, veterans disability and supplemental security income, and nursing-home care through Medicaid).

The most controversial weapon in Johnson's arsenal was the Office of Economic Opportunity (OEO). It was his effort to empower the poor. When LBJ had asked Congress to establish OEO in 1964, he knew he faced one of the toughest legislative battles of his presidency. He had chosen Phil Landrum, a conservative Democrat from Georgia, who was familiar with rural poverty in his district and had authored the Landrum-Griffin Act (a law that curbed union power), to be floor manager in the House. With Landrum, Johnson hoped to blunt some of the savage opposition he anticipated from conservative southerners.

To head OEO, Johnson had picked Sargent Shriver, John Kennedy's brother-in-law, who had been the first director of the Peace Corps. LBJ admired Shriver's skills as a political salesman and sought to capitalize on the popularity of the Peace Corps. In putting the early phase of the program together, Shriver had enlisted Adam Yarmolinsky, my predecessor as McNamara's special assistant at the Defense Department.[1] Yarmolinsky was expected to become Shriver's deputy once Congress established OEO.

As the OEO bill reached the floor of the House in August 1964, a tight vote was expected. The North Carolina delegation and several House Democrats it had recruited as allies demanded a commitment that Yarmolinsky would have no position in the Office of Economic Opportunity in exchange for their support. Their problem was the alleged Communist affiliations of his parents and Yarmolinsky's own alleged radical sympathies during his youth. Shriver, fearing defeat, told the President on August 7, 1964, that he believed the bill could not pass unless Yarmolinsky was sacrificed.[2] In three wild days of House voting, Landrum had to give governors veto power over Community Action programs, accede to a loyalty oath for Job Corps enrollees, and announce on the floor of the House that Yarmolinsky would have no role in the poverty program: "I have been told on the highest authority that not only will [Yarmolinsky] not be appointed, but that he will not be considered if he is recommended for a place in this agency." The final House vote of 226–185 approving the bill proved much wider than anticipated and raised sharp questions about the decision to sacrifice Yarmolinsky to the North Carolina delegation.

At the President's press conference on the day after the House passed the bill, a reporter said, "I want to ask a question about Adam

Yarmolinsky. . . . He had been with the Department of Defense—"

President: "He still is."

Reporter: "I thought he had been working . . . on the poverty bill."

President: "No, your thoughts are wrong."

Reporter: "I was also asked to ask you, sir, if he was going back to the Pentagon. . . ."

President: "He never left."

A week later, the President was asked about "some published columns from various sources" about Yarmolinsky. He responded tartly:

> I would think that probably you ought to seek the columnist and see what . . . [his] source . . . is. Mr. Yarmolinsky is employed by the Defense Department. . . . No one, to repeat, to emphasize, no one, at any time, any place, anywhere, suggested to me anyone for any of these places [OEO jobs]. The first information that I had that Mr. Yarmolinsky was, in effect, appointed to one of these places that did not exist was the columnist rumor that you talked about. I was informed by . . . Mr. Shriver that he had made no recommendations to anyone, that he had not recommended Mr. Yarmolinsky to anyone associated with me, or with me, and did not plan to.

As all this had gone on, I was sitting in the Pentagon, in the Office of the Special Assistant, a post I'd held for months since the public announcement of my appointment to succeed Yarmolinsky. The Saturday morning after the House vote, McNamara called me into his office. I told him I was shaken by the treatment of Yarmolinsky and I couldn't understand why the President had given an answer so obviously at odds with the facts. "That's not the point now," he told me. "The important lesson here, Joe, is this. When the President, or one of his major programs, is involved, none of us is important. Everyone's expendable."

OEO went on to launch such popular programs as Head Start to offer poor children preschool education and follow through to preserve their gains in the initial school years, the Neighborhood Youth Corps to provide job skills, and college work-study programs. But OEO also spawned the Community Action Program (CAP), which established organizations in cities, towns, and neighborhoods across America to organize the poor to help themselves. Many local officeholders believed that CAP bankrolled radical blacks and whites to upset the balance of political power in their communities. OEO also set up VISTA (Volunteers in Service to America), which sent young college students and graduates into poor urban and rural areas to teach people how to read, write, take care of basic hygiene, and muster some self-respect. Inevitably, these socially conscious young men and women raised the political consciousness of the poor.

Confrontations with elected officials over the activities of poverty warriors irked Johnson and often angered him. Yet so long as they did not jeopardize other Great Society initiatives, he was willing to weather the political flak, because he knew the poor had to organize to be heard.

When a member of Congress or governor complained that VISTA volunteers were getting into politics, as Senator Robert Byrd (D-W. Va.) did on behalf of local officials, Johnson nodded agreement and moaned about the lack of control at OEO. But in the privacy of his own official family, the President confided that it was about time some of these local politicians heard from the poor in their communities.[3] After a couple of businessmen expressed concern about the community action agency in Harlem in New York City, Johnson said to me, "You know the way to do something about Harlem? Make these rich Wall Street bankers drive through Harlem to and from work every day so they see the poverty instead of riding on an air-conditioned train drinking martinis and talking to each other about how much money they make."*

Born of brutal political labor, the Office of Economic Opportunity sparked vicious back-alley fights. As community action programs gave the black urban poor a local political voice, mayors (most of whom were Democrats) demanded control over CAP agencies in their cities and the funds that Shriver was disbursing. Shriver, who almost seemed to enjoy taunting them, refused, insisting that he was enforcing the law's mandate of "maximum feasible participation" by the poor in OEO programs.

For a while the President resisted the pressure from the mayors. He wanted the poor to have the political clout to goad big-city machines to be more responsive. But by the end of 1965 LBJ feared that community action organizations were jeopardizing other Great Society efforts. The Teacher Corps, his program to encourage college graduates to teach in urban ghettos and poor rural areas, was starved of funds because members of Congress feared the teachers were political organizers in academic drag. A scandal in Harlem's HARYOU-ACT

---

* Johnson's belief in personal experience wasn't limited to Wall Street bankers. He once told me that "the way to end urban pollution is to make the auto company executives and their wives ride around Detroit in non-air-conditioned cars during the summer. Then," he added, "they'll damn well solve the problem."

raised his concern about corruption in other big-city CAPs. Johnson also began to worry that the Community Action Program might be the nucleus of a political force the Kennedys would use against him.

To complicate matters, Shriver sent to the President a memo on October 20, 1965, sketching grandiose plans "to end poverty in the United States, as we know it today, within a generation." The proposals covered everything from housing to a negative income tax and ranged far afield from OEO's immediate concerns.[4] Johnson regarded the memo as unrealistic. Worse yet, he saw it as a Kennedy manifesto that Shriver had written for eventual leak to the press. He thought it was meant to demonstrate that Shriver and his brother-in-law Robert wanted to invest far more in the war against poverty than the President.

Johnson's distrust was heightened by a public altercation between Shriver and Budget Director Charles Schultze that same fall. Schultze wanted to ease friction with mayors. *"We ought not to be in the business of organizing the poor politically,"* Schultze wrote to the President. He suggested that OEO stop sponsoring local elections to poverty boards, soft-pedal its conflicts with local elected officials over representation of the poor on such boards, and step up efforts to put the poor to work in nonpolitical jobs. Schultze's memo was in part inspired by Vice President Humphrey's anxiety that the Community Action Program threatened the entire Great Society, needlessly and recklessly antagonized local officials, and would be a major campaign issue in 1966. At the bottom of Schultze's memo Johnson penciled, "O.K. I agree. L."[5]

When Schultze passed the word to OEO, Shriver objected. The dispute erupted in the newspapers, most sharply on the front page of *The New York Times*. Furious, LBJ told me to get Schultze and Shriver to desist from fighting in the press. Both responded with angry memos to the President. Schultze believed that Shriver had deliberately leaked stories to inflame the situation and Shriver thought that the White House, perhaps the President himself, was putting out stories to undermine him. In his memo, Shriver hinted at his own distrust of Johnson and implied that the President was undercutting him.[6] The President was convinced that Shriver was going his own way. Both the President and Vice President suspected that Shriver was building an organization to help Robert Kennedy take the White House in 1968. This distrust simmered in a cauldron of conflicting bureaucratic ambitions, as the Departments of Labor, Agriculture, and Health, Education, and Welfare jockeyed to take over OEO programs related to their areas of concern.

In this atmosphere, the President instructed me in "strictest confidence" to look at dismantling OEO and moving its programs to other existing government departments and agencies. He wanted to accomplish this without any legislative action in order to avoid a bloodbath on Capitol Hill. On December 18, 1965, I sent the President a proposed reorganization, which Attorney General Katzenbach said we could adopt without going to Congress. With the President's approval, Shriver could delegate all OEO functions to various departments, as he already had done with some. To deflect the political reaction, I suggested that the President give the responsibilities of the OEO director, including supervision of the Community Action programs, to the new secretary of Housing and Urban Development. I also recommended Shriver as the new secretary. I warned Johnson that "The reorganization of the War Against Poverty is potentially the most politically explosive act the Administration could take, even though it makes good organizational sense." Nevertheless, he was sufficiently interested to have the Justice Department draft the necessary papers.[7]

The President eventually decided not to spend any political capital on reorganizing OEO. He didn't want to precipitate a nasty bureaucratic war within his administration or a political brouhaha on Capitol Hill. He preferred to move successful programs out of OEO one by one, and drop the ineffective ones. He did not wish to give Shriver's brother-in-law Robert Kennedy and congressional liberals any ammunition to accuse him of shorting the needs of the poor because of the Vietnam War.*

I always believed that Shriver was loyal to LBJ, but Johnson himself blew hot and cold on his OEO Director. At the end of a day in which LBJ said he "was pretty disgusted at" cabinet officers more interested in protecting their turf than in producing results and several senators who ran for cover on a controversial labor vote, he told Shriver, "Sarge, you're the only one that's not letting me down. The rest of them are just fighting—the party, the programs, the senators and everybody—I'm glad somebody is looking out for what they believe in."[8] Nevertheless, Johnson couldn't look at Shriver without trying to see whether Robert Kennedy was in the shadows behind his brother-in-law.

●

---

* Eventually, most OEO programs were transferred to other government departments. As black militants moved from the streets to City Hall, they brought Community Action under tight local political control, proving once again that where one stands depends on where one sits. In 1981, Congress abolished the Community Services Administration, which was the last independent vestige of OEO.

Mounting an aggressive war against poverty was certain to be contentious. The pursuit of beauty might have been expected to win the President accolades. In Lyndon Johnson's presidency, even that would be controversial, as we discovered in the battle over highway beautification in 1965.

To Johnson, environmental legislation* was a profession of faith in the power and beauty of nature. To traditional concepts of preservation he added his "new conservation" of restoration and rescue, designed to salvage as much as possible of what urbanization and transportation systems had already destroyed. In his special message in 1965 on Conservation and Restoration of Natural Beauty,† the President asked Congress to enact a highway-beautification bill. The bill would give the federal government power to require states to ban billboards and exposed junkyards along highways. States failing to do so would lose all federal highway funds. Johnson hoped to bypass state and local governments, which were easily influenced by the dollars of the billboard lobby.

For months before, the President had Bill Moyers in secret discussions with Phillip Tocker, head of the Outdoor Advertising Association of America, and Donald Thomas, a Johnson family attorney, whom the billboard lobby had hired. In trying to produce a consensus bill, they shaped one so weak that it left the President little room to negotiate during the tough fights in the committees and corridors of Congress.

Johnson fought aggressively, however. He egged on Commerce Secretary Connor with handwritten notes: "Jack. All industry, labor and public service organizations . . . should be enlisted . . . get their help. . . . Let's get all garden clubs working—with Mary [Connor] and Lady Bird giving them encouragement by appearances." And he pushed his staff. Just two weeks after I joined the White House, he told me to "Take over the highway beautification bill. I want you to get it out of the Senate and through the House!"[9] At one time or another before and after that telephone command, I learned that he'd

---

* The Clean Air and Air Quality acts, the Water Quality and Clean Water Restoration acts, the Solid Waste Disposal Act, and the Motor Vehicle Air Pollution Control Act were among the major laws he pushed through Congress.

† The theme of Johnson's message fits the eve of the twenty-first century as snugly as the mid-1960s: ". . . modern technology, which has added much to our lives, can also have a darker side. Its uncontrolled waste products are menacing the world we live in, our enjoyment and our health. The air we breathe, our water, our soil and wildlife, are being blighted by the poisons and chemicals which are the by-products of technology and industry. . . . The same society which receives the rewards of technology, must, as a cooperating whole, take responsibility for control."

given the same message to Moyers, Jack Valenti, Horace Busby, Lee White, Larry O'Brien, and John Connor.

By early September 1965, reluctantly responding to White House pressure, the Senate Public Works Committee developed a bill, but it was even weaker than the one the President had submitted. The committee bill gave the states sole power to regulate billboards and junkyards.

The following Saturday afternoon Johnson called a staff meeting in the Oval Office with Doug Cater, Jake Jacobsen, Valenti, Busby, Harry McPherson, White, Dick Goodwin, and me, to plan strategy for the House of Representatives. The meeting began as a general discussion of White House congressional relations, with LBJ alternately praising, condemning, and needling us.

"You're a much superior staff to Kennedy's," he said, "But that's as a staff. As individuals, you're not superior in developing relations with Congress." To LBJ, that task was everyone's "most important job. When Members of Congress come here to the White House, you gather in a corner and talk to each other. You should be talking to them. Finding out what's on their mind. How they tick. Pushing our legislative program. Seeing what you can do for them." He urged each of us to "have congressmen to breakfast or lunch, so they can go back and tell their colleagues, 'I told the White House the other day.'"

When we did talk to members of Congress, Johnson said, we were so full of ourselves that we didn't listen to what they said. "You just want to brag to each other and the President about 'What I told the committee chairman.'" Well, he confided, "When I was a young congressman, Speaker Sam Rayburn got me a meeting with President Roosevelt to give me a chance to get the President to support a project in my district. When I came back, I said to Mr. Sam, 'I told Roosevelt this and I told Roosevelt that.' When I finished, Mr. Sam looked at me, and said, 'Lyndon, I know what you went to tell the President. But what did the President say to you?'" Johnson laughed and added, "Well, I felt like a Goddamn fool. And each of you should feel that way when you come back here and tell Larry O'Brien or me all the things you told a congressman. What I want to know is what he said to you. Is he going to vote with us? Or against us? Does he want something? What can we get if we give it to him?"

Johnson chided Dick Goodwin for heading off to Martha's Vineyard and "leaving your President to save the highway beauty bill." Then he told a story about three men sitting around telling each other about the ugliest sound each had ever heard:

The first man said, "I slipped in the carpentry shop where I was working, got caught so I couldn't move, and fell over backwards on the buzz saw table. Well, that damn buzz saw was buzzing along coming closer and closer to my head. I wanna tell you, the ugliest sound I ever heard was that buzz, buzz, buzz from the saw."

The second man said, "That's nothing. I was walking along the railroad track. I tripped and my legs got tangled under one of the ties between the tracks. This train came along, I just lay there flat as I could." Sitting in his rocker, Johnson held his legs out straight and arms at his side, physically mimicking a man lying flat and stiff under a train. "And that train kept comin' and comin' and rolled over me. Well, the ugliest damn sound I ever heard was the chug-a-chug-chug, chug-a-chug-chug, chug-a-chug-chug of that train as it rolled over me."

The third man then told of his experience. "You fellows don't know what an ugly sound is. I was in bed with this beautiful woman in the middle of a wild weekend with her, when her husband came home early. I jumped up, put on my underwear, grabbed my pants, and raced to climb out the window, pants in hand." Johnson was gesturing wildly to illustrate how the man was scrambling. "My underwear got caught on the window ledge and I was hanging half out the window when her husband got there. He grabbed my balls with one hand, and pulled out his pocket knife with the other." Johnson held his left hand out in front of him, fingers theatrically clenched. Then Johnson joined the thumb and fingers of his right hand as though holding a pocket knife, and raised that hand to his mouth. Then he roared, "The ugliest sound I ever heard was the click, click, click as he tried to open the blade of that pocket knife with his teeth."

Johnson and all of us burst into laughter, until tears came to our eyes. As we finally settled down, he turned to Goodwin, "Well, the ugliest sound I heard this week was the swish, swish, swish when Pat McNamara [Chairman of the Senate Public Works Committee] cut off Goodwin's pecker." Goodwin had been one of many of us trying to get a stronger bill out of the committee.

We were still laughing when Lady Bird joined us for the strategy session. The President gave each of us a number of House members to contact. That all the stops were out was clear from the assignments he gave to Lee White and me: get Internal Revenue Commissioner Sheldon Cohen, one, to see if he could lengthen the time over which billboard owners were permitted to depreciate their billboards (thus reducing their annual tax deduction for depreciation), and two, to audit billboard owners to make sure they were denied investment tax credits on their billboards.[10] Johnson felt betrayed by the billboard interests and he had decided to take them on.

We worked hard over the next few weeks. Johnson ordered me to halt any consideration of closing unnecessary Veterans Administration hospitals and to suspend controversial actions contemplated anywhere in the government so as not to offend anyone in the House "until we get our beauty bill."[11]

Johnson called a special meeting to urge every cabinet member to help get votes of key House and Senate members for his beauty bill. He drove the staff (and himself) relentlessly. He told us repeatedly that he wanted this bill for Lady Bird. "You know I love that woman and she wants that highway beauty bill," and "By God, we're going to get it for her."[12]

But such thrashing about was costly. Johnson wanted this one so badly that he had each of us running in different directions. In a memo of September 12, 1965 (in which I reported that IRS Commissioner Cohen didn't want to go after the billboard owners on depreciation but might nail them on the investment tax credit), I urged the President to "Place the burden clearly on one person to get this straightened out on the Hill. I recommend Larry O'Brien." The situation got so confused that a few days later O'Brien sent an unusual memo to the President:

> I must inform you that our performance to date on the Highway Beauty bill has fallen far below the standards of our usual work. . . . I am very much concerned about our confusion, about our unnecessary harassment of friendly members, and about irritations which can prove damaging with other bills. The billboard lobby, of course, is opposing us, but in contrast with most lobbies we confront on major bills, it is singularly ineffective and . . . nearly all the problems we have had and will have result from our own bungling.

O'Brien went on to chronicle a series of tactical gaffes, many of which he laid at Johnson's feet.[13]

In September the Senate passed a diluted version of the already unsatisfactory bill reported by its Public Works Committee. The most tense votes came in the House during the late-evening and early-morning hours of October 7 and 8. The 7th was the night of Johnson's gala entertainment and party to celebrate the accomplishments of the "Great 89th Congress," at the end of which he was to go to Bethesda Naval Hospital to have a gall-bladder operation the next morning. The only chance for a bill was now, so he kept the House in session well into the evening. While senators and their wives celebrated at the White House and enjoyed the entertainment at the State Department, the House debated the highway beautification bill.[14] The party ended before the final House vote, taken at about 1 A.M. on October 8.

That evening, however, Johnson got a break. House Republicans made highway beautification a partisan issue and, despite all our tripping over ourselves, House Democrats gave us a bill. The Senate passed the House bill a few days later. When the battle was over, though, Congress had given states the power to regulate billboards and junkyards, and the Secretary of Commerce could withhold only 10 percent of federal highway funds from states refusing to impose any controls. By and large, credit for the weak bill was given to the billboard lobbies. But much of the fault lay with the President for the one inept legislative experience I witnessed and participated in as a member of his staff. From our point of view, however, defeat was better blamed on the money of the billboard lobby, and LBJ was content to let it rest there.

In signing the bill on October 22, he expressed his disappointment and determination:

> This bill does not represent . . . what the national interest requires. But it is a first step and . . . though we must crawl before we walk, we are going to walk.
>   . . . we are not going to allow [the billboard interests] to intrude their own specialized private objective on the larger public trust.
>   Beauty belongs to all the people. And so long as I am President, what has been divinely given to nature will not be taken recklessly away by man.

Shortly after becoming President, Johnson had urged Lady Bird to use her power as First Lady to get something done and "not fritter it away." He had suggested she pick a couple of projects and make them happen. She had selected two of his, but had made them her own: Head Start and beautification. So Johnson had put Lady Bird out front on the beauty bill, in part because he thought it would help pass the legislation and in part because it was important to her. But he came to believe that he had left her too exposed, particularly when, during the House floor debate, Kansas Republican Robert Dole had suggested that "Lady Bird" be substituted for "Secretary of Commerce" wherever the phrase appeared in the bill. LBJ did not want Lady Bird to get hurt in the course of his political battles and he never put her as far out front again.

FIVE

Scrambling

To get Congress to enact and fund Great Society programs as he escalated the war, LBJ had to hold off asking for a tax increase as long as possible. He also had to avoid imposing wage and price controls. Stemming inflation under these circumstances sent him scrambling to hold down wages, prices, and the federal deficit. It demanded all his powers of persuasion and manipulation, and often called for sheer muscle. The first test came during the 1965 steel-industry labor negotiations, just a few weeks after he announced the military buildup.

On August 17, 1965, at about 7:30 P.M., the President called me to join him right away. I hustled down the hall to the Oval Office. He was with I. W. Abel, the newly elected president of the United Steelworkers of America. A strike deadline was two weeks away. The outcome in steel would set the pattern for labor disputes to come in other major industries. The President handed me a paper Abel had given him, setting out the union's position in its ongoing contract negotiations with ten of the nation's major steel companies.[1]

As Johnson signaled me to sit down, Abel was saying, "These are commitments, Mr. President. Commitments I made to the members who elected me. After what we gave up in the last round of negotiations, we've got to make a stand."

Johnson leaned forward in his rocker, "You're starting to sound just like Dick Russell [senior Senator from Georgia and leader of the southern Democrats in the Senate]. He sat on that very couch talking to me about my civil rights bill in 1964. I asked him not to filibuster.

" 'We've got to make a stand somewhere,' he said. He sounded just like you," Johnson added, knowing how comparison with the Georgia Senator would nettle Abel.

"I told Dick Russell the story about the Negro boy, in bed with this white gal. Well, he's there in bed a-humpin' away when they hear a sound downstairs and then this voice. 'It's my husband,' this little white gal says. 'Hide. Hide. Get out of here. He'll kill you and then he'll kill me. Hurry! Hurry!'

"Well, that Negro boy, he bolted out of bed, ripped open the first door he could get his hands on, got in the closet, and she slammed it shut."

At this point, Johnson bolted from his rocker, stood upright, arms stiff at his side, legs straight, tight together, back and shoulders ramrod straight.

"Well, it was the linen closet and this poor Negro boy, he was pinned, standing just like I am, between the shelves and the door. He just couldn't move."

Johnson then began gesturing again. "Then this gal's husband bursts in shouting, 'Someone's here. Someone's in the bedroom.'

" 'No one's here,' his wife says. 'No one.'

"With that the husband starts furiously opening doors. First the bathroom door. Then his clothes-closet door. Then her clothes-closet door. Then he finally opens the linen-closet door. And here's this Negro, standing erect"—at this point Johnson resumed his erect posture, arms stiffly by his side—"buck naked, scared to death.

" 'What the hell are you doin' here?' this little white gal's husband shouts, fire in his eyes.

" 'Everybody's gotta stand somewhere, boss,' this Negro boy answers."[2]

When the laughter subsided, the President looked into Abel's eyes. "Everybody's gotta stand somewhere," he repeated slowly and softly, leaning into the labor leader. "Well, Dick Russell had to stand somewhere in 1964. And just like that Negro boy he wanted to keep down, he was stuck there in the closet when the Senate voted to end his filibuster. Mr. Abel, I know you gotta stand somewhere. But you gotta stand where you can move around a little. Not just pinned in the linen closet."

Johnson turned to me, "Go over these proposals with [Gardner] Ackley [Chairman of the Council of Economic Advisers] and [Otto] Eckstein [the CEA member expert in the steel industry] and let me know what you all think."[3]

Eckstein's brief analysis of Abel's paper told the President what he undoubtedly suspected, but didn't want to hear: Abel's demands were far from what the steel companies had offered, and the companies would follow any such wage and benefit hike with a hefty price increase. The President called me shortly after 11 P.M. the evening he read Eckstein's memo.[4] "Learn everything you can about steel. Meet every day with [Secretary of Labor] Bill Wirtz, [Secretary of Commerce John] Connor, and Ackley. Keep me informed each day of what's happening with the negotiations. I'm afraid," he added, "that this one's going to end up here." But he didn't sound afraid; his tone seemed to welcome the challenge.

The President's objectives were clear but difficult to achieve: no steel strike (a 1959 steel strike was widely credited with touching off the 1960–61 Eisenhower recession), a settlement within the administration's wage-price guideposts, and no increase in steel prices. The Council of Economic Advisers had established the concept of wage-price guideposts in 1962: wage and benefit increases should be kept at or below the economy's overall rate of productivity growth, and prices should remain stable or be reduced. The guideposts were intended to encourage increases in productivity and to deny management the excuse that wage and benefit boosts automatically justified price increases. The 1964 Economic Report to the President set the first numerical wage guidepost at 3.2 percent, its estimate of the nation's annual rate of productivity growth.

As a strike appeared likely,[5] Johnson began to make his determination public. On August 25, less than a week before the threatened strike, Johnson declared at his press conference: "I expect . . . responsibility in the current wage negotiations and . . . continued stability in steel prices."

The following morning the President met with Connor, Wirtz, Treasury Secretary Joe Fowler, Ackley, and me for over an hour. Johnson thought highly of Abel and believed the labor leader would want to act in the public interest, but he was concerned about the promises Abel had made to union members. Johnson regarded R. Conrad Cooper, the chief negotiator for the steel companies, as a henchman of Roger Blough, the United States Steel chairman, whose arrogance in increasing prices in 1962 had spurred an angry President Kennedy to call businessmen "sons of bitches." Johnson made it clear, however, that he was not going to get into any name calling; more seasoned than JFK, he would distinguish himself from the young President.

Johnson feared that Commerce Secretary Connor, a former chief executive of a Fortune 500 company, might suggest to steel management that a price increase would be acceptable, especially when Connor reported that Roger Blough considered the "President's comment at the press conference about 'price stability' . . . very troublesome to management." Johnson also worried about Wirtz's bias toward labor.[6] So he directed Connor to tell steel management that the administration believed the companies could agree to a 3.2 percent wage-and-benefits package without any increase in prices,[7] and he told Wirtz to let the union know that a 3.2 percent increase was all the administration would tolerate. Wirtz reminded him that the unions had been critical to his landslide election and were key allies in passing Great Society legislation; he warned that unions would take "mighty offense" at being fenced in by the wage-price guideposts. Ackley tartly remarked, "There won't be any Great Society unless we hold the economy in step and maintain a real growth rate of the kind we're now getting."[8]

The next day William Simkin, the head of the Federal Mediation and Conciliation Service, on his own initiative suggested to each of the parties a settlement in excess of the wage guideposts. The President had gone to the LBJ Ranch to celebrate his fifty-seventh birthday, but Simkin's action was so dangerous to our objectives that I wired him there, suggesting he send personal emissaries to Pittsburgh to set the parties straight.[9]

Johnson called me from the ranch.[10] He wanted to send Senator Wayne Morse and LeRoy Collins to mediate the steel dispute. Collins was an obvious choice: a former federal mediator of racial disputes, he understood how to manage a tense situation. Johnson's selection of Morse, however, came as a surprise. The Oregon Democrat had voted against the Tonkin Gulf resolution and had remained an outspoken critic of LBJ's Vietnam policy.

But Johnson and Morse were Senate pros. A split on one issue, however wide, didn't block them from working together when they found common ground. Though he didn't always follow his own advice, Johnson more than once told me, "Never let a political battle get personal. You never know when you'll need today's enemy as tomorrow's ally."*

Johnson trusted Morse's judgment on labor issues, and the Oregon legislator was respected by his Senate colleagues on these matters. Johnson told Morse[12] that he wanted some independent judgment about whether presidential intervention could help here. What the President did not tell Morse was that if he had to resort to a Taft-Hartley injunction to block a steel strike for eighty days (an action labor would vehemently denounce) he planned to name Morse

---

* When Morse's cattle did well at the Montgomery County Fair in Gaithersburg, Maryland, Johnson in congratulating him said, "I wish you knew as much about international relations as about the genetics of cattle raising."[11]

to chair the fact-finding board the law required. That would assure Morse's support if Johnson had to go to Congress to settle the dispute.

At Johnson's direction, I briefed Morse and Collins at the White House that Saturday afternoon. I asked Morse if he was comfortable arguing the importance of holding down wages and prices in wartime when he himself opposed direct American involvement in Vietnam. "The fact that I'm opposed to the war doesn't mean that I'd take a personal advantage of it," Morse explained. "We're in the war now and the American people must recognize that so long as this is our national policy, they've got to do their best, particularly where they hold enormous amounts of economic power, not to further unravel the country."[13]

When Johnson called me after midnight Sunday, I reported that Morse and Collins had made no progress in Pittsburgh, and believed "that, left to their own devices, [the parties] will not be able to reach a settlement."[14] Johnson decided to return to attend a breakfast meeting that Monday morning, August 30, with Morse, Collins, Simkin, and his cabinet advisers, and to invite Eisenhower to the White House later that afternoon.

The breakfast began promptly at 8 A.M. The President tested the idea of calling the parties to the White House. Wirtz was opposed. Connor was unenthusiastic. Morse and Collins, however, believed that only direct presidential pressure on the parties could avert a strike. Johnson agreed. The union planned to strike the next day at midnight, when the contract expired. The President had very little time even to get a postponement of the strike date. Johnson told Connor and Wirtz to invite management and labor representatives to the White House for a meeting that afternoon at 1 P.M.[15]

Johnson had photographers cover the beginning of his Cabinet Room meeting with Cooper, Abel, and their negotiating teams.[16] He told the parties he wanted "a noninflationary settlement." He asked them to remember "our boys in Vietnam, many of whom are dying there for freedom. Before you butt heads, stop. Look. And think. Think about your country." If they couldn't agree by the strike deadline, then the President wanted a postponement of the strike. He was well armed with the costs of a steel strike in lost jobs, increased imports, and the general threat a strike or inflationary settlement posed to the economy.[17] He then sent the negotiators, including Cooper and Abel, off to the Executive Office Building, across from the White House. "The room I'm providing for your negotiations is Room 275, the suite of offices I occupied as Vice President. That's how important I think these negotiations are."[18] He told them that secretaries Connor and Wirtz were available to help.

After the meeting, the President told me he wanted to open a secret back channel between the parties, independent of Wirtz and Connor. He asked me to have UN Ambassador Arthur Goldberg, who as an attorney had represented the steelworkers, get in touch with the union. Clark Clifford, who numbered the Republic Steel Corporation among his clients, was to contact the companies. Wirtz and Connor were never told of this channel; both would have withdrawn from the effort (and perhaps resigned their jobs) had they learned of parallel negotiations, so Johnson had me meet secretly with Clifford and Goldberg in the military aide's office in the East Wing of the White House. Johnson told each set of negotiators that everything depended on them—and them alone. He indicated to Clifford and Goldberg that he had no confidence in Connor and Wirtz, and at the same time told Connor and Wirtz that he was depending solely on them to settle this strike on his terms.

That afternoon, Johnson met former President Eisenhower at the White House.[19] He had me brief the General on the negotiations, and by the time the two leaders faced the press together, Eisenhower was recounting sad tales of his experience during the 1959 steel strike. It was a clever ploy: Eisenhower had been badly burned by the protracted 1959 steel strike, had no love for either side, and, as a military hero, underlined the importance of restraint during a time of war.

Word of that meeting was rushed to the negotiators, but Abel, Cooper, and their colleagues received no other news. Johnson had ordered all communication with the outside world cut off. The cloistering and public pressure had the desired short-term effect. A few hours after arriving at the White House, the parties agreed to extend the strike deadline for eight days. The President arranged to announce the postponement at precisely 9 P.M. so the networks could carry it on live television without interrupting their scheduled shows. Abel and Cooper, flanking Johnson, stoically nodded as the President told the nation that the negotiations were resuming at 10 P.M.

Later that evening, the President privately called Abel over to his office. He said that, like the labor leader, he had run in tough elections and had made many promises during his campaigns. While the President understood that Abel had to go as far as possible in fulfilling the promises he had made to the steelworkers, the national interest must come first. Johnson said that if Abel put the national interest first here the President would put Abel's interests first when he had an opportunity to do so.

The negotiations went into the late-night and early-morning hours of each day for the rest of the week, a good one for the President. Congress was acting favorably on his Great Society proposals.

Each evening, I would report to the President on the steel negotiations. He was in an expansive mood, and he usually drank several glasses of scotch and soda during our discussions, which sometimes ended over after-midnight dinners.[20]

As the negotiations continued, the President used the secret Arthur Goldberg and Clark Clifford channels to check on what Wirtz and Connor were reporting. Johnson felt that the union and the steel companies might be a little more likely to trust Goldberg and Clifford and perhaps even to discuss compromises with them. Johnson alerted me, "You watch what Clark suggests. He represents Republic Steel, and if he suggests something he thinks will move the companies, it will be what they really want because when it's over Clark will want to be in a position to tell his clients he got them something."

On Wednesday, Clifford reported to me that the steel companies would raise their offer to the union if the President would permit selective price increases in product lines where there was no Japanese competition, thus avoiding the danger of increasing imports. That evening Wirtz said the union was convinced that if the administration would "wink" at modest price increases, the companies would enrich their proposal. Former Treasury Secretary Douglas Dillon, now close to Roger Blough, called me to say that "some selective price increases" would help move big steel.

The President was adamant when I told him of these conversations: "No price increase," he said in his small green den. "None. Zero," he repeated as he made a circle with his right thumb and forefinger. He told me to tell Clifford and Connor to "give that message to [Roger Blough] in a tough way" and "turn him upside down and shake him before he makes an ass of himself again. He can go to 3.2 without a price increase."[21]

The next morning, the situation remained stalemated. The President met again with the negotiators. He gave them much the same pep talk he had in the Cabinet Room a couple of days before,[22] but this time he added a personal plea: with all the problems on his desk—the war, the economy, poverty, civil rights—he wanted to spend the upcoming Labor Day weekend with Lady Bird: "I plead with you to come to an agreement so I can go to the ranch and see Lady Bird and we can all enjoy the last weekend of summer." If the parties came in with a sound settlement, the President said, he'd invite them all to the Inauguration in January 1969.

Late the night before, I had told the President that as much of a problem existed between Commerce Secretary Connor and Labor Secretary Wirtz as between the parties; they couldn't even agree on the cost of particular benefits. Johnson decided to make that problem our opportunity. Through Clifford and Goldberg we had learned that each of the parties had come to regard the corresponding cabinet secretary as its ally. The President told me to sit down and conduct a negotiation between the cabinet secretaries, get them to assign the same costs to various benefits, come to an agreement, make them sign the agreement, and then present it to the parties. Around midnight on Thursday night and into Friday morning, the President met with Connor and Wirtz, telling each to negotiate with the other, with me as the mediator, and come up with an agreement they could both sign: "If you two can't agree, how the hell can we expect Abel and Cooper to agree?"[23]

The negotiations had already taken their toll on Connor and Wirtz. On his way to my office, Connor, shaking his head in disgust, told White House deputy special counsel Larry Levinson, "What a way to make a living." Wirtz was so tired that he fell asleep in my office as I was talking to him.[24] Nevertheless, from midnight until 1 A.M., I began to hammer out some agreement between Connor and Wirtz, but they were still quarreling about numbers. At around 1 A.M. on Friday morning, I met with Johnson and several others, and at 2 A.M. we went over to dinner in the mansion,[25] all the while conducting a nonstop discussion of how to get a settlement. After dinner Johnson sent me back to mediate between Wirtz and Connor.

I worked most of the morning with Wirtz, Connor, and Ackley in the Executive Office Building. Finally, the cabinet secretaries reached an agreement within the wage-price guideposts and signed it. I called the President: "If they can agree," he said, "then they must have found common meeting ground for the parties. I'll be right over." The President came over at about 2:30 P.M., met with the three of us, and told Wirtz and Connor to present their proposal to the parties.[26]

The President left the Executive Office Building, but he was so close to a settlement he couldn't sit still in his office. He walked around the White House grounds, chatted with reporters, looked over a new teleprompter, and had an animated meeting with two new speechwriters, Bob Hardesty and Will Sparks. At 4:40 P.M. I called to tell him that the parties had approved the Connor-Wirtz settlement. Johnson asked me to bring the steel negotiators to his office and told Bill Moyers he wanted to announce the settlement live at the top of the evening network television news at 6:30 P.M. Anxious to tell someone his good news, he then opened the door to his outer office, and with a grin stretching from ear to ear, he looked at his secretaries, Juanita Roberts, Marie Fehmer, and Vicky McCammon, and made victory circles with the thumbs and forefingers of both of his raised hands. A few minutes later, I brought the steel negotiators into his office.[27]

Amid smiles and congratulations, Johnson led the way into the Flower Garden, where photographers took pictures, and then we all walked over to the White House theater, where the President announced the settlement, live, on all three networks.[28] He delivered the message that no price increase was justified. When we returned to the Oval Office, the President started toward the door to go to the south grounds for his chopper,[29] then turned back to his desk, sat down, looked through a pile of photos taken over the past few days by his personal photographer, Yoichi Okamoto, pulled out one with me in it, wrote "To Joe, With thanks, LBJ," and handed it to me, smiling.

We were exhausted from the ordeal of five days of nonstop negotiations, but exhilarated by our success, which confirmed the belief in our minds and Johnson's that the President could get anyone to agree and that we could exert enormous influence over labor negotiations in the future. Cooper thanked Johnson for his "dedicated, tireless, and even-handed efforts." Abel praised him for his devotion to "free collective bargaining" and wrote that "we certainly think of you as our President."[30]

As Johnson worked to hold the steel labor contract within his wage guidelines, he had to battle Congress over its attempt to thwart his effort to curb non-Vietnam defense spending. On November 9, 1964, less than a week after Johnson's election, McNamara had flown to the LBJ Ranch[31] with several new initiatives, including a list of almost one hundred military installations he wanted to close to save a billion dollars a year. On his return from the ranch, McNamara told me he had secured the President's approval, but "the only time I've ever seen the President's face pale appreciably was when I showed him the list," which included four installations in Texas, the Brooklyn Naval Ship Yard and Army Terminal, and Glasgow Air Force Base in Montana, a major employer and source of income for Senate Majority Leader Mansfield's home state.

From the moment McNamara announced the closures on November 19, 1964, an attack force of senators and representatives assaulted the White House and the Pentagon. But the Defense Secretary held firm and the President took the position that these were McNamara's decisions. "I will not review them, I will not overrule him," Johnson said to complaining senators.[32]

Congress, however, wasn't going to get caught by surprise again. In the Military Construction Authorization bill sent to the President in August 1965, Congress provided that no Defense Department installation could be closed until the Secretary of Defense gave the House and Senate Armed Services committees 120 days notice; moreover, notice had to be given between January 1 and April 30 and, if Congress adjourned before the 120 days ran out, the secretary had to start all over again the following year.

Johnson considered the bill an improper legislative encroachment on executive power. He knew it would end his ability to close unnecessary bases and cut fat out of the defense budget. He asked Lee White and me to put together a draft veto message on August 19. On Saturday morning, August 21, the President had me assemble his advisers to discuss whether he should veto the bill and to review a draft message. These included Deputy Attorney General Ramsey Clark, Cy Vance, White House counsel Harry McPherson, Congressional liaison Barefoot Sanders, Clark Clifford—and newly confirmed Supreme Court Justice Abe Fortas.[33] Vance, stating his own view as well as McNamara's, felt that the provision would make it impossible to run the Pentagon efficiently. Clark and McPherson thought the bill was probably unconstitutional, confirming Johnson's instinct that Congress was intruding too deeply into his prerogatives as Commander-in-Chief.

Johnson most wanted Fortas's view on the constitutionality of the restriction. Fortas believed it was clearly unconstitutional and that the Supreme Court would so find. Relatively fresh from Harvard Law School, where professors left the impression that Supreme Court justices lived and worked in ivory towers, I was surprised to see Fortas discussing a constitutional question that might come before the Court and even speculating on the Court's likely action.

The President was determined to win this fight. To Johnson, that meant he had to be as sure as he could that he had the votes on Capitol Hill. But if members of Congress did not sustain his veto and the constitutional test moved to the courts, Johnson wanted to see that he had the votes in the Supreme Court, or at least an articulate advocate there. Then, if ever again he had to face Congress on a constitutional issue of this sort, the members would accord him a little more respect and enough votes to sustain his veto.

Toward the end of the meeting, the President called me to check on its outcome.[34] He wondered what compromise we thought he might work out with Congress. There was a consensus that if the notice to Congress was reduced to sixty days and the restrictions on its timing eased, the President should sign the bill. Johnson wanted McNamara to visit the chairmen of the Senate and House Armed Services committees, Richard Russell of Georgia and Mendel Rivers of South Carolina, respectively, to solicit their agreement to this compromise. Johnson then gathered the White House staff and divided up the entire Congress among us, with instructions to call assigned members, inform them of the veto, and see what they would do. Fortas, Clifford, Ramsey Clark, and I returned to my office to put the final touches on the draft veto message, which the President released that afternoon.[35]

The statement seemed to hit all of Johnson's points: the Attorney General's opinion that Congress had stepped beyond its constitutional role to "raise and support" armed forces, the inability of the Congress to deal with the multitudinous details of executing laws, the $1 billion annual savings already achieved by closing bases, the need for flexibility in a nuclear age, and even a touch of history, quoting James Madison on the floor of the House during the first session of the first Congress in 1789: "If there is a principle in our Constitution . . . more sacred than another, it is just that which separates the Legislative, Executive and Judicial powers."

But the statement did not mention two central concerns of the President. Johnson used to say that "an individual rarely, if ever, does anything for just one reason." One of the keys to persuasion and success in politics and government, he told me, was to figure out as many reasons as possible why an individual might take certain action or vote a certain way. And always remember, Johnson would say, "A man in a tough situation rarely reveals the real reasons why he does something." Some of us on the staff used to say that if we figured out a dozen reasons why LBJ took some action or other, we probably didn't know the most important one.

So it was with the veto of the Military Construction bill. Of the many reasons set forth in his veto message, perhaps the key ones were never mentioned. Johnson simply didn't want any more inhibitions than the minimum necessary on his freedom to reduce non-Vietnam defense spending and to act in Vietnam. On their face, restrictions on the executive's ability to close military bases had nothing to do with Southeast Asia. But Johnson knew that the restriction could be a troublesome precedent in the future.

McNamara's discussions with Russell and Rivers elicited their agreement to a sixty-day notice period and more flexible timing for giving notice. But, as we on the White House staff made our congressional calls, it became clear that members would readily sustain the President's veto and accept thirty days' notice with no restrictions on timing. Once satisfied he had the votes, LBJ said he would accept only a thirty-day restriction. When I mentioned that McNamara was selling Russell and Rivers on a sixty-day-notice provision, Johnson said, "On whose authority?"

"I thought that was what you suggested during the meeting Saturday," I said gingerly.

"Maybe that's what you thought, but that's not what I said. I suggest you start *listening* to what I say instead of *thinking* what I say. Thirty days is the maximum notice period the President will accept. You tell Bob that."

When I called McNamara to tell him, I feared the worst. "Goddamnit," he responded, but added to my surprise and education in the ways of this President, "I feared something like that would happen when he decided to have all the members called. I've made my deal with Russell and Rivers, but I left a little leeway. I told them that this is what I'd recommend to the President and that I thought he'd take it. I'll just tell them he won't take anything more than thirty days. They can count too and they'll realize he has the votes."

In early September, Congress passed a revised Military Construction Authorization Act that permitted base closures on thirty days' notice, which could be given at any time. When he signed the bill, Johnson praised the Congress and expressed his "refreshed faith in our institutions of government."

Johnson's decision to hold off a tax increase also set us on a scavenger hunt to find money for the federal treasury. Soon after he announced the Vietnam buildup, the President asked me to speed up sales of excess government stockpiles of strategic materials.[36] After World War II, with shortages fresh in its mind and the cold war getting chillier every day, the government had accumulated millions of tons of materials like aluminum, copper, zinc, molybdenum, and rubber. From his experience chairing the Senate's Preparedness Investigating Subcommittee, Johnson knew how industries had sought to increase government stockpile purchases to maintain prices during times of recession and to recoup profits lost to lower-priced imports. Indeed, to help his own farm constituents, Johnson had made sure that the government warehoused plenty of wool and long-staple cotton.

As President, LBJ saw stockpile surpluses as a source of revenue. When I reported that we planned to sell $550 million in fiscal 1966 and $700 million the following year, the President penciled across my memo: "Joe, shouldn't we set goals, call in Cong leaders, incl chr of committees [whose approval was required for some sales], & sell 1 Bil [each year] if possible."[37]

The big bucks were in aluminum: 1.4 million tons of excess aluminum could be sold for close to $700 million. For some time, the General Services Administration had tried unsuccessfully to get the aluminum industry to cooperate in a program to sell some of this stockpile. Finally, on October 25, 1965, prodded by the President, the General Services Administration informed the major aluminum companies that it planned to sell 100,000 tons of stockpile aluminum.[38]

Four days later, on a Friday, Ormet Corporation, a small aluminum producer and subsidiary of Olin Mathieson Chemical Corporation, announced an increase in the price of its aluminum. Reynolds Metals Company and Kaiser Aluminum and Chemical Corporation, two of the big three, promptly raised prices. The third, Aluminum Company of America (Alcoa), was studying the situation, but was expected to join the parade.

That evening Otto Eckstein, as acting chairman of the Council of Economic Advisers, fired off a cable to the President, who was at the ranch recuperating from gall-bladder surgery. Eckstein's cable pointed out that this was the fifth price increase in two years and the industry's after-tax profits were at near-record levels. The companies should be reducing prices, Eckstein emphasized, not raising them. Noting that a rise in aluminum prices would make it easy for other metals to go up, Eckstein urged Johnson to act.[39]

The President was thundering when he called me from his bedroom the next morning at 8:50 A.M.[40] He had been depressed since leaving the hospital. He was annoyed that his recovery was not proceeding faster and hurt by the ridicule to which he was being subjected for having exposed to the world his big stomach scar from the operation. He had been trying to assure everyone that he had not had another heart attack; the gesture had misfired.

He was also irritable because of the strict diet doctors had put him on. Johnson loved to eat. Though he was often put on diets, he was always breaking them. He tried all sorts of nonfattening dishes, but diet tapioca pudding was just about the only low-calorie food he enjoyed. His most successful effort was during this convalescence. The presidential daily diaries record Johnson's pride at dropping from more than 220 pounds to 209, then 208, 207½, 206¾, 203 (a point at which LBJ proudly exclaimed that he was wearing a suit he had not been able to get into since 1958), and by mid-December, 191¾, probably his lightest weight during his presidency. The loss of every pound was painful. Johnson, who liked lots of gravy, would complain about tasteless meals: "What's a broiled veal chop? Those old green beans, same old squash, tossed salad—I'm against anything that's tossed." He would ostentatiously display the looseness of his jackets, exaggerate the decline in his waistline, and refuse to let Dr. Burkley look at the scale when his weight went up.[41] In the end, he succumbed to his love of food and enormous appetite (even when he ate diet puddings, he often consumed two or three servings). When his stomach expanded so that even his tailored suits couldn't disguise his true girth, Johnson wore a girdle.

This morning there was fury in his words. He wanted to flood the market immediately with whatever amount of stockpile aluminum was needed to break the price. Johnson also called Commerce Secretary Connor and asked him to urge industry executives to roll back their price increases. Connor argued that the increases were justified and that in any case the President didn't have "dictatorial authority . . . to order price reductions." This further incensed the President, who told him, as he slammed down the phone, "I'll get Bob McNamara to do it."[42]

Johnson reached McNamara at St. Paul's School, a New England prep school, where his son was playing in a football game. McNamara reminded the President that he had cleared the trip earlier in the week and protested that he was not seeing enough of his son. Johnson said, "Well, you should see more of your son. But you know, your country really needs you and you're up there at some Goddamned football game."

McNamara returned later that evening, and we began laying out a plan to use the aluminum stockpile to roll back the price.[43] Both McNamara and I were taken aback by the intensity of Johnson's wrath. What I didn't know at the time was that this had been a terrible day for LBJ: as a result of a map-plotting error two American pilots had destroyed a friendly village of Vietnamese civilians; his daughter Luci, who was eighteen, had told him she was going to marry Patrick Nugent and the President and Mrs. Johnson thought their youngest daughter was too young to get married and was making a serious mistake; and Johnson had seen Peter Hurd's portrait of himself, which he had hated. He called it "the ugliest thing I ever saw." Mrs. Johnson said afterward that she didn't expect to endure an encounter so grim if she "lived to be a thousand."[44]

On Monday morning, I called the President to report on the situation. He was still in bed at 10:51 when we talked,[45] frustrated by his slow recovery and complaining about his diet. He sounded weary but furious, this time at a story in *The New York Times*, headlined, "JOHNSON, ANGRY, MOVES TO RETAIN ALUMINUM PRICE." Under the subhead, "Was 'Sputtering Mad,' " this sentence appeared: "Mr. Johnson, who in recent weeks has repeatedly stressed the need to avoid inflation, was said by Administration sources in Washington to have been made 'sputtering mad' by the move." The President asked me whether I had talked to any reporters from the *Times*. I hadn't. Then he ripped into Eckstein. "That sonuvabitch sends a cable down here that would make any President see red. Then when I do what he wants, he goes around bragging about how mad he got the President." Johnson worked himself into a towering rage over the phone as he told me that "I am not . . . never have been . . . never will be . . . sputtering mad" and how terrible it was for the foreign leaders to see the American President so portrayed. I had to bite hard into my own hand to restrain laughter as the President shouted angrily again, "Do you hear me? I am not now, never in my life have been, and never will be sputtering mad!"

Angry or not, Johnson saw the sale of stockpiled aluminum as a tantalizing three-cushioned shot: it would make clear his intention to roll back any inflationary pricing moves, put some money in the federal treasury, and help our international balance of payments by reducing the need for imports.[46]

Johnson wanted to have and eat his cake. He wanted to dump stockpiled aluminum on the market without admitting he was doing it at this time to break the price. Since the industry was already fabricating aluminum at full capacity, we decided to present a stockpile disposal as essential to meet growing demands of the Vietnam War and mitigate balance-of-payments problems. Should anyone ask, Johnson wanted forceful denials that any stockpile release was designed to undercut the industry's price increase.[47] *The New York Times* reported the following day:

> Aluminum companies would not comment . . . on reports that President Johnson was considering use of the national aluminum stockpile as a tool to force rescission of the price rise. . . .
> Privately, however, industry sources tended to doubt that the President would, or could, take such drastic action.

When Alcoa, the industry giant, raised its aluminum prices, the President ordered us to put enough stockpile aluminum on the market to break the increases. But we didn't know how much that was. On November 6, McNamara announced a release of 200,000 tons from the stockpile. When company executives stiffed us on the price increase despite some tough talk from McNamara, the President told me to announce release of an additional 100,000 tons of aluminum.

That did it. On November 10, Alcoa rescinded its price hike. Within hours, the rest of the aluminum industry followed Alcoa's rollback.

Johnson asked McNamara to praise industry fulsomely at a press conference, and the Secretary hailed this "act of industrial statesmanship," adding, ". . . we do an injustice to these executives when we

say that they would act only when clubbed. . . . These . . . leaders of
the business community . . . don't have to be clubbed into a sense of
responsibility."[48]

Shortly thereafter, the government and the industry reached an
agreement to dispose of all excess aluminum in the stockpile. The
industry was relieved to have this ax lifted from over its head and the
administration was pleased to get the money from sale of the stockpile.[49]

As we stuck our finger in the economic dike to stem the aluminum price rise, another hole opened when the Anaconda Company,
the world's largest copper producer, raised the price of copper. CEA
Chairman Ackley wired the President at the ranch: ". . . we can't
welcome a copper increase in the middle of the aluminum crisis,"
especially when "copper companies are far more profitable than the
aluminum companies."[50]

With the aluminum battle barely ended, the President ordered
me to reassemble his key economic advisers and put together a plan to
roll back the price of copper. On Friday evening, November 12, I
rounded up what were becoming the usual firefighters on price
increases—McNamara, Fowler, Connor, Katzenbach, Ackley, Eckstein, and others, including David Ginsburg, a Washington lawyer
whom Johnson remembered from World War II when Ginsburg
served in the Office of Price Administration.[51] It quickly became
apparent that we were woefully uninformed about the copper market.

When I called the President about our concern, he told me about
"a little man" who had worked on the staff of the Senate Preparedness
Investigating Subcommittee who "knew more about copper than any
living being. Joe something or other. Find him and get him down
there to help you." Johnson couldn't remember his last name, but he
remembered what he looked like. Frantically, I ran down subcommittee staffers and found out that I was looking for Joseph Zimmerman,
who now lived in Peter Cooper Village in Manhattan and had a weekend home in Connecticut, where I located him that Saturday. He was
astonished that the President knew he existed. Since leaving the subcommittee staff, he had become a metals trader in New York and, yes,
he still knew a great deal about copper.

I had Zimmerman flown to Washington on a White House Jet
Star that afternoon, and at four o'clock he walked into the Cabinet
Room for a meeting with McNamara, Fowler, Katzenbach, Ackley,
Bundy, and me.[52] After recovering from his initial shock, Zimmer-
man gave us an education on the copper industry. Copper shortages
had come about as a result of growing demand, unrest in copper-

producing foreign countries, and labor disturbances at home. American copper companies were reluctant to raise prices because they feared substitution (ironically mostly by aluminum). But, Zimmerman stressed, copper prices were set in world markets, with Chile the price leader.

That afternoon, I expressed my doubts to the President that we could do anything about the price of copper. "It's a world price. For starters, we'd have to get Chile to roll its price back."

Johnson didn't blink. "Find out what it will take to get [Eduardo] Frei [President of Chile] to roll the price back. We need to send someone special to meet with Frei." He immediately decided on W. Averell Harriman, the veteran American statesman, as the ideal man to make it clear to Frei that reducing the price of copper was of personal importance to the President. He wanted me to put Harriman on a plane that afternoon to meet with Frei as soon as possible. When I suggested that such a strenuous journey on short notice might be difficult for the seventy-four-year-old diplomat, Johnson chuckled and whispered into the phone, "You just call him up and get a car over to his Georgetown house. Ol' Averell likes women. You just tell him what the President wants him to do. And tell him we'll put a couple of pretty nurses on the plane and they'll start working on him as soon as wheels are up and by the time he gets to Santiago he'll have it up!" Johnson was chuckling loudly. "Then you put together the rest of the program that Zimmerman suggests. If we have to, we'll roll back the world price of copper!"

On Tuesday, November 16, our cabinet group met again, with Zimmerman coming down from New York to put the final touches on a program. During the meeting in my office, the President stopped by just before 8 P.M. to bless the program and thank Joe Zimmerman.[53] Zimmerman was so touched tears rolled down his cheeks.

The next day, McNamara announced a program to release 200,000 tons of copper from the stockpile, control copper exports, suspend the import duty on copper, and ask the New York Commodity Exchange to increase margin requirements on copper trading to stem inflationary speculation. I informed Anaconda of the Harriman mission to Chile and the President's willingness to bargain with Frei to get him to hold the price of copper. Two days later, hailing these moves, Anaconda rescinded its price increase and the other companies followed.[54]

But there was to be no respite for LBJ on the economic front. On the morning of December 31, 1965, Bethlehem Steel Corporation announced a $5-per-ton increase in the price of its structural steel. An industry-wide increase would quickly fan out across the economy. It would also set a foul precedent, coming on the heels of the industry's noninflationary labor settlement and the administration's subsequent success in holding down aluminum and copper prices.

LBJ took Bethlehem's action as a personal slap in the face, since during the September labor negotiations he had made it clear that no increase in steel prices was warranted. What particularly galled Johnson was that Bethlehem executives had picked New Year's Eve for their announcement, a Friday, when, the President said, "They probably thought we would all be out partying somewhere. I want to call these bastards war profiteers. That's exactly what they are."

As soon as Johnson saw the story of Bethlehem's announcement on the news wires at the LBJ Ranch, he ordered Gardner Ackley to condemn the price hike publicly[55] and ask Bethlehem Steel's top executives to come to Washington on New Year's Day. When Bethlehem ignored Ackley's invitation, Johnson wanted to issue a stinging statement, among other things accusing the steel company of "making money off of the sacrifices of our boys" in Vietnam.[56] After some discussion, the President agreed to a softer statement, urging Bethlehem to meet with the Council of Economic Advisers "right away" and "to consider the larger national interest, to weigh the impact of unnecessary price action against the sacrifices of our men in Vietnam, and to act accordingly."[57]

It was the first time that the President had so publicly entered a price-rollback battle at its earliest stages. Once he had done so, we had to win. "The worst thing for the American presidency," Johnson said, "would be for one of these steel magnates like Roger Blough to beat the President of the United States." At Johnson's direction, shortly before midnight on New Year's Eve I contacted Edmund Martin, Bethlehem's chairman, and he agreed to come to Ackley's office the next day.[58]

The next morning, the White House phone at my home rang at 7 A.M. "What's happening with steel?" the President asked. "Have you heard from any companies? Or anyone in the cabinet?"

As I drearily looked at the clock and saw the time, I reminded the President that it was New Year's Day. He ignored that remark, grousing instead that there were no congressional statements in the newspapers or on the wires supporting his move against Bethlehem. Then we discussed strategy for the meeting with Martin that afternoon.

At the meeting, Martin gave little justification for the increase and no indication that he would rescind it. When I reported this to the President, he told me to make certain that the government did not buy "one Goddamn ounce" of steel from Bethlehem or any company that raised its price.[59] The President and I got into another argument about calling the Bethlehem executives "war profiteers." This time what slowed him down was my comment that such a charge would put him in the same position as President Kennedy after he called corporate executives "sons of bitches" during his 1962 battle with big steel and tore apart his relations with American business.

The next day, LBJ sent a telegram to Martin and the heads of the seven other largest steel companies asking them to "put the interest of your country first." He added pointedly, "I am not announcing this wire so that you and your associates can consider the interest of your country and your company with complete freedom."[60]

But Johnson also wanted to put some public pressure on the steel executives. LBJ used to say, "Men are moved by love and fear, and the key to persuasion is to find the right measure of each to move them the way you want to." So, as he dispatched the telegrams, he directed Ackley and me to give a background briefing to the press. He wanted attribution to "high administration officials" not to "White House sources. . . . You cannot say White House sources," since in his telegram he had indicated that he would not put public pressure on the executives. The President knew precisely the points he wanted made: "excessive profits . . . the fact that in ten years steel had gone from a $645 million export surplus to a $600 million import deficit . . . all my advisers—the Secretaries of Treasury, Commerce, Labor and Defense and the CEA—think the increase is unwarranted . . . the role of steel in price inflation . . ."

LBJ overruled my arguments against calling the Bethlehem executives war profiteers. He instructed me to say, "They are laying themselves open to warranted charges of profiteering." He made me repeat the words back to him over the phone. "Now, do you have it?" he demanded. "Say it exactly that way."[61] He was so determined I decided to make the charge in the press briefing, in order to forestall the President's making it and damaging himself. So I said, "I think also that with what Chairman Ackley described yesterday as soaring profits, and with a very difficult Vietnam situation that might require additional military action, moving at this time the Bethlehem people do leave themselves open to the charge of profiteering."[62] The next morning the front pages of both *The New York Times* and *Washington Post* reported that, as the *Times* wrote, "Government officials labeled the Bethlehem action 'profiteering' from the war in Vietnam."

U.S. Steel, the industry giant that had gone to the mat with John Kennedy, had not made a decision. At the President's direction, I asked the company's chairman, Roger Blough, to meet with McNamara before he acted. Blough indicated that U.S. Steel was contemplating raising structural steel prices only $2.75 per ton, with reductions in another line to mitigate the structural increase. The President was satisfied with the result. Immediately after U.S. Steel's announcement, Bethlehem rescinded its price increase. Johnson had won another holding action.

Some weeks later at a meeting with businessmen, one of them complained to the President about the "profiteering" charge. I was standing next to Johnson. He looked surprised. He said he considered the statement reprehensible. He assured the businessman: "If I find out some damn fool aide did it, I'll fire the sonuvabitch!"[63]

Six months after his decision to pursue the Great Society and the war without a tax increase, it almost seemed as if LBJ could hold down prices and wages by the force of his presence and personality. But there would be no time to rest on the laurels of the aluminum, copper, and steel price victories. They would turn out to be only three of scores of price and wage battles in a presidential jawboning effort the likes of which the American people had never seen. And, in late 1965, as we took comfort in the achievement of the noninflationary union agreement with big steel, not one of us could know that would be the last major wage settlement within the guideposts.

SIX

Guns and Butter

LBJ'S DETERMINATION to pursue both the war and the Great Society without a tax increase didn't sit well with William McChesney Martin, Chairman of the Federal Reserve Board of Governors. The Fed has authority independently to determine the nation's money supply and can effectively set interest rates, thus quickening or slowing the economy's pace. The President's only leverage over the institution is his power to appoint its seven members, including the chairman, for fixed terms with the advice and consent of the Senate. Johnson appreciated the power of the Fed and the financial community's esteem for Bill Martin, who had been appointed by President Truman in 1951.

Johnson's populist instincts made him think of interest rates in terms of their effects on small farmers, small businessmen, and poor people forced to borrow money to make ends meet. He was suspicious of eastern bankers and the financial establishment of which Martin was a preeminent icon. He told the chairman that he came from a part of the country that liked low interest rates "all the time." Martin responded that he too favored low interest rates—"as low as conditions of inflation, deflation, or stability—which is my preference—permit them to be," but not all the time. That kind of candor formed the basis for a mutual, but wary, respect between the two men. Relations between them remained cordial until December 1965.

In mid-1965, Martin had begun dropping hints that he might

favor higher interest rates to tighten credit, slow the economy, and avoid inflation. As Martin kept hinting, CEA Chairman Gardner Ackley fired off memos to the President arguing strenuously that no tightening of credit was warranted; money was needed to keep the economy growing, consumer and wholesale prices were pretty steady. On October 4, Budget Director Charles Schultze wrote the President that, contrary to normal procedure, he had, in preparing the budget, instructed his staff not to discuss the budgetary outlook with the Fed. "Quite apart from security considerations," he wrote, "I am afraid that *the budgetary outlook* [increases in Great Society programs and Vietnam spending] *would be used as an excuse to tighten up on monetary policy.*" When Treasury Secretary Joe Fowler also weighed in with concerned warnings that the Fed might tighten credit, the President called a meeting of the Quadriad* for October 6.[1]

Fowler began the meeting by reporting, "There's a lot of discussion of pressures to get [interest] rates up."

"What pressures?" the President asked, feigning surprise.

Finance companies wanted more money, banks were complaining about the difficulty of getting the money people want, "so they concluded let's exact higher rates," Fowler responded. "Tom Gates [Chairman of Morgan Guaranty Trust Company] is thinking about raising some rates," he added.

The President wondered aloud whether there ought to be some private conversations with key bankers or whether he should make a public statement about the importance of keeping rates down.

Sensing that Johnson's comments were designed to smoke him out and that he'd been cut out of the budget process, Martin said he thought it would be important to know how much was going to be spent in 1966, "particularly by McNamara on the war."

Johnson said it was impossible to predict. "It could be $10 billion, it could be $3 to $5 billion." Realizing he should assuage Martin and downplay the war's cost, he added, "McNamara says it very likely will be less than $5 billion for the rest of [fiscal] 1966." Under the circumstances, Fowler and Ackley said they wanted to "hold the line" on interest rates.

Martin said he didn't know enough about the situation to be confident about what to do. But he confessed that he leaned toward increasing rates.

Johnson thought it was important "at this time to keep from

* The Quadriad consisted of four key economic officials: Fed Chairman Martin, CEA Chairman Ackley, Treasury Secretary Fowler, and Budget Director Schultze. I usually attended Quadriad meetings with the President.

driving rates up." He noted that he'd seen firsthand the havoc that high interest rates level on the poor and small farmers and businessmen. Ackley and Schultze agreed.

Martin, looking directly at the President, said, "If we thought you were right we'd all do the same thing. But the question is, whose crystal ball is right?"[2]

The discussion failed to elicit Martin's commitment not to raise rates. But, as word of the meeting leaked through the financial community and as Fowler made public the administration's view, interest rates retreated.[3] Within the administration, the belief was widespread that Martin would not decide what to do until after release of the President's budget and legislative program in January 1966.

Then, on November 29, 1965, Fowler and Ackley alerted LBJ that Martin had privately expressed an intention to vote to increase the discount rate (the interest rate at which the Fed lends money to banks), if any regional Federal Reserve Bank proposed such action. Three regional bank boards were to meet on Thursday, December 2, and Ackley was certain that at least one, and perhaps all three, would suggest a discount-rate hike. He saw the Fed Board as split 3 to 3, with the seventh member undecided but leaning toward a rate hike.[4]

Johnson asked Ackley to try to turn the undecided member against a rate hike and he told me to get a sense of how key members of Congress would line up on the issue.[5] On Tuesday, November 30, the White House revealed that the President planned to meet with the Quadriad "in the very near future." This was an attempt to signal Martin to wait until after the meeting before deciding whether to increase the discount rate. Martin had another idea.

On Friday, December 3, at Martin's urging, the Federal Reserve Board voted 4 to 3 to raise the discount rate. Acknowledging the legal independence of the Fed, Johnson "particularly regretted" that the board's action was taken before his budget and legislative program were known. He expressed concern that the cost of credit would rise for "homes, schools, hospitals, and factories," and promised to "do my best to give the American people the . . . well-integrated economic policy to which they are entitled."

While the President's view was moderately expressed, he was quite angry with Martin and incited key Democratic legislators to attack him. From his ranch, Johnson burned up the wires to Washington, asking one member of Congress after another, "How can I run the country and the government if I have to read on a news-service ticker that Bill Martin is going to run his own economy?" Senator William Proxmire (D-Wisc.) called for hearings "to determine what action must be taken to prevent this creature of Congress from endangering the nation's prosperity and from doing so in defiance of the President of the United States." Goaded by Johnson, fellow Texan Wright Patman, Chairman of the House Banking and Joint Economic committees, excoriated Martin for "thumb[ing] his nose at the President, the Congress, and the American people." He attacked the "folly of allowing a handful of banker-dominated members of the Federal Reserve to dictate the economic future of the country."

On Monday, December 6, I flew down to the ranch with Martin, Fowler, and Ackley. Sitting on the lawn in front of the ranch house, LBJ at first probed for any way of turning Martin around. He quickly saw that there was none. Nevertheless, the President was charming and in a teasing mood during the meeting, at lunch, and for much of the afternoon. As a result, the meeting and the later press conference were superficially amicable.[6]

But Johnson made sure hearings were held in Congress, and he urged Proxmire, Patman, and others to keep the heat on the Fed. Most important, he replaced C. Canby Balderston (whose term expired January 31, 1966), one of Martin's majority votes on the Fed Board.

The replacement of Balderston was delicate for LBJ. Martin was threatening to resign if Johnson put another liberal on the board. As New York Times economic reporter Eileen Shanahan wrote at the time, "Martin has long been telling all who talk with him that he would resign if he ever found himself consistently in the minority." Johnson's two prior appointments, James Robertson in 1964 and Sherman Maisel in 1965, had voted against the rate hike. Johnson now wanted to tilt the balance of power against Martin, but he didn't want Martin to quit. Having an establishment Republican banker as chairman would be an enormous asset in the days ahead, especially if Johnson could hold him in check with a "low-interest-rate man."

Martin suggested that Johnson appoint Atherton Bean, a Minneapolis businessman serving on the board of a District Federal Reserve Bank. Martin tried to sell Bean to the President in an evening meeting on February 1, 1966. He called him "too fine a man for anyone to think of him as my man, or yours."[7] But Johnson was taking no chances. The President had in mind a liberal, Andrew Brimmer, an Assistant Secretary of Commerce at the time. He knew Martin could not leave the board over Brimmer's appointment—because he was black—even if the balance of power might shift against him. Moreover, with Brimmer, Johnson would become the first President to name a black to the Federal Reserve Board.

When Johnson suggested Brimmer to Martin, the Chairman complained that he was too young, and would be the fourth economist on the board and that was too many.[8] But LBJ knew he had Martin.

LBJ also wanted to be sure he had Brimmer. On the brink of announcing the nomination, Johnson became concerned about whether Brimmer shared his sense of the overriding importance of low interest rates. The President asked if I was "absolutely certain that Andrew Brimmer will vote to hold interest rates down," or whether someone as brilliant and persuasive as Martin would overwhelm the young economist.

"Has he gotten so involved with big business in the Commerce Department that he's forgotten what it's like to be a Negro?" Johnson asked.

"I think Brimmer favors low interest rates. That's what Gardner Ackley tells me," I replied.

The President shot back, "*Thinking so* is not good enough. I want you to *know so*. Brimmer doesn't go on the board until we *know*."

I called Ackley and others who knew Brimmer well professionally. Brimmer was reluctant to talk to them about what his policies would be once he became a member of the Fed. I made it clear to the economists that if Brimmer considered it inappropriate to discuss his view on these subjects the President might consider it inappropriate to put him on the board.

I reminded Ackley of LBJ's distinction between thinking and knowing. The first time I told the President I thought I had a congressman's vote on a bill, he snapped, "Don't ever *think* about those things. Know, know, KNOW! You've got to *know* you've got him, and there's only one way you know." He raised his right hand and closed his fingers in the form of a fist. He looked at his right hand and said, "And that's when you've got his pecker right here." Johnson then opened his desk drawer, opened his fist as though he were dropping something, slammed the drawer closed and smiled.[9]

The President had a private talk with Brimmer. He concluded, as he later told me, "Andy Brimmer hasn't forgotten what it's like to be Negro, to be a small farmer, to be a candy-store owner, to be a corner druggist, who needs to borrow money to keep his business going without paying exorbitant interest to the New York bankers."

The President had one more call to make. Russell Long of Louisiana chaired the Senate Finance Committee, which would have a lot to say about how the Senate would handle the Brimmer nomination. Long had a favorite white candidate from his home state. When Johnson told Long he intended to nominate Brimmer, Long demanded, "What the hell am I going to tell the people in my state?" "Tell them he's from Louisiana," LBJ replied.* [10]

Brimmer's swearing-in, after swift Senate confirmation, had a sweet touch from Johnson. At his suggestion, Brimmer asked Federal Reserve Chairman Bill Martin to administer the oath of office. [11]

The Brimmer appointment would help temper the Fed, but to have both butter and guns, Johnson had to negotiate the political and economic rapids without a tax increase and without inflation. That meant keeping the defense budget, including Vietnam costs, as low as possible.

As early as August 20, 1965, the President had written himself a note: "McNamara's got to find ways to drag his feet on defense expenditures." Pressed by LBJ, McNamara got the defense budget down to $60.5 billion, by arbitrarily assuming that the war would end on June 30, 1967, the final day of the fiscal year. Without that assumption, McNamara warned, defense spending should be pegged at $63 to $65 billion. Even with the assumption, Johnson might have to ask Congress for more money later in the year. [12]

To help justify his defense budget, the President sent McNamara to the history books. The Secretary's research gave LBJ the benchmarks he needed: during the three years of the Korean War, the Defense Department had requested $164 billion; Congress appropriated $156 billion; Defense spent only $102 billion. Throughout that war, unspent military balances rose from $11 billion to $62 billion. Moreover, in the course of fourteen months, President Truman had submitted two regular defense budgets and four requests for additional funds.

With this precedent, LBJ decided on a defense budget of $60.5 billion, with McNamara publicly stating that the amount was sufficient for a war that would end on June 30, 1967. The budget did not provide for any pipeline of materials or personnel or long-lead-time items that might be needed after that date. Later in the year, substantial supplemental funds would be requested to take care of such needs, and by that time it was conceivable (though unlikely) that the war might be over, but in any case, several Great Society programs would have been enacted and funded.

The Democratic liberals were insisting that the President not slow his domestic programs, and his allies in the labor movement were especially vehement. Andy Biemiller, organized labor's top lobbyist, sat in my office for an hour on December 23, 1965, delivering

---

* Brimmer was in fact from Louisiana, something Russell Long hadn't known.

a stern message from AFL-CIO president George Meany, who believed "that the Great Society programs must not be gutted because of the war in Vietnam." It wasn't that the labor movement questioned the President on the war; like LBJ himself; it wanted both to fight the Communists in Southeast Asia and to fund an era of social progress.[13] Those liberals who did question the war seemed willing to mute their criticism so long as the Great Society programs continued.

Johnson did not always share the outlook of his liberal allies, such as Senators Joseph Clark (D-Pa.) and Gaylord Nelson (D-Wisc.) who wanted big increases in all domestic spending. He planned to continue to fight for the Great Society, but he felt that it was essential as a matter of political strategy to control expenditures. Otherwise, he believed, "the Republicans and right wing Democrats in the Congress" would gut the Great Society programs and use the war as an excuse.[14] Except for Vietnam, Johnson held his fiscal 1967 budget to a small increase of less than one percent above fiscal 1966; most of that increase involved health, education, and social service programs, which went up sharply.

As Johnson's intention to go pedal-to-the-floor with his Great Society became clear and evidence accumulated of a step-up in the economy, Budget Director Schultze "strongly" recommended a $5 billion tax increase, and CEA Chairman Ackley sent the President a memo saying that he leaned in the same direction. When the President returned Ackley's memo to me, he asked that Ackley, Fowler, and Schultze produce tax proposals on a most discreet basis. "Caution them not to go into detail with staff & keep away from all reporters," his handwritten note said.[15]

As his economic advisers suggested some sort of tax increase, LBJ sent Fowler to talk to Wilbur Mills (D-Ark.), Chairman of the House Ways and Means Committee, the starting point for tax legislation in the Congress. Mills told Fowler that the administration's budget should hold civilian expenditures at the prior year's level. "The full impact of Vietnam expenditures," he said, "should not be put in the fiscal 1967 budget," and any spending above.$105 billion should "only be attributed to the Vietnam expenditures." Mills wanted no part in any tax increase but he was amenable to some modest tax adjustments: stepped-up withholding of personal income taxes, accelerated collection of corporate taxes, and extension of auto and telephone excise taxes. These measures promised to raise some revenue, but not much. Senate Finance Committee Chairman Russell Long gave a diagonal nod of support to these adjustments. Both Mills and Long confirmed Johnson's suspicion that no tax increase could be passed and they emphatically refused to support one.[16]

The President recommended these adjustments and others, and the Congress enacted them into law by mid-March 1966, less than sixty days later. Modest as the adjustments were, however, both Mills and Long demurred when Johnson suggested a signing ceremony. Even these changes were, like all tax increases, unpopular.[17]

As the President pushed and pulled with the budget and the tax increase, he was also developing his legislative program. Beyond our very first discussion in the pool as I had treaded water, the President offered little guidance. He would occasionally say that he wanted "a program for the cities," or an "Asian Development Bank," or "something to help the Negro male and his family." At other times he spoke of a "fair-housing bill," or a "consumer program to help housewives buying groceries and veterans buying cars and homes." But he expected me to put the flesh on the bones "with the finest minds in the country." He wanted the best ideas "without regard to the politics. You let these intellectuals get me the ideas. I'll worry about the politics." He would often add, when irritated, that "The trouble with the Democratic party is that all the intellectuals want to be politicians and all the politicians want to be intellectuals."

Over that summer and fall, I set up task forces to develop legislative programs in transportation, job training, air and water pollution, population and family planning, income maintenance, tax reform, education, public assistance, urban affairs and housing, health care, crime, foreign aid, civil rights, and agriculture. We sought ideas from a broad sweep of individuals, from United Auto Workers President Walter Reuther to Yale University President Kingman Brewster, from economists like John Kenneth Galbraith and Barbara Ward to writer John Steinbeck and former Secretary of State Dean Acheson, from reports of government commissions and galleys of unpublished books.[18]

I asked Vice President Humphrey to sit in on our task force on the cities. In December, Johnson read a press report that quoted Humphrey as saying LBJ was considering a program to select certain cities to be rebuilt as demonstrations of what could be accomplished. He called me and asked me "how in the hell" the Vice President found out we were working on that. I told him that I had invited Humphrey to meet with the urban-affairs task force because he'd been a mayor himself. The President roared into the phone wires: "You are never, never to let the Vice President attend any meeting on the legislative program. He has Minnesota running-water disease. I've never known anyone from Minnesota that could keep their mouth shut. It's just something in the water out there."

The President told me to tell Humphrey to stop talking about "a Marshall plan or demonstration plan or any other plan for the cities. The President will talk about what he wants to do in the State of the Union message and he doesn't need the Vice President to try to commit him to some crazy, Goddamned expensive idea that Congress will never approve anyway." I called Humphrey that day.[19] He was remorseful, hoping he hadn't blown our cities proposal. He had not; but Johnson never again let me involve Humphrey in preparing legislative programs.

On December 29, 1965, I took the President through a loose-leaf book that outlined suggested new programs, entitled "The Great Society—A Second Year Legislative Program." We were working in his office at the LBJ Ranch. The President sat behind his desk, leaning back in his chair; I was off to the side turning the pages so he could see them (the loose-leaf binder was folded open, standing on its long edges).

We were serving up plenty of butter to go with the guns, a grand design, but no more grandiose than the President's September 16, 1965, statement had been: "We mean to show that this Nation's dream of a Great Society does not stop at the water's edge: and that it is not just an American dream. All are welcome to share in it. All are invited to contribute to it." As he went through my proposals, Johnson approved a vast international health initiative (which, among other things, set the goal, eventually achieved in 1980, to eradicate smallpox from the face of the earth by 1975), and international population, education, and food programs.

To fulfill his commitment "to reshape and reorganize the Executive Branch to meet more effectively the tasks of the Twentieth Century," we proposed Operation TRIM (Tighten, Reorganize, Invigorate, Modernize), including a Department of Natural Resources (he liked it, but disapproved after we could not put the political pieces in place in either the Executive Branch or Congress). We also suggested organizing the Department of Housing and Urban Development and reorganizing the Department of Health, Education, and Welfare (approved); moving the Small Business Administration to the Commerce Department (disapproved as "politically naïve"); a single Atomic Energy Commission Administrator (disapproved); overhaul of the Civil Service System (approved); a four-year term for House members to run concurrently with the presidential term (approved); and electoral college reform (approved). In civil rights, he okayed proposals for fair jury selection, protection of civil rights workers, and fair housing.

LBJ was excited about a new Department of Transportation and auto, highway, and tire safety programs. He was lukewarm about public funds for a commercial supersonic transport plane, granting grudging approval because it was the hot button for the powerful Washington senators, Warren Magnuson, who chaired the Commerce Committee (on which we were dependent for our auto-safety program and most consumer legislation), and Henry (Scoop) Jackson, a key supporter on Vietnam and environmental programs.

The President lit up when we came to the Demonstration Cities program, a five-to-ten-year effort to transform "the slum core [of several cities] into a modern area with a total approach—new homes, schools, parks, community centers and open spaces," as well as health care, transportation, and police protection. He was enthusiastic about several new parks (including California Redwood, Indiana Dunes, and North Cascades), programs for the preservation of historic buildings and sites, a national trail system, a scenic roadways system (Johnson wanted to build picnic areas along roads so drivers and their families could stop, rest, and commune with nature), a clean-rivers demonstration program, and tough new clean-air legislation.

In health, Johnson approved measures to encourage comprehensive health planning at the local level, modernize hospitals, increase the number of doctors graduating from medical schools, train paramedics, and (in response to a plea from the Kennedy family) create a Committee on Mental Retardation.

In education, LBJ approved programs to stimulate school construction and modernization in poor areas, a cold war GI bill, and school lunch and breakfast programs. He greatly expanded a proposal I made to enrich kindergarten and summer programs for poor children ("We've got to get them educated and keep them busy while they're young"). Johnson's support of school meals for poor children had been prompted by a Denver priest, Father Charles Woodrich, who had been unable to get anyone in the federal government to listen to him except White House aide Larry Levinson. Father Woodrich had been part of an experiment in Denver under the poverty program during which one secondary and three elementary schools were provided lunch at a sharply reduced cost, while neighboring schools charged full prices. Where the lower-priced meals were served, attendance improved, attention span extended, and dropout rates and disciplinary problems dropped significantly.[20] LBJ decided to expand Father Woodrich's experiment.

As he agreed with a proposal for campaign-reform legislation, the President gave me a brief lecture on money and politics. His view of campaign financing was complex and ambivalent. He was acutely aware of the importance of money in politics and he knew how to raise millions. He used those funds not only for his own reelection, but to assist congressmen who supported his programs. He knew the legal limits of fundraising and how to skirt them. One evening in the green den off the Oval Office, Clifton Carter, a Texas aide he had named as executive director of the Democratic National Committee, proudly told Johnson that an hour earlier in the White House he had received a $50,000 contribution (in cash, the way many political donations were made in those days) from a man Carter did not identify in my presence, but whom the President knew. Johnson reprimanded Carter, telling him that it was illegal to accept political contributions on federal property. A few minutes later the three of us walked over to the living quarters. "Come here," the President signaled as he took us both out on the north portico. Raising his arm and pointing out across the lawn and Pennsylvania Avenue, he said to Carter, "Do you see what's over there?"

"Lafayette Park," Carter responded.

"No. Beyond that," the President said, gesturing vigorously.

"The Hay-Adams Hotel," the forty-seven-year-old Carter said like a schoolboy searching for the answer the teacher wanted.

"Do you know why they built the Hay-Adams Hotel?" the President asked. "They built it so that people like you could have a place to go to accept political contributions."

But this afternoon at the ranch Johnson talked about "how demeaning, how Goddamn demeaning it is for the President of the United States, the President of all the people, to go, hat in hand, to a few wealthy contributors and beg for money. It's wrong! Wrong! WRONG! And we've got to do something to stop it."

Johnson believed that all federal elections should be publicly financed. But he didn't think it was possible to pass public financing in the House, because about 150 members ran without any opposition. In any given year, he said, "more than 200 hope to run with no opposition. Public financing guarantees an opponent to just about every House member. And you can't pass a bill when you start with two hundred members against it."

Finally, the President approved U.S. participation in the Asian Development Bank, a bicentennial commission, rent-supplement funding, extension of unemployment benefits, increasing the hourly minimum wage, truth-in-packaging and truth-in-lending, repeal of the federal statute permitting states to have right-to-work laws, and a modest anticrime program. And at the end, he okayed a series of special messages to Congress.

It was an extraordinary experience. In less than two hours, this

President had blessed a massive second-year program that would astound the Congress and the country when he unveiled it in his State of the Union message on January 12, 1966.[21]

The budget and legislative program that Johnson would present in January 1966 would amount to a public declaration that he was going to get his Great Society while he fought the war. It took all his smarts, and all his staff's patience, to figure out how to tell that to the American people just the way he wanted to.

LBJ turned preparation of the State of the Union into a wild melee of conflicts over ideas and even writing styles. On November 15, he asked department and agency heads to send me any material they thought should be included in his State of the Union message. At the same time, Jack Valenti was gathering ideas for the foreign-policy section of the message from selected outsiders.[22] Everybody from cabinet members to lower staff bickered over programs and dollars as the President played Solomon. It irritated him that Congress had the power to dispose of his recommendations, but he enjoyed anticipating how key chairmen would react and he loved plotting how to win them over.

On November 27, Valenti requested an okay to talk to Dick Goodwin, who had left the White House staff a few months before, about helping draft the message. The President said, "No." On December 7, Valenti sent me a note, "[the President] specifically objected to the man you and I had discussed doing any work on it. I intend to press the suggestion again real soon—but he flatly refused to let him work on the draft now."[23] While Johnson neither liked nor trusted Goodwin, he admired his speechwriting talent and had tried to dissuade him from resigning. A month later, dissatisfied with our prose, the President told Valenti he could seek Goodwin's help.

Goodwin began drafting in early January. The speech was scheduled for January 12. Senators and congressmen called to get their pet projects mentioned. Cabinet officers, like Treasury Secretary Fowler, hung in close to make sure that the words (in his case on the economy and tax adjustments) were exactly the ones they wanted the President to speak.[24] The President reviewed at least a half-dozen drafts between January 5 and 11. About 4 A.M. on the morning of the day the speech would be given, as the President slept, we sent to his bedroom door what we thought was the final version. I went to sleep on the couch in my office and Goodwin went to his hotel, utterly drained. He was so angry about the endless revisions of his drafts and the President's refusal to deal with him face to face that he declined Johnson's invitation to accompany him up to the Capitol for delivery of the message. Goodwin later told me, "It was just too much. I couldn't go through with it. I was exhausted and disgusted with the way I was treated."

At about 7:15 A.M., Valenti, Moyers, Watson, Jacobsen, and I, but not Goodwin, were summoned to the President's bedroom.[25] He said the message was "getting there," but he was still not happy. He ordered a complete reorganization and he wanted it cut by a third.

The President told Valenti and me to do the revisions. We grabbed some coffee and locked ourselves in Horace Busby's old office.[26] The message, to be delivered that evening at nine, would be more than five thousand words long after editing and had to be put on teleprompters before delivery, a process that in those days could take more than a couple of hours. As Valenti and I worked, people were pounding on the door, wanting to see what was happening to their words and ideas. We ignored them. We began feeding Johnson redone pages of the message during the late morning. He reworked it and we had it retyped. That afternoon in the Oval Office, he reviewed the message with Clark Clifford and Abe Fortas, calling out revisions to Valenti and me. We were in Valenti's office adjacent to the President's, listening on Valenti's speaker phone as he shouted the changes; the President refused to invite us into his office, which would have made our work somewhat easier.[27]

In the course of all this, Johnson insisted on inserting a vague sentence about his intention "to ask Congress to consider measures which . . . will enable us effectively to deal with strikes which threaten irreparable damage to the national interest." The sentence was a deliberate slap at Republican Mayor John Lindsay, who was settling New York City's transit strike with a wage increase far above the guideposts. Lindsay was ignoring administration signals that such a deal would set a dangerous inflationary precedent.

That evening, Johnson electrified the Joint Session of the House and Senate with his barrage of new legislative proposals. Calling for a program from the second session of the 89th Congress at least as ambitious as he had asked of the first, the President was interrupted fifty-nine times by applause. Most interruptions were genuine, but just in case, LBJ had told White House aide Marvin Watson to begin clapping at the end of certain lines to help spark the applause. Valenti's charge was to count the number of applause interruptions so that it would be immediately available to the press for inclusion in their stories.

The applause was loud—some Democratic members even whistled and cheered—when the President called for a four-year term for House members to run concurrently with the President's. Later the

President wryly remarked that no one had noticed House Judiciary Committee Chairman Emanuel Celler sitting on his hands. Celler was afraid the House would forfeit too much of its institutional independence if its fortunes were so closely tied to a President's political performance. House Republicans wanted the chance to increase their numbers in off-year elections when a Democrat occupied the White House. The senators, of course, wanted no part of a four-year term, which would permit representatives to run against them without forfeiting their House seats. The proposal went nowhere.

Johnson's insistence that the war not intrude on his dream of a Great Society pervaded his message:

> We will continue to meet the needs of our people by continuing to develop the Great Society. . . . I have come here to recommend that you, the representatives of the richest Nation on earth . . . bring the most urgent decencies of life to all of your fellow Americans. . . . There are men who cry out: We must sacrifice. Well, let us rather ask them: Who will they sacrifice? Are they going to sacrifice the children who seek the learning, or the sick who need medical care, or the families who dwell in squalor now brightened by the hope of home? Will they sacrifice opportunity for the distressed, the beauty of our land, the hope of our poor? . . . I believe that we can continue the Great Society while we fight in Vietnam. But if there are some who do not believe this, then, in the name of justice, let them call for the contribution of those who live in the fullness of our blessing, rather than try to strip it from the hands of those that are most in need.

As to the war that tortured him, Johnson had this to say:

> The war in Vietnam is not like [World War II and Korea]. . . . Yet, finally, war is always the same. It is young men dying in the fullness of their promise. It is trying to kill a man that you do not even know well enough to hate. . . . Therefore, to know war is to know that there is still madness in this world.

At the mansion later that evening, we relaxed over drinks and a late dinner and watched television on the three sets in the President's bedroom.[28] LBJ was pleased by his reception on the Hill. In his shirtsleeves, pacing around in front of the TV sets, waving his arms, he dismissed congressional leaders who told television reporters that he was putting too much on their plates. He knew it was unlikely that he would ever again have a Congress with so many liberals, and he said he intended to see they worked for their constituents.

The next morning, *The Washington Post* carried a headline and lead that Johnson would have written for himself: "U.S. CAN CONTINUE THE 'GREAT SOCIETY' AND FIGHT IN VIETNAM, JOHNSON SAYS—LBJ HANDS CONGRESS MASSIVE WORK LOAD—With an agenda rivaling the original Great Society program in scope, President Johnson last night laid before Congress a staggering work load for 1966."

Columnist Mary McGrory wrote that LBJ wasn't thinking small, and "Anybody who wants to take from the poor to fight the war in Asia will have him to fight." Johnson's message had exhilarated the capital. After his long, frustrating, sometimes self-pitying convalescence at the ranch, LBJ was back in the saddle.[29]

But Lyndon Johnson was riding two horses at the same time and it wasn't clear how long he could continue this feat. All during the autumn and early winter, as he was preparing his domestic program, the U.S. commitment in Vietnam grew and his advisers searched for some way to get the North Vietnamese to the table for peace talks.

McNamara, then Bundy, and finally Rusk, with varying degrees of ardor, were urging the President during the latter part of 1965 to institute a bombing pause over North Vietnam. Fortas and Clifford were opposed. And Johnson had serious reservations. He thought nothing short of the fear of losing the war would bring the North Vietnamese to the negotiating table, and he worried that they would take advantage of a pause to step up shipments of supplies and troops to the South. Nor did he trust Soviet Ambassador Anatoly Dobrynin, who had suggested a bombing pause to Bundy as a step toward negotiations. Nevertheless, in one of the most hesitant actions I saw him take, the President instituted a pause on Christmas Eve 1965. He mounted a frenetic diplomatic push, through every available public and private channel, including the Russians and East Europeans, to get the North Vietnamese to negotiate. But Ho Chi Minh, the North Vietnamese leader, refused to come to the table.

Pressure mounted to resume the bombing, and on January 29, 1966, the President held a National Security Council meeting to review the situation with the Joint Chiefs of Staff. He asked me to attend. My notes show that the Chiefs pressed him for resumption of the bombing and for many more troops. Army Chief of Staff General Harold Johnson urged that the President "surge troops in, doubling and tripling the number of men there [then about 225,000], declare an emergency and call up the reserves." But General Johnson and the other Chiefs put their "highest priority on resuming bombing." Johnson pressed the Chiefs to describe the benefits of bombing. They talked in general terms about intercepting supplies and troops from North Vietnam. Johnson was skeptical and he voiced the doubts of Senate colleagues, noting that "Senator [Eugene] McCarthy [D-Minn.] wants to know how much [the bombing] really stops" and that "a number of senators have said the bombing has no effect."[30]

Everyone present assumed the bombing would be resumed whatever case the Chiefs made (I wrote the President that afternoon, "the case made . . . for resumption . . . was totally unconvincing," but I suggested he get a good lawyer to argue the case to Congress and the public[31]) and it was, on January 31, 1966. But the President rejected recommendations of the military that he lift the restrictions on targets. Johnson continued his prohibition against bombing Hanoi and Haiphong.

At the NSC meeting, Johnson had looked tired and concerned. He had worried about whether the bombing pause would endanger American lives in South Vietnam. Now he worried that we might needlessly endanger our pilots or spark a wider war. And the war was beginning to take a toll. Each casualty caused him personal pain. He was also showing his frustration at being diverted from pursuit of the domestic ambitions he had announced so grandly two weeks earlier.

That January I noticed something else: Lyndon Johnson had stopped drinking. He made no announcement about it; indeed, I don't think he wanted anyone to know. But his concern about not being at full capacity every second of every day for fear he would have to make a decision about our troops in Vietnam had led him, with very rare exceptions, to stop drinking the Cutty Sark scotch he so enjoyed in the evening. After that, even on occasions when Lady Bird or one of the doctors would encourage him to have just one drink to relax, LBJ almost always refused.[32]

SEVEN

Going for
the Great Society

JOHNSON'S QUEST for the Great Society dominated the second session of the 89th Congress as it had the first. Resolved not to let the escalating war slow him down, he sent an array of legislative proposals to Capitol Hill. Then for hours on end, he pressured, persuaded, and pleaded with the Democratic leadership at weekly breakfasts, and with committee chairmen and recalcitrant members in scores of phone calls and face-to-face meetings, to get laws back to him for signature. With remarkable speed, Johnson pushed through Congress laws for child nutrition, truth-in-packaging, bail reform, mine safety, urban mass transit, national parks and seashores, clean rivers, international education, auto, tire, and highway safety,* and a host of other matters.

He gave special attention to his proposals to create a department of transportation and to rebuild American cities, because of his interest in them and the controversy they sparked.

When the President had told me in the swimming pool at the ranch that the first step in getting the federal government's transportation act together was to establish a single cabinet department, he had

---

* In the late summer of 1967, when Lyndon Johnson received a new-model Lincoln, which Henry Ford sent him each year, the dashboard was padded, many switches were recessed and their placement reorganized. Johnson bitched unmercifully about the unfamiliar dashboard and interior styling until someone pointed out that most of the changes had been mandated by his Transportation Department administering his auto-safety legislation.

a much better sense than I of the nasty street fighting ahead. For more than a century and a half, Congress had been taking charge of the nation's transportation system—providing funds to build westward-bound roads for nineteenth-century pioneers, regulating railroads and trucking, opening inland waterways and harbors, constructing airports and setting airline rates and routes, and in the 1950s establishing the Highway Trust Fund to finance highway systems.

By the 1960s a crazy quilt of agencies and bureaus crossed wires and pandered to congressional committee chairmen. No single executive had the authority to shape and conduct a coherent policy that promoted the public's interest in modern, cheap, and fast transportation.

LBJ was set on changing this chaotic situation and shifting the center of power from Congress to the executive. He wanted to combine the more than thirty agencies and bureaus that funded transportation and protected safety in a cabinet-level Department of Transportation, which would have 100,000 employees and a $6 billion budget—and be responsive to the President.

Johnson handled with dispatch agency heads reluctant to relinquish their autonomy to the new department. Treasury Secretary Fowler wanted to retain the Coast Guard in his department. He took his plea to the President. After setting forth the history of the Coast Guard and its relation to other Treasury Department functions like customs and currency control, Fowler rested his case. Johnson smiled and said, "Joe, what is it? Do you have a boat, a yacht, a plane you want to keep? Is it the Coast Guard mess you want to keep? Do you like to wear the Coast Guard uniform? Are you an admiral in the Coast Guard?" At first a little embarrassed, Fowler began smiling as the President rattled off his questions. Johnson himself began smiling, then turned to me and said, "Old Joe, he just doesn't want to give up all those mess boys at Treasury and those boats he can go on in the summer. Well, whenever he needs a boat, make sure he can have the *Sequoia* [the presidential yacht]." Fowler laughed with the President, surrendered the Coast Guard, and wholeheartedly supported the effort to establish the new department.[1]

The President spent hours talking to interest groups and transportation experts on how to put the department together. At one point, I backed off a suggestion that he had abruptly dismissed as naïve. "I didn't hire you to 'yes' me," he snapped. "You disagree with me, you let me know it. Don't back off just because I say something." He was determined to make certain he understood all sides of this controversial proposal. He turned the Oval Office into a parade ground for competing views, and his phone wires burned with calls to people all over the country—businessmen and labor leaders, left and right, Democrats and Republicans, northerners, southerners, easterners, westerners. "It's not doing what is right that's hard for a President. It's knowing what is right." He said it so often that he made it sound trite.

He'd try the railroad position on the truckers, then go back to the railroad people with the truckers' position, testing, probing, sucking up facts and opinions like a giant vacuum cleaner. Johnson continued to consult and ferret out opposing views even after he'd made up his mind, but before he revealed his thinking, because he didn't want to be surprised by any opposition, fail to muster all possible support, or miss any opportunity to overwhelm or undermine an opponent he could not persuade. He was a political and intellectual baker, kneading with those enormous hands until every aspect of the proposal was explored; once confident of that, he would put the bread in the oven.

As Johnson got comfortable with the broad shape of the department he would propose, he told Lee White and me to meet with transportation industry leaders. With varying degrees of enthusiasm, executives from railroads, airlines, and inland-waterway carriers supported the idea. The ailing maritime industry, both labor and management, worried about their federal subsidy and wanted no part of any consolidation.[2]

Then I met with William Bresnahan, head of the American Trucking Association. That evening I told the President of the meeting, "With some modifications of the secretary's power, the truckers are enthusiastic supporters. They're all for it."

LBJ smiled knowingly, his eyes brightened, and he said, "Joe, we're going to get our Department of Transportation! You know why?"

I had no idea. He gave me a patronizing look, and almost whispered, "Because of the truckers. When the truckers deal on the Hill, they deal one on one"—Johnson paused for effect and leaned toward me—"and only in cash." He slapped his leg approvingly.

But moving the bill through Congress was not quite as easy as I thought it would be that evening.[3] The fight in the House centered on whether to include the Maritime Administration in the new department. Anxious about the loss of shipping jobs, AFL-CIO President George Meany sent a telegram to each member declaring that a vote to put the Maritime Administration in the Transportation Department would be considered an antilabor vote.[4] Maritime lobbyists choked the Hill with fear that LBJ would find it easier to reduce shipping subsidies. The House voted to keep the Maritime Administration out of the new department.

On the Senate side, the proposal to establish a new department ran into John McClellan, a stony-faced, crafty Arkansas Democrat who chaired the Senate committee with jurisdiction over the bill. McClellan wanted the administration to relax its demanding standards for approving waterway-navigation projects before he would move the bill. So, after holding the first series of hearings, McClellan couldn't find time even to meet with me.[5]

I reported my frustration to the President one night over dinner in the mansion. Johnson suggested that I leak off the record to a friendly reporter that "there are some who say McClellan is holding up the Transportation Department because he wants the Corps of Engineers to build a dam on land he owns so he'll get a lot of money when the government buys the property."

"Is that true?" I asked.

Johnson leaned back in his leather chair and told me this story:

"The first time Mr. Kleberg* ran for Congress, he was back home making a tub-thumper campaign speech against his opponent. I was sitting on the steps at the side of the platform, listening.

"Mr. Kleberg said: 'It isn't easy, but I guess I can understand why the good citizens of the hill country might let themselves be represented in Washington by a man who drinks too much. It isn't easy, but I guess I can even understand why the good citizens of the hill country might let themselves be represented by a man in Washington who carouses with city women while his wife and children are back here working the land. But, as God is my witness, I will never understand why the good people of the hill country would let themselves be represented by a man who takes female sheep up into the hills alone at night!'

"Well," the President said, "I jumped up and shouted, 'Mr. Kleberg, Mr. Kleberg, that's not true.'

"And you know what Mr. Kleberg did?" Johnson asked as he looked into my eyes. "He just looked down at me and said, 'Then let the son of a bitch deny it!' "

Johnson and I both laughed, then he paused and said quietly, "You just let John McClellan deny it."

Without our having to resort to the leak, McClellan began meeting with me. We'd haggle back and forth and I'd report to the President. Finally, I got angry. McClellan told me he was having trouble producing a quorum at committee meetings to mark up the bill.[6] But when I pressed other members to go to the meetings, I discovered that

---

* Richard Kleberg, part owner of Texas's huge King Ranch, was the congressman who first brought LBJ to Washington as an aide.

McClellan had been telling them they didn't have to show up. Johnson laughed. "You know something," he said, "John McClellan is teaching you more about politics in two months than your old boss Tom Dewey* learned in two presidential campaigns."[7]

When I finally came to an agreement with McClellan on easing standards for Corps of Engineers water projects, I returned to the Oval Office and proudly reported to Johnson that I had a deal and McClellan would move the bill. As I described the agreement, Johnson was sitting behind his green leather-topped desk and I was standing to his left, leaning on the cabinet that encased the AP and UPI wire-service tickers that constantly clicked away in his office. "Open your fly," Johnson ordered. I just smiled, knowing he wasn't serious but surprised nonetheless.

"Unzip your fly," he said rising from his green chair, "because there's nothing there. John McClellan just cut it off with a razor so sharp you didn't even notice it."

Johnson hit a button on his phone. "Get Senator McClellan for me."

As Johnson was telling me what a bad bargain I'd struck, McClellan got on the phone. "John," the President said, "I'm calling about Joe Califano. You cut his pecker off and put it in your desk drawer. Now I'm sending him back up there to get it from you. I can't agree to anything like that. You've got to realize that the transportation system of this country needs something besides more highways in Arkansas."

Eventually the Transportation Department bill, including the Maritime Administration, passed the Senate. In conference, the Maritime Administration came out, but just about everything else LBJ wanted stayed in. Johnson was so annoyed with the maritime corporate executives and union leaders that he refused to invite them to the signing ceremony.†[8]

The problems exposed by the Watts riot had put the stamp of urgency on LBJ's desire to mount a concerted assault on slum conditions in America's cities. The first step had been to get the Congress to create a Department of Housing and Urban Development. In persuading Congress to act, the President kept his own counsel about whom he might name secretary. Nevertheless, on September 9, 1965,

---

* Dewey was the New York governor who ran twice for president on the Republican ticket and was defeated both times. He headed the law firm with which I was associated before entering government service in early 1961.
† Fifteen years later, in 1981, Congress moved the Maritime Administration into the Department of Transportation.

when the President signed the bill creating the new department, urban America's most severe problems festered in swelling black ghettos
and most observers had expected him to nominate Robert Weaver, the
black Administrator of the Housing and Home Finance Agency.

In late October, I alerted Johnson to a provision in the law that
required him to designate a secretary or acting secretary by November 9. He balked at making any decision while Congress was adjourned. To my surprise, he said he hadn't settled on Weaver. Before
he picked anyone for this hot spot, he said, he wanted to have "his
pecker in my drawer," everything on the Hill lined up, and every
person and interest group who favored the appointment ask him to
make it.

Weaver came to see me on October 27,[9] armed with documents
he said the President had to sign within two weeks to establish the
new department and designate its secretary. I said that the President
was not operating under any such deadline. Weaver was astonished.

When I spoke to LBJ, he asked me to get an Attorney General's
opinion that the President was not required to take any action by
November 9. Unfortunately, Katzenbach concluded that the law required the President to act. If Johnson didn't either name a new
secretary or designate someone to act temporarily, Katzenbach feared
chaos among lawyers who would expect to see the secretary's signature on millions of dollars of housing and urban-development loans
and bonds.[10]

Katzenbach's opinion was not what the President wanted.
Johnson called to tell me that he had another lawyer with him who
said he didn't have to do anything, "not one damn thing" until he
made a decision in due course. "You and Katzenbach are my lawyers;
you're supposed to help me not harm me. Now find another way to
look at this." When I argued with him, he asked whether I had read
every word of the law and legislative history. Of course I hadn't. Nor
had Katzenbach, so we took another look.

Weaver, meanwhile, kept asking to have his papers signed. If he
was not at least named acting secretary, he said he would resign from
the government. Johnson wasn't budging. He had several concerns.
In mid-October, the House had rebuffed his attempt to fund Rent
Supplements, a Great Society program to pay the difference between
the monthly rent of the working poor and 25 percent of their income.
The defeat was blamed on draft regulations which Weaver had prematurely made public and which, Republicans charged, provided rent
subsidies for people whose incomes were too high. At the time,
Johnson privately blasted Weaver for his "political stupidity" in having anything on paper until Congress provided the funding.[11] He

ignored the fact that he would have roasted Weaver unmercifully had the housing administrator not been ready, upon getting the appropriation, to award the first rent supplements.

Johnson was also wary of difficulties he might face in gaining Senate confirmation for the nation's first black cabinet secretary, particularly for a post focused on the cities in the bitter aftermath of the Watts riot. Weaver was not personally popular on the Hill, and Senate Majority Leader Mike Mansfield didn't think well of him. The President feared that Weaver, in an acting capacity, might stumble during the congressional adjournment and thus turn his confirmation into a contest requiring a heavy expenditure of presidential capital to get it through.[12]

Katzenbach and I sought out that last refuge of desperate lawyers, the dictionary. The law provided that the positions and agencies to be moved into the new department "shall lapse." Katzenbach wrote an opinion that "The term 'lapse' is commonly used to connote a gradual process (e.g., Webster's New Int'l Dict. (2d ed.) 'to pass . . . gradually,' " as distinguished from overnight change. From that, Katzenbach imaginatively concluded that there was no need for the President to make a selection by November 9.[13] The President now had the opinion he desired. He ordered all copies of the earlier one destroyed and insisted that both Katzenbach and I sign the new one.

When I told Weaver of the Attorney General's opinion, he was flabbergasted.[14] He said that "the whole world" expected him to be named either secretary or acting secretary by November 9; if nothing was going to happen, it would be "embarrassing, downright humiliating"; he'd have to resign. I urged him not to do anything rash that might jeopardize his chances to be the nation's first black cabinet officer. He was still angry when he left my office, but he did commit himself to sit tight.

That evening, when I reported to the President at the ranch,[15] he snapped, "Let him resign. If he's that arrogant, the hell with him. You just tell him to resign. Call him tonight and tell him." I argued with the President, but he was adamant. Nevertheless, I did nothing that evening, hoping he would let matters settle.

The President called the next morning[16] and asked if I had Weaver's resignation, "Did you get it? Did you get it?" When I said I hadn't, he snapped, "Goddamn it. Get it. Have him deliver it to you this afternoon."[17]

Weaver came over to my office late that morning.[18] He had decided to hang in. To his bewilderment, I suggested he consider resigning. I said that the President was not going to act until Congress reconvened in January and that he intended to consider several can-

1. The LBJ ranch house, pool, and hangar.

2. Breakfast with the Congressional leadership in the White House living quarters in August 1965. Around the table (*from left*): Jake Jacobsen, Hale Boggs, Russell Long, Hubert Humphrey, Carl Albert, George Smathers, me, Larry O'Brien, House Speaker John McCormack, the President, Senate Majority Leader Mike Mansfield, Marvin Watson. Jack Valenti (*far right*) on the phone. LBJ used the poster board on the easel to show the status of his Great Society legislation in Congress.

3. LBJ telling Humphrey on September 22, 1965, of the reorganization that would take all civil rights responsibilities away from the Vice President. Nicholas Katzenbach, Lee White, and I attended this meeting.

4. A break in a November 26, 1965, budget meeting to talk about growing stronger and healthier grass at the LBJ Ranch. *From left:* an unidentified agricultural expert, Deputy Budget Director Elmer Stats, Charles Schultze, LBJ, me, Jack Valenti, ranch foreman Dale Malechek.

5. Jack Valenti and I locked ourselves in this office to work on the President's 1965 State of the Union message minutes after Johnson had ordered a rewrite and just a few hours before he was scheduled to deliver it.

6. LBJ and New York Governor Nelson Rockefeller—a mutual admiration society in the Oval Office in early 1966.

7. LBJ giving me changes to a special message to Congress in January 1966.

8. In the sitting room of the White House living quarters, discussing the escalating cost of the Vietnam War in May 1966. *From left:* me, Senate Minority Leader Everett Dirksen, Robert McNamara (*back to camera*), LBJ, and Senate Majority Leader Mike Mansfield.

9. A meeting on the legislative programs in the den adjacent to the Oval Office in June 1966 with (*from left*) me, Larry O'Brien, Treasury Secretary Henry (Joe) Fowler, and LBJ.

10. President and Lady Bird Johnson walk to the helicopter on the South Lawn of the White House grounds en route to a July 4th weekend at the ranch in 1966. Press Secretary Bill Moyers and I are behind them.

11. Walking from the West Wing Office to the White House living quarters for a working lunch. *From left:* Robert McNamara, former Budget Director Kermit Gordon, LBJ, CEA Chairman Gardner Ackley, me, and Joe Fowler.

12. The embarrassing White House dinner with Joan Crawford. Cathy Douglas is on my right. Don Hewitt, then "CBS Evening News" executive producer, is on Crawford's left.

13. At the President's desk in the Oval Office working on the message to Congress to request food aid to ease the famine in India.

14. LBJ in a phone conversation with Commerce Secretary Alexander (Sandy) Trowbridge on March 8, 1967, about his desire to reinstate the investment tax credit, as Joe Fowler and I look on.

15. LBJ with his Cabinet on April 5, 1967. *From left:* Secretary of State Dean Rusk, Secretary of Defense Robert McNamara, Postmaster General Lawrence O'Brien, Secretary of Agriculture Orville Freeman, Secretary of Labor Willard Wirtz, Secretary of Housing and Urban Development Robert Weaver, Secretary of Transportation Alan Boyd, Secretary of Health, Education and Welfare John Gardner, Secretary of Commerce Alexander Trowbridge, Secretary of Interior Stewart Udall, Attorney General Ramsey Clark, Secretary of Treasury Henry Fowler.

16. A meeting in the Cabinet Room during the Arab-Israeli Six-Day War. *From left:* Chief of Naval Operations Admiral David McDonald, LBJ whispering to me, Robert McNamara, Deputy Defense Secretary Cyrus Vance. Army General Earle Wheeler, Chairman of the Joint Chiefs of Staff, has his back to the camera.

17. Press Secretary George Christian, LBJ, and I revising a presidential statement on legislation to forestall the threatened rail strike in July 1967.

18. On the evening of July 24, 1967, in the Oval Office, working on LBJ's televised statement on the Detroit riots. *From left:* Supreme Court Justice Abe Fortas, Robert McNamara, me, Army Secretary Stanley Resor, Army Chief of Staff General Harold Johnson.

19. LBJ at his blackboard in August 1967, setting forth the case for his tax surcharge in a meeting with key members of Congress in the State Dining Room at the White House.

20. LBJ introducing my mother and father to Italy's President Giuseppe Saragat at a White House state dinner on September 19, 1967.

21. Briefing LBJ on the 1968 legislative program in the living room at the ranch in December 1967. Stan Ross, a member of my staff, is in the background.

22. In the White House living quarters, reviewing the final draft of the 1968 State of the Union message on the eve of its delivery. *From left:* Jim Jones, Harry McPherson, LBJ, me, George Christian, and Larry Levinson.

23. LBJ visits with my sons, Joe III and Mark, in the Oval Office on July 2, 1968. Jim Jones is in the background.

24. A February 1968 meeting with Ramsey Clark and Senator John McClellan on the Safe Streets and Right to Privacy acts. That's Yuki, the mongrel pup that Luci found at a gas station and LBJ loved, jumping from McClellan to the President.

25. Sitting in the Flower Garden with Luci Johnson and the President on March 28, 1968, just before the lunch at which LBJ first told me he was thinking about not running for reelection.

26. District of Columbia Mayor Walter Washington, in the den adjoining the Oval Office on the morning after the assassination of Martin Luther King. He is asking the President to move Army troops into the nation's capital to restore and maintain order, as George Christian, Harry McPherson, and I listen.

didates for the new post. Weaver eventually agreed to return to his office and compose a letter of resignation. That afternoon, as Weaver was en route to my office, the President called.[19] I reported, "Weaver is on the way over now with his resignation."

"What the hell is he doing that for?" the President asked. "I don't want him to resign!"

"You told me to get him to resign!"

"I don't want him to resign!"

"My God! What am I supposed to do?" I asked in exasperation.

"You tell him not to resign. That's what you do. What the hell is he resigning for? Tell him I have a list of names, he's on it, and I'm going to make a selection in January when Congress comes back."

"Mr. President, after what he's been through, he may just hand me his resignation and walk out."

"You have no authority to accept his resignation," Johnson said. "You tell him, if he wants to resign, he can't resign to you. He's got to resign to the President. Tell him he has to give it to me."

Weaver entered my office, letter in hand. He looked so broken— his dreams of a lifetime had been shattered over the past twenty-four hours—that I thought he might welcome the news. When he offered his handwritten letter of resignation, I said, "The President doesn't want your resignation."

Weaver was utterly confused, so disconcerted and agitated he spit his words out. "No," he said, "I'm through. I don't want any more of this. I'm through." He tried to put his resignation letter in my hand or leave it on my desk.

"I can't accept your resignation. I have no authority to. You've got to give it to the President."

"What have these last few days been about? What's going on?" Now he was enraged. "How the hell can I see the President? He's at the ranch."

"You can call him," I said pointing to the phone on my desk.

Weaver shook his head, took his letter with him, and said he'd think about it. That night, Weaver called me. He sounded exhausted and tipsy. He wasn't happy with me or the President. But when the President called me late that evening to check on the situation,[20] I was able to report, "He's not going to resign. He'll sit it out."

Black leaders, many of whom I'd asked to urge Weaver to hang in, united behind him. Whitney Young and Roy Wilkins told me they were not interested in the job, that it should go to Weaver; singer Lena Horne's father, Frank, organized prominent blacks to write and call in support for Weaver. All the black and liberal organizations I contacted wanted Weaver.[21]

LBJ knew it would be dicey to put the first black in the cabinet as Secretary of Housing and Urban Development after the Watts riots. He avoided hanging Weaver out as "acting secretary," a situation in which Weaver would be anxious, vulnerable, and prone to make some mistake. He went through a review of other candidates. Johnson delayed until virtually every major black and liberal leader had asked him to name Weaver so that he could remind them that he'd done something for them. Then he carefully lined up Senate support for Weaver and picked an outstanding deputy secretary.

Finally, on January 13, shortly after Congress convened, Johnson announced his choice of Weaver to be the first Secretary of HUD, and Robert Wood, an urban expert from the Massachusetts Institute of Technology, to be his deputy. On January 17, the Senate Banking Committee reported them out after a hearing of little more than an hour; the full Senate unanimously confirmed them that same day.

In the course of orchestrating this Senate love fest for the first black cabinet officer, the President left the new Secretary numb. He made it clear he could break or make Weaver—by doing both. He gave me a glimpse of the trait that sometimes drove him to crush and reshape a man before placing him in a job of enormous importance, much the way a ranch hand tames a wild horse before mounting it. To Johnson, this technique helped assure that an appointee was his alone.[22]

With the new department in place, Johnson turned to designing a program to rebuild America's slums. United Auto Workers President Walter Reuther had given Johnson a sense of the way to launch that effort in a September 17, 1965, meeting in the Oval Office. Reuther's idea was to make Detroit and a few other cities examples of the way decaying center cities could be rebuilt through teamwork by all segments of the community—business, labor, government, blacks and whites. The goal was improved housing, employment, schools, police, transportation, health care, recreation, and urban life in general. Only the President and the federal government, Reuther had argued, could lead such an undertaking.[23] Reuther's concept captured the President's imagination. After the meeting, Johnson told me he wanted to turn America's cities into gems and bring all Americans together to rebuild slum neighborhoods.

Johnson's dream was far more ambitious than anything contemplated before. The federal government's efforts in cities had previously focused on housing. By the mid-1960s, however, urban problems extended far beyond the dilapidated buildings housing seven million families. Schools were inadequate, as were health care, transportation, and recreational facilities. With a new department to lead the effort, Johnson was ready to tackle them all, rebuild entire slum neighborhoods in American cities and in the process provide jobs for the unemployed in the ghetto. Instead of urban renewal programs that moved poor people out of their neighborhoods and homes, he envisioned a program that would allow them to stay there, in remodeled or new dwellings, with jobs, police protection, recreation, and community health centers.

In its final form, Johnson's proposal expanded the number of cities to six large (500,000 people or more), ten medium (250,000 to 500,000), and fifty small (less than 250,000) so that the program could reach as many states and congressional districts as possible. Local and federal Great Society programs would be an integral part of every plan. Cities would have to involve all elements of the community, including poor residents, and promote racial integration of housing. The federal government would pay the cost of preparing plans; upon approval, the federal government would pay the lion's share of executing them.[24]

The President's proposal was a far bigger bite than the Congress seemed prepared to swallow. By mid-May, the key House subcommittee, chaired by Democrat William Barrett of Pennsylvania, was poised to gut the bill,[25] and there had been no movement in the Senate. Southern Democrats and Republicans took the bill's title, "Demonstration Cities," which I'd selected to capture the hopeful concept of a city demonstrating its capacity to rejuvenate its slums, and threw it back in the President's face, as bowing to black urban demonstrators and rioters. They also objected to the bill's desegregation requirements. Liberals thought the bill's $2.3 billion was too little; conservatives thought it was profligate. Members of Congress and mayors feared their cities would not be chosen. *The New York Times* wrote the program's obituary in its editorial column on May 15: "President Johnson's legislative techniques, often justly praised, have failed him badly in his attempt to rebuild the nation's urban centers. All signs on Capitol Hill suggest that the 'demonstration cities' program is dead." Within the administration, sentiment grew to take a wisp of a bill and settle for just the $12 million planning phase.[26]

But Johnson had no such intention. At the Democratic congressional leadership breakfast on May 31, 1966,[27] he called the Demonstration Cities bill "the most important domestic measure before the Congress and to the future of the American cities." He instructed Larry O'Brien and me to identify the trouble and "get the legislation passed." He was, he insisted, going to get his Demonstration Cities bill *this* year from *this* Congress. "So get the Vice President and Weaver out there revving up the interest groups. Turn the House committee around and get them to report out our bill. Then tell them to hold it, because the House won't want to take up any legislation this controversial in an election year unless they're sure the Senate will act. So we'll have to get the Senate to act first."[28]

I reminded the President of the problems in the Senate. The subcommittee chairman, John Sparkman (D-Ala.), facing a reelection campaign, wouldn't touch the bill with its racial-integration baggage, much less lead the way. Democrat Paul Douglas of Illinois, a liberal who supported the legislation and ranking member of Sparkman's subcommittee, was himself in a tight race against a popular Republican, Charles Percy, and couldn't give the bill the time it would require.

That left Maine Democrat Edmund Muskie, a member of Sparkman's subcommittee and an intelligent and canny legislator. But, I pointed out, Muskie probably didn't have a single city in the state of Maine that would be eligible for the program.

"Well, he has one now," the President said.

"What one?" I asked.

"Whatever one he wants." Johnson chuckled. The President thought Muskie was perfect to carry the legislation.

O'Brien and I first worked to turn the House subcommittee around. In a steamy room off the Speaker's Office, crowded with other subcommittee members, Speaker McCormack, Majority Leader Carl Albert, O'Brien, and I argued for over an hour with subcommittee chairman Barrett. Finally, Barrett agreed to move our bill—if we could get the legislation through the Senate before going to the House floor.

When I reported to Johnson, he told me to "get off my ass, get O'Brien off his ass, and see Muskie. You shouldn't be sitting in your office, you should be sitting in his."

O'Brien and I saw Muskie on June 22.[29] Muskie expressed concern about the program's complicated financing and the difficulty of establishing close working relationships required among so many federal departments. The next day, he was flying to his home in Kennebunkport, Maine, for the July 4 recess and we agreed to resume the discussion when he returned.

When I told the President, he said if we waited until Muskie returned we wouldn't have a bill. At his direction, I asked Muskie to meet with O'Brien, the Vice President, and me in my office on his way to the airport.[30] Muskie came and over small steaks and iced tea we moved closer together, but did not reach agreement. We decided to work over the recess and resume discussions with the Maine Senator when he came back.

This time the President was annoyed. After telling me how naïve I was about nailing things down, he said that O'Brien and I should "get up to Maine" and have an agreed bill before Muskie returned to Washington. Though Muskie clearly didn't want to be bothered over the recess, he agreed to see O'Brien and me on July 6 at his Kennebunkport home.[31]

On that morning, O'Brien and I flew in a small plane to Pease Air Force Base in New Hampshire. The weather was so foul that our Air Force pilot was not certain whether he could land there, or in Boston or New York. We told him we had to see Muskie. He then checked back at the White House. Learning of the call, Johnson ordered the plane to land at Pease. We did, greeted by fire trucks, ambulances, and the base commander, who feared that we would crash in the near-zero visibility. We drove to Muskie's home, where, over lobster stew prepared by Muskie's wife, Jane, we sat for several hours and hammered out a bill.

But we still lacked one vote in Muskie's subcommittee for a majority. Senator Thomas McIntyre, a Democrat from New Hampshire—a state with few, if any, eligible cities—was up for reelection and feared a vote for a bill with a $2.3 billion price tag would alienate his frugal constituents. The President met with McIntyre on July 19. The New Hampshire Senator asked him to downplay the closing of Portsmouth Naval Base, which employed many of his constituents, until after the election. He also wanted some pictures with the President for his campaign. The Senate subcommittee was scheduled to vote on the Demonstration Cities bill less than a week later. LBJ wanted to help McIntyre and hoped the New Hampshire Senator could help him.[32]

After a brief walk around the south grounds for pictures, Johnson told me that McIntyre would support the bill if some way could be found to reduce the price tag. I suggested that we could have a specific amount authorized for just the first three years—$12 million for the planning grants, another $900 million for the next two years of the program (which was all we had requested for that period), and leave the amounts unspecified for the remaining three years. The President told me to let McIntyre propose such an amendment to Muskie's bill, so he could go back to New Hampshire and tell his constituents that he had reduced the amount from $2.3 billion to less than $1 billion.[33] With that, the Senate subcommittee was able to report the bill with a 6–4 vote, rather than have it fail on a tie. The Senate passed the legislation on August 19.

Having survived attacks from conservatives, the Demonstration Cities program now faced an onslaught from liberals. The most serious threat came from a set of hearings held by Connecticut Senator Abraham Ribicoff, with big political assists from New York Senators Robert Kennedy and Jacob Javits. Ribicoff's hearings spotlighted the plight of ghetto blacks. They quickly turned into a media circus as witnesses and subcommittee members pummeled the administration for not doing enough for the cities. The President saw them as a Kennedy-inspired attack, which Ribicoff was willing to front because "Abe wants to be America's first Jewish Vice President." Johnson thought that Kennedy and Ribicoff well knew that Congress wouldn't even provide the money he had asked for, much less the gargantuan amounts they wanted. He refused to deal directly with either senator, but he personally cleared every cabinet member's statement before the subcommittee.[34]

To divert publicity from the hearings, Johnson went on a three-day swing through the Northeast to plump for his Demonstration Cities bill and trumpet programs he had passed. In Syracuse, New York, he announced a number of measures to strengthen urban programs, then tossed rhetorical darts at the Ribicoff hearings, Kennedy, and Congress:

> I want to say to the Congress this afternoon: Give us action . . . and American cities will be great again. . . . Give us funds for the Teachers Corps. . . . Give us more resources for rent supplements. . . . Give us the means to prosecute the war against poverty. . . . Give us the child nutrition act. . . . Give us the hospital modernization bill. . . . Give us the money for urban mass transit. . . . Give us a just minimum wage. . . . Give us better unemployment insurance . . . [and on and on].

Despite the first round of hearings, which ended on September 1, Johnson was able to get the House committee to report out a new Demonstration Cities package very close to the Senate version. Then the House Republican Policy Committee decided to make it a party matter to kill the bill. To counter this, Johnson mobilized Fortune 500 businessmen to send telegrams and issue a statement urging passage of the bill. From the White House, we mounted a campaign to gain newspaper editorial support.*

* At one point, the President asked me to call Joseph Pulitzer, the editor and publisher of the *St. Louis Post-Dispatch*, to get him to write an editorial attacking Missouri Democratic Senator Stuart Symington for criticizing our bill. Symington found out about the call, chewed me out, and complained to the President. Symington

LBJ feared that Ribicoff's second round of hearings, rumored to include such inflammatory figures as black power advocate Floyd McKissick and other witnesses pressing for more money, would kill the Demonstration Cities bill on the House floor. At Johnson's direction, I called Ribicoff, who agreed to postpone the hearings until after we got the bill passed, because he thought "the cities bill was the most imaginative proposal in the whole area" and he didn't "want to do anything to injure it."[35]

Our head count for the House vote was close. At a meeting in the Speaker's Office on October 6, the Speaker and Democratic leadership said they needed one more public push from the President. Johnson was holding a press conference that day and I had sent him a note urging him to plug Demonstration Cities. When the Speaker raised the same issue during the meeting, I called the White House, hoping that the President had done something. O'Brien later said I didn't even have to speak because the grin was so wide on my face as I was holding the receiver.[36] In response to a reporter's question, the President had said, "I think it is one of the most important pieces of legislation for the good of all American mankind that we can act upon this session." After beating back a series of crippling amendments, the House passed the Demonstration Cities bill at 10 P.M. on Friday October 14.

On November 3, 1966, the President signed the bill in the East Room. In his statement, he referred to it as the "Model Cities" Act. He ordered all members of his administration to use that title from then on. After the ceremony, as we were walking back from the East Room, he said, "Don't ever give such a stupid Goddamn name to a bill again." I smiled. So did he. But I got the message, and he knew it. In any case, despite my gaffe in titling the bill, the Johnson magic had once again prevailed.*[37]

Johnson's efforts on behalf of blacks drew complaints from Mexican-Americans that the administration was neglecting their needs. At a White House press conference in March 1966, LBJ was asked if he had "heard . . . that Mexican-Americans feel they should have more attention."

They are right, he responded. They "are entitled to more con-

---

later told me Johnson had expressed complete surprise and decried his inability to control "rogue elephant aides who get too big for their britches."
* In its final version, the law largely conformed to the President's original proposal, but did not include a provision to promote housing desegregation. After 1966, more conservative Congresses refused to appropriate enough money for the program. In 1974, Congress converted Model Cities into a general urban renewal program.

sideration. . . . They have been discriminated against in housing, in education, in jobs." He promised "to do everything I can to improve their lot."

With that, he sent me off on a search for qualified Mexican-Americans to fill government posts and to organize a conference in Texas for Mexican-Americans comparable to the White House Conference on Civil Rights, which blacks wanted only for themselves. The President suggested I host a dinner in the White House mess for Mexican-American leaders to discuss the conference. I held the dinner on May 26, 1966, with five top leaders.*[38]

When the President joined us around 8 P.M., he shook everyone's hand, sat down, talked about growing up with Mexican-Americans, and said, "Tell me your complaints and problems. I want each of you to talk to me."

The leaders weren't shy. Alfred Hernandez said his people were disappointed that no Mexican-American was on the Equal Employment Opportunity Commission. Several chimed in that Mexican-Americans had no one representing them in the administration.

Johnson jumped in. "One of my closest secretaries, Yolanda Boozer [a Mexican-American], sitting right here with me [he had brought her along], is a fine and able representative," he insisted. "She's as close to the President as you can get," Johnson continued. "She opens my mail, my personal and top-secret letters, letters that only she and the President see, every day." Then he paused, and added, "She'll help you anytime you call. Send her your letters and she'll bring them right to me."

The guests were agog. Bert Corona said none of them had any idea that the President had a Mexican-American so close to him. He wanted a picture of Yolanda Boozer to let "some of my people know this."

Johnson listened to the group for an hour. After his departure, we continued our discussion. Around 11 P.M., the President invited us to join him and Mrs. Johnson in the living quarters to see the White House. When we arrived, Johnson conducted a grand, bombastic, uproarious tour of the White House living quarters, sending ushers scurrying to bring drinks to everyone as we walked through various rooms. The group grew increasingly boisterous. The Mexican-Americans moved from room to room in wide-eyed amazement, rais-

---

* Agustin Flores, chairman of the veterans group G.I. Forum; Dr. Hector Garcia, the Forum's founder; Bert Corona, acting president of the Mexican-American Political Association; Roy Elizondo, representative of the Political Association of Spanish-Speaking Organizations; and Alfred J. Hernandez, national president of LULAC (League of United Latin American Citizens).

ing their glasses as they shouted, "Viva LBJ!" Johnson, who was the only one among us not drinking, was completely relaxed, relishing the chance to open the White House to these men.

In the Lincoln bedroom, Johnson urged everyone to try "the bed Abraham Lincoln slept on. Go ahead, bounce on it!" Everyone did. Then we went to the theater on the ground floor of the East Wing to see four short films, including one on the President's Mexican trip. Mrs. Johnson and Lynda slipped off to bed as the President ordered more drinks served to his guests in the theater. The Mexican-American leaders cheered and applauded after each movie ended and erupted in more shouts of "Viva LBJ!"*[39]

Fearing that inflation would endanger the Great Society programs he was moving through Congress, Johnson pushed me constantly to move on some price or other, as he read reports from the Council of Economic Advisers, or noticed some increase on the AP or UPI wires. Shoe prices went up, so LBJ slapped export controls on hides to increase the supply of leather. Reports that color television sets would sell at high prices came across the wire. Johnson told me to ask RCA's David Sarnoff to hold them down. Domestic lamb prices rose. LBJ directed McNamara to buy cheaper lamb from New Zealand for the troops in Vietnam.[40]

The President told the CEA and me to move on household appliances, paper cartons, newsprint, men's underwear, women's hosiery, glass containers, cellulose, chlorine, air conditioners, and caustic soda, which is used to make soap and paper. He ordered the government to stop buying wooden furniture in order to hold down lumber prices, which accounted for many thousands of ugly gray plastic and metal desks in federal offices. When a price increase couldn't be rolled back, he wanted it delayed. Johnson was everywhere, a Dutch uncle with a thousand thumbs plugging holes in economic dikes to hold off the floodwaters of inflation.[41]

When egg prices rose in the spring of 1966 and Agriculture Secretary Orville Freeman told him that not much could be done, Johnson had the Surgeon General issue alerts as to the hazards of cholesterol in eggs. "Everyone in government should be expressing

---

* The following April LBJ appointed Vincente Ximenes, a leading advocate for Mexican-Americans, to the Equal Opportunity Commission. He later appointed Dr. Hector Garcia as the first Mexican-American to sit as a U.S. delegate to the United Nations. At Johnson's suggestion, Garcia made his maiden UN speech in Spanish. LBJ spoke to a cheering White House Conference of Mexican-Americans in Texas. He came there from signing a treaty returning Chamizal, a small territory, to Mexico, thus ending a hundred-year dispute between the United States and it southern neighbor.

concern about the cholesterol deposited on the heart from eating eggs," the President suggested, and he began to sprinkle his own conversations with references to the dangers of eating eggs. Later that year, he told McNamara to substitute medium for the large eggs the Pentagon was purchasing.[42]

LBJ was so consumed with the threat inflation posed to his domestic agenda that in March 1966 he ordered Freeman to hold a press conference to cheer an unexpected drop in food prices. *The New York Times* reported, "It was the first time in memory of Federal farm officials that a Secretary of Agriculture indicated that he was pleased with a decrease in farm prices." Democratic members of Congress from farm states and leaders of farm organizations dashed to the White House to protest. Johnson nodded as they deplored Freeman's political indiscretion and then said pointedly, "Farm prices must be out of sight if Orville Freeman's complaining publicly about them!"

Johnson reached for every lever, but the effort was necessarily uneven, and as 1966 progressed, the administration was scrambling like a quarterback under a defensive blitz. By midyear, *The New York Times*, which had been supporting Johnson's jawboning, said in an editorial that "use of the guideposts [and these ad hoc agreements] has been capricious and unfair," and several economists were questioning the effectiveness of our scatter-shot approach.[43]

Though Johnson often complained about lacking leverage over prices and wages, he was wary of touching one product over which the government had substantial pricing power. That was oil. In late 1965, Buford Ellington, the Director of the Office of Emergency Planning, had argued that residual fuel-oil import quotas should be lifted because there was no "national security" justification for them. Johnson wasn't prepared to accept his advice, but he didn't want to leave any tracks. So I was sent off to persuade Ellington to agree to relax, rather than terminate, quotas.[44]

LBJ's problem was not so much his Texas oil pals, since domestic refiners had begun to drop out of the residual fuel market in favor of higher-quality products. Far more serious was labor leader George Meany's opposition to any relaxation for fear that lower-priced fuel oil would hurt union coal miners. Against Meany, Johnson had to balance House Speaker John McCormack and the New England congressional delegation, which wanted import quotas lifed because of the high consumption of residual fuel oil in their states. Both organized labor and McCormack were loyal to the President on Vietnam and the Great Society. When I reported to the President that the relaxation would "hold the prices" of residual fuel oil and coal, but block any increases, he felt he could walk the line and relax the oil-import quotas.[45]

By the end of 1966, petroleum prices were up and still rising, and major oil companies had posted record profits. CEA member Jim Duesenberry proposed to hold prices down by increasing import quotas and other steps, but Interior Secretary Stewart Udall resisted.[46]

LBJ had told me repeatedly that he didn't want to get involved in oil. So the night I got word of the impasse, I met with the President alone. "No matter how much we increase quotas and reduce the price of oil," he said, "I'll be accused of favoring the oil industry. I've never intervened to help the domestic oil industry and I'm not going to intervene to hurt them." He told me I could "guide" Duesenberry, but not to "get personally involved because you are my voice on these matters."

I encouraged Duesenberry to meet with Udall, which he did. But Udall knew LBJ wouldn't get even his pinky caught in this cookie jar, so he refused to take any action, and oil-import quotas were not further relaxed.[47]

In 1966, I suggested to the President that we needed a wage and price czar to lead the jawboning effort. He was concerned that naming a czar would invite fears of wage and price controls and set off the inflation he was trying to avoid. One June evening over dinner, however, after making a rare comment that I looked tired, he said, "If you get yourself a price czar, get someone in whom you have absolute confidence, someone you'd give Mark and Joe [my sons] to if you died, someone as discreet as Lady Bird."

The candidate in the back of my mind actually came close: John Robson, a law-school roommate and close friend, with good judgment, not interested in publicity, and an Illinois Republican who had helped elect Congressman Donald Rumsfeld and was aiding Charles Percy in his run for the Senate. On July 14, 1966, I brought a nervous Robson into the green den adjoining the Oval Office to meet Lyndon Johnson.[48]

The President talked about the difficulties of fighting inflation. Robson responded that he'd been told a lot about the problem, but he had no experience in government or economics.

"No one was born knowing how to walk," Johnson said, "but you gotta learn to walk sometime." Then leaning a little into Robson, "You gotta live to learn. And the grindstone of life can be a lot better teacher than a Yale or Harvard education," Johnson added acidly. Robson had attended Yale and Harvard as he well knew.

Robson repeated his concern about lack of experience.

Johnson moved closer to Robson's face. In an almost fierce whisper, staring at him, he said, "I need you more than I need a company of Marines in Vietnam."

"I'd be proud and honored to assist, Mr. President. I just hope you recognize my limitations."

We then discussed what to call Robson and where to put him. The President decided not to make him an identifiable White House staffer. He intended to characterize the assignment publicly as studying the impact of federal procurement on the economy from an office in the Bureau of the Budget. Sensing Robson's disappointment at not being formally on the White House staff, Johnson observed that the Bureau's authority and scope were such that "they can even get into the President's bathroom."*[49]

In 1966 the greatest threat to LBJ's efforts to wrestle the feisty economy to the mat came from the prediction of a wild 19 percent jump in capital spending on plant and equipment. With unemployment plummeting to 3.7 percent in February, news of a sharp rise in capital investment put pressure on Johnson to seek a tax increase or face higher interest rates, encouraged by a jittery Federal Reserve Board.

Congress would counter any request for new taxes with demands to cut domestic spending. Johnson wanted to avoid that, especially with so many Great Society proposals awaiting congressional action and plans to send more to Capitol Hill. So he decided to grab the government and nation by the scruff of the neck in order to slow down capital spending and borrowing.

On March 7, Johnson sprayed these orders at me in the Oval Office:

> Have [Federal Power Commission chairman] Lee White†
> slow down [construction] permits [for private power facilities]. Get Boyd to slow down approvals on all [highway]
> construction. . . . Tell [Health, Education, and Welfare Secretary] Gardner that if he doesn't slow down spending [on hospital construction], we'll have another 1929. We're going to have to take our time on everything, except Vietnam
> . . . talk to Wood and Weaver about housing construction. . . . Ask Vance to slow down [Army] Corps of Engineers projects and anything not needed in Vietnam and get

* Robson went on to serve in the Ford administration as Chairman of the Civil Aeronautics Board and in the Bush Administration as Deputy Secretary of Treasury.
† Johnson moved White from the White House staff to chair the commission in March 1966.

[Interior Secretary] Udall to slow down a little [on power
and conservation projects]. . . . On the Hill, we've got to
get our appropriations bills through, but once we have the
money, we must slow down on spending. Get the SEC [Se-
curities and Exchange Commission] to slow down approval
of new stock issues [which corporations use to raise capital
for new investments]. . . . Tell Connor we want to look at
the EDA [Economic Development Administration]
projects. . . . Tell Agriculture we want to look at water
control and rural electrification projects, to slow their approval. . . . Call in the hundred biggest spenders in the
government and ask them to hold up their plans a little bit
and call in the top lending people to ask them to temporize
a little on approving loans.[50]

During another rapid-fire talk, Johnson snapped, "There are 30
key people in the entire Goddamn government—just 30 key people.
Spend an hour with each of them. Ask them . . . 'What are you doing
[that you can stop] to heap gasoline on the fire?' "[51] Each time we
spoke, I wrote madly away in my notebook and then passed the
President's instructions around the government.

Johnson was concerned that Treasury Secretary Fowler would
not move aggressively on the big banks (by, among other things,
increasing or withdrawing federal deposits) to reduce their lending for
plant and equipment. He compiled figures comparing the rise in interest rates and other economic indicators during Fowler's tenure as
Treasury Secretary to their rise in the previous decade. Then he called
Wright Patman (D-Tex.), the combustible populist chairman of the
House Banking and Currency Committee. "Wright, there's something you've just got to know. Interest rates have risen faster under
Joe Fowler than under any secretary in this century."

"Something's got to be done about that, Mr. President!" Patman
shouted over the phone.

"That's why I'm telling you," Johnson continued. "If I were
you, I'd send him a blistering letter and have him up to testify.
You've got to build a fire under him."

"You're absolutely right, Mr. President."

Standing at the President's desk, I could visualize Patman—the
most vocal proponent of low interest rates in Congress, an implacable
foe of Wall Street bankers and Martin's Fed—his face siren red, his
whole body trembling with rage.

"You know, Wright," Johnson went on, "unless Fowler starts
moving, the New York bankers will just keep raising interest rates
and rolling in the money."

"I'll write him, Mr. President!"

Patman sent Fowler a scathing letter the next day. The Treasury Secretary called the President and me as soon as he received it. Johnson suggested Fowler tell Patman that he would put pressure on the banks "or else he'll turn your hearing into a Texas-barbecue."[52]

Johnson directed the Federal Housing Administration, the Veterans Administration, and the Federal National Mortgage Association to slow funds for housing. He called the nation's governors to the White House to urge them to control their own capital spending. He invited 150 big businessmen to a White House dinner.[53] After the meal, Johnson asked any who favored a tax increase to raise their hands. Not a hand went up. Well, he said, smiling, if they didn't want a tax increase, then they'd better trim back their plans for capital spending.[54]

Johnson also instituted an unprecedented requirement for presidential approval of every borrowing by any federal agency. Dismissing Treasury officials' concerns that his effort to exercise such control could disrupt orderly sales of federal paper and cause chaos in some financial markets, from September 1966 until well into 1968 Lyndon Johnson personally reviewed and approved every issue of federal paper to borrow money.[55]

Johnson tried to make sure the government did its part by slowing federal spending and borrowing. He launched major Great Society programs with minimal amounts. "Congress is like a whiskey drinker," he told me. "You can put an awful lot of whiskey into a man if you just let him sip it. But if you try to force the whole bottle down his throat at one time, he'll throw it up." And, he might have added, if that man suspects that you want to get the whole bottle down him, he might not take the first sip.

Nonetheless, the congressional disposition to bankroll pet projects of powerful members and enact politically popular bills kept adding to the budget. Congress passed budget busters that Johnson found impossible to veto, such as a GI bill of rights for cold war veterans and a federal employee pay increase far more costly than he had requested.

The President took out some of his frustration on me: "[We're] getting the hell beat out of us" on the budget because "you don't know enough members of Congress . . . get to know more congressmen and senators." When I said I'd speak to Larry O'Brien right away, Johnson said, "I'm talking to you. You do it. You got to learn to mount this Congress like you mount a woman."[56] Johnson worried that the economic situation and congressional budget busting on political pork, like highways and dams, would kill particularly vulnerable Great Society projects, like funding for his National Endowments for the Arts and Humanities and Hirshhorn Museum and Sculpture Garden.

When he got frustrated by the difficulty of controlling big government expenditures, the President would become acutely sensitive about cutting small costs, everything from turning the lights out in the White House to insisting that cabinet officers use slower, cheaper aircraft to save fuel on short trips.[57] Nothing was exempt and there wasn't a nose that couldn't be cut off to spite a face. Marvin Watson was the President's preferred instrument for these economy sprees. Johnson knew that Watson would do exactly as he'd been told, whereas most other top aides might temper the President's more outrageous instructions—or, as I often did, conveniently forget them in the hope that he would.

During one of the budget meetings in my office, the President was looking sourly at my phones. I didn't realize what had caught his attention until the next morning when Army Signal Corpsmen arrived. They told me that Watson had ordered the number of my phone lines reduced from six to three as part of an economy drive. Five secretaries spread over two shifts and Larry Levinson, as well as myself, used those phones. Two days after the number of lines were reduced, House Speaker McCormack tried to call me repeatedly, and the lines were always busy. The Speaker complained to presidential secretary Juanita Roberts. She reported the complaint to the President immediately. Johnson chewed out Watson for such "damn fool frugality that could cost us our legislation in the House," and by that afternoon not only were the six lines restored: two were added.[58]

On another occasion when some office space opened up in the West Wing basement, Watson sent the President a memo asking, "May I take the space . . . and move various secretaries and other personnel from this floor?" Johnson checked the "No" line and wrote across the bottom of Watson's memo, breaking pencil points, "Hold until further notice & let some sec[retaries] go. It is disgusting the # we have. L."[59] With that, we went through a (mercifully brief) purge of secretaries.*

Short of increasing taxes, Johnson also worked the revenue-raising side of the budget as no other President had. If it wasn't nailed

---

* No detail was too small for Lyndon Johnson's attention. He approved most White House party guest lists, menus, even seating arrangements. He once called from the ranch to tell me, "Have the janitor clean the red rugs on the second floor every hour" (this was the carpet in the hall corridor outside the Oval Office and other main-floor West Wing offices). "Keep the ash trays in my office and in the area where the red rugs are clean," and "Tell the secretaries that there are to be no conversations in the hall. If they want to talk, they should talk on the telephone and not stand in the hall."[60]

down, LBJ was ready to sell it. We sold stockpiles of strategic minerals (bringing in almost $1 billion in fiscal 1966), timberlands, mining rights, and excess real estate. Johnson created Participation Certificates, which represented pools of various federal low-interest loans made, for example, to help localities build sewers and hospitals, developers build housing, and veterans buy homes. He sold these certificates to individuals and institutions, decreasing the budget deficit by $2.9 billion in fiscal 1967.

But spending slowdowns, government property sales, price- and interest-rate jawboning, and budgetary legerdemain, as shrewd, imaginative, and energetic as Lyndon Johnson was, could not alone tame the pent-up economic forces set loose by the expanding war and his tenacious pursuit of the Great Society.

A contract negotiation in mid-1966—between the International Association of Machinists and Aerospace Workers (IAM) and five major airlines (Eastern, National, Northwest, Trans World, and United)—proved to be the Achilles heel in the President's jawboning program, and signaled that LBJ's ability to control economic events was ebbing.

Tempering wage and benefit demands was decidedly more difficult and less effective than holding down price increases and interest rates. Union leaders are elected by their members and the surest route to remain in office is a settlement big enough to discourage future opposition. Moreover, Johnson's populist instincts tilted him toward the workingman's side, and Democratic party politics rendered unappetizing bare-knuckled scraps over wages with organized labor.

The IAM wanted 5 percent annual increases in wages and benefits. The airlines had offered 2.8 percent. Within these competing demands, Johnson hoped to mediate a settlement acceptable to both sides and close to the 3.2 percent wage guidepost.[61] As the strike deadline approached in the spring of 1966, Johnson invoked the Railway Labor Act to provide a sixty-day no-strike period, during which a presidentially appointed board would recommend a settlement package. Johnson then placed a call to Oregon Senator Wayne Morse.[62] Morse was committed to the wage-price guideposts, but he was so opposed to sending American soldiers to fight in Vietnam without a congressional declaration of war that he was privately talking about impeaching Johnson. (Just two months later he would announce his opposition to LBJ as the party's candidate in 1968 and his support for Robert Kennedy instead.)

"Wayne," Johnson began, chuckling, "I know you want to have

me impeached. It's not just Vietnam. It's all the tough jobs I keep asking you to do."

I could hear Morse's loud, hoarse laugh over the phone.

Johnson then asked Morse to chair the airline labor-dispute board.[63]

On June 5, Morse's board proposed an annual wage and benefit increase of 3.5 percent, close to the 3.2 percent guidepost, but far below what the IAM sought. Johnson quickly endorsed the report. The next day the union rejected it and attacked Morse.

Led by its tough president P. L. (Roy) Siemiller, the IAM struck the airlines the moment the no-strike period ended. Although the strike had no serious impact on the economy, it was a major inconvenience for the middle and upper-middle class, and for senators and representatives themselves, so Congress began to thrash around to do something.

As Johnson sensed that Congress would lay on the President responsibility to make the final decision to end the airline strike,[64] he made one last push for a settlement. On the morning of July 29, he gave his pitch to the parties in the Cabinet Room: "You men around this table can find a solution equitable to both parties better than anyone else. . . . I invite you to go over to the Executive Office Building and continue your collective bargaining."[65]

That evening the parties produced an agreement that the President could announce as (just barely) "within the general framework" of the Morse board report. The union vote on the proposed agreement was scheduled for that Sunday, July 31.

After the announcement, Johnson went to Camp David for the weekend with some close friends. On arrival, he was elated at the settlement, offered everyone a nightcap and retired at 1 A.M., feeling good and relaxed. Rare for him, LBJ slept in that morning, and had two stacks of hotcakes at a noontime breakfast. I killed his good mood when I called shortly after 3 P.M. to tell him, "It looks like the union's playing games; it's not urging its members to approve the contract."[66]

Johnson woke me up on Sunday at 7:20 A.M. to discuss the ratification vote. At 9:15 when I told him that we had serious trouble, Johnson asked me to get up to Camp David. I arrived after 1 P.M. and the President took me to the swimming pool.[67] As reports came in that IAM members in the East were voting to reject the settlement, he told me to call union and political leaders out West, where the time was two to three hours earlier, and ask them to urge the machinists to approve the settlement. A favorable vote in the West might offset the accumulating adverse vote in the East. On my way to the phone, a bee stung the small toe on my left foot. As I sat down at the phone, my toe swelled almost to the size of a golf ball and I began to have a mild anaphylactic reaction. Johnson had a White House physician check my breathing and put an ice bag on my toe. He told me to "Keep sipping water and keep making those calls," and he told the physician to sit near me and "watch him constantly" in case my reaction got worse. Fortunately, it didn't, but it wasn't any easier to make those calls with a nervous Navy doctor staring at me.

The calls were to no avail as union members overwhelmingly rejected the contract. As an angry Congress considered legislation to block a strike, the parties came to an agreement union members approved. Ackley put it at 4.9 percent,[68] far in excess of the 3.2 percent guideposts. IAM President Siemiller irresponsibly—but correctly—bragged that the airline settlement "destroy[ed] all existing wage and price guidelines now in existence." So far as organized labor was concerned, as the summer of 1966 came to a close, the guideposts were indeed dead.

Business was not far behind. The Inland Steel Company raised its prices on strip and sheet steel. Other companies rushed to follow, ignoring pleas from CEA Chairman Ackley asking them not to follow Inland's lead.[69]

Along with other events, the airlines labor settlement and the steel price increase compelled the President to face the limits on his own power to manipulate the economy and to consider wage and price controls and action on the tax front.

That same August, Johnson asked me to explore, on a "top-secret-eyes-only basis," whether he had authority to impose wage and price controls without congressional action. I gave the assignment to Robson, with instructions to research the issue himself. Any leak of Johnson's interest in the subject would spark a round of sharp price increases. Emphasizing that the issue was not free from doubt, Robson concluded that in a national emergency declared by the President, the 1917 Trading with the Enemy Act might be invoked to impose wage and price controls without going to the Congress. Robson noted that Harry Truman's 1951 Korean War declaration of national emergency was technically still in effect. I passed his memo along to the President.

The President quoted from the memo in an Oval Office conversation with Katzenbach. Katzenbach was concerned that a court might overturn presidential action to impose controls, unless Congress promptly passed a law confirming it. In other unorthodox uses of the Trading with the Enemy Act, like Roosevelt's bank holiday, Congress had ratified the President's actions. The Attorney General eventually gave these views to LBJ in an eyes-only memorandum, no copies of which were left at the Justice Department. Katzenbach wanted a "free hand to support any such action" the President took, so he didn't want a memo in the files revealing any doubt about the President's authority to act, or expressing a view that would put the government on the short end of a lawsuit challenging wage and price controls established by presidential executive order.[70]

I held a series of secret discussions among the President's economic advisers, including Supreme Court Justice Abe Fortas. The President attended a number of them. He particularly wanted some indication how the Supreme Court would rule on presidential imposition of controls without congressional action. Fortas thought that the question was close and the outcome might well depend on the severity of the situation at the time the matter came before the Court.

In the end, the questions of legality became moot. Virtually all of Johnson's advisers recommended against imposing wage and price controls because of the difficulty of enforcing them. The vehement opposition expressed by those who had helped administer economic controls during World War II and the Korean War was persuasive to Johnson. Besides, he couldn't afford to ignite a congressional firestorm that might jeopardize his domestic programs.[71]

During that summer of 1966, the President confronted the prospect of a fiscal 1967 budget deficit triple the $1.8 billion he had predicted in January, and that was without the whopping additional funds needed to finance the war. With unemployment below 4 percent and pressures on interest rates continuing, Johnson's advisers knew some kind of tax action was appropriate, but they were divided on what exactly to do. Some wanted a modest personal and corporate income tax increase. Others preferred to suspend the investment tax credit (a special tax break for business investment in plant and equipment) in order to slow capital spending and hit only business.[72]

On August 8, Johnson met with Democratic and Republican congressional leaders to see how they felt about an income-tax increase. House minority leader Gerald Ford reacted instantly, "You'd have trouble getting more than fifteen votes." Ford's Democratic counterpart, Carl Albert, trumped him, "You wouldn't even get that many!" Senate Finance Committee Chairman Russell Long and House Ways and Means Committee Chairman Wilbur Mills told Johnson they opposed any tax increase, but might go along with suspending the investment tax credit.[73]

In a perfect world, Johnson believed, a tax increase might make sense if coupled with an agreement from Federal Reserve Board chairman Martin to lower interest rates. But Johnson feared that a tax increase sufficient to satisfy Martin would precipitate a recession. In any case, he wasn't about to put his Great Society programs on the cutting block by asking for taxes he couldn't persuade Congress to enact.

The stock market then took its sharpest dive of the year. Johnson followed the market each day and often timed and phrased announcements to evoke a favorable impact on stock prices. He wanted the market during his administration to be the highest it had ever been. Ackley warned Johnson that the steep drop was another portent of an impending financial crisis and urged suspension of the investment tax credit.[74]

Johnson wanted all his advisers to sign a memo recommending the action. On the Friday before Labor Day, I gathered Ackley, Katzenbach, Schultze, O'Brien, Ginsburg, Fowler, and McNamara in my office. Each of us initialed the memo to the President.[75] Johnson asked Congress to suspend the credit and Congress swiftly gave him what he requested. Suspension of the investment tax credit cooled pressures on capital spending, undercut inflation, and slowed the climb in interest rates, but it did little to reduce the deficit and did not silence discussion of a tax increase.

Moreover, Johnson's strategy was taking a toll on his credibility. Many economists were beginning to wonder whether he was serious about reining in inflation, as they questioned the fairness and long-term effectiveness of the administration's frenetic efforts to hold down prices and interest rates, and watched organized labor bury the wage guideposts in large settlements like the IAM contract with the airlines. Rising war costs and funds for Great Society programs were stretching the outer limits of the President's ability to manipulate the federal budget.

Johnson's extravagant rhetoric announcing new programs belied the modest funds he requested to begin them. Conservative members of Congress distrusted him because they believed that he was hiding his real intentions just to get a foot in the door. The Great Society's liberal advocates were frustrated because he wasn't asking for enough to smash the door open. And Congress was providing even less. There was a gnawing sense that, however many fingers LBJ was able to put in the dike, without a tax increase he could not much longer prevent the waters from flowing over the top.

EIGHT

The Great 89th

WHEN THE 89th Congress adjourned on October 22, 1966, Johnson's legislative accomplishments were already monumental. Indeed, with the President asking for 113 major measures and getting 97 passed, the second session of the 89th Congress had exceeded the output of the first, in which 87 measures were requested and 84 passed.

Johnson's legislative revolution was taking the federal government into the modern world on the side of the little person. Its achievements included the war on poverty; health care for the elderly and the poor; aid to education for poor children; voting rights; immigration reform; and regional heart, cancer, and stroke research facilities in every section of the nation. Johnson had delivered support for the arts throughout the country, environmental protection for air and water, mine safety for workers, model cities, rent supplements, and urban mass-transit systems. He had opened the way for a new rehabilitation program for drug addicts, support for training health professionals, vocational rehabilitation, a teacher corps, and bail and civil procedure reforms for the courts. He had put consumer protection on the national agenda with auto, highway, and tire safety, truth-in-packaging, and protection for children from unsafe toys and hazardous substances. A 1964 tax cut would eventually unlock six years of economic growth and prosperity which would spawn such profits and wages that federal revenues would increase, thus making it possible to fund the Great Society.

149

On October 15, in an East Room ceremony, LBJ received a glowing report from House Speaker McCormack and Senate Majority
Leader Mansfield about two years of towering legislative progress
from "The Great 89th," as he called this Congress.* On October 24,
Larry O'Brien and I released a report to the President cataloging the
array of measures that he had proposed and Congress had passed. By
any standard, the grand total of 200 measures proposed and 181
passed, for a batting average of .905, was unprecedented and not
likely to be surpassed. Still the President was disappointed by what he
viewed as lack of appreciation of his achievements, and he yearned for
more recognition.

He took off on a spectacular trip through Hawaii, American
Samoa, New Zealand, Australia, the Philippines, South Vietnam,
Thailand, Malaysia, and Korea. Just before he departed in a helicopter
from the south lawn of the White House,[1] Johnson showered me with
presents: gold buttons for a blazer, gold cuff links, a gold Zippo
cigarette lighter, a gold tie clasp and an electric toothbrush—all with
the presidential seal. In Seoul, Korea, a crowd of two million people
greeted him. Swept up in the euphoria, he later told an audience of
American and South Korean servicemen that his great-great-
grandfather had died defending the Alamo. *Time* correspondent Hugh
Sidey wrote that LBJ had no relatives who fought at the Alamo and
Johnson good-humoredly cracked, "If Hugh Sidey had a crowd of that
size, he would have claimed George Washington was his great-great-
grandfather."

Johnson was enthusiastically received everywhere, and came
away convinced that Asia was the future. He poured out his feelings
on the Far East to some of his staff: "I think history fifty years from
now will say that the sleeping giant in America awakened and turned
its eyes toward the Golden West—they have the manpower, the
resources—Indonesia and Southeast Asia have everything you need
in the world. They have the largest area in the world. . . . This is the
way of the future . . . unlimited resources untapped . . . two-thirds
of the people . . ."[2]

While in Asia, Johnson kept an eye on events at home. Traveling
in very different time zones, he called me at all hours to give instruc-

---

* Johnson even had a song written to celebrate this Congress, with this chorus: "We
salute you Congress for a job well done/Making our Society a Greater one/We
salute you Congress for you further the theme/That brings us to the era of America's
dream/Oh, the Great 89th will always be remembered/Yes the Great 89th has left
its mark/No Congress before ever opened the door/To the future like the Great
89th."

tions and receive reports. During his journey, the President came up with the idea of a triumphal tour of the country to sign major Great Society bills Congress had passed. A whirlwind trip just before the November 8 election would highlight his accomplishments and give him a chance to help Democratic candidates for Congress and several statehouses. At his direction, I worked out arrangements for the House and Senate to postpone sending several bills to the White House to provide adequate time for the President to sign them during his national tour. Also at Johnson's instruction, Sherwin Markman and other White House aides were dispatched to find the nation's greatest shopping center for the Truth-in-Packaging signing; the right spot in Minnesota, the land of ten thousand lakes, for the Clean Water Restoration Act; a location in Boston for Model Cities (to help Speaker John McCormack's nephew Edward in his bid to be governor of the Bay State); a good location in Chicago for the neighboring Indiana Dunes National Lakeshore (to help incumbent Senator Paul Douglas); a place in the heart of North Dakota, a wheat-producing state, for Food for Freedom; and on and on, for a hectic, long preelection weekend. Johnson thought he had a clever way to campaign for Democratic candidates without appearing to be too political, something that he wished to avoid because of the importance of bipartisan support for the Vietnam War.[3]

The trip was set to begin on Friday, November 4, two days after he returned to the White House. Candidates across the country adjusted schedules for the President's anticipated arrival, and in some places, like Seattle, where Markman had found a huge shopping center, workers started constructing platforms.[4]

But the President began to have second thoughts. He sensed that many congressional Democrats, particularly those swept into office by his 1964 landslide, might take a beating. He didn't want to be identified with their defeat or have their losses blamed on support of his Great Society programs. He also feared that rushing through eleven cities in four days would look too much like a circus.

Yet he still ached over the lack of appreciation from the people for his achievements and longed to find a way to gain their recognition. On the night before returning to Washington, in his fourteenth-floor Westward Hotel suite in Anchorage, Alaska, Johnson launched into a long and sometimes bitter monologue, while a few aides and secretaries listened:

> I am willing to let any objective historian look at my record. If I can't do more than any[one else] to help my

country, I'll quit. FDR passed five major bills the first one hundred days. We passed 200 in the last two years. It is unbelievable. We must dramatize that in the two days of signing to come. I would have several signings—in the East Room at 10, in the Cabinet Room at 11, in the Fish Room at 12, in my office at 1, and I would do it for two full days, and I would give them [reporters] statements two days before I did it so they can write their stories. . . . There never has been an era in American history when so much has been done for so many in such a short time. . . . Several Presidents have passed education bills. I passed eighteen. . . . In medical care, we passed twenty-four bills—in all the years before they passed seventeen. . . . In conservation we have passed twenty major bills. . . . We are the only administration in history that has done anything about dirty water . . . truth in packaging. . . . We must tell people what we have done.[5]

Johnson's decision to abandon the signing trips did not go over well. Incumbent Governor Pat Brown of California, faced with an uphill fight against Ronald Reagan, had cancelled a whistle-stop train tour of Los Angeles County to receive the President; he had to hustle to fill his schedule. In Illinois, Senator Douglas worried that Republican challenger Charles Percy would now trounce him.

If that had been the end of it, Johnson would have been blamed for not campaigning, but better to accept that than be faulted for campaigning and losing. Moreover, he would gain just as much publicity, possibly more, by signing the bills in the White House. But he refused to let the matter end there.

The next day a reporter asked whether "cancellation of your big campaign trip" meant the President wouldn't do anything to help Democratic candidates. Johnson responded tartly, "First, we don't have any plans, so when you don't have plans, you don't cancel plans. . . . The people of this country ought to know that all these cancelled plans primarily involve the imagination of people who phrase sentences and write columns, and have to report what they hope or what they imagine." With this incredible answer—in the face of a score of disappointed politicians in ten states publicly reshuffling their schedules—Johnson made his credibility a bigger story than his legislative achievements as 1966 ended. *New York Times* columnist Tom Wicker, who sympathized that LBJ "has absorbed in relative silence more—and more unfair—criticism than most Presidents ever have to hear," wrote sadly that "the credibility gap is becoming the vulnerable heel of Achilles Johnson."

What may have sparked Johnson's irritation at the press was the gathering clouds—how much harder it was to pass each new proposal, the depth and viciousness of the developing white backlash, and the swelling anger of black ghetto youths. There was rising concern about the Vietnam War, which by the end of 1966 had killed 6,500 Americans and wounded 37,000, as the U.S. troop contingent there rose to 385,000. After civil rights, the war took the heaviest toll on Johnson's political capital and popularity. While most Americans still hoped to win the war, they also wanted to end it as soon as possible—and more were questioning its morality. After a short burst of enthusiasm in the summer of 1965, mounting casualties, fear of inflation, and stalemate were frazzling people's nerves. And the credibility gap on small matters was eroding the people's confidence and trust in their President.

The first major storm came with the results of the midterm elections. The President's party lost forty-seven seats in the House of Representatives, three seats in the Senate, and eight statehouses.

Less than a week after the midterm elections, the President had to decide whether to sign a popular anticrime bill Congress had sent him in a burst of preelection jitters. Republicans and southern Democrats, eager to flex their muscles and embarrass Johnson, saw the rising crime rate in the nation's capital as the perfect political tablet on which to write a "tough" bill and overrule Supreme Court decisions viewed as soft on criminal defendants.

House members had passed the bill in 1965. It bristled with mandatory sentences, permission for cops to question suspects and material witnesses for several hours before arraignment, and an antipornography provision, under which an individual could be convicted of a crime without being granted a full hearing on the issue of obscenity. Shortly before the November 1966 elections, the Senate had passed the House bill and sent it to the President.

Most presidential advisers recommended a veto, but Katzenbach and Hoover urged Johnson to sign the bill.[6] Overwhelming congressional support for the legislation and politics (a veto could lead to charges that Democrats were soft on crime) made the call close.

As on so many other close ones, Johnson consulted Abe Fortas, who recommended a veto. Fortas believed the pornography provisions were clearly unconstitutional and that the Supreme Court would so rule. He also considered the provisions authorizing extended questioning of suspects and witnesses prior to arraignment unconstitutional but could not predict with certainty what the Court would decide. He thought the mandatory sentences unwise, but probably constitutional. After the President talked to Fortas, the Supreme Court Justice and I structured the veto message.[7] On November 13, 1966, Johnson vetoed the bill with the message we had drafted.*

During November, LBJ pressed forward on one of his most controversial initiatives, despite sharp criticism from powerful allies. Johnson felt strongly that as a component of his war on poverty birth-control information and devices should be made available to poor people who wished to have them. He believed that promotion of family planning, at home and abroad, was a positive duty of government.

Previous presidents had either opposed mounting government birth-control programs, finessed the issue, or gingerly approved a little research on population control. Johnson himself had waited until he was elected in his own right to unveil his position. Then, in his January 4, 1965, State of the Union message, Johnson had said, "I will seek new ways to use our knowledge to help deal with the explosion in world population and the growing scarcity in world resources."

Six months later, in a speech marking the twentieth anniversary of the United Nations, Johnson had asked the world organization to "face forthrightly the multiplying problems of our multiplying populations. . . . Let us act on the fact that less than $5 invested in population control is worth $100 invested in economic growth." That same month, the Supreme Court struck down as unconstitutional a Connecticut statute prohibiting the distribution of information about contraceptive devices and their use. During the year, the administration, largely through the Office of Economic Opportunity and Department of Health, Education, and Welfare, had begun to make contraceptive devices and information available to married women who asked for them.

In 1966 the administration began to educate the poor about birth control, and Johnson got Congress to increase funds for family planning. HEW Secretary Gardner ordered birth-control information and devices given to anyone requesting them, married or not.

Johnson also moved aggressively on the international scene to make family planning the policy of other governments. He had put food-grain aid to India on a month-to-month basis because India, relying on the U.S., had neglected its rural economy and failed to promote family planning. As the 1965–67 Indian drought and famine worsened, all the President's agricultural and foreign policy advisers

---

* A year later, the President signed a D.C. crime bill revamped to meet some of his objections, with a statement Fortas also helped draft.[8]

urged him to expand food shipments to India immediately. But Johnson wanted India to take care of itself—improve its agricultural production, end food hoarding, and control its population. He also felt that the United States should not bear the aid burden alone. Many Johnson advisers and prominent friends of India, including Ambassador-at-large Harriman, did not share the President's perspective, and they relentlessly pressed him to ship enormous amounts of grain to India.

Fed up, Johnson assigned me in early 1966 the task of coming up with a food-for-India program before Prime Minister Indira Gandhi visited him in March. According to our own experts, the Indians needed eleven to twelve million tons of grain in 1966. I sent the President a memo on February 3, proposing a compromise I'd worked out with Agriculture Secretary Freeman and others: a stopgap shipment of grain before the Gandhi visit, after that six million tons, plus an additional two-thirds of five million tons, with other countries to contribute the rest. Johnson exploded all over my memo. "No, *Hell* no," he wrote. "Ask Freeman if he has lost his mind? No! No! No! Maybe ⅔ of 10 [million tons] but not 6 [million tons] + ⅔ of 5 [million tons]. He must be working for India?"[9]

When the hotline rang that afternoon, I picked it up and, before I could say, "Yes, Mr. President," Johnson shouted, "Are you out of your fucking mind?" He was so agitated with my being "duped by the pro-India lobbyists in the administration" that to maintain my own perspective I had to recall what his long-time aide Cliff Carter had told me soon after I had arrived at the White House. "To work for this man, you've got to remember two things," Carter had warned. "You're never as good as he says you are when he praises you and you're never as bad as he says you are when he chews you out."

In due course, when all the dust had settled, Johnson sent 3 million tons of grain to India before the Gandhi visit and asked Congress to approve an additional 3.5 million tons after that. Johnson asked other countries to satisfy India's remaining need. Before he sent his message to Congress on March 30, 1966, though, Johnson had met with Gandhi,[10] and he reported that "The Indian government believes that there can be no effective solution of the Indian food problem that does not include population control. The choice is now between a comprehensive and humane program for limiting births and the brutal curb that is imposed by famine. As Mrs. Gandhi told me, the Indian government is making vigorous efforts on this front."

In mid-October 1966, the President had Labor Secretary Wirtz receive on his behalf the first Margaret Sanger Award in World Leadership. The award was named after the founder of Planned Parenthood, a most aggressive proponent of contraception and a special target of the Catholic hierarchy. It was a tribute no other President would have risked accepting.

All this set the stage for a stinging attack from the nation's Catholic bishops when they met in Washington the week after the midterm elections. On the whole, Johnson enjoyed an amicable relationship with the Catholic hierarchy. They applauded his work for the poor and the old, and appreciated his consideration of parochial schools in the Elementary and Secondary Education Act. But the church had long held that the rhythm method—limiting intercourse to times when a woman was not fertile—was the only morally permissible means of birth control. The Pope had reaffirmed that position early in the year, and though the American clergy were not as conservative, the bishops regarded government birth-control programs warily.

Late in the afternoon on November 14, Father Francis Hurley, the top staffer for the National Catholic Welfare Conference and the bishops' liaison with the White House, rushed me a copy of a statement that the American bishops had just released. The bishops charged that the administration was coercing the poor to practice birth control:

> On previous occasions we have warned of dangers to the right of privacy posed by governmental birth control programs; we have urged upon government a role of neutrality whereby it neither penalizes nor promotes birth control. Recent developments, however, show government rapidly abandoning any such role. Far from merely seeking to provide information in response to requests from the needy, Government activities increasingly seek aggressively to persuade and even coerce the underprivileged to practice birth control. . . . We decry this overreaching by government. . . .
>
> . . . In the international field, as in the domestic field . . . international programs of aid should not be conditioned upon acceptance of birth control programs by beneficiary nations.[11]

One bishop charged that the administration had ignored an earlier letter from the hierarchy protesting its policies. The bishop did not say to whom the letter had been addressed, but Hurley told reporters that it had been sent to war-on-poverty director Sargent Shriver, a Catholic. Shriver had simply acknowledged the letter, without answering the points it raised.[12] *The New York Times*, like most other papers, played the coercion charge on page one: "Roman Cath-

olic Cardinals and Bishops of the United States charged tonight that
the Johnson administration was putting pressure on the poor to practice birth control."

The President wrote "Terrible" at the bottom of my memo reporting these events and started my next day with spirited complaints
about the Catholic bishops. He talked of the "fine relationship" he
had with the church hierarchy, his support of poverty programs and
human dignity for blacks, which the church very much wanted, and
the help he had given parochial schools. "The first thing the Pope said
to me was that I was a doer, not a talker," Johnson said, referring to
his meeting in New York in October 1965. He told me to call the
bishops and say that the "President is entitled to better treatment,"
that providing birth-control information was not coercion and "tell
them, 'please don't attack the administration that's helped you so
much.' "13

Johnson was also annoyed that Shriver had not given the bishops
a substantive response to their letter. He suspected that the bishops
had not attacked Shriver personally because he was a fellow Catholic
and a Kennedy in-law. Johnson knew, but refused to acknowledge,
that the bishops felt compelled to speak out because he had declared
himself so forcefully in favor of government promotion of birth control at home and abroad—no fewer than twenty-three times since his
1965 State of the Union message. He had Shriver deny the coercion
charge, assure the public that he would act immediately if any such
incidents were reported, and respond to the hierarchy's earlier letter.

I called Father Hurley and reminded him, "If the bishops ever
have a problem, all they have to do is call the agency head involved
and if they don't get a call back, just call me and I'll pass along their
concern to the President." I offered to meet with Detroit Archbishop
John Dearden, the new leader of the American bishops, to make sure
he understood the administration's "open-door" policy. I passed along
the President's "disappointment that [the bishops] had to go to the
newspapers without any prior consultation with us."

Hurley said he anticipated a continuing problem: the bishops
believed that for government simply to provide birth-control information to the poor was inherently coercive. He volunteered that a
forthcoming bishops' statement on civil rights would be totally in
accord with the President's policies. Their statement on peace in Vietnam would be "dove-like," he warned, but it would explicitly oppose
"peace at any price."14

Unsatisfied, the President wanted me to "work out something"
so he could pursue his policies without attack from the bishops. He
told me to meet with Hurley that evening. Johnson said he was not

"going to deny contraceptives to any poor person who wanted them," and he was "not going to piss away foreign aid in nations where they refused to deal with their own population problems." But he considered it "important to make peace with the Catholic bishops because before long they may be the only allies we have on Negro rights and the poverty program."

He also wanted me to find out whether the group of bishops who wrote the statement included Richard Cardinal Cushing, Archbishop of Boston and a Kennedy family intimate. "See if it was Cushing who advocated it." Johnson bet that the attack, without any mention of Shriver, whose OEO program was most involved, might have originated with the Kennedys, "probably Bobby."[15]

That evening as the President entered Bethesda Naval Hospital for surgery to repair damaged scar tissue from his 1965 gall-bladder operation and remove a polyp from his throat, Hurley delivered a letter from Archbishop Dearden conveying "prayers for the speedy recovery of the President and the continuance of his good health."[16] When I read the letter to the President over the phone, he said, "If the bishops want my speedy recovery, they can stop attacking me in the press." Hurley and I had another long talk. He assured me that Cushing had nothing to do with the bishops' statement and we came up with an uneasy truce: if the President and the administration would portray their efforts in terms of "the population problem" rather than "birth control" or "population control," Hurley would do all he could to get the bishops to lie back. The more general characterization could be seen to encourage producing more food, redistributing wealth, and using the rhythm method, rather than simply distributing contraceptives.[17]

I quietly met with Archbishop Dearden at Catholic University to say that the administration's doors were always open for conversation and to ask him to temper his criticism.[18] Dearden was cordial but made no commitments. Nevertheless, those meetings, coupled with reports of serious splits in the Catholic hierarchy and among Catholic moral theologians and parish priests on the issue of birth control, calmed the President.

But nothing deterred him from his objective. In the fall of 1967, he decided to join more than two dozen world leaders in a statement on population stressing the importance of family planning to "the enrichment of human life, not its restriction . . . [to free] man to attain his individual dignity and reach his full potential."[19]

Two months before the statement was made public, Johnson had me secretly send it to Father Hurley to point out that nowhere did it refer to "birth control" or "contraceptives," and tell him the President insisted on that out of respect for the American bishops and hoped they would in turn respect his views. Hurley promised to work to that end, but he couldn't be sure how the bishops would react.[20]

When the statement was issued on December 11 at the United Nations, the American bishops were silent. The President was delighted.

The Democratic party's loss of congressional and gubernatorial seats did not inhibit LBJ from extending the reach of his long arms, as he made clear in the case of the Penn-Central merger.

When he became chairman of the Pennsylvania Railroad in 1963, Stuart Saunders, a businessman whose impeccable attire and cherubic countenance provided cover for his tenacity and political street smarts, was determined to consummate the biggest railroad merger in American history: his new company and the New York Central Railroad. Saunders had pioneered railroad mergers in 1958 and 1959, successfully combining the Norfolk & Western and Virginia Railways. He was obsessed with doing the biggest ever, the Penn-Central.

In 1962 the railroads had submitted a merger plan to the Interstate Commerce Commission (ICC), whose approval was needed to close the deal. Representing the United States, the Justice Department vehemently fought the consolidation on antitrust grounds. On April 6, 1966, the ICC overrode the department's objections and approved the merger. Competing railroads asked a three-judge federal court for an injunction. The Justice Department took no position before this court and the judges refused to block the merger. The competing railroads then went to the Supreme Court.

In November 1966, as Thurgood Marshall, then Solicitor General of the United States, prepared to file his brief with the Supreme Court, Stuart Saunders called me. He had commitments, Saunders claimed, from Robert Kennedy when he had been Attorney General, and from President Johnson, that if the ICC hearing examiner approved the merger, the Justice Department would support it or at least withdraw its opposition. Saunders was a little fuzzy about the time, place, and specifics of the President's commitment, but he sent me a copy of Kennedy's signed pledge.[21]

Saunders had met with Kennedy on August 21, 1964. Two weeks later, then Acting Attorney General Katzenbach had written Saunders enclosing a memorandum signed by Kennedy on his final day as Attorney General:

> I did tell Mr. Saunders that I would inform my successor by memorandum which I would place in the De-

partment files that, if the [ICC] hearing examiners' recommended decision should be contrary to the Government's position and favorable to the merger and the merger applicants have by that time formulated terms for inclusion of the New Haven in the proposed Penn-Central system . . . then . . . it would be my recommendation that the Department of Justice not continue opposition to the merger beyond that point. *

Katzenbach's letter to Saunders volunteered, "I might add that I am in agreement with his conclusions."[23]

When I pressed Saunders about the President's commitment, he responded vaguely. According to Saunders, Johnson had said if the railroad executive ran into any problems delaying the merger, he should get in touch with the President, who would "move things along." Saunders had seen the President on a number of occasions, but the only evidence of any conversation was a letter from Saunders thanking the President for hearing him out at a July 1964 meeting. The letter simply expressed the hope "that some way can be found to change the opposition of the Department of Justice to this merger"— hardly evidence of any commitment.[24]

Ramsey Clark had been named Acting Attorney General when Katzenbach became Undersecretary of State in late September 1966. He knew of no Johnson commitment and didn't consider Kennedy's memo binding on the government. Kennedy had written: "I pointed out . . . that I could make no commitment which would bind my successor." Despite Kennedy's memo, Clark noted, Justice had opposed the merger before the ICC long after the hearing examiner's March 1965 decision recommending approval.

Clark also knew that Kennedy had agreed to support the Penn-Central merger just as he was entering the New York Senate race, that Saunders was a heavy Democratic money man, and that the merger was popular in New York so long as the New Haven Railroad's commuter service to New York City was protected, something Saunders had promised to do.[25]

The President was at the ranch Thanksgiving week 1966. On the Monday evening before the holiday, I sent him a memo setting out

* As Senator from New York, Kennedy stayed involved. On November 25, 1966, Peter Edelman, a top aide, called the Justice Department to tell then Acting Attorney General Ramsey Clark that "the Senator" wanted to make sure Clark was aware of Kennedy's memo, familiar with Katzenbach's attitude toward the merger, and knew that the Senator "still favors the merger and feels that any delay will be harmful to the public interest."[22]

the situation. "In the absence of any indication from the White House," my memo concluded, "Ramsey would file before the Supreme Court recommending that the case be remanded to the ICC for further hearings. . . . This, in effect, would delay the merger and would be interpreted by Saunders as a violation of an agreement he feels he has with the Administration and with you personally. . . . If you do not desire him to recommend remand of the case, it would be necessary for me to talk to him within the next day or two."[26]

On Thanksgiving Eve, Jake Jacobsen called me from the ranch. The President, Jacobsen said, had made no commitment to Saunders, but Kennedy's memo "sure sounds like it does commit." The President wanted me to talk to Katzenbach.[27] Claiming to speak for himself but obviously passing along something the President had suggested, Jacobsen said he didn't know why the Justice Department had to file any brief with the Supreme Court.

I met that evening with Katzenbach and Clark. Katzenbach considered Kennedy's "memo pretty well a commitment." Again, Clark disagreed. When I suggested that perhaps no brief need be filed, Clark reacted strongly: the U.S. had opposed the merger before the commission and "when the largest merger in the history of the United States is before the Supreme Court and the United States is a statutory party, the United States is obligated to give the Court its views of the case."[28]

The President called late that evening. When I reported, he told me to get Katzenbach, Clark, CEA Chairman Ackley, Labor Secretary Wirtz, Secretary of Transportation–designate Alan Boyd, and Commerce Secretary Connor together the next day. He wanted either no brief or one that reflected Boyd's position. He knew Boyd favored the merger, but with me he simply made the point that if any brief was filed it should support the views of the head of the department charged with responsibility for transportation policy.[29]

At 9 A.M. on Thanksgiving Day, I met in my office with the group.[30] Before us we had a copy of the latest draft of the Solicitor General's brief. Boyd argued that the Transportation Department, not Justice, should set the position for the U.S. government. The Transportation Department, he insisted, thought the Penn-Central merger should go forward as soon as possible.

Clark disagreed; he had problems with the merger and thought that the Justice Department should decide what the United States said in court. To him, it was a matter of principle: the Solicitor General should determine what goes into Supreme Court briefs.

I reported my difficulties to the President. That afternoon, Johnson phoned Fortas. Johnson taped this conversation, but there is a handwritten notation on the Presidential Daily Diary: "belt [of conversation] destroyed on President's instruction." Later that afternoon, the President called me[31] and said "the best lawyer I know says" there's no need for the Supreme Court to send the case back to the ICC and the brief should indicate that the agencies responsible for transportation policy believe the merger should be consummated immediately. Johnson felt the best thing would be to file no brief at all; but if all the lawyers thought one had to be filed, then it should be written along the lines he suggested.

Johnson called Fortas again. LBJ then told me[32] that Fortas thought the Justice Department had become overbearing on matters within the substantive responsibility of other agencies; Boyd should determine what the government says to the court about transportation-policy matters, and the brief should reflect Boyd's view of the merger. He asked me to talk to Fortas about it.

When Johnson had earlier spoken of advice he was getting from "the best lawyer I know," I had thought his reference was to Donald Thomas or A. W. Moursund, two personally close Texas attorneys. I knew the President felt free to talk to Fortas about almost anything that troubled him, including constitutional issues that might someday come before the Court, but this was different. Johnson was talking to Fortas about what to put in a brief about to be filed with the Supreme Court in a pending case.

Before I could decide what to do about the President's extraordinary request, Fortas called me at home over the White House line. I told him my Thanksgiving had been ruined by the President. Fortas said, "Years ago, after I started working for this man, I began celebrating Thanksgiving on the day before. He ruins every Thanksgiving Day." Fortas then repeated what the President indicated he had said.

At Johnson's direction, I called Solicitor General Thurgood Marshall, who was in Atlantic City for Thanksgiving, to talk directly to him about his brief. I made no mention of Fortas or the advice he had offered the President. Marshall balked at what he considered an intrusion on his turf; he felt there was no way he could refrain from presenting his views to the Supreme Court in a case of this magnitude.[33]

The President also told me to have Boyd speak to Marshall, and to have Ackley, who supported the merger, visit the Solicitor General and send him a memo. Ackley did so and reported that "Marshall is obviously unhappy with the situation in which he finds himself, and would like to find a way out. But he is being pressed very hard in the other direction by his staff." Ackley also noted that Marshall does genuinely find it "inconceivable that the Solicitor General could fail to take a position before the Supreme Court."[34] But the discussions and memos had an impact: Marshall agreed to write a new brief.

The new brief did the trick. The Justice Department abandoned its opposition to the merger, and added these sentences: "We emphasize that, in questioning the Commission's procedure, we do not quarrel with the merits of the Penn-Central merger proposal itself. Indeed, the agencies of the Executive Branch that have substantive responsibilities for the formulation of economic and transportation policy believe that the merger is in the public interest and that its consummation should be promptly effected." That was a far cry from the draft we reviewed in my office on Thanksgiving morning; that draft had raised all sorts of questions about the merger and asked that the case be sent back to the ICC for a whole new round of proceedings.[35] Now, the Solicitor General was arguing that the Court could retain jurisdiction over the case and simply have the ICC quickly correct certain procedural technicalities to permit the merger to proceed.

Throughout most of this Thanksgiving weekend, Stuart Saunders had been staying at the Hay-Adams Hotel across Lafayette Square from the White House. When he called me the Monday morning after Thanksgiving,[36] I said the President had worked on the problem over the weekend and Saunders would be pleased with the government's brief.

Despite the Solicitor General's urging, on March 27, 1967, the Supreme Court did indeed remand the case to the ICC. Astonishingly, Justice Fortas participated in the Court's decision. In a dissenting opinion in which Justices John Harlan, Potter Stewart, and Byron White joined, Fortas argued that the merger should go forward without further ICC proceedings. Fortas even quoted the portion of the Solicitor General's brief that made the very point he had suggested the President have the Justice Department put forth: "The United States . . . does not challenge the merger itself. Indeed, the Solicitor General has represented to the Court that 'the agencies of the Executive Branch that have substantive responsibilities for the formulation of economic and transportation policy believe that the merger is in the public interest and that its consummation should be promptly effected.' "

On January 15, 1968, the Supreme Court finally approved the merger. Justice Thurgood Marshall, whom LBJ had appointed to the Court in the interim, recused himself because of his prior appearance before the Court in the Penn-Central case. Despite having advised the President on the case, Fortas saw no reason to do the same. Indeed, he wrote the Court's opinion approving the merger.

•

In November, even after the midterm elections, Johnson could
bask in his ability to outmaneuver the Catholic bishops and position
the Supreme Court to give him the decision he wanted. But as the
winter of 1966–67 came on, he would be braced by chilling political
winds, particularly from the press, members of his own party, and a
Congress much less agreeable than the Great 89th. And the war half
a world away would continue to distract him and drain his energies as
it took more American lives and diverted more of the nation's resources.

Sleepless Nights

NINE

The Press and
the Credibility Gap

LYNDON JOHNSON'S affair with the press ranged from ardent to embittered suitor. During the honeymoon years, he sought out reporters for long talks and walked them around the south grounds of the White House. In time, he began to distrust most of them. He loved the games he played with reporters, but was infuriated about leaks he hadn't planted himself and doubts about his credibility that his game playing invited. He knew more about government and Washington than anyone else, and he was aggravated that the press didn't automatically recognize the fact. He couldn't understand when *The Washington Post* "turned on" him—that's how he termed occasional editorial criticism of some program or policy, or even an unflattering photo or an acerbic Herblock cartoon. He and *Post* president Philip Graham (who died in 1963) had been such close friends and Johnson felt he had been especially nice to Graham's widow, Katharine.[1]

Even so, he could never get enough of the news he so mistrusted. He had the bulldog edition of *The Washington Post* picked up each evening. The weekly newsmagazines, due on the stands on Monday, were usually delivered to him late Sunday afternoon. He would call on Sunday evening or very early in the morning to ask about some story in a newsmagazine or newspaper. When I hadn't yet seen it, he'd say, "You can't be a top presidential aide unless you read the paper and keep up with the news."

He had three television sets in his office, three more in the green den next to it and three each in his bedrooms at the White House and ranch. The AP and UPI wire-service tickers clacked away in the Oval Office, and an Army Signal corpsman delivered him wire-service copy at least every hour at the ranch. He read *The Washington Post, New York Times, Washington Evening Star, Baltimore Sun*, and *Christian Science Monitor* every day, and other major papers which he varied week to week but which included at least one from Texas, as well as a White House clipping service.[2]

The President read the wire-service tickers in his office many times each day—bending deep down into the machine, pulling at the rolls of paper, impatient for the next line of type. It became a contest to get my hands on a story first, so that by the time he called I could tell him I'd already done something about it. When I noticed that Lee White didn't have wire stories delivered to his office, I asked, "How the hell can you function without reading the tickers?" White replied, "I don't need them. I've got the best ticker reader in the world working for me in the Oval Office. He'll call immediately if there's anything I need to know."[3]

Johnson had three television sets put in my office and wire copy delivered to me every thirty minutes. I shouldn't have been surprised. In early July 1965, when I was still at the Pentagon and responsible for providing support to the White House, Jack Valenti called. The President wanted everyone on the White House staff to have a portable radio that they could carry around in their pockets at all times, and a card listing the frequencies for network radio news stations in each major city, so that from anywhere any staffer could tune in on the hour or half hour to the national news. Eventually, I selected Sony as the best pocket-sized radio, and provided Marvin Watson 24 radios, 72 batteries (3 extras for each radio) and 25 laminated cards with network radio frequencies in all major cities in the U.S.[4] By the time I got to the White House a few days later, the President had installed in my office a radio, operated through a telephone speaker behind my desk, set with direct feeds from ABC, CBS, NBC, and Mutual, so it would pick up only the hourly news broadcasts with no distracting music in between.

LBJ wanted the press to report stories the way he saw them. He would ask me, "What's the headline in this message?" or "What's the lead off this speech?" When AP or UPI led with something other than what he wanted, he'd hit the POTUS line and tell me to get the lead changed. He was especially miffed that the press often judged his war on poverty by the size of the OEO budget instead of the many more billions spent for health, education, housing, and cash benefits for the poor.[5]

And he didn't like stories about his aides. He was always praising Roosevelt's aides and their "passion for anonymity." When his aides received publicity, Johnson would remind us, "There's only one person elected here, only one name on the ballot, and it isn't Califano or McPherson."

In early 1967, Johnson approved my speaking before Sigma Delta Chi, a professional society of journalists. I sent him a draft of the speech for his approval. It was largely about government management, but included an illustration of what we were learning from our new systems-analysis techniques: that of the 7.3 million people then on welfare, after accounting for children, their mothers, and the old, blind, and disabled, only some 50,000 fathers and no more than 300,000 mothers could be put to work.[6] Neither of us anticipated the publicity the welfare numbers would set off. *The New York Times* gave it front-page coverage, network television picked up the story, and so did every paper in the country. Every time the President saw me the next day, he needled me about waking up to my face on the *CBS Morning News* and *Today* show, and seeing it again each half hour. When *The New York Times Magazine* was doing a piece on me entitled "Deputy President for Domestic Affairs," he refused to release any pictures of the two of us together, and ordered me not to provide the magazine with any pictures he had given me.

The first time I was quoted in a way the President didn't like, I made an excuse about being quoted out of context and LBJ told me about A. W. Moursund, one of his blind trustees. An enterprising *New York Times* reporter had gone to Judge Moursund's office in Johnson City and told his secretary, "I'd like to see the judge." The secretary buzzed Judge Moursund. Moursund asked, "Does he want to hire a lawyer?" She asked the reporter. He said, "No." Judge Moursund asked, "Does he want to buy an insurance policy?" No, he didn't. "Does he want to buy some land?" No, he didn't. "Well, what does he want?" She said, "He wants to interview you since you are trustee for President Johnson." Moursund said, "Well, you tell that young fellow that I am not in the interview business."

"You just tell these reporters you're not in the interview business," Johnson said to me. "Then you won't have to worry about getting misquoted."[7]

He would urge us to turn around reporters who were writing unfavorably about him. A woman reporter who covered the White House wrote some stories Johnson considered critical of him. He told White House counsel Harry McPherson, "What that woman needs is you. Take her out. Give her a good dinner and a good fuck."[8]

McPherson sighed, shrugged, and continued with his conversation. But periodically the President would ask McPherson if he'd taken care of the reporter. Every time she took even the slightest shot at the President, he'd call Harry and tell him to go to work on her. Finally, McPherson took the female reporter out to dinner and schmoozed her about LBJ. He dutifully reported to the President that he had taken her to dinner. A few days later she wrote some admiring lines about McPherson.[9] That evening I was in the green den with the President and a couple of Democratic senators who knew McPherson from his days as counsel to the Senate Democratic Policy Committee. One of them asked LBJ about McPherson. The President lit up, then leaned over and intently staring at the Senator said, "He's a fine young man, but I'm a little concerned about his family. You know, Harry's been taking out this bitch of a reporter and screwing her, and I worry about his wife and children."*

LBJ went on repeated tears about leaks. We were under instructions to do memos for the record of our conversations with reporters and send them to him with a copy to the press office. The order was based on the reasonable premise that the press secretary and the President could do a better job if they understood the interests of the White House press corps. But Johnson also intended to inhibit us from talking to reporters. In any case, he suspected that his aides were not writing memos on all their conversations. He decided to put in another system as well. The President ordered Marvin Watson to tell the White House operators to ask everyone who called his top aides to identify themselves and their affiliation. There were no direct lines in those days, so all calls went through the general number, 456-1414. Watson and LBJ tracked reporters' calls to staffers.

The situation was a setup for the witty Mary McGrory, who was then writing for the *Washington Evening Star*. On January 16, 1966, she published her column in the form of a letter to Watson asking that

---

* LBJ made a similar suggestion when I advised him of the problems James Gaither, an aide on my staff, was having with Edith Green, the irascible Democratic congresswoman from Oregon who chaired a key house education subcommittee. Green was trying to torpedo the administration's program to encourage innovative elementary and secondary education programs. Johnson became irritated with our inability to deal with her. In exasperation one evening he said to me, "Goddamn it. You've been trying to drag me into this thing when I've got a hundred other problems. Well, I'm going to tell you how to get our bill. There's no point in my calling that woman. Gaither is a good-looking boy. You tell him to call up Edith and ask her to brunch this Sunday. Then he can take her out, give her a couple of Bloody Marys, and go back to her apartment with her. Then you know what he does? Tell him to spend the afternoon in bed with her and she'll support any Goddamn bill he wants. Now if he wants to help his President, that's what he should do instead of writing these whiney memos every night."[10]

he not credit me with ten calls from her, because on the last two she "was merely trying to tell [Joe Califano's] secretary that [the] deadline had passed." That column was expensive for both Watson and me. Watson found himself out on a limb as LBJ, pretending to have known nothing about it, rescinded the order he'd given. And I doubt that the President ever stopped believing that I had inspired McGrory's column.

Even minor leaks irritated Johnson. In January 1967, he had a grand black-tie dinner for the Vice President, Speaker of the House of Representatives, and Chief Justice of the Supreme Court.[11] Among the guests were sixty-seven-year-old Supreme Court Justice William O. Douglas and his new twenty-three-year-old wife, a bright and very attractive blond woman, who sat on my right. On my left was 1940s film superstar Joan Crawford. The Douglases' recent marriage—she was his fourth wife—had caused a sensation in Washington.

The dinner was Cathy Douglas's first formal occasion at the White House. Crawford was drunk and, as dinner progressed, she became increasingly irritated as people kept approaching to introduce themselves to Mrs. Douglas. Most didn't even notice Crawford, and I could feel the movie star boiling. Crawford began to make increasingly nasty remarks about Cathy Douglas's lack of sophistication and her youth, to the embarrassment of the other guests. After the salad course, the waiters placed glass plates with finger bowls on them in front of each place. Cathy Douglas was busy greeting the people that continued to stop by to say hello, so she did not immediately remove the finger bowl and doily from her glass plate.

Suddenly, Crawford reached across me, grabbed the finger bowl and doily from Cathy Douglas's plate, and put it to the side. "They don't put the dessert in the water," she said to Douglas.

Douglas ignored her, as did I. But the gossip columns carried various versions of what had happened and Johnson chewed me out for leaking it because he believed it demeaned the White House and his guests. Eventually, he was persuaded that I hadn't, but that probably Interior Secretary Stewart Udall, also at the table, had.

Johnson often complained about reporters who attended White House parties. Normally, the social office invited about twenty to twenty-five reporters to large White House receptions. "I can't even swallow a mouthful of food without having a reporter watch to see if I chewed it properly before swallowing," he'd say. "All we're doing is inviting five hundred guests, standing them up against the wall, and then making them be gracious to the twenty-five reporters who come up and ask them questions like 'Are you happy here? Why are you here? Will you come next time? Are you a friend of the family? Isn't the service here worse than it used to be? Isn't the coffee weak?' ''[12]

The President's obsession about leaks had its amusing moments. When a Task Force on Education, chaired by University of North Carolina President William Friday, reported in the summer of 1967, the President told me to leak its report, along with the distinguished membership, both of which had been kept secret. The report had concluded that the administration's education programs should continue to be concentrated on poor urban and rural students,[13] a view LBJ fervently espoused and one contrary to the positions of both the Republican party and the National Education Association. He wanted me to make sure the leak could not be traced to the White House.

It took a couple of weeks to get the report leaked, but finally, through an intermediary, I placed it in the hands of Marjorie Hunter of *The New York Times*. On August 21, 1967, she wrote what I thought was a great story that ran as the second lead on the front page.

That morning, Doug Cater, who was the President's aide on education matters, came into my office, reduced almost to trembling because of the way the President had chewed him out about the leak. Cater was trying to find out who had done it.

"I did," I told him.

"Well, I'll never tell him," Cater loyally responded.

"*He* told me to put it out," I said.

Later that morning,[14] I showed the story to the President. "Here's the story on the Education Task Force you wanted me to get out. Have you seen it?" He grunted yes, and never mentioned it again to me, or Cater, or anyone else.

But there were more serious problems than the odd trivial leaks or the President's game playing. By late 1966, the credibility gap was eating away at the administration. As McPherson said at a working meeting on the 1967 State of the Union Message, "The President is simply not believed."[15]

Vietnam was at the center of it. It had begun all the way back with Johnson's speech at the University of Akron on October 21, 1964. He had said, "We are not about to send American boys nine or ten thousand miles to do what Asian boys ought to be doing for themselves." The number of troops in Vietnam had gone from under 20,000 when he made that statement to 385,000 by the end of 1966. Some were recalling Franklin Roosevelt's 1940 presidential campaign promise, "I have said this before, but I shall say it again and again and again: Your boys are not going to be sent into any foreign wars." Johnson's response to criticism of the escalation—that American troops were, in fact, doing what Asian troops could *not* do "by themselves and alone, resist the growing might and grasping ambition of Asian communism"—was considered lame by his critics. And the Gulf of Tonkin resolution was by no means the formal declaration of war Congress had given Roosevelt in December 1941.

Johnson's credibility problems were built upon Eisenhower's and Kennedy's. Eisenhower's State Department had lied when it denied that the President had known U-2 pilot Gary Powers was on a spy mission when his plane was shot down over the Soviet Union in 1960. Kennedy's administration initially dissembled on the Bay of Pigs invasion, and his Defense Department stated, just before it revealed the Cuban missile crisis, that the Pentagon had "no information indicating the presence of offensive weapons in Cuba," as Kennedy feigned a cold to return to the White House to deal with it. And early on the Kennedy administration had put out such misleading reports on the number of troops in Vietnam that Pentagon reporters used to joke that there were more soldiers in Saigon bars than the government admitted having in the entire country. Shortly before Kennedy's assassination, several stories were published about his credibility problem.

Johnson widened the credibility gap, particularly on Vietnam, with unrealistically low budgets and unduly optimistic reports on the war's progress. He created problems for himself in other areas as well. A charade in late 1963 and early 1964 had led the press to believe that Johnson considered it impossible to produce a budget under $100 billion; he had then produced one well under that, and below even Kennedy's last budget. His fixation with keeping his options open on any new policy venture until he had every political stone turned and set in place was, in good part, why he was such an effective legislator. But the misleading body language played badly with the press corps and the public, who like to bear witness to the struggles and machinations of their presidents. Johnson added to his problems with his habit of keeping even small things secret until the last minute—travel plans, minor appointments—and then changing his plans or appointees if a leak had occurred and denying that he'd made any change.

LBJ blamed much of his credibility problem on the Communists. Angry about stories in *The New York Times*, he'd complain about how easily the Communists manipulated the paper on the Vietnam War. In October 1966, Johnson talked at Camp David over dinner about how concerned he was of "Communist infiltration." He said he knew the Communists "had heavy influence in the networks (except ABC) and on several columnists." A year later, he told me that the "commies have succeeded in creating great doubt about the credibility of the government," including himself, Humphrey, Rusk, McNamara, and national security adviser Walt Rostow. Eventually, he concluded that the only fair paper was the *Christian Science Monitor*.[16]

The credibility problem was exacerbated because LBJ became the most gullible victim of his own revisionist claims. He would quickly come to believe what he was saying even if it was clearly not true. Thus, after the event, he convinced himself that Humphrey had wanted to get out of overseeing the administration's civil right's efforts, and that he had not told me to solicit Weaver's resignation.

On Saturday, February 11, 1967, after a relaxed dinner in the White House living quarters with several friends, including Texas Congressman Jake Pickle, his wife, and me, we watched part of a David Susskind show. Some participants questioned the President's credibility. When it was over, LBJ wound up on "the press's credibility gap." He said "the credibility gap comes from four completely false stories and one that was half true." The first involved the newspaper stories that the President's first budget could not be under $100 billion. "I never said it couldn't be under $100 billion. Someone in one of the departments said it, and by the time the press got through with it, the story was all twisted." Rather than admit their mistake, Johnson added, "they attacked my credibility."

The next was a story about speeding in Texas. The newspapers reported that "an AP photographer clocked the President as going over 80 miles per hour." "I actually drove past the AP and UPI photographers en route to church while they were talking to each other on the side of the road. They didn't even see me," Johnson insisted. When the Secret Service car "far behind me" reached the photographers, the photographers followed the Secret Service, never passing them. "On the trip, according to Secret Service records," Johnson concluded, "I averaged forty-two miles per hour."

The third "completely false" instance was "cancellation of the Boston-Austin cross-country trip following the Asian trip." Johnson admitted that we had sent advance men out, but "I never firmly committed myself to the trip, and until the President says, 'We are going,' no trip is scheduled."

Johnson's half-true example was a press report charging that "not all planes lost by the military have been reported." The story was critical of information coming out of the Pentagon, especially on Vietnam. Johnson said that what the report had failed to note "is that of course not all planes lost are reported, only those lost on combat missions. When a plane crashed in Texas it wasn't reported, nor was it reported when one was lost because of normal wearing out."

The President couldn't remember the other "completely false" instance. I'd heard most of this routine before, and had witnessed the authentic increase in the President's conviction each time he recited it, so I reminded him of the "sputtering mad" story during the aluminum controversy. "That's it," he nodded and recounted the incident as he now remembered it. In this latest version, he accused the press of dreaming up the "entire story." He solemnly declared to us, close friends and associates, that "I have never been sputtering mad in my entire life."[17]

TEN

State of the Union
1967

IN THE SPRING of 1966, Lyndon Johnson was looking forward to another Great Society State of the Union message. He told me not to limit my search for ideas to the East and West coasts. "The trouble with you Harvard liberals," he said, "is that you think there are no brains in the middle of the country." He urged me to "Get some water experts. You don't know a Goddamn thing about water or power. In Brooklyn you think water comes out of a faucet and electricity out of a socket. Find out about water and power and about clean rivers for farmers and cities." So during the spring, summer, and early fall of 1966, accompanied by various White House aides, I visited several university centers—among them Chicago, Austin, and New Orleans, as well as New York, Cambridge, and Los Angeles. We talked to almost one hundred experts from sixteen universities, as well as from the Ford Foundation and *Scientific American*. We produced a three-inch-thick book of ideas.[1]

On November 8, 1966, Johnson received my memo summing up our work. That was the day he also heard from the American electorate. In the 89th Congress, Johnson had enjoyed a progressive, not merely Democratic, majority in the House of Representatives. Democrats retained a substantial majority, 248 to 187, in the new 90th Congress. But Republicans gained forty-seven seats, mostly at the expense of liberal Democrats. It was going to make it exceedingly difficult for Johnson to muster a majority for his agenda. The Senate margin had also slipped, though a number of the new Republicans were as liberal as the members they replaced.[2]

The President was mulling over what to do. Programs such as the war on poverty and model cities, which had survived key House tests by far fewer votes than conservative Republicans had gained, were in jeopardy. The composition of the powerful Rules Committee and even helpful procedural rules put in place by the 89th Congress were endangered.[3] Vietnam was taking its toll on federal resources. It was clear that the nation could fund both the war on poverty and the war in Southeast Asia. But it wasn't clear that the American people were willing to do so.

Johnson also had problems within his own party. Throughout 1966, he kept the pressure on for desegregating elementary and secondary schools and hospitals under the 1964 Civil Rights Act. The southern governors and congressmen were livid at the federal intrusion into their "states rights," imposing integration faster than the people of their states would accept it. Henry Wilson, White House staff liaison with the House of Representatives and a North Carolina native, was alarmed at the depth of the reaction to the administration's guidelines for desegregating schools. He warned the President that it "could be deep enough and strong enough to wreck the very foundation of our relations with the Congress."[4]

After the November 1966 election results, Missouri Governor Warren Hearnes smelled blood. At a post-election meeting of Democratic governors at White Sulphur Springs, West Virginia, he raised the question of whether LBJ should be the party's candidate in 1968. Along with most southern governors, Hearnes believed the administration's civil rights policies were destroying the Democratic party in the South.

Democratic governors in the South and border states demanded a meeting with the President. Johnson invited them to the ranch on December 21, 1966. In the late morning, HEW Secretary Gardner talked to the governors about the purpose of the desegregation guidelines and the way his aides were enforcing them. On the way to lunch, Gardner told the President that he had failed to get through to the governors. Johnson told him not to feel bad. "They want to go back to slavery. You're not going to get through to them."[5]

The lunch went pleasantly enough, but in the afternoon Hearnes led an assault on Johnson's policies for the better part of two hours. He briefly questioned the advisability of U.S. involvement in Vietnam, but for the most part he attacked the administration's energetic push to desegregate schools. Then other governors warned Johnson that his policy was ruining the party in the South. Some went so far as to imply that the President was a traitor to his heritage.[6]

When I arrived at the ranch the next day, the President was still steaming. He thought that Alabama Governor George Wallace (who had not attended the meeting) with his demagoguery threatened the civility of every community in America and was adding to the pressure on southern and border state governors to resist desegregation. Red-faced, he almost shouted at me. "Niggah! Niggah! Niggah! That's all they said to me all day. Hell, there's one thing they'd better know. If I don't achieve anything else while I'm President, I intend to wipe that word out of the English language and make it impossible for people to come here and shout 'Niggah! Niggah! Niggah!' to me and the American people."[7]

I was at the ranch to go over the full menu for his State of the Union message and legislative program. In one set of proposals, I was suggesting a program to help build and refurbish community centers for older people. Johnson wanted to be sure the centers offered hot lunch. "That way, it gives people a reason to get out, and when one dies, she'll leave a piano, another will give a chair, and soon it will be a great place for old folks to get together."

Then the President reminded me that he wanted to do something to improve the lot of the elderly in nursing homes. For months the President had been agitated about the need to produce the finest nursing homes for senior citizens. He had seen some filthy ones and the experience had disturbed him. As Medicaid and Medicare began funding nursing-home care, he didn't "want good taxpayer dollars spent to keep people in ratholes." He had set up a task force to develop proposals for his legislative program.[8]

I remembered Johnson's meeting with the task force in the Fish Room near the Oval Office. Seated around the table were doctors, housing, finance, and health experts, and New York architect Lewis Davis. The President sat down in a chair at the end of the mahogany table. He looked somberly around the group and began softly, describing the squalor of the nursing homes he had seen. His voice got louder and angrier, "Fire traps, rat traps, a disgrace . . . no one of you would let your mother near one." As his voice rose, he began talking about how we were not honoring our father and mother as the Bible teaches, we are dishonoring them, and disgracing ourselves.

Then his eyes lit up as he continued: "I set up this group because of those experiences. I want nursing homes that will be livable, happy places for people to serve out their old age, places where there will be a little joy for the elderly, but most of all places that take care of their special needs." He mentioned the need to have "flat floors, and grades, so that wheelchairs can easily be used," and "special handles on bath-tubs and showers so the old people can use them safely and with a little dignity."

Then, to mark the point, Johnson said, "And when you design toilets . . ." he leaned on his left rump, put his elbow on the arm of his chair, took his right arm and hand, and strained to twist them as far behind himself as he could, and while grunting and poking his hand out behind his back, he continued, ". . . make sure that you don't put the toilet paper rack way behind them so they have to wrench their back out of place or dislocate a shoulder or get a stiff neck in order to get their hands on the toilet paper." The President brought his right arm forward and, still tilted on his left haunch, added, "Stick it right there alongside them or in front of them so it's easy to reach."[9]

Now Johnson wanted many of the task force recommendations included in his legislative program.

When I proposed revamping estate-tax laws to close loopholes and raise billions, he asked me how many wills would have to be rewritten. "The changes will only increase taxes for wealthy people," I responded. Johnson snapped, "That'll still make everyone mad." He cut me off when I started to argue. "We couldn't possibly pass it, because most Americans think they're going to make a lot of money and leave it to their kids when they die and they'll all think it's going to affect them."

The President liked the recommendation to lower the voting age to eighteen, but said, "Wait until next year for that."*

I suggested legislation to require tobacco companies to reveal the tar and nicotine content of cigarettes in their packaging and advertis-ing. Johnson had always been reluctant to move aggressively on cig-arettes. He often remarked how hard he had found it to quit smoking after his heart attack. Perpetually at odds with the South over deseg-regation, he didn't want to make political life any more difficult in tobacco-growing states like Virginia, North Carolina, Georgia, and Kentucky.

As I pressed my case, I lit a cigarette from one of the two to four packs I smoked each day (working for LBJ had increased my smoking from one to as many as four packs a day; by early 1967 I carried regular cigarettes in one pocket and menthol in another so I could continue to smoke when my throat grew raw).

---

* On June 27, 1968, Johnson proposed a constitutional amendment lowering the voting age to eighteen. After enactment by the Congress and ratification by the states, his proposal took effect beginning with the 1972 elections.

Johnson pointed his finger at me, chuckled confidently, and said, "The day you quit smoking those things, I'll send your bill to Congress."*

While he was worried generally about his legislative prospects, Johnson saw one opportunity in the new Congress. He had supported truth-in-lending legislation to give borrowers the full cost of credit simply and clearly. But he hadn't been able to pry the bill out of the Senate Banking Committee. Its sponsor, Paul Douglas, was not a strong legislator and the committee's chairman, Willis Robertson of Virginia, had been vehemently opposed. Both senators had lost their reelection campaigns. When Johnson spotted the bill on my list of Unfinished Tasks, he said he wanted a strong push for truth-in-lending, with the committee's new ranking Democrat, William Proxmire (Wis.), as its sponsor.†

As we went over more than a hundred ideas that afternoon, I kept thinking: There will never be enough for this man; he adopts programs the way a child eats rich chocolate-chip cookies.[10] They came to him every which way. Earlier that year, my son Joe had swallowed a bottle of aspirins and I had rushed him to Sibley Memorial Hospital. The President, frantically trying to reach me, finally ran me down.

"What are you doing at the hospital?" he asked. After offering to help, Johnson said he'd always worried about children getting into medicine bottles and hurting themselves. "There ought to be a law that makes druggists use safe containers," he said. "There ought to be safety caps on those bottles so kids like little Joe can't open them." That prompted the proposal for the Child Safety Act, which Congress eventually passed in 1970, which is why it's so difficult for Americans to take the tops off pill containers.[11]

As Johnson was trying to decide whether to load new programs into his State of the Union message and onto the first session of the 90th Congress, Senate Majority Leader Mansfield was urging the Senate committee chairmen to make a "top-to-bottom" evaluation of major federal programs. One sentence in Mansfield's letter to the chairmen caught Johnson's political eye: "A complete restudy by the Senate could provide not only a basis for adjustment of legislation . . . but also a check on the equity and efficacy of the administrative interpretations and practices which have developed."

Two days later, on New Year's Eve, without mentioning Mans-

---

* I didn't quit smoking until October 28, 1975, fifteen months before I became Secretary of Health, Education, and Welfare.
† The Senate passed the bill in 1967 and the House in 1968, when Johnson signed it into law.

field, Johnson made it clear at a press conference at the ranch[12] that new programs would be forthcoming from the administration.

> . . . We must continue the war against our ancient enemies just as we are continuing it in South Vietnam—until aggression ceases; and until we can provide each child with all the education that he can take; until we can see that our families have a decent income; until we can secure the measures that are necessary to improve our cities, to curb pollution, to reduce poverty.
>
> I think this Nation with a gross national product of some $700 to $800 billion can afford what it needs to spend. And I shall so recommend.

Privately, Johnson offered an additional reason: "If we don't keep them [members of Congress] busy up there doing our work, they'll drive us crazy down here investigating and evaluating us."

As Johnson continued to maintain his guns-and-butter posture, he realized he'd be presenting Congress with a request to increase taxes. Indeed, he had come to consider such action essential to preserve his domestic programs, as projections for the fiscal 1967 and 1968 deficits climbed into the double-digit level.[13]

At this point, all of Johnson's cabinet advisers except Willard Wirtz favored a tax increase, but they couldn't agree on how much or when it should take effect. Suspension of the investment tax credit had had an immediate dampening impact. When Ackley lowered his estimate of the economic growth rate for calendar 1967 from 4 to 3.1 percent, several advisers feared that an early tax hike would provoke a serious recession.[14] The mixed economic signals heightened Johnson's instinctive skittishness about putting the economic brakes on too fast. He was cornered between the economic rock and the political hard place: he confronted a mounting budget deficit crying out for action to reduce spending, increase taxes, or both, and a sluggish economy that such action might shove into recession.

Johnson reluctantly concluded that he had to ask Congress for more taxes. He took on what he knew would be a bare-knuckled, knee-groin political fight with the more conservative Congress, settling on a four-pronged approach: a 6 percent surcharge* on individual and corporate income taxes effective July 1, 1967, with a low-income exemption, and three actions to offset any dampening economic impact of such an increase: a big boost in Social Security

---

* A surcharge is a tax on a tax. If an individual's taxes are $100, a 6 percent surcharge increases them by $6.

benefits effective the same date (but with no Social Security tax increase until eighteen months later), restoration of the investment tax credit, and (he hoped) substantial easing of the Fed's monetary policy. The Social Security benefits alone would lift 1.4 million Americans above the poverty line, largely through an enormous increase in the minimum benefit.

Not until the eve of the State of the Union message did Johnson's advisers agree to the program he wanted. Once again, the President told me to have each—Fowler, Schultze, Ackley, Wirtz, Connor, Clifford, McNamara, and me—initial a memo recommending the program. [15] As I passed it around the table in my office, Clifford asked, "Does he want it notarized and sworn to?"

By Sunday, January 8, we had the State of the Union in pretty much final shape, ready for cabinet review the next day. To keep his decisions secret, Johnson's instructions were explicit: Each cabinet officer, except Rusk and McNamara, was to come to my office alone, read the final draft in my presence, and give me his comments. Rusk and McNamara could see drafts in their own offices. Only Fowler was to see the section requesting a tax increase; only Connor and Wirtz the section recommending the merger of their departments into a new Department of Business and Labor. The passages where LBJ would propose the 20 percent average Social Security increase with a 59 percent hike in the minimum monthly payment, and a multibillion-dollar expansion of Medicare to cover the disabled, were to be left out so no one would see them. All these precautions were taken to avoid leaks on the day before the President was to deliver the message. [16]

On and off during the day, the President, who had a schedule of the cabinet visits, popped into my office. He had lunch with White House congressional liaison Henry Wilson to review one last time how the changed lineup in the House would affect the legislative program. [17]

That evening just before eight, as I reported to him on the cabinet review of the message and showed him the initialed memo recommending the tax increase, the President autographed a picture of the two of us with my two sons, when he had given them a beagle a few weeks before, "To Mark and Joseph Califano, From their friend, Lyndon B. Johnson." [18] That's how I knew he was pleased with the legislative program.

The State of the Union message was scheduled for the evening of January 10, the date selected to avoid interfering with Senator Dirksen's birthday party on the 11th, and after a review of the television schedules to avoid driving particularly popular shows off the air. [19] "I don't want millions of people looking at me for an hour and thinking,

'This is the big-eared son of a bitch that knocked my favorite program off the air,' " Johnson said.

The President delivered the message before a joint session beginning at 9:30 P.M. Remarkably, some of his strongest applause came when he expressed his intention to stand firm in Vietnam. Not surprisingly, no one applauded when he unfolded his request for a tax surcharge. Though this message was sober, he once again startled the members with the length and breadth of his legislative requests: the increase in Social Security benefits, expansion of Medicare, merger of the Commerce and Labor departments, Safe Streets Act, extension of Head Start to three-year-olds and a follow-through program after entering school. Other initiatives included requests for a number of consumer-protection measures, a Corporation for Public Broadcasting and federal funds for public television, an air-quality act, help for migrant workers and American Indians, the first prohibition of age discrimination (for those from 45 to 65), Selective Service reform, action on pending civil rights legislation covering jury selection, protection of civil rights workers, employment and fair housing, and increased funds for model cities.

The President devoted a special portion of the message to an impassioned appeal to ban all wiretapping and bugging except in national-security cases. Just about everyone heartily applauded except Robert Kennedy, who sat with his arms folded and his lips tightly sealed.

And on Vietnam he tried to close the credibility gap. He abandoned the arbitrary assumption that the war would be over at the end of the fiscal year and estimated Vietnam expenditures realistically. He gave a candid assessment of the situation:

> I wish I could report to you that the conflict is almost over. This I cannot do. We face more cost, more loss, and more agony. For the end is not yet. I cannot promise that it will come this year—or come next year. . . .
>
> How long it will take I cannot prophesy. I only know that the will of the American people . . . is tonight being tested.

After the message, we returned to the White House living quarters for drinks and sandwiches and listened as commentators talked about the "sober message" and the President's continued determination to go forward with his Great Society.[20]

The next morning, though, criticism began to flow in. Martin Luther King wired that the President hadn't given enough time to civil rights and expressed concern about an administration retreat.

New York Times columnist James Reston called it a "guns and margarine speech." Labor grumbled about the proposed departmental merger. During the first hour, trading volume on the New York Stock Exchange broke all prior records, with the market dropping sharply.[21]

The President called on the hotline. Impatient with his critics, he wanted to stir up support for his legislative programs. "The cabinet is no good in this area . . . get the messages out as fast as possible and get hearings held on our legislation . . . pick out the ten leading businessmen to support the merger of Labor and Commerce . . . get the word out that the surcharge is under $5 a month for most people . . . get out the budget figures to the networks, UPI, AP . . . now that it's [the tax surcharge] done, let's get it [supported]. Senators and Congressmen—Ford, [Senator Vance] Hartke [D-Ind.], Russell Long—are giving us hell. No one is for us. Ask Long to get a statement in the [*Congressional*] *Record* today. Let's get more propaganda today . . . divide up the press [and get our story out]. . . . The message was 69 minutes, eleven minutes for applause and I didn't have to stop and wait for it. Listen to the tape . . . get McNamara, Fowler, Connor, Boyd, and Meany pushing our tax proposal and the merger. . . . Get Meany and his people over here this afternoon. . . . Tell Louis Martin [a key LBJ operative in the black community] to get the civil rights message out and Cliff Alexander [deputy special counsel to the President] to call King. . . ."[22]

Later in the day, I told LBJ that CBS president Frank Stanton had called to say "the President looks wonderful. The color picture was excellent. His delivery was never better in a television speech. He has never looked better on television in his life." I added that Stanton liked the content and thought the Labor-Commerce merger made "abundant good sense."[23] The President grunted, "Stanton doesn't have any vote, not one Goddamn vote to get our programs and tax bill passed," and hung up.

The President had tried unsuccessfully to lure Stanton into his administration to take over the United States Information Agency. At one point, LBJ, frustrated by his inability to persuade Stanton's boss, CBS Chairman William Paley, to let go of his right hand, said, "Goddamnit, Bill, if you don't tell Stanton to get down here, then you've got to take the job yourself."* When Johnson couldn't get a full-time

---

* LBJ had more success with another request he made of Paley while he was in the Senate. As Paley told me the story, for years Johnson had pestered him to designate the Johnsons' Austin TV station a mandatory buy for advertisers who purchased network time. Paley had refused. At 6 A.M. Austin time on the morning after the November 1954 elections, in which Democrats gained control of the Senate, Paley's private line rang in his New York City apartment. "Bill," Johnson said to the CBS

hold on such talent, he often demanded part-time work. From Stanton, he wanted help with his television appearance. Perpetually dissatisfied that he did not come across well on television, Johnson kept seeking to master the medium. That's what inspired his choice of former NBC Chairman Robert Kintner for the White House staff (a move destined to fail, as it did, for no one who had been chief executive of a major corporation could revert to the demands of being a staffer under Lyndon Johnson).

That evening the President met with Meany and the other powerful labor leaders for over an hour in the Cabinet Room to discuss the merger of Labor and Commerce. He had broached the idea to Meany in an Oval Office meeting I attended on the evening of January 5. Meany had committed to support the merger. But the concept ignited unexpectedly fierce opposition from other AFL-CIO Executive Council members. In February, Johnson rushed me to an AFL-CIO Executive Council meeting in Miami to urge them to hold off any vote on the merger, for fear the proposal would go down by a two-to-one margin. In early March, the President had the entire council for lunch, where he made one more pitch. But there was no give.[24]

At that point I urged the President to call Meany on his commitment and press the AFL-CIO president to come out publicly for the merger. Johnson turned to me, teacher to student, and said: not only would he not do that, but he didn't want anyone ever to know that Meany had committed to him. "It's just like a member of Congress," Johnson added. "You can't ever ask a man to do something that will jeopardize his job." Then, in exasperation, he repeated one of his common refrains, "You've never even run for any office. I just wish every damn White House aide had to run for dogcatcher in some county. Then you'd understand." Johnson tossed the stillborn merger of Commerce and Labor to a committee for further study and never mentioned his January 5 meeting with Meany. Instead, he accepted criticism for making a rare legislative blunder.[25]

By early 1967, crime had burst out of the closet as a national issue, so shortly after delivering the State of the Union, Johnson sent Congress a special message on his anticrime program. He believed that over the long haul equal opportunity, jobs, education, health care, and housing would do more to slow rising crime than immediate efforts to improve law enforcement. Nevertheless, as citizen concern

---

Chairman, "you are talking to the next majority leader of the United States Senate, and I want that station to be a mandatory buy!" This time, Paley acceded to Johnson's request.

and political pressures closed in on him, he concluded that the federal government had to stake out a larger role in fighting crime.

His program would have a distinctive LBJ brand on it, starting with the name of its centerpiece bill to aid local law enforcement. Burned by the title Demonstration Cities Act, Johnson had repeatedly told me to be "Goddamned careful what you call these bills. Don't name them at midnight when you're tired and should be doing something like answering mail or returning calls. Do it in the morning. And then count to ten."

I had suggested "The Safe Streets Act" because that's what people were worried about—safety on their streets and in their homes. Ramsey Clark argued that there was no way we could make the streets safe and therefore we shouldn't give the bill that name. He wanted to call it the "Crime Control Act." With an impish smile, the President made a "Solomon-like" decision in his bedroom one morning. "Tell Ramsey I'll call it 'The Safe Streets and Crime Control Act.' That way he can't complain, you can't complain, and then in all my statements you just call it the Safe Streets Act."

When I sent Harry McPherson an early draft of the message, I wrote, "Please get mean and nasty before you start working on it, since the President wants a tough anticrime message." The President worked over the first version we showed him—he wanted it "sharpened" and "changed . . . to soften the 'sociological' bent of the message."[26]

Recognizing that local governments did, and should, bear most of the responsibility for controlling crime, Johnson proposed to help them with federal grants to improve their police and criminal-justice systems, to encourage research and innovative law-enforcement programs, and to build modern crime labs, police academies, and community correction centers. He also asked Congress for tough laws to control guns and organized crime, more money to fight drugs, and a unified federal corrections system. He urged states and cities to try innovative approaches, such as treating alcoholism as a disease rather than punishing it as a crime in the absence of other crimes or disorderly conduct. Finally, Johnson unveiled the details of his Right of Privacy Act, to ban all wiretapping and electronic eavesdropping, except in national-security cases and even then to prohibit use in court of the evidence obtained.

LBJ held strong views on wiretapping, bugging, and spying—indeed, on any invasions of privacy.[27] President Kennedy had installed a peephole in a door between the Oval Office and its anteroom so that his secretaries could, without interrupting him, decide whether to send in a call and keep track of his visitors. Upon discovering that his secretary Juanita Roberts and some aides like McGeorge Bundy used it to look in on him, Johnson because so infuriated that he jammed a pencil into it, not even waiting overnight for White House carpenters to seal it.[28]

Before Johnson became President, government agencies, including the FBI and Internal Revenue Service, wiretapped and bugged extensively, largely without the public's knowledge. Starting early in his administration, Johnson made clear to anyone who would listen his distaste for such activities. In June 1965, he had issued a memorandum to cabinet officers and agency heads prohibiting wiretapping except in national-security cases. In February 1966 I had sent the President a memo to solicit his position on a bill to prohibit all private wiretaps and restrict wiretapping by federal and state officials to certain crimes. In commenting on alternatives I set out, the President wrote, "I like this best" next to "a *complete ban* on all taps, even in national security cases." Where I mentioned that the Justice Department was studying the constitutional aspects of "the use of nontelephone electronic 'bugging' devices," Johnson wrote, "Urge legislation to stop this."[29]

In May 1966, Missouri Democratic Senator Edward Long, chairman of a subcommittee investigating electronic eavesdropping, had skewered Internal Revenue Service Commissioner Sheldon Cohen for IRS eavesdropping and wiretapping. The President asked Cohen for an explanation. Cohen outlined the situation and concluded that the IRS practices are "simply not [wrong] . . . in the eyes of the law or of reasonable people." Johnson was hardly satisfied. He broke the points of several pencils as he scribbled at the end of Cohen's memo: "Sheldon—Stop it all at once—and this is final—no microphones—taps or any other hidden devices, legal or illegal if you are going to work for me—L—."[30]

Like so much else about Johnson, his stand and actions on wiretapping and bugging were filled with sharp contradictions. As President, he had a Dictabelt taping system on all his phones—in his bedrooms and offices at the White House and the LBJ Ranch—so that he could signal his secretary to record a call. He used the system to capture crucial conversations with foreign leaders, cabinet officers, White House aides, and prominent outsiders like senators and business and labor leaders. He voraciously read FBI and foreign intelligence reports filled with information that could only have been obtained from bugging and electronic eavesdropping. LBJ disliked and mistrusted FBI Director J. Edgar Hoover, but he bent over backward to accommodate him. Seeing what Hoover passed to him about other powerful figures, including John Kennedy, LBJ assumed that his own life was the subject of a secret FBI file in the Director's office. Though he was amused by reports Hoover fed him, the President thought there was something "weird" about the FBI Director's obsession with the personal lives of other people.[31]

Johnson took satisfaction in the contrast between his position and that of Robert Kennedy, who had been elected Senator from New York in 1964. In late 1966, following reports that the FBI had used electronic surveillance on defendants in several criminal cases (including Johnson's former Senate aide Bobby Baker), the Supreme Court remanded one of those cases to a lower court for retrial. Ramsey Clark ordered an investigation, which revealed widespread eavesdropping by the FBI. Hoover responded that Attorney General Robert Kennedy had authorized and encouraged these activities. Kennedy denied Hoover's charge, claiming that he had authorized only wiretaps in national-security cases and didn't know about widespread FBI wiretapping and eavesdropping in other situations. Johnson privately sided with Hoover. He told me, "I have heard that Bobby listened to these conversations. . . . Hoover called Bobby, asked him to stop it."[32]

With LBJ gobbling up every charge and denial, Justice Department sources leaked to *Washington Post* reporter Richard Harwood a 1962 Robert Kennedy directive, prohibiting "improper, illegal and unethical" investigative practices. The directive did not spell out limits on wiretapping and did not specifically ban bugging, but Harwood wrote in the *Post* that, broadly interpreted, Kennedy's order restricted wiretaps to national-security cases and banned bugs. He reported that the FBI had ignored Kennedy's order. Johnson fumed at Harwood's stories and considered the *Post* reporter a Kennedy apologist. But his most vehement spurt of anger was directed at Jack Rosenthal, Katzenbach's and Clark's special assistant for public affairs (who years later would become editorial-page editor of *The New York Times*). Johnson told me Rosenthal had been "rifling [Justice's] files to leak some stuff to help Bobby." He told me to call him and "ream his ass."[33] (I never did and Johnson never asked whether I had.)

Against this background, it was not surprising that Johnson took delight in drafting the section on privacy in his crime message and insisted that I point up his position in all my press briefings.

The President's difficulty in deciding when to ask for a tax surcharge and figuring out how to persuade Congress to pass it increased the pressure for higher wages. The Vietnam War made work stoppages in key industries unacceptable. Organized labor balked at any inhibitions on its right to strike and believed that rising prices and corporate profits justified sizable wage increases. All these forces came to play on Johnson when, just three days after he had submitted his State of the Union message, the National Mediation Board gave up trying to settle a bitter dispute between the major railroads and six shopcraft unions representing 140,000 workers who serviced railroad cars.

Since this would be the pattern-setting contract of 1967, Johnson had to seek a low settlement—and this without disenchanting organized labor, the most powerful soldier who remained with him in the trenches, fighting both the war on poverty and the one in Southeast Asia. At the same time, Johnson couldn't tolerate a nationwide strike.

On January 28, he invoked the Railway Labor Act to block a strike for sixty days and set up a mediation board to seek a settlement. He named David Ginsburg to chair the board. As expected, Ginsburg's board recommended a low settlement. The unions rejected it with a defiant statement from the International Association of Machinists, headed by Roy Siemiller, the firebrand who had embarrassed the President during the 1966 airline strike. The union was now free to strike on April 13.

Three days before the strike deadline, on a Sunday night, the President returned from Camp David for a meeting in the Cabinet Room with his key advisers. All the unions, except for Siemiller's IAM, had agreed to extend the no-strike period. Even AFL-CIO President George Meany had been unable to get Siemiller to agree to any extension.[34]

Boyd, Ackley, McNamara, and Vance sketched the paralyzing impact of a strike on the economy, war effort, and morale of troops in Vietnam. They and Wirtz wanted the President to ask Congress to legislate an extension of the no-strike period in order to give collective bargaining one more chance. Clifford disagreed, saying, "to delay a strike for twenty days is to take a great right a working man has away from him . . . the right to strike." Fortas thought, "the stove is too cold" for any move by the President, beyond making a statement "to alert the nation" and call upon the parties in the railroad dispute to reach agreement. Clifford and Fortas wanted to let a strike arouse public opinion and lay a foundation for legislation if a national emergency was indeed created.

The President asked me to set up meetings the next morning with the congressional leadership and key committee members and to draft both a message to Congress with a resolution postponing the strike for twenty days (during which the President would name another mediation board) and a statement along the lines Fortas had suggested.[35] He would decide which course to pursue the next day.

The following morning, the President set out the alternatives for the bipartisan leadership. Republican senators reminded him of his promise in his 1966 State of the Union message to recommend broad legislation to protect the nation in emergency strike situations. Raising his voice, Senate Republican Policy Committee Chairman Hickenlooper asked, "When do we face up to labor's destructive power? We must face up to the arrogance of labor!"

"If I had a solution," Johnson said, "I would submit it."

House Minority Leader Ford asked, "Why does the country have to be at the mercy of a limited segment of the labor movement? Others [among railroad unions] agreed to settle [reasonably]. Why wasn't the crisis foreseen? Why do you have us here at so late a date?"

Johnson was effective, but as I sat watching the Republican congressional leaders, I could feel the changed atmosphere. They had some legislative muscles after the midterm elections and they enjoyed flexing them to put the President on the defensive.[36]

LBJ then faced Democratic and Republican members of the House Interstate and Foreign Commerce and Senate Labor and Public Welfare committees, most of whom depended on organized labor for campaign contributions and workers. Any bill to extend the no-strike period would have to pass muster in these committees. Senator Edward Kennedy suggested that the President should bring the union leaders to the White House, "publicly ask [them not to strike] and be turned down publicly."

Once burned by Siemiller and not certain whether Kennedy's suggestion was intended to be helpful or mischievous, Johnson dismissed it. "The President should not have to see each labor leader in the country."[37]

The President sent his bill to delay the strike for twenty days to Congress that afternoon and Congress passed it the next day.

Johnson wanted to name as the special mediation panel chair U.S. Court of Appeals Judge Charles Fahy, who had been the first general counsel of the National Labor Relations Board during the Roosevelt administration. When I approached Fahy, he thought he should retire to take on this task because "it would be inappropriate for me to do so while I am also an active federal judge." I disagreed. Unable to convince him otherwise, I checked with the President because Fahy had such a good civil rights record that he might prefer to keep him on the bench. Noting that there were plenty of pro–civil rights judges he could get confirmed for the federal appellate court in the District of Columbia, Johnson picked Fahy to chair the mediation panel.[38]

The Fahy panel reported to the President on April 22, the eve of Johnson's departure to Germany for the funeral of Konrad Adenauer, the first Chancellor of the German Federal Republic. The panel recommended wages and benefits higher than Ginsburg's board had, but still did not meet the unions' demands. Both sides rejected it. LBJ issued a public plea for the parties to reach agreement and he took AFL-CIO President George Meany to Germany with him,[39] thus relieving the labor leader of any immediate pressures from Siemiller and also providing an opportunity to make Meany an ally, or at least neutralize him, in the inevitable congressional battles ahead.

The Fahy panel and railroad management and labor testified before the Senate Labor Committee on April 24. All committee members urged the parties to accept the panel's recommendations, but the parties remained far apart.

On the afternoon of the Senate hearing, the President called from Germany to tell me to assemble his advisers, specifically including Fortas, and send him a cable with our recommendations. He also told me to make sure "flowers go out to Dirksen" (who was hospitalized with the flu) and to call "Ev and tell him 'The President called me from Germany just to make sure he was kept informed every hour about your condition. The President is terrifically upset about it.' "[40]

That evening, I met with the Fahy panel, Wirtz, McNamara, Boyd, Clifford, and Fortas.[41] When Fahy saw Abe Fortas at the conference table in my office, he was visibly shaken. I realized immediately that his man, who felt it necessary to retire from the bench to take on this assignment, was appalled to see a Supreme Court justice joining the deliberations; indeed, Fahy winced each time Fortas spoke. Clifford hung in for continued collective bargaining; all the others thought the President "should put the best face on what would essentially be . . . compulsory arbitration," a course anathema to labor. Senator Wayne Morse, whom I spoke to after the meeting, was "unalterably opposed to compulsory arbitration."[42]

I cabled the President in Germany with the legislative options. "[W]hatever we propose," I wrote, "it is likely that the issue will revolve around an attempt by the Congress to put as much of the monkey on your back as is possible," for example, leaving it to the President to trigger an imposed settlement.[43]

The President called as soon as he returned to the White House on the afternoon of April 26. The Democratic leadership was quite jumpy about the situation. They wanted more than just another extension; they wanted a proposal that settled the dispute. Johnson feared that a combination of politically motivated Democrats and Republicans might try to pass legislation authorizing the President to seize the railroads, something he didn't want to do, but a solution organized labor preferred to any legislated settlement.[44]

The next day Johnson's advisers agreed that he should ask Congress for a ninety-day extension of the no-strike period, during which a new mediation board would seek an agreement. Failing that, the board would prepare a final statement based on the Fahy recommendations, which would take effect at the end of the ninety days. Johnson anticipated trouble in the House with this proposal. So, before sending a bill to Congress, he sought to line up Morse and Mansfield on the Senate side and to temper the opposition of the AFL-CIO.[45]

Johnson needed all his persuasive talents in a May 3 cat-and-mouse meeting with George Meany. UN Ambassador Goldberg, a former labor lawyer who was a key proponent of the bill Johnson planned to send Congress and who opposed seizure,[46] and I were there as his props. The President began by giving Meany a box of cigars that the President of Paraguay had given him and regaling the labor leader with a story about Sam Rayburn. As they began discussing the administration's bill, Meany balked at anything other than government seizure of the railroads. Goldberg pointed out that seizure was in effect a perpetual injunction; under the President's proposal, the new board could modify the Fahy proposals. Johnson told Meany that without his bill he feared Senator Jacob Javits and other Republicans would press for some permanent emergency strike legislation extending the Taft-Hartley law to railroads and other labor disputes.

Meany responded that "Javits is just trying to embarrass you." He didn't think Javits's proposal would go anywhere. But Johnson's comment had its impact on the AFL-CIO president, since many members of Congress and editorial writers were clamoring for broad-based emergency strike legislation.

Meany admitted that "somewhere down the road this railroad situation has to be settled," but he felt that the "solution may be nationalization."

Johnson said, "I must have a procedure to keep [the parties] talking . . . [the five-member board I will now propose] gives me the machinery. . . . The top three people will be pro-labor . . . the Republicans in Congress want me to go much further. . . ." Then, leaning into Meany, he added, "George, all we're talking about here is a few lousy pieces of silver . . . if you don't go along with his, you will soon be hollering, 'Come help us!' "

Meany paused before he responded. What Meany did not even suspect was that Johnson intended to put him on this five-man board. That made it imperative to persuade Meany not to oppose the bill so strenuously that he would find it impossible to accept the appointment.

Meany indicated that while the five-man board might be "the best approach" for the President, that did not mean he could support it.

"Don't oppose it too damn much," Johnson pleaded and asked Meany not to testify against it.

Meany said, "I won't testify unless I have to testify."

That wasn't good enough for what Johnson had in mind. "George Meany can't testify because he needs to be influential in this dispute," Johnson said tauntingly.[47]

After meeting that evening with bipartisan congressional leaders, the President sent his proposal to Congress and told me that he was going to Texas for a few days. He wanted me to "Send a copy of the message to Morse . . . get him to say it's a pretty dangerous situation for the nation . . . get Mansfield to come out in support of the proposal . . . get someone to give a speech tomorrow on how good the boards have been that have been working on this [and] how glad he is to live in a country which cares this much about collective bargaining . . . get full committee hearings started immediately . . . get columnists in to see you this afternoon . . . [Bill] Lawrence, [Rowland] Evans, [Drew] Pearson, [Washington] Post and [New York] Times editorial writers and get them thoroughly briefed . . . get someone to attack Javits and someone to say how disgraceful it is for the Senate to be so tied up . . ."[48]

The Senate Labor Committee reported Johnson's bill on June 6 and the full Senate passed it the next day. The House was another matter. On the afternoon of June 14, during the acrimonious debate on the House floor, the President sent me to California to meet with academics to gather new ideas for the 1968 legislative program.* Larry Levinson, who picked up my end of the bruising effort to drive Johnson's rail bill through the House, had dinner with the President that evening. House Majority Leader Carl Albert was worried about a seizure amendment sponsored by Brock Adams, a Washington Democrat. At dinner, Johnson asked Levinson to have Wirtz send Albert a letter attacking the amendment, so the Majority Leader could read it on the House floor during the next day's debate. After dinner ended

---

* Warren Christopher, a Los Angeles lawyer, set up the dinner meeting at Chasen's. The President called during the meal and told me to bring Christopher back to Washington that same evening. Johnson planned to interview Christopher, whom Ramsey Clark had recommended for the deputy attorney general's post; and, if he liked him, to nominate him on the spot. He did, and a pleasantly surprised Christopher got the job the next day.[49]

at 10:36, Levinson called Wirtz, waking him at home to relay the instruction.

The next morning, the President called me down to his office and asked to see a copy of Wirtz's letter. When I answered that I didn't have one, Johnson hit the speaker phone button on his desk and told the White House operator to get Wirtz. When Wirtz got on the phone, the President asked him where the letter to Albert was. "I got this call from Levinson," Wirtz explained petulantly, "but I wasn't sure it was really your instruction."

The President exploded. "Let me tell you something," he bellowed, leaning over the speaker phone. "If you get a call from the cleaning woman who mops the floors at three A.M. and she tells you that the President wants you to do something, you do it! Now you write that letter and bring it to Albert yourself. I don't have time to make all these calls and you know Goddamn well that I tell my aides to pass on instructions from me all the time." With that, Johnson hung up. The letter was delivered to Albert, copy to me, within an hour.[50]

With Congress deadlocked, union workers began to walk off the job at 12:01 A.M. on Sunday, July 16. The President faced the reality of a nationwide rail strike, as he kept one eye on Newark, New Jersey, where the worst racial rioting since Watts had broken out. As food supplies were threatened, commuter lines snarled and McNamara publicly decried the danger to our troops in Vietnam, the President made another plea to the congressional leadership and Congress finally acted to end the strike.[51]

As Johnson had privately assured Meany, he appointed a real labor man to the special board: Meany himself. For chairman, he chose Wayne Morse. Johnson told Morse he had gotten the "black bean." Morse asked what the black bean was. The President told him about members of a Texas military expedition in the mid-nineteenth century who got captured in Mexico by soldiers. Since there was not enough jail space, with eyes closed each had to pick a bean from a plate. Those with the white beans went to jail; those with the black ones were executed. IAM President Siemiller bitterly denounced Morse as "the biggest strike-breaker in the nation."

Nonetheless, Morse produced a unanimous report that both Meany and former American Telephone and Telegraph Chairman Frederick Kappel signed. Johnson had named Kappel as the business member on the board; it was the kind of appointment LBJ delighted in. Businessmen saw Kappel as quintessentially Republican, one of their own. Yet AT&T's business was so critically dependent on the Federal Communications Commission that the President had enormous leverage over him.[52] While Kappel could disagree with the President (and he did publicly express reservations about the report), he dared not create any serious problems. Johnson wanted a report tilted toward labor with a distinguished businessman's endorsement. He got it. The union almost immediately accepted the report. The railroads refused, and the settlement was imposed upon them in October 1967, thus ending the dispute—but at a higher level than Johnson sought, reflecting his declining power to shape economic events.

In late 1968, Morse would understand what LBJ had meant by the black bean. That November, Republican Robert Packwood defeated Morse in his Senate race, largely because organized labor had turned against the Democratic incumbent.

ELEVEN

Who Shall Serve
in Vietnam
When Not All Serve

JOHNSON'S ANGUISH about the war was heightened by the unfairness of
the draft. He saw it as another injustice visited on the less fortunate
and minorities, and he struggled for a fair method to determine who
should go to war when all do not go.

In 1951 during the Korean War, Congress had tried to disguise
this question by renaming the 1948 Selective Service Act the "Universal Military Training and Service Act." But there was nothing
universal about the draft. By the time LBJ was forced to resort to large
draft calls, the unfairness of the Selective Service System—riddled
with exemptions and deferments, administered erratically by 4,100
virtually lily-white local draft boards—stood in sharp relief against
the war's increasing unpopularity. Facing the need to ask Congress to
extend the draft law before its expiration in July 1967, the President
had established the National Advisory Commission on Selective Service in 1966 to review the system and recommend how to distribute
the heavy burden of waging war fairly among the affluent and the
disadvantaged.

Johnson immersed himself in every aspect of the commission's
work, beginning with the selection of its members.[1] Since he was
particularly concerned about the unfair burden minorities bore, LBJ
chose Burke Marshall, John Kennedy's Assistant Attorney General
for the Civil Rights Division, to chair and two blacks, John Johnson,
publisher of *Ebony* and *Jet*, and civil rights activist Vernon Jordan. He
also named labor leaders; college presidents, including Kingman

Brewster of Yale; women as different as Oveta Culp Hobby, publisher of *The Houston Post*, and Anna Rosenberg Hoffman, a member of FDR's inner circle; John Courtney Murray, the distinguished Jesuit priest and moral theologian; businessmen; a judge; and a couple of loyal friends, George Reedy and Warren Woodward, to keep him informed from the inside.

He insisted even on approving all key staff members. One was the commission's general counsel, Charles Rangel, a black lawyer from the United States Attorney's office in the Southern District of New York, who had been wounded in combat and awarded the Bronze Star as a platoon sergeant during the Korean War.[2]

In February 1967 the commission recommended a sweeping overhaul of the way men were drafted: a lottery system of random selection, drafting nineteen-year-olds first and working up (rather than the existing system of drafting twenty-six-year-olds first and working down). A reorganization was also urged to curb the wide discretion of local draft boards to exempt and defer. By eleven to seven, the commission voted to end college-student deferments.[3] Here was a system more to LBJ's liking, one in which rich and poor, black and white, would face the same odds of military service in young adulthood.

Army General Lewis Hershey was for all practical and political purposes the Selective Service System. The seventy-three-year-old had been its director from before World War II. He had serious reservations about the commission's recommendations. When I was alerted to this, I set up a meeting with McNamara and Hershey. By memo, I asked the President if I could imply that he agreed with the commission. Johnson circled the word "imply" and wrote, "No— Don't quote me or imply. . . . Let's get his best judgment free of influence." In the meeting, Hershey said that he could go along with random selection and drafting the youngest first, although they were not his preference. He was intensely opposed to any reorganization that reduced the power and discretion of local draft boards.[4]

When I reported back to the President, he said he wanted to "go with Hershey where we can" and thus was prepared to leave the local draft boards with wide discretion if Hershey placed blacks and Mexican-Americans on them, as Johnson had ordered in December 1966. Hershey agreed and, six months later, with pressure from the White House, two hundred blacks, ten Hispanics, and sixteen American Indians had been named to local boards, with assurances of many more to come.[5]

In early March the President proposed to Congress a random selection system that began with nineteen-year-olds first. He intended to eliminate all graduate school deferments except for medical and dental students, but he called for a national debate on college deferments before he decided what action to take. Johnson buried the commission's proposed reorganization in a management study, but committed himself to making local boards *"truly representative of the communities they serve."* His message to Congress stressed his critical consideration:

> . . . we must continue to ask one form of service—military duty—of our young men. We would be an irresponsible Nation if we did not—and perhaps even an extinct one. . . . The Nation's requirement that men must serve, however, imposes this obligation: that in this land of equals, men are selected as equals to serve. . . . A just nation must have the fairest system that can be devised for making that selection.

Extending the law for four more years, Congress endorsed drafting the youngest men first and left the President power to end graduate school and occupational deferments. But it continued undergraduate college deferments and refused to allow the President to establish random selection without further legislation.

Congress also unleashed its anger at draft-card burners and others who tried to impede the Selective Service System. The new law ordered the courts and Justice Department to give precedence to prosecuting draft-law violators, and required the Attorney General to bring to trial all cases referred by Hershey for prosecution or explain in writing to Congress why he didn't. Johnson shared the members' irritation. When I noted in a memo that this provision stemmed from the "intense feeling . . . that Justice does not move fast enough against draft violators," Johnson wrote, "I agree. L."[6]

Each time the media ran stories or pictures of young men burning their draft cards or disrupting local boards, the President became exercised. On October 20, 1967, the eve of antiwar demonstrations at the Pentagon, the President took me into his office just before 7:30 P.M., and called me over to the tickers near his desk. He pulled the paper from the roll to show me UPI 208, a wire-service report that several individuals had left 992 draft cards at the Justice Department. He began jabbing at it with his finger and shouted, "I want a memo to the Attorney General tonight. I want the FBI investigating."[7]

That evening, as we sat in the living quarters before dinner, the President called General Hershey and delivered a monologue about the need to punish draft protesters. At times he was infuriated; at others he seemed genuinely struggling to understand what could drive a young American to burn his draft card. He wanted to know who "the dumb sonofabitch was who would let somebody leave a bunch of draft cards in front of the Justice Department and then let them just walk away." If Ramsey wouldn't act, the President wanted Hershey to do something about draft-card burners and people disrupting the Selective Service System.

Over dinner, the President talked about the antiwar demonstration at the Pentagon planned for the coming weekend and worried that "Communist elements" would take advantage of the situation to "make sure that there will be big trouble in the Negro ghetto." He wondered whether to deploy Army troops around the White House and how much of the 82nd Airborne should be alerted to deal with the demonstration. For a time he thought about issuing a statement—earlier he had even dictated one sentence to me, "I have instructed all governmental authorities charged with the responsibility in this matter to see that the law of the land is obeyed and enforced." But he decided not to, because he concluded it would achieve little beyond additional publicity and controversy.[8]

In fact, Johnson had reason to be concerned. The demonstrators' avowed purpose was to "shut down" the Pentagon. Although they could not agree on how to accomplish this—some advocated nonviolent civil disobedience, others a violent assault—all wanted to strike a blow at the institutions carrying on the war, including the Selective Service System. The week before the march in Washington, protesters in Oakland, California, had both clashed with police and passively resisted them in an attempt to close down that city's Army induction center. Smaller confrontations had occurred across the country.

The Justice Department had been monitoring and reporting to the President on the planned demonstration since early October, and it too was concerned about far left and Communist involvement. Johnson decided to prepare for the worst. He had troops, including regular Army soldiers, marines, and police, deployed or on the alert to protect the Pentagon, the Capitol, and the White House. Army troops were even secretly stationed in the basement of the Commerce Department, so they could rapidly assume positions surrounding the White House if such action became necessary. To avoid detection, the soldiers drove into the Commerce Department parking area in civilian clothing in groups of two to four in private cars, with their uniforms, equipment, and weapons in the trunks, over a period of many hours.[9]

There were some skirmishes, but the demonstrations were generally peaceful. The Pentagon continued to function, and no riot erupted in Washington's black ghettos. On Sunday, October 22, the President and Mrs. Johnson went to church, and afterward drove around the Lincoln Memorial, where the demonstrators had first assembled. The President was full of curiosity. He wanted to see what the remaining hippies looked like—their dress, sex, and ages, their flags, bed rolls, blankets, flight bags, and flowers. Then LBJ drove to the Pentagon, and unnoticed, he looked over the Mall entrance of the building and the road to it bounded by soldiers.[10]

The next week, the President received a raw intelligence report that protesters had urinated on the lawns in front of the Pentagon and some female protesters had tried to unzip the flies of soldiers standing to block their path and taunted them, "Wouldn't you rather fuck than fight?" Johnson immediately told me to leak it to columnist Joseph Alsop, a staunch supporter of the Vietnam War and an angry critic of the demonstrations. Johnson wanted Alsop to see the report's description of youths having intercourse on the Pentagon lawns and urinating in unison on command, and the signs that demanded, "LBJ, pull out like your father should have done." When I sent the President a report that the taxpayer costs of the demonstration and cleanup exceeded one million dollars, he told me to release it to the press.[11]

The draft-card burnings and disruptive protests increased. When I told Johnson that many were burning obsolete draft cards or Xerox copies, he became even more furious because the Justice Department had no violation of law to prosecute. But Hershey had gotten an earful and he, at least, was going to act as he thought he should and believed his President desired.

Less than a week after his call from LBJ, Hershey ordered the immediate induction of anyone registered for the draft who interfered with the Selective Service System. He asked the President to issue an executive order to authorize immediate induction of those who interfered with the system, burned, mutilated, or forged a draft card, or obstructed the operation of a local draft board.[12] In early November, Hershey's order became public and touched off spirited controversy.

Hershey's tough line certainly conformed to the President's mood, but it was filled with constitutional and practical difficulties. LBJ's heart may have been with Hershey, but he knew he couldn't act on emotion alone, and his instincts were against using military service as a form of punishment. He had me seek the advice of others on his staff. Larry Temple, a conservative Texas attorney, considered any such executive order "ill-advised" and of "doubtful" legality.[13] Abe Fortas, speaking to a group of students at Colgate University, also attacked Hershey's policy, saying that Hershey is "a law unto himself and responds only to his own conversation." Fortas was right, but he didn't know that the President had wound Hershey up to begin with.

I added my own concern. I urged the President to stay out of the public controversy. On November 18, Johnson began an off-the-record meeting with Hershey and Clark in a testy mood. He complained that Clark had prosecuted only 1,300 out of 7,300 men who had been arrested for failing to report for induction. Clark replied that many should never have been arrested, that their failure to report was inadvertent, and that he was doing all he could under existing law. Johnson snapped back, "If you need more laws, submit your suggestions at once!" Hershey complained that a judge had released protesters who were blocking the door to the main Selective Service headquarters. Johnson wanted the name of the judge. Nobody gave an inch.[14]

After the meeting, Johnson sent Ramsey Clark a list of all the criminal statutes on sabotage, espionage, and interference with the government. He had asked me to have White House aide Matthew Nimetz prepare the list because of his growing concern about the increase in antiwar demonstrations, particularly those affecting public appearances by him and some cabinet members, and intelligence reports of Communist and Socialist Worker party involvement. I had sent it to him the evening before. His eyes-only memo to Clark began:

> In connection with your investigations of possible illegal acts committed by individuals or groups seeking to impede actively, forcibly, and violently Government policies in Southeast Asia, you should bring to the attention of all United States Attorneys the following statutory provisions, together with judicial decisions relevant to their application, as well as any other criminal or civil laws you believe to be relevant.
>
> You should instruct all United States Attorneys of our firm policy that the right of free expression and dissent be in no way infringed. You should instruct them that it is also our firm policy that persons who violate the law—for examples, by disrupting peaceful meetings, preventing public officials from carrying on their work, impeding the operations of the Armed Forces and the Selective Service System—will be prosecuted to the full extent of the law.

After signing the memo, Johnson added this handwritten note: "If you need further legislation in this connection, please submit suggestions at once."[15]

In early December Johnson got word of an unfavorable New York Times story about Hershey and the administration's draft policy that was coming up. He decided to have Hershey and Clark issue a joint compromise statement on the draft: individuals who did something improper affecting their own status (e.g., burned draft cards) would be inducted as soon as possible; individuals who violated federal law by doing something against the system generally (e.g., obstructed recruiting or a Selective Service board) would be promptly prosecuted by a special unit Clark would establish in the Justice Department; U.S. Attorneys would turn related local law violations over to local authorities immediately. Johnson approved every word of the joint statement before its release on Saturday, December 9, 1967.[16]

The statement preempted the *Times* story. Unfortunately, an agreement I had negotiated that neither Clark nor Hershey, nor their subordinates, would talk to the press was violated. With each side putting its spin on the joint statement (and accusing the other of the first breach), the issue was more confused than ever and the administration appeared to be speaking out of both sides of its mouth. As I reported to the President, "Hershey is saying he will accelerate the draft . . . of registrants who violate the Selective Service Act in ways that do not affect their own status. The Justice Department is saying that such registrants cannot have their draft status accelerated, but must be prosecuted under the criminal laws."[17]

On December 21, 1967, Yale University President Kingman Brewster wrote Johnson on behalf of the Ivy League presidents: "We realize, as you do, the threat of spreading civil disobedience, and would support any lawful effort to assure the orderly processes of recruitment and selection for military service. However . . . fundamental values of due process of law will remain in serious jeopardy unless you make it clear that the draft is not to be used as punishment and that draft boards are not to become extra legal judges of the legality of acts of protest."[18]

The President spoke to me about Brewster's letter on December 24, the morning he returned to Washington from a hectic world trip, and again on Christmas Day. By early on the 26th, he had decided that I would respond on his behalf and try to get our house in order. While meeting that day on an international balance-of-payments crisis, Johnson reworked drafts of a letter I had prepared. He eventually approved (as did Hershey and Clark) the "Dear King" letter I sent out, which stated:

> . . . the Selective Service System is not an instrument to repress and punish unpopular views. Nor does it vest in draft boards the judicial role of determining the legality of individual conduct. . . . [The joint Hershey-Clark] statement sets out the cardinal principle that lawful protest activities, whether directed to the draft or other National issues, do not subject registrants to acceleration or other special administrative action by the Selective Service Sys-

tem. . . . It is also fundamental to the preservation of our liberties that the laws of the land be respected and obeyed. Violations of law cannot be countenanced. Where violations occur, the judicial system must be invoked. This basic concept, too, is clearly set out in the Joint Policy Statement. . . . General Hershey has informed me that he adheres to these views. [19]

The President hadn't found it easy to check his anger and help with this letter, when he heard echoes the evening before of the chant outside the White House: "Hey, hey, LBJ! How many kids did you kill today?" But the letter put the matter to uneasy rest.

Johnson continued to worry about the draft's unfairness, what he saw as its coddling of the affluent middle and upper classes. Blacks and Mexican-Americans, he said, did not have nearly the same opportunity to escape the draft through higher education and occupational deferments—at least, the President emphasized, not until each child who desires a college education can get one without regard to the "thickness of his daddy's wallet."

So, in February 1968, Johnson eliminated most graduate school deferments, except for medical, dental, and divinity students, beginning with those who had entered graduate school in the fall of 1967. He also abolished the bloated list of occupations automatically eligible for deferments, such as glassblowers, engineers, and metallurgists. Even more consequentially, the President changed his mind about drafting the youngest first. When I sent him a memo in mid-December recommending he begin to do so, Johnson charged back, "I don't want to draft 19 year olds first as General Hershey, Secretary McNamara and Joe Califano prefer. I want to draft everyone that graduates from college. Start at age 23, if not enough, go to 22, then 21, then 20 and lastly 19."[20] These decisions made the draft fairer, but because the impact was to put American middle and upper-class children at much higher risk, the President had dramatically raised the political stakes for himself.

TWELVE

Six-Day War

HALFWAY THROUGH 1967, as Johnson had wrestled with the economy, Vietnam, an increasingly difficult Congress, and mounting antiwar protests and struggled to reform the draft and avoid a nationwide rail strike, Israel attacked Egypt. The Arab-Israeli Six-Day War presented a politically sensitive and delicate situation for LBJ. American Jews were big financial supporters of the President and big political supporters of his Great Society. On the other hand, many liberal Jews were leading the growing opposition to Johnson's policies in Vietnam.[1]

Israel started the Six-Day War in a surprise attack on June 5 and by June 7 had destroyed the Egyptian Air Force on the ground, demolished most of Egypt's tanks in the Sinai, and captured the Jordanian sector of Jerusalem. The Arab countries, notably Egypt, Jordan, and Iraq, had provoked the attack by ordering a UN peacemaking force out of Sinai, closing off the Gulf of Aqaba (blocking access to the Israeli port of Elath), calling for a "holy war" against Israel, and signing a pact against it.

Many American Jews feared that the State Department would consider Israel the aggressor and its attack unjustified. The political problem reached white heat when, shortly after fighting broke out, State Department spokesman Robert McCloskey told reporters, "Our position is neutral in thought, word, and deed."

The American Jewish community worried that any invocation of the Neutrality Act by the President would, as David Ginsburg warned privately, "prevent the Israelis from raising money in the United States through Israeli war bonds and probably through many other means." They also feared that a posture of neutrality would prevent the U.S. from shipping supplies to Israel. Even Abe Fortas called me to express his own "deep reservations about the applicability of the Neutrality Act to this situation."[2]

Johnson ordered White House Press Secretary George Christian and Rusk to back the administration away from McCloskey's statement, but many American Jews remained anxious about reports that LBJ was displeased with Israel for precipitating the war. Johnson, nettled that he had to confront a Middle East crisis, became even more agitated by the pressure from American Jews. The President told me to call his friends—New York lawyer and businessman Arthur Krim, MCA Chairman Lew Wasserman, and New York attorney Edwin Weisl, among others—to assure them privately that he stood with Israel and urge them to get that word out and the Jewish community off his back.[3]

But LBJ had problems on his own staff. Larry Levinson and Ben Wattenberg, then a White House speechwriter, sent the President a memo on June 7, urging him to reassure "a mass meeting of American Jews tomorrow at 2 P.M. in Lafayette Park" across from the White House. Levinson and Wattenberg thought a presidential message of support for Israel would "neutralize" the State Department's neutrality statement "and could lead to a great domestic political bonus . . . the Mid-East crisis can turn around a lot of anti-Vietnam anti-Johnson feeling, particularly if you use it as an opportunity."[4]

As soon as he'd read the memo, Johnson called Levinson in my office. He told him how disappointed he was in some of his Jewish friends, their reactions to "what was being done in these days of crisis," their lack of trust in him. A little while later, Levinson left my office as the President was coming out of the Oval Office. Spotting him, Johnson jutted out his right fist and yelled down the hall, "You Zionist dupe! You and Wattenberg are Zionist dupes in the White House! Why can't you see I'm doing all I can for Israel. That's what you should be telling people when they ask for a message from the President for their rally." LBJ turned abruptly and stormed off to the mansion. Levinson stood there "shaken to the marrow of my bones," as he later said.[5]

Johnson handled the international aspects of the crisis coolly. On June 8, when Israeli planes attacked the U.S. Navy communications ship *Liberty* in international waters off Gaza, killing thirty-four Americans, Clark Clifford urged Johnson to be "tough," to "handle" the incident "as if the Arabs or Russians had done it." He wanted

Johnson to insist that the government of Israel "punish the Israelis responsible." Clifford thought it "inconceivable that [the attack] was an accident." Rusk urged that the President seek reparations, punishment, and an assurance of no repetition. The Secretary of State considered the attack "incomprehensible." Privately, the President subscribed "one hundred percent" to Clifford's views.[6] Publicly, however LBJ did not dwell on the incident, stoically accepting an Israeli apology and reparations.

By June 10, when a United Nations cease-fire took effect, Johnson had spoken with Soviet Premier Alexei Kosygin several times on the Hotline, which had never before been used in a crisis. The Israelis had conquered the Gaza strip, Sinai peninsula, West Bank, and Golan Heights. Johnson insisted only on a cease-fire; he did not call for a withdrawal of Israeli forces, leaving that to future negotiations.

Johnson's handling of the Six-Day War brought him no respite from a Congress increasingly divided over racial issues, the Great Society, and Vietnam. On June 7, the House voted down the administration's bill to increase the debt limit, thus threatening to bring the federal government to a halt because it couldn't borrow any money after June 30. It was a major setback for the administration, and compounded Johnson's difficulties with Ways and Means Committee Chairman Wilbur Mills, who had reluctantly managed the bill on the House floor at our insistence. The President wanted a list of the Democrats who had voted against. When he saw certain liberals on the list, including Richard Ottinger, whose district included part of the wealthy New York suburb and county of Westchester, he asked why they had voted against the increase. I told him that most of them had done it as a protest against the war, which they thought was shorting domestic programs. "Okay," Johnson said, "I want you to tell Ottinger that there's plenty of money for domestic programs, especially housing. Tell him we're prepared to put a public housing project right in the middle of his fancy Westchester district to demonstrate to him and his constituents how much money there is for domestic programs. Maybe that'll help him to vote an increase in the debt limit."

THIRTEEN

Burn, Baby, Burn!

THREE DAYS AFTER the Six-Day War ended, Johnson nominated Thurgood Marshall to be the nation's first black Supreme Court justice. Since his days as a teacher and National Youth Administration worker in Texas, Johnson had understood the importance of role models to demonstrate to black and Mexican-American children (as well as to white adults) that they could aspire to any job in the United States and do it just as well as anyone else. Marshall was ideal; even before President Kennedy had placed him in a judgeship in 1961 and Johnson had named him Solicitor General, he had won twenty-nine of the thirty-two cases he'd argued before the Supreme Court, including, on behalf of the South Carolina plaintiffs, *Brown v. Board of Education*, which in 1954 struck down the "separate but equal" doctrine that had perpetuated racially segregated schools.*

In the fall of 1966, when Johnson had moved Attorney General Nicholas Katzenbach to the Undersecretary of State post George Ball had vacated, he had named as Acting Attorney General Katzenbach's deputy, Ramsey Clark, whose father, Associate Justice Tom Clark, had been on the Supreme Court since 1949. Johnson told the younger Clark that he could not make him Attorney General because his father

---

* Johnson was peacock-proud of another role model he often claimed to have discovered: Barbara Jordan. In January 1968, when she was serving as the first black elected to the Texas Senate, he named her to his Commission on Income Maintenance Programs. Jordan later became the first black woman elected to Congress from the South.

would have to resign from the Court to avoid any conflict of interest and the President "didn't think that would be right." LBJ made that same point to a number of others, assuming what he had said would get back to Tom Clark and would lead him to step down from the Court.[1]

Johnson was hesitant about naming Ramsey Clark Attorney General, in any case. Since Clark was a Texan and his family was close to the Johnsons, the President thought he might be accused of cronyism, especially because of the thirty-eight-year-old Clark's youth and (despite six years with Kennedy and Johnson) his lack of stature. He was also concerned about Clark's judgment. So he perched Clark on the hot tin roof of "Acting" for five months while he took a measure of the man and let the Congress and press see him perform.

As the weeks turned into months, on more than one occasion I urged the President to name Ramsey his Attorney General because he'd been in the "Acting" capacity too long. "That's a Harvard recommendation, not a Brooklyn one," he said. "There are two jobs in this man's government that you want only your mother to fill—and even her not on every day: Commissioner of Internal Revenue and Attorney General."[2] This comment was not surprising; several of us on the White House staff thought that the only person Lyndon Johnson truly trusted was Lady Bird, and she only 90 percent of the time.

Though Johnson was never entirely comfortable with Ramsey Clark, the promise of a vacancy on the Supreme Court proved irresistible, and on February 28, 1967, he nominated him to be Attorney General. Two hours later, Justice Tom Clark said he would resign from the Court at the end of its term in June. I assumed Johnson would choose Marshall to fill the vacancy. Then one morning in his bedroom, he kicked off a lengthy discussion with me and others about whom he should appoint to the court. He mentioned several possible black nominees, then mused about whether he should appoint the first woman. Rare for her, Lady Bird broke in. She thought that "Lyndon has done so much" for blacks, "why not indeed fill the vacancy with a woman." A few women were discussed, including Shirley Hufstedler, then a judge in California.* The President was momentarily intrigued with the idea, but in short order he settled on Marshall and sent his name to the Senate on June 13, the morning after Tom Clark formally retired.†

---

* In 1968 LBJ named Hufstedler to the U.S. Court of Appeals for the 9th Circuit.
† The Senate confirmation process for Marshall was protracted by the standard of those days, but he was confirmed on August 30 by a 69–11 vote, over strenuous

Marshall's nomination—and the appointments of Weaver and Brimmer, the 1964 and 1965 Civil and Voting Rights acts, the Great Society social programs and the obvious commitment of the President—could not calm the mean streets of urban ghettos. In the two years since Watts, the anger of (mostly) young blacks had erupted in serious disturbances in more than two dozen American cities. Then in the month following Marshall's nomination, riots in Newark and Detroit outraged and frightened the entire nation. Hundreds of young blacks, shouting, "Burn, baby, burn!," set fire to buildings in their own neighborhoods. The senseless deaths and tragic destruction in those two cities slapped Lyndon Johnson with a violent reminder that his ambition to do something for poor blacks, whether one side or another thought it too much or too little, might in any case be too late. Just as he had after Watts, he was forced to face the fact that he might be losing his race against the ticking clock of expectations that the promise of his own legislative achievements and rhetoric had wound up.

On the evening of July 12, 1967, Newark police had arrested a black cab driver for a traffic violation. A rumor that police had beaten the driver to death swept through the city's black ghetto. Rioting erupted on that steamy summer evening and reached such destructive fury the next night that New Jersey's Democratic Governor Richard Hughes termed it a "criminal insurrection."

The President wanted to stay out of Newark, but Hughes was one of his strongest supporters. He called the New Jersey Governor at midday on July 14. By then several were dead, hundreds were in custody, scores of fires had been set, looting, violence, and property destruction were rampant, and Hughes had ordered the state National Guard into the city. "I just wanted you to know that . . . everyone here wants to support you and give you any aid," Johnson told Hughes. "You just let Ramsey Clark or Mr. Hoover [know what you need]." Hughes told the President he intended to restore order with his own resources.[3] By the next day, fifteen were dead and a thousand under arrest. Sniper fire disrupted police, national guardsmen, and firefighters. But Hughes held firm in his determination to handle the situation locally, and the President was relieved that the New Jersey Governor did not ask for federal troops.

On Saturday afternoon, July 15, the UPI news ticker reported that Vice President Humphrey had called Governor Hughes and "of-

---

opposition of southern senators led by North Carolina Democrat Sam Ervin, who attacked Johnson for nominating such a liberal "judicial activist" to sit on the nation's highest bench.

fered federal aid." Johnson wanted me to talk to the Vice President immediately to tell him that "He has no authority, spell it out, N-O-N-E, to provide any federal aid to Newark or any other city, town or county in America." Johnson fretted that any such offer would be read as using Great Society programs to reward rioters. I passed along a softened version of the President's message. Should Humphrey hear from Hughes, I told him to refer the Governor to either Ramsey Clark or me.[4]

The next day, the Associated Press reported that the Vice President had offered to send U.S. marshals to Newark. Johnson didn't need a phone to talk to me from his bedroom to my office in the West Wing. He wanted Humphrey gagged for good, forbidden to talk to any governors before he "brings down the Administration."[5]

"I've been good to Hubert, haven't I?" Johnson asked me plaintively, and then posed a series of outlandish rhetorical questions. "Why do you think he's doing this to me? Do you think he just wants to torture me? Do you think he spends his weekends trying to figure out how to make my job more difficult?" I called Humphrey, who couldn't believe the wire-service report and was annoyed that the President would give any credence to something "so ridiculous on its face."[6]

On Wednesday, July 19, Governor Hughes called the White House to report that Newark was under control. At a cabinet meeting that same day, Johnson urged his top officials "to do more on the problems with minority groups and with the cities," and "When members [of Congress] complain about riots, ask them what they're doing to build programs like model cities and rent supplements." The President repeated his refrain, "We are not getting our story over," and then set up a group, chaired by the Vice President and composed of several cabinet officers, Charles Schultze, and me, to consider what else the administration could do for the cities and blacks in the ghettos.[7]

After the cabinet meeting, LBJ met with NAACP executive director Roy Wilkins and Urban League executive director Whitney Young. He warned them that the House's antiriot bill and Senate opposition to Thurgood Marshall's Supreme Court nomination were bad omens for his legislative program. The two moderate black leaders seemed at a loss. Young said they were concerned about "the whole pattern, not just about Newark" and that they could not control the "young people." I was struck by their despair. The nation was at flash point with pent-up frustration and anger, and these leaders seemed bewildered by the rush of events. They had led so many successful battles for civil rights in the courts and Congress. Now they were at bay, numbed by their lack of influence.

The President told his visitors that he understood their problems, that he wished the country to be "tolerant, but . . . we must control crime." Then he treated them to a recitation of his Great Society's achievements, the amount of money he had gotten Congress to commit to antipoverty programs, "$25.6 billion this year, up from $12 billion in 1963." Johnson rushed on. "The school systems of the cities have failed . . . these young Negroes aren't being prepared for jobs" and they couldn't even become apprentices because "they aren't allowed in the labor unions." He saved his most acerbic comments for the liberals. "We are now divided. We've got liberal, progressive forces going down different roads. [Senators Abraham] Ribicoff and [Robert] Kennedy are embarrassing [HUD Secretary] Weaver," instead of helping him with his cities legislation. "I'm a progressive. I'm not a liberal," Johnson told them. "A liberal is intolerant of other views. He wants to control your thoughts and actions." Then Johnson leaned forward on the arm of his rocker, moving closer to the black leaders. "You know the difference between cannibals and liberals?" He asked. "Cannibals eat only their enemies."

Wilkins suggested that "Communists are involved" in inciting blacks to riot. Oh Lord, I thought, Johnson didn't need to hear that, with the reports that Hoover was sending him. The President nodded. He said Hoover was "checking on the [source of snipers'] rifles in Newark." Then, to my relief and surprise, he brushed Wilkins's concerns about Communists aside and asked Wilkins and Young to help him on the Hill and get other black leaders to join their efforts. Johnson said that House Minority Leader Gerald Ford was playing politics, trying to cut poverty funds by connecting them to Newark. To the contrary, he said, we have to deal with "ignorance, poverty, and disease."

Johnson described the "cabinet task force" that he'd set up under the Vice President on "the urban Negro and the city." When Wilkins suggested that the President add OEO Director Shriver, Johnson responded that it was a "cabinet task force and Shriver is not in the cabinet." I had to hold back a smile; Johnson was furious with Shriver because Newark Mayor Hugh Addonizio and Governor Hughes had complained to the White House that poverty-program workers were involved in the riots and might even be inciting them.[8] Their complaints had played to LBJ's recurrent suspicion of the Kennedy in-law and his frustration that, despite all he was doing for blacks, he could not elicit from them the passionate response they gave Robert Kennedy.

That evening I sent the President a summary of a presidential task force report on the cities. Its basic thrust was an urgent call for programs "to encourage integration—by race and income." It was a gloomy assessment: by 1983, the nation's major cities would be 40 percent black and 40 percent poor; twenty cities would be majority black and have even more poor residents; and central cities would continue to deteriorate without a major infusion of social programs and a concerted integration effort.[9] Not only had the Newark violence and arson taken twenty-six lives, injured fifteen hundred, and burned hundreds of homes and stores, Johnson thought correctly as he mulled over the report, its ashes threatened the programs that he believed would offer hope to the nation's cities and the young blacks living in them.

The congressional reaction to the racial violence in Newark and other cities was swift and harsh, fulfilling some of Johnson's darkest predictions. Earlier, on July 19, over the administration's opposition, the House had overwhelmingly passed a bill making it a federal crime to cross state lines to incite or participate in a riot. Johnson considered the antiriot bill politically opportunistic and useless since it could do nothing to prevent riots.

The following day things in the House got even worse. In his 1967 special message to the Congress on Urban and Rural Poverty, Johnson had proposed the Rat Extermination Act, to launch a rodent eradication and control program in cities to protect ghetto children from being bitten and terrified by rats. The legislation had moved with so little effort through Congress that we assumed easy passage when it came to the House floor three days after the Newark riots ended. But southern Democrats and Republicans greeted the bill with a torrent of ridicule and refused, by a vote of 207 to 176, even to debate it. They called it a "civil rats bill," conjured up to create a "rat bureaucracy," "rat patronage," and a "high commissioner of rats." One suggested that the President should "buy a lot of cats and turn them loose"; others cracked that the next thing Lyndon Johnson would want was legislation to eradicate snakes, squirrels, bugs, and blackbirds.

The President was appalled. He issued a scathing statement that afternoon, calling the House action a "cruel blow to the poor children of America" and noting that "thousands of those children—many of them babies—are bitten by rats in their homes and tenements. Some are killed. Many are disfigured for life. . . . We are spending Federal funds to protect our livestock from rodents and predatory animals. The least we can do is give our children the same protection we give our livestock." He called on the House to reconsider its action and sent me to the press office to display pictures of babies grotesquely disfigured by rat bites. That evening, Johnson reminded me that during the summer of 1966, when we had first discussed the bill, the House would never have killed it with such ridicule; the temper of the country, he said, was turning against the ghetto blacks because of the riots.*

Newark's fires were dying out when Detroit suffered the nation's worst disturbance since federal troops had been required to quell a race riot there in 1943.† Shortly before 4 A.M. on Sunday, July 23, police raided an after-hours drinking club on the city's West Side. There were again rumors, this time that police had beaten a man and a woman.

On edge, LBJ ordered me to keep a close eye on Detroit that Sunday afternoon as we worked on the presidential yacht *Sequoia*, drafting the tax message he was to deliver to Congress on August 3. We were sailing the Potomac from Mount Vernon to Washington. When Johnson got back to the White House that evening, the FBI was reporting intensifying riots.[10]

Just before 3 A.M. on Monday, Michigan's Republican Governor George Romney called Ramsey Clark to report on the deteriorating Detroit situation (20 injured, 650 arrested, 150 fires) and to suggest that he might need federal troops. Clark awakened the President with this news and Johnson ordered Army troops put on alert.[11]

Romney called Clark several times during the early-morning hours, finally indicating that he would be "recommending" that the President send federal troops to Detroit. The conversations were wary on both sides. Clark suspected that the Michigan Governor was engaged in political maneuvering.[12] Clark's suspicions turned on LBJ's amber lights. Fortas had breakfast with the President[13] and turned his amber lights to red. He kept them flashing.

During Newark, Governor Hughes and Lyndon Johnson had communicated over clear lines of mutual trust. Here the static of presidential ambition and political suspicion fouled the lines. Romney was a moderate and popular "Republican with a conscience," in his

---

* LBJ mounted a strenuous effort to turn the House around, mobilizing big-city mayors and civil rights groups. As a result, the House eventually reversed itself and added a rat extermination program to the Partnership for Health Act, which the President signed on December 4, 1967.

† In June 1943, thirty-one people died in Detroit rioting. When Michigan Governor Harry Kelly declared that he was unable to maintain order and asked for help, President Franklin Roosevelt dispatched federal troops to stop the violence.

third term as Governor. As yet undeclared, he was campaigning for his party's 1968 presidential nomination against the acknowledged but undeclared front-runner, Richard Nixon. LBJ considered Romney a more potent rival than Nixon.

Unsure how to handle the riot, Romney fueled Johnson's distrust with his ambiguous calls to Clark. Wire-service stories out of Detroit provided conflicting reports. Around 5 A.M., AP reported that the President had ordered troops into the city. At 5:37 A.M., UPI reported that Romney claimed that Clark had promised to send troops. Less than twenty minutes later, UPI reported that no troops had been ordered into Detroit. At 8:35 A.M., AP reported that Romney had announced that he had asked for troops, that the government had agreed to send them, and that he had withdrawn the request "because of the situation in the rest of the country," an apparent reference to minor disturbances in other cities.[14]

Johnson considered Romney's implication, that federal troops might be needed elsewhere in the country, irresponsible and provocative, and part of a partisan political strategy to blame the riots on him. Gerald Ford, who was also from Michigan, had been touting this line, and the Republican Coordinating Committee issued a statement that very day, charging that "[W]idespread rioting and violent civil disorders have grown to a national crisis since the present Administration took office."

Johnson could have ignored Romney's vacillation and political maneuvering. He had the constitutional and legal authority to deploy troops. He had only to determine that the situation was out of control, order the rioters to disperse, and if they did not, send in troops. But the recent occasions on which a president had acted unilaterally had been to enforce federal court orders that state authorities had defied: Eisenhower to desegregate the schools in Little Rock, Arkansas, and Kennedy to open the way for James Meredith's admission to the University of Mississippi. Those were quite different situations. Moreover, Johnson did not like to use military troops in domestic disorders. He believed that local and state authorities should maintain order. He couldn't stand the thought of American soldiers killing American civilians.

Instead, Johnson and Fortas set in motion a strategy that would require Romney to comply meticulously with two federal statutes they considered tailored to the situation. One permitted the President to deploy armed forces "upon the request . . . of its [a state's] governor" to suppress "an insurrection." The other permitted deployment of troops "to suppress . . . domestic violence" that deprived persons of their constitutional rights, where "the constituted authorities of that State are unable . . . to protect" those rights.

Romney was reluctant to "request" the President to deploy troops and he refused to admit that he was "unable" to maintain order in Detroit. Johnson insisted on a written request. Finally, Romney sent a telegram to the President, "I hereby officially request the immediate deployment of federal troops. . . . There is reasonable doubt that we can suppress the existing looting, arson and sniping without the assistance of federal troops."[15]

Johnson responded within minutes to what he termed Romney's "official request" by dispatching troops to Selfridge Air Force Base near Detroit. But in his telegram to the Michigan Governor, the President made it clear that the troops would be available to "assist local and state police and the 8000 *Michigan* National Guardsmen under your command" and that he was acting *"on the basis of your representation that there is reasonable doubt that you can* maintain law and order in Detroit." LBJ added the italicized words himself.[16] Desperate for his own eyes and ears on the scene, Johnson dispatched Cyrus Vance, who had left the Pentagon to return to private law practice, and several government officials to Detroit to assess the situation before deciding whether to put Army soldiers on the city's streets.

In a subsequent wire to Clark, Romney said, "Time could be of the essence. There is no evidence that any organized state of insurrection presently exists against the government here; there is also no evidence that it does not. We cannot state unequivocally that the situation will not soon be contained; we most emphatically cannot say it will be under existing circumstances." But, Romney noted, "In 1943 the failure to supply federal troops at the critical period in Detraoit [sic] caused a great deal of unnecessary bloodshed."[17] Romney's maddeningly vague analysis and pointed reference to the cost of delay in 1943 convinced Johnson that he was being set up. The President sent me to get *New York Times* reports of the 1943 Detroit race riots, to see how Roosevelt had handled the deployment of troops then.

That evening, at the weekly Democratic congressional leadership meeting, Johnson reviewed his tax bill and his proposed reorganization of the D.C. government, which he hoped would help "relieve in the Nation's capital" the kinds of tensions which set off riots in other cities, but his preoccupation was with the situation in Detroit.

The President read a UPI ticker aloud: "Republican Party leaders called big city rioting a national crisis today. They demanded a full investigation by Congress and more forceful action by President Johnson." The Republican report, seeking to lay the rioting at LBJ's feet, asserted there had been organized planning behind the riots, and urged the President to support the antiriot bill. By now, Johnson was certain that the Republicans had set a political trap. He told the Democratic leaders around the cabinet table, "Local order is a local proposition. . . . The FBI has found no evidence of outside intervention . . ." and "no shred of evidence" of Communist participation. He added that he was trying to do something about the situation with his Great Society programs, but "Congress spends millions of dollars worrying about little calves, but not about little kids."[18]

Though he didn't mention it during the meeting, LBJ was stung that Eisenhower had endorsed the Republican statement. He told me to let General Andrew Goodpaster, a key channel to Ike, know what the President was doing and ask whether the former president understood how partisan the statement was. Goodpaster eventually replied that Ike had not meant to criticize President Johnson for causing disturbances and the "only thing General Eisenhower could suggest was that the President might like to appoint a high level commission to look at this thing right away."[19]

After the meeting, Johnson came to my office to join Fortas, McNamara, Army Chief of Staff Harold Johnson, Clark, and Army Secretary Stan Resor. He took Fortas, McNamara, Clark, and me to the White House pool for a quick swim, and then back to the Oval Office. At 9 P.M. we all went to dinner, joined by J. Edgar Hoover, Secretary Resor, General Johnson, and White House press secretary George Christian. We were interrupted repeatedly by reports on Detroit.[20]

We returned to the Oval Office, and at around 10 P.M. Vance called to recommend, with Romney's concurrence, that the President federalize the Michigan Guard and send Army troops into Detroit. The President put him on the speaker phone. As Vance described the situation, we all asked lots of questions. LBJ was the most skeptical. He challenged Vance's assessment. Vance told him bluntly that the situation was growing more serious by the minute. When General John Throckmorton, who was accompanying Vance, explained how he planned to deal with the riot, Johnson said he didn't want troops to carry any ammunition. "We can't do that," Throckmorton insisted strenuously. Johnson backed down somewhat: he would let them carry ammunition, but he did not want their guns to be loaded except on the orders of a regular Army officer on the scene. And then he noted sadly, "Well, I guess it is just a matter of minutes before federal troops start shooting women and children."

The President asked whether the Michigan Guard could be assigned to deal with the sniping incidents and federal troops kept out
of situations where they might have to shoot. "I'm concerned,"
Johnson said, "about the charge that we cannot kill enough people in
Vietnam so we go out and shoot civilians in Detroit." Throckmorton's
reassurance that "We will only shoot under the most severe provo-
cations" did not satisfy him.

Johnson also reminded everyone that by federalizing the Guard,
he would be responsible for its conduct. Newark had taught him that
the National Guard could do more harm than good in racial disturbances, first, because it was almost entirely white (blacks at that time
were a tiny 1.15 percent of the Guard nationwide, a factor that increased tensions when they entered black ghettos to restore order)
and, second, because guardsmen were poorly trained for riot control.[21]

Johnson directed Vance to make one final plea to the rioters for
law and order. He asked whether helicopters could drop leaflets urging them to calm down before troops were sent in. There wasn't time
enough for that, he was told. So the President asked that loudspeakers
be used in all riot areas for a last-minute appeal.

Hoover challenged the President on any delay. "They've lost all
control in Detroit, and Harlem will break loose in thirty minutes," he
said. "They plan to tear it to pieces."

Johnson, who had been standing, leaning over the speaker phone
on his desk, slumped to his chair and signed the proclamation ordering the rioters to disburse and setting the stage to send in the troops.
He moved to the green den to review a statement Fortas had been
drafting for television that evening.

The statement was a product of Abe Fortas *presidential con-
siglieri*, not Abe Fortas *presidential counselor*. The President wanted
to stick it to Romney, and Fortas was encouraging him. The seven-
minute statement mentioned Romney fourteen times, spelled out to
the minute when the President received Romney's wire (10:56 A.M.)
and when he responded (11:02 A.M.), emphasized the "undisputed
evidence that Governor Romney of Michigan and the local officials in
Detroit have been unable to bring the situation under control . . . law
and order have broken down in Detroit, Michigan. . . . The Federal
government in the circumstances here presented had no alternative
but to respond, since it was called upon by the Governor of the State
and since it was presented with proof of his inability to restore order
in Michigan."

I suggested that the statement read like a partisan attack. Johnson
didn't buy that. The Republicans were trying to blame him, and he

wanted it understood it was Romney who couldn't keep order. Fortas
sided with the President. McPherson came in. Fortas asked him if it
was too tough. McPherson thought Fortas and the President were
talking about the statement's condemnation of the rioters, so he answered, "No."[22]

The statement went out as Fortas had drafted it. Johnson signed
the executive order to move the troops into Detroit. We raced over
to the theater on the first floor of the East Wing, and the President
read the statement on all three television networks, with Hoover,
Clark, McNamara, Secretary Resor, and General Johnson standing
behind him.[23]

Early the next morning, CBS President Frank Stanton called me
to critique the President's performance. Obviously, Stanton began,
the President had to send in the troops and it is a nasty situation,
but "the television side of the job was not well handled." Stanton
thought the "[eye]glasses and lighting were bad. It was a mistake to
have McNamara, Clark, and the others stand behind him. They look
like props." Then Stanton turned to the text of the statement. "It was
unnecessary to needle Romney . . . [with the governor's] failure to
control the situation . . . [using the times] 11:02 and 10:56 was
beneath the office of the President."[24] I reported Stanton's remarks to
LBJ; I'm sure he believed that I had prompted some of them. He said
curtly, "I had the best damn constitutional lawyer in the country
write that statement."

I passed along one other comment. Martin Luther King had
wired his dismay at the "blind revolt against the revolting conditions
which you so courageously set out to remedy as you entered office."
King thought the President should offer a program to create a job for
everyone, black and white, in the cities.[25] Johnson told me to call King
and tell him we were preparing such a program, but that King should
work harder to get Congress to pass his legislation already on Capitol
Hill.

The riots in Newark and Detroit heightened concern at the White
House that subversives might be encouraging, or at least exploiting,
the violence. Hoover's FBI and other intelligence sources fed the
President reports of Communist involvement, rumors of Chinese
Communist funding, and ominous predictions of even more dreadful
disturbances to come.[26] Militants, like Rap Brown and Stokely Carmichael, preaching a message of hate and violence against the white
establishment, were gaining influence among young black men, playing on the despair of their ghetto life.

The President would read Hoover's reports and mutter about

Communist support of black radicals, but he was more afraid of a white backlash in Congress and across the nation. A white majority, shaken and repelled by black violence, would be increasingly reluctant to be just, much less generous, to poor blacks, and this attitude augured serious trouble for the Great Society.

In this atmosphere of anger, resentment, and suspicion, the President, on July 27, decided to establish the National Advisory Commission on Civil Disorders.[27] He wanted to announce the commission in a nationwide television address that evening, a few hours after he had decided to establish it and before the rioting in Detroit had ended. At the same time, he wanted to proclaim the following Sunday, July 30, a national day of prayer for reconciliation. I expressed reservations about the whole idea because I feared the press reaction would be: "The cities are aflame, the country's coming apart, LBJ can't get a tax bill, so what does he do? Set up a commission and say a prayer." Moreover, the President planned to load the commission with liberals who wanted more money spent on Great Society programs than the President was asking—and he was asking more than the Congress was prepared to give. To me the commission had the potential to be a political Frankenstein's monster and it was almost inevitable that Lyndon Johnson would sour on his hasty creation.

But he brushed aside my concerns. He wanted this commission to help whites understand the plight of black ghetto dwellers and help assure blacks that he was working to alleviate their plight. He also wished to preempt congressional investigations he feared would inflame the situation and castigate him—from the right, for pandering to the rioters, and from the left, for not doing enough.

For the commission's membership, Johnson chose a group that he thought would understand the plight of blacks and speak out boldly, including Republican Senator Edward Brooke of Massachusetts, a black; Roy Wilkins; and, as vice-chairman, New York City Mayor John Lindsay. At the same time he wanted the commission to acclaim his accomplishments and promote his legislative agenda. Getting the kind of report he wanted meant he had to control the commission. For this, he chose Illinois Governor Otto Kerner, a Democrat, as chairman. His choice was ostensibly based on Kerner's experience as a former U.S. Attorney and National Guard general. Privately, though, Johnson knew that Kerner longed for a federal judgeship, and the President suspected Kerner was such a loyal Democrat that in the early-morning hours of November 9, 1960 he had helped assure that John Kennedy had the votes he needed to carry the state and win the presidency. Johnson expected Kerner to perform no less a service for him.* For insurance, LBJ called his trusted kitchen cabinet adviser David Ginsburg, who was embarking on his first family vacation in years, back from Seattle to be the commission's staff director.

In announcing the commission, Johnson tried to navigate the mine-filled waters of the right and left. He condemned rioters and urged that they be punished, but, he warned, "It would compound the tragedy . . . if we should settle for order that is imposed by the muzzle of a gun. . . . The only genuine, long-range solution for what has happened lies in an attack—mounted at every level—upon the conditions that breed despair and violence." He chastised those in Congress "who would have us turn back" and who had ridiculed his bill to exterminate rats in city ghetto slums.

Two days later, in meeting with the commissioners, the President asked for a penetrating analysis of the riots, examining everything from police training and subversive involvement to such root causes as unstable families, joblessness, lousy education, and dilapidated housing. In an exuberant charge he said, "Let your search be free, untrammelled by what has been called the 'conventional wisdom.' As best you can, find the truth, the whole truth and express it in your report."

By the next day, when order was finally restored in Detroit, 40 people were dead, more than 2,000 injured, 5,000 arrested, and 5,000 left homeless. The only solace for the President was in the conduct of the troops he had dispatched. As he said privately, "None of you will ever know how it feels to send federal troops into the cities until you yourself send them in. It makes chill bumps to think of the possibility of the National Guard shooting citizens and citizens shooting back at them. I think it is a tribute to General Throckmorton that no soldier has been shot. No citizen has been killed as a result of the regular forces which are in Detroit."†[28]

There was widespread editorial criticism of the President's comments about Romney. Johnson went on the offensive to prove that it was the Governor who had played politics and the President who had acted prudently. The White House leaked a chronology of events, Attorney General Clark released a statement and backgrounded the press, and the President publicly defended his performance. Romney

---

* LBJ nominated Kerner for a seat on the U.S. Court of Appeals for the 7th Circuit in March 1968 and he was promptly confirmed. Johnson believed that the Nixon administration's indictment of Kerner in 1971 for conspiracy, bribery, perjury, mail fraud, and income-tax evasion was Richard Nixon's way of getting even with the man who Nixon believed helped steal the 1960 election for Kennedy. Kerner was convicted on February 19, 1973, shortly after LBJ died.

† Unfortunately, one person later died as a result of action by regular forces.

tried to respond. He held a press conference and backgrounder, but he quickly lost the public ground to the White House. On August 2, to the President's delight, one syndicated columnist wrote, "Five nationally prominent GOP politicians and four powerful Democratic officials have told me they believe that Gov. George Romney's presidential prospects were cremated last week in the flames of Detroit."[29]

Romney would try once more, in early September, to reconstruct events in his favor. On September 12, Johnson had a reluctant Attorney General land on the Michigan Governor again. Clark issued a short statement, which Johnson had virtually dictated: "Again, with great reluctance, I find it necessary to answer Governor Romney's grossly distorted account of events on the morning of July 24, 1967. Understanding the great stress a public official is under at such a time and having been involved on behalf of the federal government in many of our more serious civil disturbances of recent years, I would not criticize Governor Romney for his indecision if he did not persist in his distortions." Clark then flatly contradicted Romney's account of events.[30]

But there was tension within the administration. Like much of America, many cabinet members were frustrated and angry about the violence; their patience with the President's policy of restraint was reaching the breaking point. There were acrimonious exchanges at an August 2, 1967, cabinet meeting. Ramsey Clark reported that relatively few blacks were involved in the summer's riots and urged administration restraint in responding to the violence. The Vice President immediately interjected, "But there are fifty-two cities potentially about to explode." When Clark said that he had no evidence of a conspiracy since, of those arrested, very few had crossed state lines, HEW Secretary John Gardner challenged both his logic and his numbers.

Rusk expressed concern about Stokely Carmichael, who was reported to be threatening the lives of the President, Rusk, and McNamara, and Rap Brown, who was reputed to be inciting riots. He thought there must be some legal way to "take care of them." Clark said he didn't have a case against either. Humphrey said impatiently that the mayors wanted to know "why we cannot do something." Fowler, normally calm and extremely cordial, and a lawyer himself, was infuriated with Clark: "It is incredible to think you can't make a case."

The President read from letters saying that moderate blacks like Roy Wilkins weren't "voices of the ghetto" and wondered whether he should meet with some militants. UN Ambassador Goldberg thought not, noting that young radicals in the labor movement had scared

Roosevelt's administration, but, except for Walter Reuther, they have fallen into obscurity over time and "vanished down the drain." As Goldberg argued that "solutions do not come from nightsticks," the President shifted the cabinet discussion to other matters. After the meeting, however, the President expressed his disappointment with Clark: "If I had ever known that he didn't measure up to his daddy, I'd never have made him Attorney General."[31]

As if the situation in Detroit had not damaged his political ambitions enough, Romney had a more disastrous collision with the White House a few weeks later. Romney had visited South Vietnam in 1965, and had stated publicly that he believed American involvement there "was morally right and necessary."

In a television interview on September 4, 1967, Romney reversed field: "I no longer believe that it was necessary for us to get involved in South Vietnam to stop Communist aggression . . . it was tragic that we became involved in the conflict there." When the interviewer reminded him of his earlier statement, Romney replied, "I just had the greatest brainwashing that anyone can get when you go over to Vietnam, not only by the generals, but also by the diplomatic corps over there, and they do a very thorough job."

When this exchange came over the wire services, John Roche, a Brandeis professor and former chairman of the Americans for Democratic Action, who was LBJ's resident intellectual, and who was yearning to be part of the political fray, urged the President to let Romney have both barrels. The next morning, when Johnson saw the *New York Times* headline—"Romney Asserts He Underwent 'Brainwashing' on Vietnam Trip"—he had another idea. He told Democratic Chairman John Bailey to ask Romney to apologize for "insult[ing] the integrity of two dedicated and honorable men," General William Westmoreland and Republican Ambassador Henry Cabot Lodge, who had briefed Romney on his 1965 trip to South Vietnam.

And then the next day LBJ lined up some governors who had been with Romney on the 1965 trip. Philip Hoff of Vermont found Romney's statements "incredible"; former governor of Georgia Carl Sanders said Romney "may have gone off into a corner somewhere and been brainwashed privately but I don't know anything about it"; John Burns of Hawaii stated, "No attempt was made at any time to control what we said or asked." And former Oklahoma governor Henry Bellmon, chairman of the Nixon for President organization in Washington, said no "effort was being made at 'brainwashing.' The Governors were given every opportunity to raise questions and . . . the answers . . . given were full and factual."

Johnson was having so much fun that he read excerpts from the governors' statements aloud as he relaxed at the ranch on September 7 and 8.[32] When a reporter asked George Christian about Romney's brainwashing charge, the press secretary, at Johnson's direction, replied that the White House had "no reaction."

The summer riots riveted Johnson's attention on the young blacks who lashed out in self-destructive frenzy. He reached for something that would give them work and hope. Congress had passed President Harry Truman's full-employment act in 1946. It promised Americans jobs but had contained no program to provide them. Johnson had all along seen much of the Great Society—his expansionary economic policy, education and vocational training programs, community health centers, the war on poverty, the 1964 Civil Rights Act—as devoted to fulfilling that promise. Still the problem of the urban hard-core unemployed remained. LBJ had set the government off on a determined search for a program that would provide "real jobs, not make-work stuff," so these unemployed, largely black youths from single- or no-parent families could gain self-respect.

Initially, OEO Director Shriver and some others favored a public-works program to provide several hundred thousand jobs, financed by a new tax on something (gasoline was the preferred target).[33] LBJ rejected the idea. We can't get any taxes, he argued; public-jobs programs take too long to mount; we need jobs now; I want to immerse business in the problems of the urban unemployed and get some "ghetto grime under those highly polished executive fingernails."

Evidence was accumulating that training by employers was the most likely technique to get and keep someone working, far outstripping vocational training programs and the Job Corps. This led to creation of JOBS (Job Opportunities in the Business Sector) and NAB (National Alliance of Businessmen). NAB, a voluntary organization, was designed to get the nation's corporations to pledge to hire and train hard-core unemployed. The government would defray most extraordinary training costs, including health services, teaching reading and writing, and counseling in basic work and life skills. Aiming the program at the nation's fifty largest cities, Johnson's dream, as always, was ambitious. He wanted 100,000 men and women on the job by June 1969; two years later, 500,000—the sum total of the nation's hard-core unemployed. Johnson also hoped to put 200,000 poor high school students to work in those same cities in the summer of 1968.

We had begun with a pilot program in five American cities in

October 1967, and it showed early promise. My enthusiasm almost derailed it when I sent the President a memo suggesting that the White House announce a new manufacturing plant planned by Avco in Boston to hire and train the hard-core unemployed. I thought it would be a great example for blue-chip corporations in other cities. Johnson's handwritten reaction was a cold reminder of his anxiety about the Kennedys: "Let's keep these small items out of WH & particularly Boston."[34]

By the end of the year, business had demonstrated a willingness to tackle the hard-core unemployed[35]—both to do its share and to get needed workers. Unemployment was down and still declining, so training these unemployed was worth the effort for many corporations. By early January 1968, Johnson saw this opportunity clearly and he energetically promoted the formation of JOBS and NAB.

With a little nudging, Henry Ford II, chairman of the Ford Motor Company, agreed to chair NAB. That settled, Johnson wanted a southern businessman for vice chair. At around 6:30 P.M. on January 22, the President told me he had decided on J. Paul Austin, president of the Coca-Cola Company in Atlanta, Georgia.[36] He wanted Austin aboard that evening so he could announce the team the next morning, to coincide with a special message to Congress, "To Earn a Living: The Right of Every American."

When I called Austin's office, I found that he was ill at home. Johnson told me to phone him there. I spoke to his wife, Jeanne, who politely but firmly refused to awaken her husband. When I reported to the President, he snapped back that Austin had married one of the company's secretaries some years back, so certainly his wife could take dictation. Call her back, he said, tell her that the President wants her husband to be vice chairman of the most important program to create jobs in the ghetto and save the cities of this country from being burned to the ground. Ask her, can't she just type that up, with a box marked "yes" and ask him to check it, or just nod his head.

I reminded the President that she thought her husband was pretty sick.

Just do it, Johnson shot back; nobody's that sick. He hung up. Then the POTUS line immediately rang again: You stay on the line until you get an answer, he ordered.

I called Austin's wife and insisted that she take the message and get an answer from her husband. She was a little annoyed and so worried about his health that I didn't try to remain on the phone.

The President called me shortly before 9 P.M. to ask whether Austin was lined up.[37] I told him I expected to hear during the evening. He gave me hell for not staying on the line and told me to call again, "Now!"

I called and got through to Austin. Hoarse, and weak with a severe flu, he agreed to serve, which I reported with great relief to the President shortly before midnight.[38] The relief was not so much for myself but for Austin. I knew LBJ would have called him if he had given me any other answer.

The first NAB executive committee was a blue-ribbon group of businessmen, personally selected by the President. He had them to lunch in the living quarters of the White House on Saturday, January 27. A superb meal was served—special New York cut steak, fine wine, extra-rich ice cream. We had prepared some talking points, which were released to the press, but the presentation was pure Johnson. Jabbing and gesturing with his hands and arms, his face expressive of grit and excitement, Johnson challenged these fifteen titans of industry—including Henry Ford, Paul Austin, and the chief executives of Mobil Oil, Safeway Stores, International Telephone & Telegraph, and Aluminum Company of America:

> We've looked at every kind of job program—government manpower training programs, the Job Corps, vocational training and retraining programs. And we've found the one that works best. What works best is what you do best: on-the-job training. Unemployment is down to 3.7 percent. We're faced with the hard core unemployed. You all are going to have to teach them how to wash and stay clean, how to read, how to write. All the things everyone around this table got from their mommies and daddies. Only these people don't have mommies and daddies who give a damn about them. Or if they do, those mommies and daddies can't read or don't know how to help them.
>
> So you're going to have to wake them up in the morning, because they've never had anything worth getting up for before. Then you're going to have to scrub them. Then you're going to have to teach them real basics: reading, writing, arithmetic. Then you're going have to train them to work in your companies. Then you're going to put them to work in your factories and stores and offices.

Johnson looked slowly around the table, half preacher, half tough guy, roaming back and forth across the line between exhortation and threat:

> This is no bullshit meeting. We're going to have assignments and commitments for you to deliver on. Henry

Ford has committed to chair this program. Paul Austin has committed to be vice-chairman. They've committed to provide executives from their companies to help out.

As the President paused, one of the executives said, "This is a tough job, Mr. President."

Johnson turned to him and said, "I didn't invite you here to tell me how tough a job this is. I invited you here to get the job done. You are the only ones in the world who can do it." Then, turning again to the entire group around the table, Johnson continued:

> This economy has been so good to you that you can afford to give a little back. You can put these people to work and you won't have a revolution because they've been left out. If they're working, they won't be throwing bombs in your homes and plants. Keep them busy and they won't have time to burn your cars. And you'll be doing something as important for your country as the platoons of Marines are doing in Vietnam.
>
> Each of you will be a chairman in your city. I want each of you to commit to meet the goals we set. We're going to put people to work that never thought they could work and never wanted to work. We'll get you some Federal money to help pay the extra costs of teaching and training, but I can't do it alone. I need you, each of you. I need your commitment to make taxpayers out of these taxeaters.

At this point, James McDonnell, chairman of the aerospace corporation McDonnell-Douglas, excitedly blurted out, "I commit! Mr. President, I commit!"

Johnson looked down the side of the table at him, leaned on his elbow, stared at McDonnell, and in a penetrating Texas whisper, said, "Mr. McDonnell, you committed when you ate the first bite of my steak."[39]

The laughter broke the tension, and the National Alliance of Businessmen went to work. With the President persistently prodding NAB director Leo Beebe, a Ford executive deputized to full-time work on the project, and the White House staff,[40] by December 1, 1968— six months ahead of schedule—100,000 hard-core unemployed had been taught, trained, and put to work in cities across America, and the job-retention rate was almost 75 percent.*

* By 1991, the National Alliance of Business (the group dropped "men" from its title) had three thousand companies as members and had trained and employed hundreds of thousands of unemployed men and women.

FOURTEEN

Arm Twisting for the Nation's Capital

EVEN BEFORE the disturbance in Watts during the summer of 1965, LBJ was worried about racial violence in the nation's capital. The riots in Los Angeles, the disturbances in other cities, and then the awful destruction of people and property in Newark and Detroit moved the situation in the District of Columbia to the front of Johnson's concerns. From his election in 1964 he had sought self-government for the District; in the summer of 1967 he was determined at least to set the stage for it.

By the time Lyndon Johnson became President, he had lived in Washington, D.C., almost all his adult life; he was as much a Washingtonian as any resident of the nation's capital. While the press caricatured him as a big-handed, big-nosed, big-eared, larger-than-life, tall Texan—and he indeed loved the state of his birth and youth*—it was Washington where he and Lady Bird lived day to day. Texas was where they spent weekends and holidays. So it's not surprising that both Johnsons wanted to do something for the residents of the

---

* Johnson saw that Texas was taken care of. He made sure federal money was provided to fund the medical center in Houston, had me monitor research grants that the National Science Foundation, National Institutes of Health, and Atomic Energy Commission awarded to the University of Texas to make it "the Harvard of the West," and had me scour the government for grants and contracts for Southwest Texas State College in San Marcos (where he had gone to school). He ordered me to "go after all the *grants* that merit can justify. You are my man on this and defense placements [in Texas]." And he got Texas-based Braniff Airlines to offer nonstop flights between Austin and Washington, D.C.[1]

227

nation's capital. Lady Bird would leave a stunning legacy of floral beautification along the Potomac, the Mall, and throughout the parks. LBJ's legacy to the District of Columbia, as might be expected, was political. *

The Constitution gives Congress the power "to exercise exclusive legislation in all cases whatsoever, over . . . [the] District." The framers assumed that Congress would use that power only to protect the federal government's interests and would permit the District's residents to manage their own affairs. Indeed, after the federal government set up in Washington in 1800 residents enjoyed various forms of self-government for more than seventy years, even electing their own mayor from 1820 until 1871.

But when slavery was abolished, thousands of blacks migrated to the nation's capital and Congress temporarily suspended home rule in 1874. That "temporary" suspension was still in effect in 1965 when Lyndon Johnson decided to take home rule beyond the rhetoric of his predecessors.

Starting with Harry Truman, three presidents had routinely asked Congress for home rule for the District and, on five occasions, the Senate voted to grant it while the House failed to act. In February 1965, when Johnson asked for home rule, everyone anticipated that once again the Senate would respond favorably and the bill would die in the House District of Columbia Committee, which was dominated by conservative southern Democrats. A hundred years after the Civil War, these southern Democrats had picked up plenty of Republican allies, for the District of Lyndon Johnson's time was overwhelmingly Democratic and liberal.

As expected, the Senate passed Johnson's legislation with only minor amendments in July 1965.† Then two events led LBJ, bolstered by an almost religious faith in the right to vote, to turn D.C. home rule into a crusade: passage of the Voting Rights Act and the Watts riots, which sharpened the President's concern that the poverty of predominately black Washington was fertile soil for violent outburst.

A week and a half after the eruption in Watts, Johnson warned:

---

* In addition to reforming the government, Johnson pressed Congress to approve the Kennedy Center for the Performing Arts, a permanent Pennsylvania Avenue commission to renovate the Capital's main thoroughfare, the Woodrow Wilson Center for Scholars as a living memorial to the former president, the Hirshhorn Museum and Sculpture Garden, an international center for foreign chanceries in Northwest Washington (completed in 1991), and an attractive visitors center with shops and restaurants at Union Station (completed in 1988).
† Johnson's bill called for election of a mayor, city council, and nonvoting delegate to the House of Representatives, and a congressional appropriation to make up for the taxes the District could not levy on federal property.

. . . .in the District of Columbia . . . the clock is ticking . . . when people feel mistreated and they feel injustices . . . and they have no vote and . . . no voice. . . . Just any adventure, any danger, you can't do much worse than you are doing now. And I asked myself last night, what can I do to see that we don't have any more incidents as occurred in Los Angeles in this country. . . . So, let's act [on home rule] before it is too late.

To sidestep the southern Democrats who controlled the House District Committee, Johnson decided to invoke a rarely used procedure to allow House members to vote on home rule. Normally, a bill can get to the floor only after committees with jurisdiction report it to the full House. But House rules permit a majority of members to move a bill directly to the floor by signing a petition ordering the committee discharged of the bill. Of the prior 818 attempts to discharge a bill, only 23 had succeeded. Johnson pulled out all the stops to defy the historical odds.

The President quietly persuaded two Democratic and two Republican members of the House District Committee to file a discharge petition. Then everyone on the White House staff was set to work gathering signatures of House members. We granted favors—jobs, grants, contracts, social invitations—for them. As his birthday neared on August 27, and we were still fifty-five signatures short, the President told individual members that if they wanted to give him a birthday present they could sign the discharge petition. Finally, one vote short, at 7:45 A.M. on September 3, 1965, Illinois Democrat George Shipley's secretary called the White House Usher's Office to report that her boss was flying in from his district to sign the discharge petition; the usher who received the call notified the President, and Johnson's petition had a majority.[2]

The elation didn't last long. Most observers believed that once the Johnson bill hit the floor of the House it would pass. But the Watts riots, an exhausted Congress, and a shrewd substitute bill, which allowed home rule after a prolonged process, presented a daunting legislative challenge. By mid-September, the President appreciated the uphill battle he faced; on the 14th, he penciled a note to White House aide Marvin Watson: "Let's go to work on each signer of petition. Unless we do we are going to lose—L." As we neared the start of the House debate on September 27, Johnson contacted more members than I believe he ever talked to on a piece of legislation. If a member wanted some special consideration that was not unreasonable, we were to give it.[3] The need to win transcended home rule. A defeat would represent Johnson's first major legislative setback. As

LBJ put it one evening going over a tally sheet, "If they beat us on this one, they'll know they can win. It only takes one for them to see they can cut us and make us bleed. Then they'll bleed us to death on our other legislation." Despite our efforts, the House passed the substitute bill by fifty-nine votes.

A few months after his defeat on home rule, Johnson asked me to work with Louis Martin to put together a plan for the nation's capital. Martin was the godfather of black politics, a well-to-do black newspaper publisher, originally out of Detroit and Chicago but now living in Washington, nominally attached to the Democratic National Committee. The assignment plunged the President, Martin, and me into the racially charged atmosphere of the capital's local politics.

For almost one hundred years, the District had been ruled by a board of three commissioners, one an Army Corps of Engineers officer, all appointed by the President. Walter Tobriner, the board's President, wanted out, and local pressures were mounting to appoint to the board a black more representative of the community than John Duncan, who was regarded as a white man's black.

In May 1966, Martin and I recommended that the President replace Tobriner with Walter Washington, a black who was then the National Capital Planning Authority's executive director, and Duncan with John Hechinger, president of a family-owned chain of Washington hardware and home-fixture stores. Katharine Graham, president of *The Washington Post*, and Russ Wiggins, its executive editor, both of whom cared about the District and were deeply involved in local politics, gave the two candidates high marks.[4]

Johnson also sought advice about our proposal from James Rowe, a Washington lawyer and Roosevelt New Dealer experienced in local D.C. politics. Rowe did not believe the District "is immediately ready for a Negro" president of the Board of Commissioners, especially since that was the commissioner usually in charge of the police. "If for national political reasons the President feels he must name a Negro [president]," Rowe wrote, "I wonder if it would not be possible to announce both appointments at the same time, allocating the police to the white Commissioner."[5] Graham and Wiggins expressed similar sentiments to me because they feared the business community's reaction, and white flight from the District.

The police issue was so sensitive that by mid-June Louis Martin was suggesting that the President first place Walter Washington in Duncan's number-two slot, where Washington would pick up Duncan's duties. A few months later, Johnson could replace Tobriner with a white man, and make Washington President, retaining the same duties he had already assumed. That would leave Tobriner's white replacement with responsibility for the police. Martin thought he had Walter Washington aboard when the three of us met with LBJ. Washington told Johnson that "in this climate it wouldn't help you and it wouldn't help me, unless I got the top job and responsibility for the police and firemen." Caught by surprise, Johnson refused to give Washington the top job, and sent me back to produce a new proposal.[6]

On October 3, 1966, at Johnson's direction, Harry McPherson and I had lunch with Kay Graham and *Washington Post* managing editor Ben Bradlee to discuss the D.C. situation. They both preferred a white commissioner as president of the Board of Commissioners and suggested criminal lawyer Edward Bennett Williams, Nelson Rockefeller (if he lost reelection as governor of New York), former New York Governor Averell Harriman, former Secretary of State Dean Acheson, or Sargent Shriver. They had no strong preference for any particular black but thought Duncan should go. The following week, Mrs. Graham called me and told me that "Williams is very interested in the D.C. government. He would undoubtedly accept the post as the top D.C. Commissioner if it were offered to him."[7] Then Johnson decided to hold off any new appointments until I could see whether there was some way to reorganize the District government to offer residents a greater measure of self-determination.

In early 1967, LBJ approved my recommendation to change the structure of District government to set the stage for home rule. Using the presidential reorganization authority, Johnson decided to establish a mayor and city council, appointed by the President with the advice and consent of the Senate. A presidential reorganization plan would go not to the House District Committee, which vehemently opposed home rule, but rather to the House and Senate Government Operations committees, which were likely to be hospitable. Moreover, such a plan became effective after sixty days unless either house voted to disapprove it.

The President orchestrated three months of head counting and recounting of House and Senate committee members before he was satisfied that we could muster a majority. To ease the way on Capitol Hill, LBJ reshaped the plan to call the mayor "commissioner" and the deputy mayor "assistant commissioner," and to require that only one of the two be a District resident.[8] He wasn't taking any chances of another defeat.

By the time Johnson sent the plan up on June 1, 1967, he had the firm support of *The Washington Post* and key District residents and organizations, white and black. The *Post* was particularly important

because we expected House District Committee Chairman John Mc-
Millan (D-S.C.) to try to defeat the plan. This time Johnson would be
ready. We leaked information about certain of McMillan's dealings:
how he had helped an insurance broker who had bought him a Cad-
illac, the pressure he had put on the District not to revoke the license
of an auto dealer who had given his son a car, and his financial
involvement with tobacco interests whose District taxes he kept down.
The *Post* ran a strong editorial criticizing these dealings, as well as
McMillan's ties to District liquor, parking, and real-estate interests.
LBJ thought the editorial was a strong enough shot across the bow to
moderate McMillan's opposition.[9] It worked; the Chairman opposed
the reorganization plan, but temperately.

In early August, Johnson's reorganization plan took effect. LBJ
was immediately impatient to bring the best people into the new
District government, as we embarked upon a talent hunt driven personally by him.

In the early search for the mayor—with the plan in place Johnson
began calling the commissioner "mayor"—Johnson had us focused on
a white. The candidates included Ed Williams, Washington lawyer
Gerhard Gesell (who later became a federal district judge), and a
number from outside the District. Walter Washington, whom John
Lindsay had recruited to be chairman of the New York City Housing
Authority when Johnson did not appoint him to the old Board of
Commissioners, was on the short list for deputy mayor.[10]

Now, as we discussed candidates, it became apparent to me that
LBJ had in his own mind decided to appoint the first black mayor of
a major American city.[11] His apparent focus on a black for the
number-two job was designed to mask what he was really after, in
order to avoid any leaks that might draw opposition from members of
Congress and white District businessmen. He also wanted support
from *The Washington Post*, whose president, Katharine Graham, was
still pushing for Williams. As LBJ neared his decision, he decided
against Williams, "He's white and I want a Negro. He doesn't have
any experience in running cities. And he's been representing Bobby
Baker,* who needs him more than I do—and I don't want to be
accused of rewarding him for that."

With an enthusiastic nudge from Lady Bird, on Monday evening,
August 21, the President invited Walter Washington to come to the
White House the next day to talk about the mayor's job. On the 7

---

* Baker had been a top Senate aide to Majority Leader Lyndon Johnson. His conviction for income-tax evasion, theft, and conspiracy to defraud the federal government was on appeal.

A.M. air shuttle from New York the following morning, Washington bumped into his boss, John Lindsay, who was going to a meeting of the Kerner commission on civil disorders. Lindsay asked why his housing chairman was on the shuttle and Washington told him.

When he landed in the capital, Lindsay called me at home, enraged that the President had sought out Washington for the D.C. job. The New York Mayor had just lost two top members of his cabinet and was angered about stories that his administration was coming apart. He argued that chairing the New York City Housing Authority was more important than being mayor of the nation's capital. He demanded a meeting with the President.

When Walter Washington arrived at the White House,[12] the President offered and Washington immediately accepted. A few minutes later, the President met with Lindsay.[13] Lindsay said he would resign from the Kerner commission if Johnson appointed Washington. The President, calm, knowing he had Washington, told Lindsay that he was simply offering the mayor's job. "It's up to Washington to make a decision. The job is his if he wants it."

The President took me aside to suggest that Washington and I talk to Lindsay "to calm him down and ease the transition." Washington told Lindsay he wanted to be released from his New York post. Lindsay replied that he would not talk to Washington with me in the room. When I offered to leave, Lindsay said he would not talk to Washington except in the mayor's office in New York. That evening Washington wrote to Lindsay resigning the New York post and to LBJ accepting the mayor's job. When the President read Washington's letter, he called me to have him add a sentence, "You have emphasized that it is my decision to make and I appreciate your giving me time to consider your offer."[14]

Late that afternoon I got an urgent call from Ben Bradlee at the *Post*. "I've got reports from the Hill, the District building, and New York public-housing sources that the FBI is checking out Walter Washington." I accused Bradlee of getting the story from Kay Graham, who had been involved in the deliberations and had told the President she would support the appointment of Washington. Bradlee said he was "totally opposed to the *Post*'s involvement." My charge slowed Bradlee down, but of course confirmed his suspicion.

A few minutes later, Bradlee called and said one of Lindsay's aides in New York had told the *Post* Washington was accepting the President's offer: "I'm running with the story."

"If you do, you'll most certainly kill any chance of the Washington appointment," I said.

"That's your problem," he responded.

"It's yours too because Mrs. Graham is deeply into this one," I countered.

Bradlee called a third time. "A *New York Times* reporter is asking *us* for our biographical information on Washington," he said. "I can't let them beat me with my own Goddamn story!" Bradlee's raspy voice was now a little short and sharp. "I'm going hard with this one. It's a done deal."

"You can't run a hard story," I pleaded. By this time I'd had several conversations with the President, who was warning that if there was a leak he wouldn't nominate Washington.

Bradlee read me the first few paragraphs of his story. We argued about the wording. Finally, he softened the lead to say, "Walter E. Washington is now the odds-on choice to be the new Commissioner of the District of Columbia."[15]

That evening I was in the President's bedroom when the bulldog edition of the *Post* arrived. The lead story was on the mayor's job with a big picture of Washington. Johnson tossed the paper at me. Just below Washington's picture was a story blaming me for delaying Senator Joseph Clark's efforts to bring the poverty bill to the Senate floor. The story criticized me for going behind Clark's back to kill his $3 billion job program. "That son of a bitch!" I blurted out, referring to Clark. "He's got one helluva nerve. If his job proposal is hooked to the poverty program on the floor, it'll kill the bill!"

The President, lying against a pillow at the head of his bed, sat upright. "That's the Goddamn trouble around here," he shouted at me. "You don't give a shit what they write about your President. The only thing you care about is what they write about you!"

Uneasy, I tried to smile it off.

But the President was in no laughing mood. "Well, Walter Washington is not the odds-on choice," he said. "Maybe he's the odds-on choice of *The Washington Post*; he's certainly not the odds-on choice of the President."

I suggested that the Washington appointment had gone too far down the line to back away. LBJ said he was not going to appoint someone who couldn't keep his mouth shut. I pointed out that dumping Washington now would aggravate the credibility problem, make it difficult to get the best blacks on the City Council, and, if there ever was a riot in the District, leave the President open to a charge that it might have been better handled if he'd appointed a black mayor. The President complained again about leaks. I countered that the leaks had come from the FBI checks, or Kay Graham, with whom I knew the President had discussed Washington.[16] Johnson said someone would have had to confirm them. I realized he suspected not only Washington but also me.* It was fruitless to argue anymore that evening.

The next morning[17] the President, without mentioning Washington, told me that Thomas Fletcher, a white who had been city manager of San Diego, was his choice for deputy mayor. He wanted to talk to Fletcher that evening. It was Johnson's way of letting me know that he would stay with Washington for the top spot, a decision I have always credited to Lady Bird's pillow talk.

When I went to locate Fletcher, I discovered that he was driving his family across the country, vacationing en route to the capital for another government job. I put an all-points bulletin out on him, with the FBI instructed to mount a manhunt as if they were looking for Public Enemy Number One.

At about eleven that morning, at a traffic light in Rapid City, South Dakota, an FBI agent walked up to Fletcher's car and told him to call the White House immediately. Astonished, Fletcher went to a phone. I asked him how fast he could get to Washington. He said the following Monday. I said we needed him that evening to meet with the President. The FBI got his suit pressed and drove him to Ellsworth Air Force Base near Rapid City, where a jet fighter plane swooped him to Andrews Air Force Base outside Washington. Fletcher was in my office by 7:15 that evening.[18] I told him the President was considering him for the deputy mayor's job and brought him to the Oval Office. The President talked to Fletcher for some time, obviously liked him, and asked where he was staying that evening. When Fletcher said he would check into a hotel, the President said, "Why not stay here?" and gave him a bedroom on the third floor of the mansion.[19] The next morning the Air Force jet flew Fletcher back to Rapid City to pick up his family, twenty-two hours after he had left them.

A week later, on September 6, 1967, the President announced that he would nominate Washington and Fletcher.

The road to constituting the first D.C. City Council had just as many potholes. Picking members of the new City Council was a lesson in the futility of anyone's substituting himself for the electorate. It made the President even more ardent for home rule. We tried to weigh what the voters would have done, yet we were never able to abandon the protection of our own interests. FBI reports on some individuals forced us to make judgments better left to the ballot box. Because Johnson viewed this first council as the door to an elected

---

* As we later learned, it was not Katharine Graham who gave the story to Bradlee, but Ben Gilbert, then metropolitan editor of the *Post* and a close friend of Washington, in whom he had confided.

government in the District, he wanted an impeccable group; individuals were eliminated for marginal infractions.

As the FBI conducted its background checks, those interviewed provided material for a *Washington Post* story that named six candidates LBJ was considering for the City Council. The furor it created drove the President to distraction. He had me admonish Walter Washington about the District government and Hoover about the FBI. Hoover said the leaks were coming from the White House. Actually, the entire town was a whisper factory. As soon as the FBI interviewed people, they picked up the phone to let others know who they'd been questioned about.[20]

"If the only way we can stop leaks is to stop the FBI checks, then do it," Johnson told me. Before naming City Council members, he said, "You get them alone in your office and tell them that I'm going to subject them to the Goddamnedest, most intense FBI investigation ever conducted on anybody. If they ever did anything wrong in their lives, no matter how personal, you've got to know it. Because it will come out in the FBI checks. If they tell you, we'll keep it quiet. But tell them the FBI never will because the Bureau leaks so Goddamn much, and then they'll be publicly embarrassed as they've never been embarrassed before. That's the way to stop these stories in *The Washington Post*."

I interviewed each candidate personally. It was a wrenching experience for some as they felt obliged to reveal intimate aspects of their lives. One admitted that he had a mistress. Another told me of occasional homosexual relationships years before. Others recited even less pertinent personal experiences.

The President announced the new City Council members on September 28, when he swore in Washington and Fletcher as "Mayor" and "Deputy Mayor," for the first time publicly calling them by the titles he had been using privately since the reorganization plan had taken effect. The council majority (5-4) would be black, with a black vice chair and a white chair. The chairman Johnson selected was Max Kampelman, a Washington lawyer and close confidant of the Vice President, the only council member I hadn't interviewed.

The community and newspapers initially hailed the President's selections. But within a week Kampelman became a controversial nominee. He had been a conscientious objector during World War II, something conservative members of the Senate inappropriately related to Vietnam War protestors seeking to disrupt the draft, even though he had volunteered for a civilian starvation-research program. Kampelman was accused of using Bobby Baker to get a charter for a local bank and of inappropriate conduct in representing a client in connection with a government loan. He planned to respond at his confirmation hearing and had prepared a forceful statement. But the circumstances were such—especially when the Republicans decided to make it a party issue—that getting Kampelman confirmed would have been a protracted enterprise with the outcome in doubt.[21] Johnson was not willing to jeopardize his goal of a perfect start for the D.C. Council, especially when the threat came from someone he did not know well and who was one of Humphrey's closest allies. He had me ask Kampelman to withdraw. It was one of my most distasteful and agonizing experiences in the White House. Withdrawal was crushing to this dedicated man, and the Vice President ached with his friend's pain.[22]

But there is no time to lick wounds in any White House; and in Lyndon Johnson's White House there wasn't even time to get a Band-Aid. Once the President decided that Kampelman should withdraw, he wanted to announce the new chairman at the same time. On Tuesday evening, October 10, the day after he decided to drop Kampelman, Johnson settled on Washington businessman John Hechinger in a conversation with me in the Cabinet Room shortly before 9 P.M.[23] When I tried to reach Hechinger, he was at the symphony. About 11 P.M., Johnson called to ask if I'd talked to Hechinger. I told him Steve Pollak, presidential assistant for District Affairs, would meet Hechinger when he arrived home. Johnson said he expected Hechinger to be concerned about conflicts of interest and financial disclosure. He told me to have Deputy Attorney General Warren Christopher get in touch with Hechinger "first thing in the morning. Tell him to sit outside his house in a car and go into the house with him when he comes out to get the morning newspaper," and resolve any conflict problems.

The next morning, as Christopher met with Hechinger at the Justice Department, we checked him out. Hechinger's background was excellent and included an outstanding World War II record in the Air Force.[24] But he was in a dispute with the Internal Revenue Service involving thousands of dollars.

At about 4 P.M., Christopher called to say Hechinger would not take the job. When I reported to the President,[25] he told me to get Hechinger over to see me immediately in a White House car, so that he would have no opportunity to talk to anybody between Christopher's office and mine. I told LBJ that I didn't know whether Hechinger would come. "You get him to," Johnson said as he hung up.

Hechinger arrived in my office about fifteen minutes later.[26] He gave me all the reasons, largely related to his family business and lack of political experience, why he couldn't accept the job.

I argued with Hechinger. I told him that we had gone through an extensive search and he was the man Lyndon Johnson wanted. Throughout this conversation, the President kept calling me on the hotline.[27]

"Is he with you now, Joe?"

"Yes, sir."

"Well, make sure you tell him about how much his family has meant to the District and how much this kind of service is in his family's tradition. That ought to appeal to him."

"Yes, sir."

The phone rang again. "Is he still reluctant to go along with us?"

"Yes, Mr. President."

"Have you told him how important this is to the city? To anyone that cares about this city? Have you told him how good this would be for his business?"

"Yes, Mr. President."

The line went dead. I resumed my conversation with Hechinger. Within minutes, the hotline rang.

"Listen, Joe, pretty soon this fella's gonna say he wants to talk to his wife. When he does, don't leave the room. Just sit there looking right at him while he talks to his wife."

"Yes, sir."

About five minutes later, Hechinger said he wished to call his wife. I handed him the phone on my desk. He picked it up. He obviously expected me to leave the room, or at least move to another part of my office. As the President had "suggested," I didn't budge. At the end of the conversation, Hechinger whispered, "Junnie, I'm slipping. I'm getting the works. I've got to walk out of here right now."

Hechinger turned to me and said, "I have really enjoyed meeting you and I deeply appreciate the President's confidence in me, but—"

The line rang again. "Yes, sir."

"You tell Hechinger that you have no authority to accept no for an answer," the President said. "If he wants to turn down the President of the United States, he's got to come over here and turn him down personally."

"All right, Mr. President."

Hechinger continued. "Joe, as I said—"

I interrupted, "John, look, there's no way that I can take no for an answer. What you'll have to do is tell the President your answer face to face."

The hotline rang again.

"Yes, sir."

"Get him on over here. I've got to go to a meeting."

I turned to Hechinger. "Look, John, why don't we both just go on over to see the President right now. That was the President calling. He's over there waiting for us."

With a shrug, Hechinger walked over to the mansion with me.[28] We went up to the living quarters, where, having gotten up from his nap and showered, the President was getting dressed, putting on his tie. "Mr. President, this is John Hechinger," I said as the President emerged from the bedroom.

The President grabbed Hechinger's hand, and walked him toward the magnificent view from the southwest window of the living room, from which the Washington Monument is visible. Hechinger sighed, "Mr. President, that is a beautiful view."

"Mr. Hechinger," said the President, "it certainly is, and what I'd like to do as President is keep that view beautiful and make this whole city as beautiful as that part of it is. But I can't do it alone. I must have help.

"This past year has brought to all Americans the importance of the city and the terrible trouble we've had in our urban communities. Washington should be a model. I want to do something for Washington which will make the whole country take notice. Mrs. Johnson and I know you can do this job. I don't need a politician. Walter Washington is doing just fine in that area. I need someone who cares about this city and who is an administrator, a businessman, to chair this council. You talk about the District and the cities but now there's an opportunity to *do* something. And you don't have to worry about anyone cutting you up. There are two people in the District who can pick up the phone and talk to me. That's you and Walter Washington." The President turned to me for emphasis, "Do you hear that, Joe?"

"Yes, sir," I replied.

"And there's something else," the President added turning again to face Hechinger as the two men now sat on the couch backed against the window. "I've extracted a pledge from each member of the council that they will work closely with you so that this first pilot government gets off the ground properly and we get full home rule here."

Hechinger was overwhelmed. Johnson glanced down at his folder on the coffee table in front of them. It was stamped "top secret." Johnson looked deep into Hechinger's eyes. "Mr. Hechinger, I know this is a very difficult decision for you." Then he picked up the folder in his hand and continued, "Thank God you don't have to make the decision that I do in a few minutes. You see this folder. I have to go over to a meeting and make some decisions whether to bomb the docks at Haiphong in North Vietnam. I'm trying to fight a war over there, to bring our boys back as fast as I can. I wish I could spend more time on the problems of Washington, but I can't. I don't need you in Vietnam. I need you right here to help me make this city the way it ought to be and the way I want it to be and the way every American wants their capital to be."

"I understand, Mr. President," Hechinger said. Before he could say anything more, the President grabbed his shoulders and almost lifted him up from the couch as he rose to stand and said, "I knew you would, Mr. Hechinger. Thank you. I'm delighted that you're willing to help me and serve as chairman of the City Council."

Hechinger didn't know what had happened. The President pointed him toward the elevator and whispered quietly to me: "Call George. Tell him to get the press in his office, so that they're waiting for you. Then announce this right away before he can change his mind."

Change his mind, I thought. Poor John Hechinger didn't know what his mind was with this presidential rush.

The President continued, whispering: "When you announce him, tell them no questions, just photographs."

The President moved toward the elevator with Hechinger.

I went to the phone in the living room, and with a hand cupped over the receiver, I told George Christian I was on the way with Hechinger, and passed along the President's instructions. I caught up with the President and Hechinger as Johnson turned to him.

"John," the President said, "for some reason Joe wants to make the announcement this afternoon. Why don't you just go on with him over to the West Wing and take care of that and then you and I can get together soon for a long talk about the District and about what's got to be done here. Mrs. Johnson and I look forward to seeing a lot of you and your wife."

With that, the President held his arm, shook his hand, and sent us on our way. Just as we were getting on the elevator, the President casually said to Hechinger, "Oh, by the way. On that tax matter. Joe will have the bill at your house in the morning so you can pay it before noon."

Hechinger was so dazed he just said, "Thank you, Mr. President. Thank you very much."

John Hechinger went down the elevator to the ground floor and walked over to the West Wing. I told him we would step into Christian's office, where we would make a quick announcement and then he could call his wife.

Hechinger said fine, not realizing that the press would be standing there when we entered. As we got to the door, Larry Levinson handed him a bio we planned to distribute the press, asking him to check it quickly in the hallway. He did. It was accurate except for the spelling of his mother's name.

When I opened the door to Christian's office, the press was there. I walked in with Hechinger and Christian announced that Hechinger had agreed to be nominated as chairman of the City Council. When the picture taking was over, we went to my office, where Hechinger immediately reached for the phone to call his wife.

On Friday, October 13, two days after we announced Hechinger, the President met with the D.C. City Council, Mayor, and Deputy Mayor in the Fish Room near the Oval Office. "Now the people of Washington are about as franchised as we can get them," he told them, and continued, ignoring the talking points I'd given him:

> For the moment, it's the best we can do . . . in your hands rests the District's best hope for full home rule. . . .
>
> Now I have a story I want to tell you. They say it's one of Lincoln's favorites. There was this tightrope walker, Blondin. Suppose you could take all your worldly possessions and have them compacted into gold nuggets. You give them to Blondin as he starts to walk across the tightrope above Niagara Falls. He's got everything you own and he's walking across Niagara Falls on a tightrope with all your possessions. Now, would you sit there and say, "Blondin, walk a little faster. Or Blondin, walk a little slower. Or lean a little bit to the left. Or stoop a little more, Blondin. Or bend your knees, Blondin"? No you wouldn't. All you would do is hold your breath, pray like crazy, and if he got to the other side, you'd cheer like hell.

The President paused for effect. "Well, that's the way it's going to be around here. You're going to walk the tightrope on your own. We're going to pray like crazy. And we want to be able to cheer like hell when your work is done. Thank you and God bless you."*[29]

---

* In 1970, Congress passed legislation to give the District a nonvoting delegate to the U.S. House of Representatives, and in 1973, to provide for an elected mayor and city council.

FIFTEEN

The Going Gets Tougher

No one had welcomed LBJ's announcement that he would ask Congress for a tax surcharge. Republican opposition had been anticipated, but it hurt when the two key Democrats, House Ways and Means Committee Chairman Wilbur Mills and Senate Finance Committee Chairman Russell Long, expressed grave reservations about the need for a tax increase and doubted out loud that Congress would pass one. Mills made it clear that his price for any tax increase would be a slash in domestic spending. Coupled with a sluggish economy, such reactions led Johnson to postpone sending his request to Congress.

Throughout the winter and spring of 1967, Johnson's fears about congressional action to trim Great Society programs came to pass. Appropriation requests for model cities and rent supplements were drastically reduced. His economic advisers were divided on when to ask for a tax increase. Johnson himself was concerned about precipitating a recession. In March of 1967 capital investment was projected to be so slow that he asked Congress to restore the investment tax credit. "Every prior president I know has moved too quickly to restrain the economy," he fretted.

On June 7, Johnson called a meeting of his key advisers to discuss a new economic program. Fowler advocated a tax increase to ease tight money and blunt inflationary pressures from a rising budget deficit, which he set for fiscal 1968 at "$23 to $28 billion" without the tax surcharge. This was double the deficit that Johnson had predicted just six months earlier.

The President told them that he "refuse[d] to run a deficit of the magnitude projected." He was prepared to "slash the hell out of domestic programs, if necessary" to avoid that. "I think we need the poverty program. Personally [I'm] all for education, health, and other domestic programs, [but] I've gone as far as I can without increased support for these programs," he said. "The country and the Democratic congressmen in particular will have to choose between the domestic programs and a tax increase. . . . The cabinet and the Congress have to muster more support for these programs or they'll have to be cut back." He asked for tax and expenditure-reduction alternatives, with special attention to the impact on unemployment.[1]

I had never heard Johnson talk that way. I thought he was trying to impress Fowler with his fiscal responsibility and encourage the rest of us to fight harder for the programs and the taxes to preserve them. I sensed he was also expressing his frustration about the uncertainty, the divisions among his advisers, and the lonely fight he was facing with Congress.

On June 12 I reported to him that his advisers were still at odds over the timing of a tax hike. Wirtz and Ginsburg harbored deep reservations about any increase. Johnson wrote back to me in exasperation, "For God's sake get agreement. L."* By June 17, his advisers agreed that he should ask Congress for a tax increase after the July 4 recess. A week later, Ackley suggested that Johnson might have to ask for a larger hike than envisioned because the economy might need more restraint and the war in Southeast Asia might need more funds. From Saigon, McNamara weighed in against a larger tax increase; he did "not recommend an expansion of U.S. forces in Vietnam."[3]

Mills continued to question the need for any increase and stepped up his calls for spending reductions. Despite my pointing out that "It is abundantly clear that [Mills] is anxious to be called down to the White House by you and to be consulted on your economic proposals,"[4] LBJ refused to meet with him.

---

* Johnson perpetually complained that economists could never agree. In 1967, when the Greek military junta arrested Andreas George Papandreou, the young left-wing leader who had chaired the economics department of the University of California at Berkeley (and, in 1981, became Greece's first prime minister), I got calls from academic economists who feared for his life. I sent a note to the President urging him to intervene with the junta to save Papandreou. The President called me: "You can tell them I've told those Greek bastards to lay off that son-of-a-bitch Papandreou—whoever he is." Later, I told the President that every university economist was cheering his intervention. Johnson chuckled and said, "Well, tell all of them that this is the first issue in the history of the Republic on which all American economists seem to agree."[2]

Yet again, Johnson wanted a memo signed by everyone. On July 22, we all initialed a memo recommending a 10 percent income-tax surcharge for corporations and individuals (exempting the lowest income brackets).[5] On July 26, Johnson finally sat down with Mills in the Cabinet Room. Fowler and I were also present, and the four of us, eventually joined by Ackley, McPherson, and Levinson, went over a draft of the President's message. Mills asked Johnson, "Why is the way to get more money raising taxes in '67 when in '64 [you lowered taxes to get more money]?" He urged the President to "get some outside people to study these obsolete programs" and cut them. Johnson responded that he had closed military bases and recommended elimination of numerous obsolete programs, but Congress refused to act. "I've instructed the members of the Cabinet and heads of departments to achieve all the reductions in the cost of their departments they are able to make," Johnson added, "but it doesn't do a damn bit of good if for every dollar we save, the Congress spends two!" Mills helped draft the message, but made it clear he was distancing himself until the President delivered more spending cuts.[6]

Finally on August 3, Johnson sent his tax program to Congress, asking prompt action to head off the "clear and present dangers" of a fiscal 1968 deficit that might top $28 billion.

A $28 billion budget deficit was far larger than anyone had anticipated. Johnson had gotten a long way with his strategy of guns and butter without a tax increase. He had often said that when he asked for more taxes, "All hell will break loose on our domestic program." He was more right than he feared, as reports came in that everything, from elementary and secondary education to the war on poverty to our proposal to fund a public broadcasting system, was in deep trouble. Most members of Congress preferred cuts in spending for the poor (most of whom don't vote and none of whom have excess money to contribute to political campaigns) to increasing the taxes of the affluent (most of whom do vote and many of whom make political contributions).

Johnson began serious consideration of spending cuts to reduce the deficit, shake up the Congress with the alternatives to increasing taxes, and put pressure on Mills. McNamara proposed cuts in Defense, Budget Director Schultze in domestic programs, and Transportation Secretary Alan Boyd wired the nation's governors that the discussions between the Congress and executive branch on expenditure reductions could require slashing highway construction by as much as half beginning November 1, 1967.[7] Boyd's telegram had the desired effect as state legislators and governors urged their congressmen to support the tax surcharge. But still the tax bill remained stalled.

Apparently thwarted, Johnson admitted during a spirited November press conference, at which he wore a lavaliere microphone under his jacket and walked back and forth, "One of our failures in the administration has been our inability to convince the Congress of the . . . necessity of passing a tax bill." Then, arms and hands jutting forward as if to punch home his points, LBJ revealed some of his feelings about Mills:

> . . . one of the great mistakes that the Congress will make is that Mr. Ford [House Republican leader] and Mr. Mills have taken this position that they cannot have any tax bill now. They will live to rue the day when they made that decision. Because it is a dangerous decision . . . an unwise decision. . . . I know it doesn't add to your polls and your popularity to say we have to have additional taxes to fight this war abroad and fight the problems in our cities at home. But we can do it with the gross national product we have. We should do it. And I think when the American people and the Congress get the full story they will do it. . . . We have failed up to now to be able to convince them. But we are going to continue to try.

The next day, November 18, the British devalued the pound for the first time since 1949 and raised interest rates. To compete for money and keep it flowing into the U.S., the Federal Reserve Board promptly hiked the discount rate; commercial banks followed with increases in their prime rates. Johnson seized the crisis to push his tax bill and cut congressional add-ons to his budget. He proposed and Congress enacted a program to trim the federal payroll and some domestic spending.

But Mills's appetite for cuts in social programs was not nearly satisfied. To Johnson, the chairman seemed like a shark in feeding frenzy as he attached a freeze on welfare payments for dependent children to the administration's Social Security increases. The President met with Mills, Schultze, and me in his small green den on the evening of December 13 in a last-ditch effort to get Mills to back off. He argued that the freeze was unfair: no one could predict how many people would be on welfare; they were poor and Mills's proposal could hurt them badly.

"Mr. President," Mills said, "across town from my mother in Arkansas a Negro woman has a baby every year. Every time I go home, my mother complains. That Negro woman's now got eleven children. My proposal will stop this. Let the states pay for more than a small number of children if they want to." Mills wanted to limit the number of illegitimate or abandoned children that could receive welfare. Johnson's plea that this savaged innocents did not move him. The two men took the gloves off during much of their exchange, but the bout ended in a draw.[8]

When Mills left, Johnson turned to me, "You hear that good, now. That's what we're dealing with. That's the way most members feel. They're just not willing to say it publicly unless they come from redneck districts."

Congress adopted Mills's freeze on welfare payments and went home to celebrate Christmas without acting on the President's request for a tax surcharge.

With Congress refusing to pass his tax surcharge and Vietnam War costs driving the budget deficit to vertiginous heights, Lyndon Johnson confronted the tightest economic squeeze of his presidency. Just as it seemed matters couldn't get worse, the nation's international balance-of-payments deficit soared, threatening the stability of the dollar.

Johnson had pushed legislative, administrative, and voluntary programs to reduce the nation's balance-of-payments deficit in 1965 and hold it down. In 1967, however, Britain's November devaluation of the pound shook the financial world and undercut confidence in the dollar, and the balance-of-payments deficit broke out of control. Johnson instructed me to work with his economic team to prepare a new and more drastic program for 1968.[9]

The next few weeks were a haze of conflicting views about balance of payments.[10] To complicate matters, Johnson went on a hectic pre-Christmas world tour. His trip took him to California, Hawaii, American Samoa, Australia, Thailand, South Vietnam, Pakistan, the Vatican to see the Pope, the Portuguese Azores, and back to the White House five days after he had departed. Throughout, I wired the President on balance-of-payments issues[11] and he sent uncharacteristically long cables back (written, I eventually discovered, by Charles Engelhard, the mining tycoon and LBJ financial supporter).

Johnson arrived on the south grounds about 5 A.M. on Sunday, Christmas Eve, went to mass at St. Dominic's Catholic Church, and then called me to find out where we stood on balance of payments, budget issues, and draft protesters. He was elated about the trip, but infuriated about press carping that the frantic hops had created a circuslike atmosphere.[12] Johnson thought the criticism came from reporters who preferred to get the news "sitting on their asses in the White House lobby."

On December 30, the President convened a meeting in the Cedar Guest House, a bungalow not far from the main Texas ranch house, with Rusk, Fowler, Commerce Secretary Alexander (Sandy) Trowbridge, Schultze, Walt Rostow, Wilbur Mills, Russell Long, Fed Chairman Martin, and others. The meeting went nonstop from shortly after ten in the morning, through a lunch served on TV trays, until just after three in the afternoon. By the time it was over, we had the essentials of a complex balance-of-payments program. That evening I flew back to Washington to put it in final shape. The following afternoon, the President told me to return to the ranch because he was going to announce the program on the morning of New Year's Day.[13]

When I warned the President of the hazards of such a complicated announcement for a bunch of hungover reporters who would be annoyed about an early call for a major story on New Year's Day, he just chuckled softly. "They're too Goddamn lazy," he said. "They don't like travel and they expect to rest up while I'm at the ranch. This'll give them some work to do. Tell them we have to announce it when the [financial] markets are closed."

The next morning, at the end of his statement, the President introduced me to give a background briefing at the hangar at the ranch. As I answered questions from the press corps for the better part of an hour, he paced back and forth, sometimes in the back of the hangar behind the press corps, sometimes directly in front of the elevated platform on which I was standing. When he didn't like an answer I gave, he would elaborate on it, either climbing onto the platform or from where he was pacing. The experience was so disconcerting, and the press was so annoyed that everything I said was on background, that *The New York Times* printed a picture of me with the President standing in the back of the hangar as I spoke.*

As Johnson struggled at home, the war worsened in Vietnam. In 1967, nine thousand Americans died and sixty thousand were wounded, more than double the previous year's casualties. The military chiefs pressed Johnson to lift restrictions on their conduct of the war, particularly with respect to bombing North Vietnam. By summer, he was allowing them to go after targets in the Hanoi and

* Despite the churning and deliberate needling of the White House press corps, the nation had reason to be satisfied. Although Congress rejected several of Johnson's legislative proposals, his tough, unpopular program gave the U.S. a $187 million balance-of-payments surplus in 1968.

Haiphong harbor areas and close to the Chinese border. But for all the number of bombs and troops, all the threats to bomb more and send more soldiers, the United States was no closer to victory, and the North Vietnamese, despite higher casualties and a devastated economy, refused to come to the negotiating table.

In August of 1967, *The New York Times* published a series of editorials breaking with the administration's policy in Southeast Asia. Calling the war a "bottomless pit" in which "nothing succeeds like failure," the influential *Times* urged Johnson to stop the escalation and bombing, reject the counsel of those who wanted to step up the war even further, and, "lest a dismal situation be made intolerably worse," seek a negotiated accord. The *Times* reflected more of LBJ's worries than its editorial writers may have realized when it expressed "concern that the rebuilding of slums and other domestic tasks . . . are being sacrificed to the necessity for spending upward of $2 billion a month to feed the Vietnamese conflict."

That same month, Undersecretary of State Katzenbach testified before the Senate Foreign Relations Committee that further escalation, if the President deemed it necessary, was well within the broad resolution Congress had passed in 1964 after Hanoi's gunboats had attacked American warships in the Gulf of Tonkin. Johnson took the position that if Congress wanted to restrict his conduct of the war then it should pass a less-sweeping resolution.

On September 26, 1967, Senator Clifford Case, a normally mild-mannered New Jersey Republican, surprised his colleagues and the President by going to the Senate floor to assail what he termed LBJ's irresponsible "misuse" and "perversion" of the Tonkin Gulf Resolution to deepen American involvement in Vietnam. He charged that there was a "crisis of confidence" in the President. Johnson reacted swiftly, getting Senate Democrats and Minority Leader Everett Dirksen to defend him on the floor and criticize Case. Case's vehemence was such that even long-time opponent of the President's war policy Majority Leader Mansfield expressed surprise and reminded Case that Congress had, after all, passed the resolution.

The next day, Case's speech made front-page news, and Johnson was still boiling. He talked about the speech at the Democratic leadership breakfast.[14] "You all know that whenever most Senators look in a mirror, they see a president. Well, they tell me Clifford Case has been looking in the mirror an awful lot lately."

As the President and I walked over to the Oval Office,[15] he said, "Call Case and tell him if I want advice like that I'll get it from Wayne Morse and Ernest Gruening [the only two senators who had voted against the Tonkin Gulf Resolution]. Tell him the President doesn't need advice from someone who waits until *The New York Times* editorial board decides to change its mind." I didn't make the call and the President never expected me to.

Misgivings about the war were also torturing Bob McNamara, and he wanted out of the Defense cabinet post. After an August 23, 1967, cabinet meeting, McNamara stopped by my office to tell me that he might be recommended to replace George Woods as president of the World Bank. "Keep this to yourself," he admonished me. "The only reason I'm telling you is, for God's sake, so you don't tell the President I'm indispensable if he asks you about it."[16]

LBJ didn't want to lose McNamara. He considered him "very able . . . very sincere . . . very loyal, and very much on top of his job." But he also thought McNamara "gave too much to it" and frequently expressed to me grave concern about the Secretary's mental and physical health. On August 25, 1966, with Undersecretary of State George Ball due to resign the following month, the President brought up with me the idea of having McNamara succeed Ball. He thought it was a way of easing the strain on the Defense Secretary and keeping him in the administration. "Talk to McNamara," LBJ said, and suggest that "the finest thing for him as a selfless, dedicated lover of this land would be to take Ball's job. In effect he would be co-Secretary [of State] . . . and this would be pretty acceptable to the country."[17] I never talked to McNamara, believing that the conversation uniquely called for the President.

Johnson never pressed his Secretary of Defense to succeed Ball and he continued to worry about McNamara's health. In the fall of 1967, the President discussed it one evening with White House aide Jim Jones. "Bob's a good man," Johnson said, "but I'm concerned about his health, his mental health. That man could have a mental breakdown. I'm afraid we could even have another Forrestal* on our hands. We've got to find something else for him to do."[18] The relationship between the two men was also strained by Johnson's distrust of the judgment and loyalty (to LBJ) of several McNamara aides.[19]

McNamara told the President he wanted the World Bank post and Johnson nominated him in November. A leak of McNamara's selection later that month prompted widespread speculation in Washington that the President might escalate the war, since McNamara by now had come to be regarded by capital insiders as a moderating influence on the military.

LBJ realized that Case's comments and McNamara's misgivings

---

* James Forrestal, Secretary of Defense under President Truman, suffered a nervous breakdown and in 1949 tragically took his own life.

echoed what was being said on campuses and editorial pages across America, that they reflected second thoughts the American people harbored about the war in Vietnam. Protests had made it difficult, sometimes impossible, for Johnson and other high officials, like McNamara and Rusk, to make public appearances. That was bad enough. But Johnson knew that if protest moved from the streets to the Senate floor, church pews, and living rooms of America, he confronted a problem of profoundly different dimensions. The war was taking a severe toll on Johnson personally. He agonized over his sons-in-law who were in the Armed Forces. And when he signed letters of condolence to parents and spouses of men killed in Vietnam it was not unusual to see him weep.

By the end of 1967, looking at 485,000 troops in South Vietnam, almost 16,000 war dead and 100,000 wounded, Americans had grown increasingly uneasy about the President's policy and skeptical about administration claims of success. Some advocated withdrawal, others a dramatic escalation. Most Americans didn't know what to do about this war half a world away, but they had grown impatient with the persisting stalemate. If not victory, Americans at least wanted progress for all the bloodshed they saw on their television sets each evening. With the draft reaching deeply into middle America, more and more mothers and fathers wondered whether the risk of their sons' lives in South Vietnam's jungles was really worth it. A majority of Americans polled thought that getting involved in Vietnam had been a mistake, and approval of the President's handling of the war slipped to 28 percent. As 1967 ended, Johnson couldn't seem to deliver victory on the battlefield or negotiations for peace, no matter how many troops and bombs he committed to the effort or how many diplomatic feelers he extended to North Vietnam, and the American people were beginning to have second thoughts about him.

Nightmare Year

SIXTEEN

"I Shall Not Seek and Will Not Accept . . ."

THE GREAT UNCERTAINTY and fierce struggle fermenting among the American people was also reflected in the administration. As I looked for ideas from academics for the 1968 State of the Union message and the presidential campaign,[1] what I found was criticism of the war.[*] Virtually no one offered any support for it. The criticism of Johnson personally was stinging, but most people (at least in my presence) felt he was misguided, not insincere, in his quest for peace.

The preparation of the President's January 1968 State of the Union message and legislative program became a battleground for the President's mind. Fowler pressed hard for major cuts in domestic programs, urging what I viewed as abandonment of the Great Society. Johnson's inability to get a tax bill out of Congress strengthened Fowler's hand. In his own soundings on the Hill, the President heard several variations of the Treasury Secretary's theme. In late November 1967, he was talking about trimming social programs in order to reach an accommodation with House Ways and Means Committee Chairman Wilbur Mills. On Monday evening, December 4, I wrote

---

[*] Over the spring and summer of 1967, we visited eight academic centers around the country and met with 115 of the nation's experts in economics, chemistry, history, law, business, education, psychology, the arts, humanities, medicine, psychiatry, international affairs, architecture, population, water resources, political science, criminology, violence control, urban affairs, engineering, communications, aerospace, zoology, social service, pediatrics, geophysical sciences, sociology, and anthropology. Whatever their field, they questioned U.S. involvement in Vietnam.[2]

the President a strategy of perseverance on the guns-and-butter course:

—Repackage the tax increase to raise even more revenues, by adding excise taxes, and perhaps by further increasing the corporate tax bite.
—Present to Congress a budget which eliminates what we consider to be the obsolete programs—like . . . school milk for suburban children. . . .
—Go forward on a fairly substantial scale with new programs in the area of housing and jobs particularly, and hold the Great Society programs at least at their [current] levels. . . .
. . . Serve the package up to the Congress with a strong statement about the need to . . . move with our urgent needs at home . . . even though we have a war in Vietnam, calling upon sacrifices from the American people to provide the means to handle *both* wars. Let the Congress chop it up if they decide to do so—but force the issue in terms of will in the Congress to meet these responsibilities.

I urged Johnson to tackle Mills head on. I said I thought the chairman "wants either (or both) (1) to force . . . you to your knees, or (2) to dismantle great hunks of the Great Society."

Johnson was worried about some articles and polls questioning his leadership, so I closed my memo by noting:

Recent comments . . . and the feeling of the people about a "lack of leadership" go . . . to the complexity of the war in Vietnam, riots and disorders in our cities and a feeling of futility because the problems are so immense our society seems to be coming apart at the seams . . . in January the people will be looking to you to show them that you intend to attack these problems and—while recognizing their difficulty—you can give them a sense of hope that they are not impossible of solution.[3]

The President never mentioned the memo to me, but I watched him test the suggestions at several economic and budget meetings.

On December 28, 1967, I was at the ranch to brief the President on new programs. Except for a lunch break, we spent most of the day working.* Johnson revamped his Safe Streets bill. In the summer of 1967 his anticrime legislation had emerged from the House battered

* To thank them for their work, the President invited my entire staff: Fred Bohen, Jim Gaither, Larry Levinson, Matt Nimetz, and Stan Ross.[4]

and recast by a more conservative Congress in light of rising crime, anger at the Warren Court, and backlash from urban race riots. The House rejected Johnson's gun-control proposals, authorized more money to combat riots, and did nothing to restrict electronic eavesdropping. To get his Safe Streets legislation back on track in the Senate, Johnson felt he had to tip his hat to the conservative swing by including an antiriot provision of his own.[5]

Johnson approved a host of other measures, but his concern about the budget deficit and stalemate over increased taxes set the tone throughout our discussion. The meeting ended in great uncertainty because the President put all his decisions in limbo until he could figure out how to persuade Congress to give him his tax bill.[6]

As McPherson and I began drafting the State of the Union message, LBJ became acutely conscious of history. He wanted an analysis of FDR's and Truman's messages; he wanted analogies between Korea and Vietnam; he had us count the number of words in every such message since 1934, when FDR delivered his first crafted-for-broadcast State of the Union. The shortest was Roosevelt's that year (2,574 words); the longest, Harry Truman's in 1946 (24,000). Eisenhower's average length had been 7,610 words; Kennedy's 6,967; Johnson's to that point, 5,695. Johnson wanted to keep the message under 4,000 words and he would not review a draft unless the word count was indicated.*[7]

Also, as usual, the President would not let the message out of the White House except to Rusk and McNamara, so a parade of cabinet members came through my office, one per hour, beginning at 9 A.M. on January 16, the day before the message was to be delivered.[9] Even under such secure conditions, the President again did not want anyone to see particularly dramatic proposals for fear someone would mention them inadvertently at "some Georgetown party to some columnist who's smarter than they are." Therefore, proposals to mount the $2.1 billion jobs program and to eliminate the housing gap in America were only in the copies read by the Secretaries of Labor and HUD, respectively, since each was well aware of the proposal in his field and, by that time in the Johnson administration, each would be possessed by the fear of God that any leak would cost him his program. Everyone agreed that the message was not strong enough on crime, so tougher rhetoric was added, although the President insisted on reminding his listeners "that law enforcement is first the duty of local police and local government."[10]

In the end, the message not only defended the Great Society

---

* The final version of the message was 4,070 words.[8]

programs Congress had enacted, but urged passage of those still pending and proposed major new ones. Johnson may have been wavering in December, but in January he was still willing to spend whatever capital he had left—and it was dwindling fast—to get his work done without waiting for the war to be over.

LBJ laid another heavy workload on Congress—not only the unfinished agenda of numerous bills and the massive new job and housing programs, but new consumer bills, a major expansion of child-health programs, tougher drug laws, farm programs, medical-cost-control proposals, antipollution efforts, even some increases in domestic spending—and a big push for his tax surcharge. Four years into his presidency, he was still striving to do more. He refused, he said, to accept a jobless rate "in some areas . . . still three to four times the national average," urban crime and violence, "income for farm workers [that] remains far behind that for urban workers," "new housing construction . . . far less than we need—to assure decent shelter for every family," and "many rivers—and the air in many cities . . . badly polluted." He would not preside over a Pontius Pilate government that turned its back and washed its hands.

Johnson received the customary standing ovation as he entered the packed chamber, but he faced a more troubled Congress and nation than he had addressed in earlier messages. He had no illusions about the difficulties as he began his address, "I was thinking as I was walking down the aisle tonight of what Sam Rayburn told me many years ago: The Congress always extends a very warm welcome to the President—*as he comes in.*" His delivery was quiet, his tone almost conversational as he looked into the cameras and the eyes of his audience, sometimes leaning his elbows on the podium. With Marvin Watson's prompting, there was frequent applause, but it was largely polite. And there was no clapping when LBJ pressed for his tax increase and civil rights legislation. Enthusiastic outbursts did greet his denunciation of "rising crime and lawlessness" and the need to help assure Americans that those "who preach disorder . . . and violence" will know that "local authorities are able to resist them swiftly . . . sternly . . . and . . . decisively."

The major passages, dealing with Vietnam, civil disorder and crime, and the need to raise taxes, were a somber contrast to the optimistic sermon he had delivered in his State of the Union in 1965, following his landslide election. The can-do-anything President was subdued, conceding, even as he asked for new programs, that the poverty and pollution to which so much of the Great Society was directed "cannot [be] change[d] . . . in a day." And, despite the social progress and unprecedented prosperity of which he spoke, the President recognized that "there is in the land a certain restlessness—a questioning."

With almost 500,000 troops in South Vietnam and more on their way, Johnson spoke poignantly of his desire for peace—"If a basis for peace talks can be established . . . and it is my hope and my prayer that they can . . . we would consult with our allies and with the other side to see if a complete cessation of hostilities—a really true cease-fire—could be made the first order of business."

Standing to the side of the podium on the floor of the House, I felt an urgency as he spoke those words, almost as though he ached. What I couldn't have known then was that late that afternoon his daughter Lynda Bird Robb had brought him a bundle of letters wives of servicemen had written to her. She had read to him one from a young Texas woman whose husband had gone to Vietnam two months after their marriage and had been killed thirteen days before his tour was up. Her own husband, a Marine Corps captain, was headed for combat on March 30. Lynda told her father that she didn't think she could accept such a tragedy with the courage this woman's letter displayed. When Mrs. Johnson came into the family dining room, where the President was eating his lunch as Lynda talked to him, she thought he looked exhausted and suggested that he get some rest. He said simply that he wanted both his ladies "to wear bright colors and have professional makeup jobs for tonight" so they would look just fine, and left to rehearse his address.[11]

Six days after the address, North Korea seized the USS *Pueblo*, a spy ship stationed off its coast, and took the crew as prisoners. The next week, on January 30, the North Vietnamese mounted the Tet offensive, a full-scale assault on South Vietnam's cities, stretching over more than three weeks. The press reported it as a setback for U.S. and South Vietnamese forces, and the psychological blow rever-berated through the Congress, the public, and the administration. The military was claiming victory because they had repelled the enemy and inflicted enormous losses on the Vietcong and North Vietnamese, but even in the White House many of us had our doubts.

The administration had declared that the Communists were los-ing the war. Victory or not, the sheer ability of the North Vietnamese and Vietcong to mount such a large-scale offensive had shattered the American people's confidence in the President's word. For the first time, large numbers of Americans thought their country might lose the war.

There was a sense of siege in the White House. It was increas-ingly difficult to find public forums for the President that avoided disruption from demonstrators opposing the war or demanding more money and programs for blacks and poor people. On January 3, Senator Eugene McCarthy, the Minnesota Democrat whose campaign for the presidential nomination had not been taken seriously when he announced it in November 1967, had expressed his intention to mount a "vigorous" effort in the New Hampshire primary on an antiwar platform. That same day, former Alabama Governor George Wallace congratulated cheering supporters in California for qualifying his new American Independent Party on the California ballot in his unannounced third-party bid to unseat Johnson and roll back his civil rights policies.

The day after the State of the Union, Eartha Kitt, the black singer, shook up fifty other guests at a luncheon in the family dining room of the White House when she attacked the war and high taxes, saying, "The best of this country . . . rebel in the street . . . take pot . . . get high . . . don't want to go to school because they're going to be snatched off from their mothers to be shot in Vietnam." Mrs. Johnson, tears welling and voice trembling, responded that simply because there was a war "doesn't give us a free ticket not to try to work for better things such as against crime in the streets, better education, and better health for our people."

That same week, HEW Secretary John Gardner in an emotional meeting told the President he was resigning. "You've done more for your country than most of your countrymen will realize in your lifetime," Gardner told him. "But at this point in time, I don't believe you can lead the country. I believe you can no longer pull the country together. It seems to me that in an election year you deserve the total support of every cabinet member and a cabinet member who doesn't think you should run shouldn't be in the cabinet."[12]

Knowing now that his time was running out, Johnson almost frenetically continued to press the contentious 90th Congress for domestic reforms. On February 5, right in the middle of the Tet fighting, he sent a special message asking Congress for increased funds for elementary and secondary education, a new vocational education program, an Educational Opportunity Act for college students, and increased support for universities.

The next day, he sent Congress the fourth consumer message of his presidency, trumpeting his record (wholesome meat, auto and highway safety, truth-in-packaging, flame-resistant clothing and blankets, the National Commission on Product Safety, standards for clinical laboratories); pressing Congress to complete action on truth-in-lending, fire safety, pipeline safety, fraudulent land sales, protection for mutual fund investors, and electric power reliability; and proposing new bills: the Deceptive Sales Act, Hazardous Radiation

Act, Wholesome Poultry and Fish and Fishery Products Act, recreational boat safety legislation, and an automobile insurance study. The day after that, he sent Congress a special message on crime, urging passage of his Safe Streets Act, and the next day he sent Congress one on foreign aid.

On February 12, Westmoreland cabled that he "desperately need[ed]" reinforcements.[13] Johnson ordered 10,500 more men to Vietnam and the following day sent General Earle Wheeler, Chairman of the Joint Chiefs of Staff, there to assess Westmoreland's needs. Five days later, Communist forces in South Vietnam launched the second wave of the Tet offensive.

And still the President was determined to prove that the war would not stop him. On February 19, he wrote Senator Philip Hart (D-Mich.), floor manager of the administration's fair-housing bill, to push for final Senate action. Three days later, he resumed the spurt of special messages to Congress with one on the cities, asking for the nation's most ambitious housing act to close the housing gap in America by creating 26 million units over the next ten years. The proposals included a home-ownership program for the poor, national housing partnerships to encourage private industry to invest in low-income housing, the creation of "new towns in town" (a proposal to build entire neighborhoods on large pieces of empty urban land), hefty increases in model cities and urban mass-transit funds, and $2.2 billion for OEO. On February 27, Johnson sent his message on the farmer and rural America, calling for expanded food aid to third world nations, a National Food Bank, and expansion of food stamp, rural housing, job, and electrification programs.

In early March, LBJ's "Health in America" message proposed prenatal and postnatal care for children through the first year of life,* creation of a Center for Population Studies and Human Reproduction, and measures to contain health-care costs. On March 6, he sent a special message on the "Forgotten American," asking new social programs and a bill of rights for Native Americans. On March 8, his environmental message asked for action on water-pollution control, safe drinking water, air quality, noise-pollution control, new parks closer to cities, scenic rivers and trails, wilderness areas, and exploration of the ocean's depths. That month he also sent Congress a special message on the District of Columbia.

The President could not hurl programs at Congress and the public fast enough. He was irritable and impatient when I did not have a

---

* In preparing the child-health-care measure, the President told me that once we provided care for the first year of life and beginning at the sixty-fifth year, future presidents and congresses could gradually close the gap.

draft special message in his night reading to go to Congress the next day. In our haste, we sometimes slipped up on notifying a key committee member, an unspeakable offense in prior years. Often we put so many complex proposals out in a day that reporters were unable to write clearly about them, as our own stories vied with each other for front-page coverage. During these hectic weeks, McCarthy and his student supporters in New Hampshire worked the President over on the war, Wallace announced his third-party candidacy and stirred up the white backlash against Johnson, and an increasingly critical Robert Kennedy found fault with something in almost every proposal LBJ put forward.

There was a whirl of desperate haste about the President. I suggested more than once that he was sending messages too fast. He would say, "I want to get them up there so I can get my program passed. Time is important, especially if I don't run for reelection."[14] But I never doubted that he would run. After all, he had talked about not running in 1964.

Meanwhile, the National Advisory Commission on Civil Disorders that the President had named in the swirl of the summer riots was getting ready to nip its creator's hand. Illinois Governor Kerner had turned out to be a loyal, but weak chairman. Lindsay had pursued his own political agenda. The President had begun to turn on the commission when Lindsay told a dozen news people that it planned to issue an interim report to influence the administration's January budget.[15] When I reported that Lindsay professed to be embarrassed, Johnson had snapped, "That's bullshit. And you tell Lindsay that there's something I've learned from a long life in politics: It's a darn sight easier to slip on bullshit than it is to slip on gravel. If he doesn't stop the bullshit, he's gonna slip and break his ass."

Expecting the Kerner Commission to urge vast new federal spending, I worried about the President's response. Kerner and the commission's staff director, David Ginsburg, gave me an advance copy of the final report on February 27, 1968, at breakfast in the White House mess.[16] It was the best they could do for LBJ, Ginsburg said, but as soon as I read it, I knew Johnson would erupt. The commission recommended federal spending several orders of magnitude beyond what he had proposed, and its report contained a blistering indictment of white racism. Recognizing LBJ's accomplishments, the report still emphasized whopping spending increases, and its nameplate sentence, "Our nation is moving toward two societies, one black, one white—separate and unequal," invited criticism of the administration's efforts. Johnson would certainly read it as an attack on his work. That, I feared, would drive the President publicly to ignore or demean the commission.

That evening, I summarized the report and suggested to Johnson that Kerner transmit the report with a letter "praising your progress to date" and that the President respond noncommittally, characterizing the report as a "long and important document" and the beginning of a "national dialogue." I warned the President that time was short and coverage would be wide. The report was scheduled to be turned over to reporters on Friday, March 1, with an embargo on public release until the Sunday-morning papers.[17]

The next day, February 29 in leap year 1968, proved to be "one of those days" for the President—and for me. That morning, for the better part of an hour, we argued about his response to the Kerner Commission report. Johnson wanted no part of it. He refused even to acknowledge it, much less issue any statement I suggested. He asked me to tell Ginsburg that the report was "destroying the President's interest in things like this."[18]

We had to go over to the Pentagon for the farewell ceremony for McNamara, so I decided to wait a few hours and then take it up with him again. En route to the Secretary's office on his private elevator, the President, McNamara, and several of us got stuck between floors for almost fifteen minutes. It was the day's only amusing interlude. The sergeant operating the elevator called maintenance on the emergency phone. The maintenance man asked, "Do you have a full load?" The sergeant responded, "We sure do." The President remarked to McNamara, "This is an indication of how much the Defense Department thinks of you. They're trying to keep you until the last possible moment." When McPherson said, "Mr. President, you are surrounded by people [McPherson, Larry Levinson, Will Sparks, and me] who used to work for Mr. McNamara," the President quipped, "Yes, and you all would be surprised how low you sank in his estimation when he found out I wanted to borrow you."[19]

McNamara's farewell ceremony was conducted outdoors in such pouring rain and sleet that the Air Force flyover had to be canceled, the presidential party and most participants got drenched, and the loudspeaker system broke down so that the bulk of the rain-soaked audience heard only the last few words of the President's remarks.[20]

When we returned to the White House, Ginsburg told me that, despite the embargo until Sunday, March 3, *The Washington Post* was going to run a story on the report the next day. I accused the paper's editor, Ben Bradlee, of breaking the embargo. Bradlee claimed someone had given the *Post* a copy with the cover page, where the embargo was printed, ripped off, so he had a right to go with the story. I told Ginsburg to let the *Times* and others go with it as well so that the *Post* wouldn't have an exclusive. Informed of this turn of events, the President refused even to accept the bound presidential copy of the report privately. Ginsburg ruefully delivered it to me that evening.[21]

The public and the press, however, clamored for a response. Finally, following the stepped-up attacks from liberals and a rare veiled criticism from his friend Nelson Rockefeller, Johnson decided to end the controversy. At a press conference on March 22, answering a planted question, he said, "We thought the report was a very thorough one, very comprehensive, and made many good recommendations. We did not agree with all of the recommendations, as certain statements have indicated." Johnson noted that the report had been sent for study to the cabinet, members of Congress, governors, and mayors. The next day newspapers reported that the President had "praised" the report, even though he had not committed himself to any of its recommendations.

The President could have saved himself weeks of irritation and aggravation if he had made that same statement at the time the report was issued. Why didn't he? I later told a D.C. Bar Association luncheon[22] that the President thought the commission "overdramatized" its finding that "white racism is essentially responsible for the explosive mixture which has been accumulating in our cities since the end of World War II."

On reflection, I believe the President refused at first even to acknowledge the report because he was hurt. He shared most of the commission's goals. But he felt let down by Kerner and Ginsburg for not adequately recognizing what he had already done and for failing to point out sharply that Congress would not let him do more. When the report surfaced prematurely, he immediately suspected it had been leaked by someone on the commission to box him in. For Lyndon Johnson, that settled it.[23]

On February 27, the same day I had breakfast with Kerner to get an advance review of his commission's report, McPherson and I went to luncheon in the Secretary of State's private dining room with Rusk, McNamara, Clark Clifford (who would replace McNamara as Defense Secretary), Walt Rostow, Undersecretary of State Katzenbach, and Assistant Secretary of State William Bundy. We were to discuss a speech that the President planned to give on Vietnam at the end of March. He would also try again to convince Congress and the public that we needed a tax surcharge. That's what accounted for my presence at the lunch.

It was the most depressing three hours in my years of public service. My job left me on the periphery of the war. This was the first time since early in 1966 that I had heard the President's advisers in an intimate discussion of Vietnam. McNamara, Katzenbach, and Assistant Secretary of State William Bundy were beyond pessimism. They sounded a chorus of despair. Rusk appeared exhausted and worn down.

The President had asked us to talk about the military's request for 205,000 troops on top of the half million already there. McNamara, his face lined and eyelids darkened, was tense. He called the request "madness . . . I've repeatedly honored requests from the Wheelers of the world, but we have no assurance that an additional 205,000 men will make any difference in the conduct of the war." Katzenbach and Bundy nodded in agreement, and McNamara added, "Nobody knows whether it will make any difference. It still may not be enough to win the war. There is no [military] plan to win the war." McNamara attacked the bombing of North and South Vietnam and Laos. We were "dropping ordnance at a higher rate than during the last year of World War II in Europe," the bombing was not stopping war supplies from getting to the Vietcong, and "[the destruction] is making us lasting enemies in Southeast Asia." Katzenbach said that it was clear the request for 205,000 men could not be honored; the only question was how to handle Wheeler.

Stating emphatically, "I am not pushing it," Clifford mentioned another possibility. They should consider putting in "500,000 to a million men." McNamara was sarcastic, "That has the virtue of clarity"; an increase of that proportion would at least indicate we were seeking "to accomplish the job." But he expressed grave doubts about the military, economic, political, diplomatic, and moral consequences.

Bundy said that South Vietnam was "very weak" and "our position may be truly untenable." He suggested that plans be made for withdrawal "with the best possible face" and a credible indication that we would defend the "rest of Asia."

Rusk and Rostow seemed more optimistic. They pointed out that the enemy had suffered heavy losses and gained little ground during the Tet offensive. Rusk shared McNamara's misgivings and proposed a bombing halt over North Vietnam, although the Secretary of State wasn't certain what, if any, conditions should be attached, and he admitted a halt might accomplish little or nothing.

Clifford said that despite optimistic reports about enemy casualties during Tet, "our people and world opinion believe we have suffered a setback." He asked, "How do we avoid creating the feeling that we are pouring troops down a rathole?" Before any decision is made, Clifford thought, "we must re-evaluate our entire posture in South Vietnam."*

With the exception of Rostow, there was no certainty around the table that any number of additional troops could bring victory. Rostow believed that the bombing should continue and opposed any unconditional pause. He did not express a clear opinion about Wheeler's request for more troops, but he left me with the impression that he would have honored a good part of that request. As lunch ended, I thought that he was alone among the President's men in the belief that we could succeed in Vietnam.

McPherson and I drove back to the White House together in a state of depression. I was physically shaken. Both of us were completely drained.

"This is crazy," I said.

McPherson nodded.

"It really is all over, isn't it?" I said.

"You bet it is," McPherson responded.[24]

It was at this moment, riding in the car, that I knew the President had somehow to wind the war down and get out of Vietnam.

The next day, Johnson bestowed the Medal of Freedom on Bob McNamara as he left for the World Bank presidency,[25] in a moving White House ceremony during which both men struggled to maintain their composure. McNamara's departure was an emotional strain for the two of them. Through it all, though McNamara had become increasingly uncomfortable in the cabinet and Johnson had become increasingly concerned about his Defense Secretary's stability, the two men had developed enormous respect for each other's intelligence and dedication. For me, as well as them, that East Room ceremony brought on tears.

Nevertheless, for both Johnson and McNamara the World Bank post was the best solution. For what Johnson didn't know at the time—though he may have suspected it—was that McNamara had been actively promoting Robert Kennedy's candidacy in 1968. Early in the year, the Defense Secretary had visited Larry O'Brien in his White House office to "make a strong pitch that Bobby should run for president." O'Brien had told McNamara that he thought a major effort should be made internally to change the President's position on Vietnam. McNamara rejected that course. He said that it was imperative that Kennedy run for president and be the party's nominee.[26]

* With the benefit of hindsight, I have come to suspect that Johnson named Clifford to the Defense post because the concerns Clifford had expressed in 1965 had come to pass and the President considered his new Defense Secretary just the man to reevaluate the administration's war policy.

•

Events were closing in. On March 7, during Senate debate on the administration's fair-housing bill, liberals and moderates suddenly demanded that the Senate be consulted before Johnson sent any more troops to Vietnam. On March 10, news of Wheeler's request leaked into *The New York Times*, and over the next two days the Senate Foreign Relations Committee grilled Rusk at length during televised hearings. On March 12, Senator Eugene McCarthy got a startling 42 percent of the New Hampshire primary vote. Wheeler's request fell victim to the President's concern that more troops would not accomplish much. The battle raging in the government was now whether LBJ should announce a new bombing pause, and if so, how extensive. Having tried and failed with eight previous bombing pauses, the President remained undecided.

On March 16, Robert Kennedy entered the presidential race because, he said, "it is now unmistakably clear that we can change [the country's] disastrous divisive policies [in Vietnam and at home] only by changing the men who are now making them." Kennedy's announcement four days after McCarthy's unexpected show of strength in New Hampshire confirmed Johnson's belief, expressed privately as soon as the New Hampshire primary results became known, that the New York Senator was now sure to enter the race. While Kennedy claimed publicly that he intended to run in harmony with McCarthy, the Minnesota Senator scorned his rival as late to the fray, adding, "An Irishman who announces the day before St. Patrick's Day that he's going to run against another Irishman shouldn't say it's going to be a peaceful relationship." The same day Kennedy made his announcement, Johnson held his luncheon meeting with members of the National Alliance of Businessmen to get his ghetto-jobs program off the ground; he alerted the nation to the possibility of an austerity program and maintained his hard line on Vietnam. On the whole, considering some of the things Johnson had said to me about Kennedy, I found the President strangely detached.

Bombing-halt proposals were still under debate when LBJ asked Harry McPherson and me to lunch on March 28. We sat down shortly before three in the Flower Garden and worked for an hour in the unseasonably warm sun. The first part of the discussion was on the speech to be delivered on March 31, particularly the bombing pause and tax surcharge. The President discussed the pros and cons of the pause, unconditional or conditional, how extensive, who favored or opposed what, and why. He then turned to the surtax, trying to make it easy to understand, searching for simple examples to bring home its importance to the people, and taking on his own shoulders as much responsibility for increasing taxes as possible in order to provide political cover for Congress to act.

Then the President looked long at both of us and asked, "What do you think about my not running for reelection?" We both said he had to run, though McPherson added, "I wouldn't run if I were you." Johnson asked why we thought he had to run.

"Because you're the only guy who can get anything done."

Johnson gazed at us and said pensively, "Others can get things done. The Congress and I are like an old married couple. We've lived together so long and we've been rubbing against each other night after night so often and we've asked so much of each other over the years we're tired of each other. They'd have a honeymoon. Any one of them. I wouldn't have one." Still, that afternoon neither McPherson nor I imagined Johnson would walk away.

We went back to the Oval Office, and LBJ sent McPherson off to produce a revised draft of the speech and asked me to stay behind. He sat down at his desk and turned his chair around to the signing table behind it, as I stood to his right. He began signing routine documents, mentioning, as I already knew, that Shriver would soon leave to become the American Ambassador in Paris. The President then looked up at me and said he thought I was the person to run the poverty program when Shriver left. He had mentioned this lightly in the Flower Garden, but now he was quite serious.

The poverty program, especially with its community-action agencies, was the administration's most politically prickly undertaking because of the threat an organized and aroused poor posed to already shaky city and state political machines, on which not only mayors and governors but senators and congressmen relied. The program's problems were complicated by lack of administration. Shriver had been under so much political pressure that he was constantly shuttling between Capitol Hill, various city halls and statehouses, and among rapidly proliferating and quarrelsome antipoverty groups, leaving him little time for administration. Johnson lived in fear that some financial scandal would destroy the program.

Shriver, worn down by OEO's political wars, was increasingly pinched between LBJ and his brother-in-law who was running for president. He wanted to escape the pincers. LBJ was tickled that he could hold a Kennedy brother-in-law out of the race; to him the appointment of Shriver as Ambassador to France was made in political heaven.

All this went through my mind as I struggled to respond. Not only did I have no interest in running the war on poverty, I had already decided to leave the White House after the election, whether

Johnson won or lost. What put the stunned and nervous expression on my face was my firsthand knowledge of how impossible it could be to say no to this man.

The President said he thought the poverty job was the dirtiest in government, but that if he ran he had to be absolutely certain that the program held together until after the election, and he thought I could do that. He said he was reluctant to ask me to take over the program because he thought that running OEO was very difficult and could be a dead end, but "I'll only ask you to do it if I decide to run for reelection."

"Mr. President," I responded hesitantly, "I think I should tell you something. I hadn't planned to tell you until after the election. But I have decided to leave next year, even if you win and I assume you will. I was going to stay long enough to do your legislative program and get the messages and bills up to Congress. I think I can best serve you here by getting programs together that would give you a fresh start right after the election and—"

Johnson interrupted, looking at me as though I were crazy. "I don't want you to leave your job here. You'd continue to do that. I just want you to take over the poverty program as well—and then, if I run for reelection and win, there'd be other things for you to do. The Italians [Congressmen Peter Rodino (D-N.J.) and Frank Annunzio (D-Ill.)] are always telling me to put you on the Supreme Court, but I think you'd make a better Attorney General."

LBJ was tossing out all the political lures he could throw before me. What difference did it make, I thought, what I did for the next nine months; I was still going to leave after the election. "Mr. President, you know I'll do whatever will help you, but for myself and my family I've got to leave after next year's legislative program is on the Hill." Although I already worked countless hours at the White House, Johnson's suggestions didn't surprise me; he had insisted Larry O'Brien continue to oversee the legislative effort even after he had named him Postmaster General, and he'd kept Shriver as director of the Peace Corps during the first year of the poverty program.

LBJ asked me again what I thought about his not running for reelection. I said I thought he should run, but running with the problems he now had—the war, racial tension, the poverty program, and civil disturbances—would subject him to a lot of abuse. I was afraid if he announced he was not running for reelection the legislative program would go down the tubes in Congress.

Johnson responded that if he pulled out of the race he might have even more leverage with the Congress and the North Vietnamese. He would be above politics. He could ask the people and the Congress for what he thought was right—bolstered by the sacrifice of his own political career for the good of the country. "That's far more than I ask any congressman to do when I ask him to vote for the tax bill" or a Great Society program.

"If I don't run, who do you think will get the nomination?" he asked me.

"I have never really focused on that possibility."

"Well, focus on it now. Who do you think will get the nomination?"

"Bobby Kennedy. My guess is that he'd easily take McCarthy's people away from him."

"What about Hubert?"

"I don't think he can beat Kennedy."

"What's wrong with Bobby? He's made some nasty speeches about me, but he's never had to sit here. Anyway, you seem to like his parties."

I smiled nervously.

"Bobby would keep fighting for the Great Society programs. And when he sat in this chair he might have a different view on the war. His major problem would be with appropriations, getting the programs funded. He doesn't know how to deal with people on the Hill and a lot of them don't like him. But he'll try."

"Mr. President, if you run, I think you'll win."

"Win what? The way it is now we can't get the tax surcharge passed and Ho Chi Minh and Fulbright don't believe anything I say about ending the war."

The President spoke to me at some length about the divisions in the country. He felt he would only aggravate them if he ran for reelection. I said, "I'm afraid that if Nixon wins he would dismantle our programs. And Kennedy would be stymied on the Hill if he won."

"Whether Kennedy or Nixon won, at least the leadership would support them in the first year or so," Johnson said, adding after a thoughtful pause, "And that might provide the necessary time to heal the wounds now separating the country."

The President then admonished me not to say anything bad about either Eugene McCarthy or Robert Kennedy: "If they ask you about McCarthy, say you know him and he's a very intelligent man. If they ask you about Kennedy, say you know him and he's had a brilliant government career." This surprised me. Kennedy had shrilly blamed all the country's evils on LBJ, charging in a California speech, "The national leadership is calling upon the darker impulses of the American spirit—not, perhaps, deliberately, but through its action and the example it sets." But Johnson said he thought I had something to contribute in the future to the country and the Democratic party and he didn't want me to jeopardize my ability to do so by criticizing other party leaders.

The President was slumped in his chair and he looked very tired. He said he knew he was tired because of his eyes. "They hurt and they always hurt when I'm very tired." Then he said, "Whatever I do, I want to take care of Larry Levinson and you because you've worked so hard and loyally for me." If he ran and won, the President said he would like me to have any job in the government with the exception of Secretary of State and Defense because he didn't think I was equipped for State and he wanted to keep Clifford at Defense. "Whether I run or not, I hope I have a chance to do something for you." He said he would like to make me Attorney General for a short period of time, because he wanted me "to walk out of here a distinctly independent man."

I could think of no response. The President sighed and talked again about the "divisions in the country" and his hope for "peace in Vietnam." He looked more exhausted than I'd ever seen him. "Only Bob McNamara and George Christian know how close I've come to announcing that I would not run. Now again," he sighed, "it is very much on my mind."

I later learned that LBJ had come very close to withdrawing when he presented his State of the Union message in January, but had drawn back because he didn't want to hurt his legislative program. He had told George Christian, one of the few individuals who knew he had actually prepared the announcement, "It just didn't fit. I couldn't go in there and lay out a big program and then say, 'Okay, here's all this work to do, and by the way, so long. I'm leaving.' "

Now, in my gut, standing there watching him exhausted, I began to realize that he was leaning against running. I wanted him to run; but he wasn't going to do it. I was afraid for him. He was going to be reviled for as long as he lived, which wouldn't likely be long, because of his heart condition and because when you take from a man his reason for being you accelerate the clock. Yuki, the white mongrel pup that Luci Johnson had found abandoned at a gas station, was in the room. Normally LBJ loved to excite Yuki by holding him up high and making whooping shouts. Today, he barely noticed the dog wagging its tail.[27]

The next day was again warm for that time of year and the President asked me to lunch with him in the Flower Garden. He talked again about my taking over the poverty program if he decided to run for reelection. He didn't press as hard this time, even when I reiter-

ated my intention to leave early in his second term. He was preoc-
cupied. He spoke of the dramatic shift in public opinion on the war,
with "a lot of people ready to surrender without knowing they are
following a party line."* We talked about the tax section of the March
31 speech. He asked me to go over the economic statistics with Okun
and Fowler. He played with his grandson, Patrick Lyndon Nugent,
and press photographers came out and shot some pictures of the two
of them. We went to the Oval Office to talk about the speech.[28] You
never knew when LBJ had made a decision or what it was until he
revealed it, but I left lunch convinced that he had decided not to run
and that he would say so when he announced the bombing pause.

The address on March 31 stunned the nation. Its ending caught
most of the White House staff and cabinet by surprise.† The President had already approved distribution of speech cards on his domestic
achievements to his political supporters and an aggressive program to
gather campaign data on a variety of topics, including McCarthy and
Kennedy. White House aides Jim Gaither and John Robson were in
my office preparing materials for the campaign when Johnson made
his announcement.[29]

And he left no doubt. On the last draft, he made a final edit,
changing the sentence "Accordingly, I shall not seek—and *would* not
accept—the nomination of my party for another term as your President" to "Accordingly, I shall not seek—and *will* not accept . . ."[30]

As it turned out, Johnson had withdrawn barely in time to gather
the strength he would need for the awful days ahead.

Moments after the speech, the White House switchboard spar-
kled with calls. No one has done more to unify the nation . . . The
most moving speech a President has ever made . . . A great President,
willing to sacrifice his personal ambition for the people . . . Editorial
pages and television commentators quickly took the chorus of praise
to even higher octaves. *The Washington Post* rhapsodized that LBJ
"has made a personal sacrifice in the name of national unity that
entitles him to a very special place in the annals of American history. . . . The President last night put unity ahead of his own advancement and his own pride." When Johnson flew to Chicago the
next day, crowds whose abuse the Secret Service had feared on Sun-

---

* Johnson often said he thought the Communists were brilliantly orchestrating a
propaganda effort that seduced many American politicians and leaders unwittingly.
† The President had of course discussed his decision with his family, and he alerted
Hubert Humphrey. But only a handful of others, including Horace Busby, who
helped write the announcement; Marie Fehmer, the secretary who typed it; Arthur
and Mathilde Krim; Christian; Jim Jones; Rusk; and Fortas knew in advance.

day were cheering and friendly on Monday, with people toting home-made signs, such as the one saying, "LBJ IS A GREAT AMERICAN."[31]

Tuesday, at their weekly breakfast with the President, Democratic congressional leaders wanted to discuss the political implications of the President's withdrawal. He turned their questions aside. He said he was "tired of begging anyone for anything. I had a partnership with Jack Kennedy and when he died I felt it was my duty to look after the family and stockholders and employees of my partner. I did not fire anyone. The divisions are so deep within the Party that I could not reconcile them. I'm not going to influence the Convention . . . probably won't even go. Much to everyone's disbelief, I never wanted to be President to begin with. I'm leaving without any bitterness."[32]

Our soundings already indicated that Congress was likely to be much more amenable to his programs than we had judged. The administration's housing and truth-in-lending proposals, in mortal danger the week before, had new life, and full funding for poverty programs now seemed possible. The President pressed the leadership to act on his request for increased taxes.[33] That afternoon the Senate passed the President's tax-surcharge bill by a wider than expected margin. For the first time any of us dared remember, even North Vietnam was on the defensive. On April 3, Hanoi expressed a readiness to talk and LBJ quickly took them up on it. In an instant, the President regained a credibility he hadn't possessed in years.

And his popularity soared. On April 4, when he traveled to New York for the installation of Terence Cooke as Archbishop, bystanders cheered him as he walked up the steps to St. Patrick's Cathedral. Even New York's paparazzi were smiling and waving to him.[34] As the President walked down the center aisle, the overflowing congregation rose as one and clapped and cheered him; only Pope Paul VI had ever received a standing ovation in the cathedral.

After the service, the President spoke briefly to Jacqueline Kennedy and then stopped by Archbishop Cooke's residence directly behind the cathedral on Madison Avenue. The President asked to see Nelson and Happy Rockefeller, gave Happy a picture of the couple that had been taken at the White House, and spoke quietly to the Governor alone.[35]

Just as the helicopter was about to take off from Central Park, Johnson decided to run over to the United Nations to see Ambassador Goldberg and UN Secretary General U Thant to press for negotiations to end the war in Vietnam. On the return flight, the President was exhilarated by the welcome he had received in St. Patrick's and the support he had received from U Thant. As we arrived on the south lawn of the White House at 6:30 P.M., Johnson was looking forward to a Democratic congressional fundraising dinner in his and the Vice President's honor, where he knew he'd be greeted by a crowd as thunderously cheering as any he'd faced since the 1964 campaign. And he was savoring flash reports that the next day a Lou Harris poll would reveal a complete reversal in his rating: from 57 percent disapproval before the March 31 speech to 57 percent approval after it.[36]

SEVENTEEN

The King Assassination

SHORTLY BEFORE 7:30 that evening, as the President was talking to Robert Woodruff of Coca-Cola, a sniper shot Martin Luther King, Jr., in Memphis, Tennessee, where he had been leading a strike of sanitation workers. The President cut the meeting short, and rushed through an appointment with Llewellyn Thompson, the Ambassador to the Soviet Union who was to meet with the North Vietnamese, along with Harriman, whenever the negotiations began. At 8:20 P.M., George Christian sent in word that King was dead. The President canceled his appearance at the Democratic fundraising dinner, and he decided not to go to Hawaii (he was to leave after the dinner) to meet with Westmoreland and Ambassador to Saigon Ellsworth Bunker. The trip cancellation was announced as a postponement so we wouldn't signal our fears of the violence and trouble to come.[1]

Johnson quickly sketched out a brief statement to the nation, and Christian went to alert the press to set up in the West Wing lobby. Johnson went down to the White House barbershop to have his hair trimmed. I went with him, and as he sat in the barber chair, we edited his statement. He telephoned Mrs. King and ordered flowers sent to the funeral.[2] Before the cameras, Johnson condemned King's slaying and implored "every citizen to reject . . . blind violence," and to pray for "peace and understanding throughout this land." He asked the American people to move together toward "equality and fulfillment for all of our people."

When we got back to the Oval Office, the President switched on the three console televisions.[3] Coverage of Democrats at their dinner appeared in counterpoint to reports from Memphis. He told me to call the Vice President and congressional leaders to urge them to say a prayer for Dr. King and close the dinner down. He sent Ramsey Clark; Roger Wilkins, director of the Community Relations Service; and Cliff Alexander, now Chairman of the Equal Employment Opportunity Commission, to Memphis. He stressed to Clark that it was imperative that the FBI apprehend King's assassin.[4]

"Everything we've gained in the last few days we're going to lose tonight," he said, sighing. He went limp in the green leather chair behind the desk in the Oval Office. Johnson then began absently to sign stacks of papers on the table behind his desk, to have something to do other than confront this insane act and the violent repercussions he feared.

The President went to the mansion for dinner.[5] I returned to my office and the calls began coming in; those from the District of Columbia were the most troubling. D.C. City Council Vice Chairman Walter Fauntroy called shortly before 10 P.M. to say that he anticipated "unprecedented violence" in the city.[6] Indeed, though disturbances erupted across America that night—in black ghettos in Memphis, New York, Boston, Jackson, Mississippi, Raleigh, North Carolina, and other cities—the worst violence struck the nation's capital. Black demonstrators looted, destroyed property, taunted police, and set fires.

Johnson called me repeatedly until after 1 A.M. with names of black leaders he wanted to see the next morning: Mayor Carl Stokes of Cleveland; NAACP field director Charles Evers of Jackson, Mississippi; Mayor Richard Hatcher of Gary, Indiana; Judge A. Leon Higginbotham (whom Johnson had appointed to the Federal District Court for Eastern Pennsylvania); civil rights activists Bayard Rustin and Floyd McKissick; Thurgood Marshall; Dorothy Height of the National Council of Negro Women; Roy Wilkins; NAACP lobbyist Clarence Mitchell; and Whitney Young. He ordered me to set up a service at Washington's National Cathedral so he could attend with the black leaders; ask Washington Archbishop Patrick O'Boyle to have services for Catholics in all the churches in the nation's capital; urge John Gardner, who now headed the Urban Coalition, to encourage blacks and whites in every city to talk to each other; invite King's father to the White House; have Mrs. John Kennedy and King's widow and father issue pleas for nonviolence; invite congressional leaders to the White House meeting with the black leadership.[7]

The President offered to send a plane for King's father, but he was too sick to come. When he was told that the President's prayers were with him, King's father responded, "Oh no, my prayers are with the President." Carl Stokes considered Cleveland too tense to leave, and Charles Evers thought Jackson was a tinder box, so they declined, but both sent public messages of support to the President. Everyone else I called appeared at the White House, except A. Philip Randolph, head of the Brotherhood of Sleeping Car Porters, who was ill.[8]

As the meeting with black leaders started the following morning, Floyd McKissick, a militant, appeared at the northeast gate with two other blacks, demanding that all three be admitted to the meeting with the President. I said McKissick was the only one invited. They left in a fit of anger.[9]

The Cabinet Room meeting was tense. Hatcher was angry, not at the President, but at the way blacks had been treated for so long. The intensity of his attack on "racist" American society reflected the rage on the streets. Johnson warned that King's murder could reinforce those of both races who believe that violence is the way to settle racial problems in America. That, he said, would be a "catastrophe for the country." He urged the civil rights leaders to make this tragedy mark the time when blacks pressed forward nonviolently to take advantage of the rights King had helped win. He asked congressional leaders around the table to enact legislation he had proposed to help root out racism from America. It's been "sitting too long in the Congress," he told them.

The black leaders promised to oppose violence, but the Reverend Leon Sullivan captured their concern when he said, "The large majority of Negroes are not in favor of violence, but we need something to fight back with. Otherwise we will be caught with nothing."[10]

At the end of the meeting, the group drove in a twelve-car motorcade to the National Cathedral for a memorial service for King. Afterward, the President went to the Fish Room near the Oval Office and, flanked by black and congressional leaders, issued a proclamation declaring Sunday, April 7, a day of national mourning for King and read a statement.[11]

> The dream of Dr. Martin Luther King, Jr., has not died with him. . . .
>
> We must move with urgency, with resolve, and with new energy in the Congress, in the courts, in the White House, the statehouses and the city halls of the Nation, wherever there is leadership—political leadership, leadership in the churches, in the homes, in the schools, in the institutions of higher learning—until we do overcome.
>
> I have asked the Speaker of the House of Representatives, the leadership of the Congress, and the Congress to

receive me at the earliest possible moment . . . no later than Monday evening [April 8] . . . for the purpose of hearing the President's recommendations and the President's suggestions for action—constructive action instead of destructive action—in this hour of national need.

The President sought some goal to provide a constructive release for the pent-up frustrations and to kindle the hope that springs from evidence that the system can respond to those in need.[12] He selected fair housing.*

Johnson had pressed the Congress hard on fair housing for more than two years and he finally had gained Senate approval on March 11, 1968. But there had been little hope of getting the House to pass the Senate bill. Urban representatives, normally civil rights supporters, were besieged by middle-class white constituents who wanted to keep blacks out of their neighborhoods. From the tragedy of King's assassination, Johnson saw the opportunity to salvage a national fair-housing bill—and he was prepared to use the tragedy to get it.

That evening he sent a letter to the Speaker of the House and a personal note to House Minority Leader Ford asking them to pass the Senate bill.[13] Four days later Illinois Republican John Anderson (who later ran for President) provided the crucial swing vote in the House Rules Committee to send the bill to the House floor.

For those whites who could not understand black anger, and for blacks who had nothing left but anger, the President put aside some misgivings and moved with calculation to set King securely on a pedestal too high for white or black racists to reach. Johnson had not had the personal rapport with King he'd enjoyed with other black leaders, like Roy Wilkins and Whitney Young.[14] These leaders sought change through the traditional system and had learned how to work it. King's road was outside the system and, while Johnson never hesitated to take advantage of King's actions to advance his domestic programs, demonstrations and civil disobedience were not his preferred routes to social justice.

Under Attorney General Robert Kennedy, the FBI had been permitted to wiretap and bug King to find Communist or subversive connections, but what that surveillance had produced was a record of

---

* Over my years in the White House, the President received much more vitriolic mail for his pursuit of racial justice than for his Vietnam policies. When Johnson had sent his fair-housing bill to Congress in 1966, it had prompted some of the most vicious mail LBJ received on any subject (and the only death threats I ever received as a White House assistant). When King had gone north in 1966 to protest for fair housing, he remarked that he had "never seen such hate—not in Mississippi or Alabama—as I see here in Chicago."

King's sexual activities. The tapes did reveal that among those with whom King discussed tactics was Stanley Levison, a left-wing New York lawyer and real-estate investor whom J. Edgar Hoover considered a Communist. Reports of King's sexual activities were of gossip interest to LBJ. But King's alleged Communist ties and Hoover's harping about King's consultations with Levison worried Johnson, as they had concerned Robert Kennedy.

LBJ had ordered the wiretapping of King stopped in May 1965. The Bureau had eliminated the tap on King's home but continued for some time to bug his hotel rooms with microphones. Hoover had used information from these bugs and from informants to fill the President's mail with suggestions, like the one dated April 19, 1967, that "Based on King's recent activities and public utterances, it is clear that he is an instrument in the hands of subversive forces seeking to undermine our nation."

Johnson's concern that King might be subject to Communist manipulation had heightened that April when the civil rights leader attacked U.S. policy in Vietnam. On April 23, in a press conference at Harvard University, King had declared a "Vietnam Summer" to encourage passive resistance to the draft and the war and had hinted that he might run as an antiwar presidential candidate in 1968. The President had asked me to have Burke Marshall discreetly check with King's friends to see what was going on. Marshall reported that civil rights activists Bayard Rustin and Kenneth Clark, among others, thought King had made a "terrible mistake." Two days after the press conference King dropped any idea of running for the presidency, but he maintained his opposition to the war. Marshall warned that King intended to introduce a Nuremberg concept into the Vietnam debate by equating what American troops were being asked to do in Vietnam to what the Nazis did during World War II.[15]

Johnson could not have cared less about King's philandering. And though he was sometimes angered by King's antiwar posture, he had far more concern about the Senate Foreign Relations Committee on that score. He worried more that King's opposition to the war and his radical connections would provoke a conservative backlash, not just against King but against the Great Society, and Johnson feared that more than anything else. The President was appalled and shaken by the assassination, but he determined to use the tragedy of King's death to advance the dreams of the slain civil rights leader. At this moment of crisis, Johnson consciously decided that—for our nation's sake, to end the divisiveness and complete as much as he could of the Great Society—he had to act to enhance King's reputation.

On April 5, shortly after Johnson issued the presidential proclamation on King in the Fish Room, Mayor Walter Washington asked for Army troops to control rampant rioting in the District.[16] Stokely Carmichael had announced that morning, "When white America killed Dr. King last night she declared war on us." Roving bands of blacks looted and set fires, at some points just two blocks from the White House.

The President told me to get a "proclamation or order, whatever I need to send troops into Washington to maintain order."[17] Johnson moved troops into the District that afternoon and the Mayor imposed a curfew and banned the sale of liquor and guns. Concerned that Walter Washington had never been through anything like this before, LBJ again called Cy Vance.[18]

All afternoon and evening rioting and looting got worse in cities across the country. My office became a command center, with a large map of Washington on an easel in the center of the room, punctured by scores of red-beaded pins to spot the location of burning fires. At least every thirty minutes the White House situation room submitted reports to me on civil disorders across the country.[19]

LBJ was determined to avoid the bloodshed of Watts, Detroit, and Newark. He insisted that I speak personally to Mayor Washington, Deputy Attorney General Christopher, and Army Chief of Staff General Johnson to pass along "the President's instructions that the police, troops, and National Guard be cautioned, to the man, to use the minimum force necessary" in the District. "If humanly possible," Johnson added, "I don't want anybody killed." Senator Richard Russell of Georgia called the President to object that marines guarding the Capitol grounds had not been issued ammunition. As complaints mounted about not providing ammunition to soldiers or letting them load their rifles, Johnson repeated to me, "I don't want Americans killing Americans. I may not be doing the popular thing, or even the right thing, but no soldier in Washington has killed a citizen yet."[20]

When I wasn't eating lunch or dinner with the President or in the Oval Office, he was on the phone to me or in my office. LBJ offered Richard Daley any help he might need in Chicago; shortly before midnight on April 5th—at dinner with Judge Higginbotham, Horace Busby, deputy press secretary Tom Johnson, and me—the President told me that he had information that Daley was "marked for assassination" and to "see the FBI gets this information to Daley's police people."[21]

Johnson discussed the speech he was planning to give at a joint session of Congress. He told Busby the speech "can make or break us. The speech Sunday [announcing the bombing pause and his withdrawal from the campaign] was good and accomplished what we wanted, but King's death has erased all of that, and we have to start again." The President asked me to move into the White House living quarters.[22]

The situation in the capital deteriorated throughout the night. Eventually 14,000 regular Army, Marine, and National Guard troops joined the District's 2,800 police officers on the city's streets. Mayor Washington was intent on keeping arrested troublemakers in prison. "I don't want the people they're arresting released," he told me. "I don't give a damn what they have to do. I don't want them released tonight. Apparently the troops are starting to release some people they picked up for looting. That's just insanity. I don't give a God-damn what the Constitution says. We just can't release them and let them go out again."[23]

I passed along the reports, one more dire than the next, to the President. Remarkably, even in this situation, he didn't lose his sense of humor. That evening I gave the President a report that Stokely Carmichael, fist clenched to symbolize militant black power, was or-ganizing a group at 14th and U Streets Northwest to march on George-town, the posh Washington enclave where many newspaper columnists, television reporters, and *Washington Post* editors live, and burn it down. The President read the report aloud, smiled, and said, "Goddamn! I've waited thirty-five years for this day!"[24]

Sometime after 3 A.M. on Saturday, April 6, Vance came to the White House from his post at the D.C. government's command cen-ter.[25] Vance was plainly exhausted and in great agony from a herni-ated disc in his back. He asked for a drink. We were drinking scotch and soda when the President walked in from his bedroom in his pajamas. "No wonder the nation is going up in smoke and riots and looting," he said in mock rage. "My two top advisers are sitting around drinking!"

By later that Saturday, we had reports of rioting and looting in more than a hundred American cities. Marines and regular Army troops patrolled Washington's streets. We set up roadblocks around the White House, and stationed soldiers at the southwest gate. We were prepared to close all roads to the nation's capital. LBJ wanted me to have Louis Martin, one of his key advisers on civil rights, in my office immediately and have him stay throughout the afternoon and evening. When Martin got to the White House gate, the guards opened his trunk. They saw sets of golf clubs and all sorts of golf equipment and immediately suspected he was a looter, especially since he was black and dressed in casual clothes.[26]

A sense of how dark the day was came when Senator Robert Byrd of West Virginia called that afternoon, April 6, to go on record that the curfew should be "re-enforced immediately, and looters should be shot, if they are adults (but not killed; just in the leg)." He felt that "The time for restraint is ended," and asked why martial law had not been imposed.[27]

The President decided not to address Congress on April 8 as he had suggested in his statement accompanying the King proclamation. That would be the eve of King's funeral. If he spoke before the service, he feared that the television networks would ask those attending the funeral whether he had urged Congress to do enough and the response would be that he had not, even though Congress was balking at what measures he'd already sent up to the Hill.[28]

That Saturday evening the President had to send troops to Chicago. I brought the proclamation and executive order to his living quarters. Johnson's eyes were heavy with fatigue, his jaw sagging. Lying on his back in bed, he signaled me to hand him a pen, and signed the papers as he held them up over his head, which he was too exhausted to raise from the pillow.

The next day was Palm Sunday. The President took his daughter Luci, his secretary Marie Fehmer, Jim Jones, and me to St. Dominic's Roman Catholic Church for the 12:15 P.M. mass. As we left the church, the congregation stood without leaving their places and gave the President warm, supportive, understanding smiles and nods.[29] In Washington, the rioting had subsided, but there were reports of homelessness and food shortages. After a helicopter trip to Andrews Air Force Base to bid farewell to General Westmoreland (who had come to Washington for meetings on Vietnam when the President canceled his Hawaii trip), Johnson flew along 7th and 14th Streets Northwest, where smoke was still rising from smoldering and burnt-out buildings.[30]

In the afternoon, Mrs. Johnson called my office to invite me to have supper with the family that evening. "I'd love to, Mrs. Johnson," I said, "but I haven't been home since Wednesday night. I think I'd better go see my kids."

"I can certainly understand that, Joe," Mrs. Johnson said. "But Lyndon and I are having some people he truly likes—Lynda, Luci and Pat, [Texas Congressman and Mrs. Jack] Brooks, Vicky [McCammon]—and I'd like you to be there."

I tried to beg off.

"Joe," Mrs. Johnson said, "this is going to be a nice evening for Lyndon. This has not been a good week. You've been bringing a lot of bad news to him. I want Lyndon to see you in some pleasant circumstances. You know Lyndon sometimes can confuse the messenger with the message and I wouldn't ever want that to happen to you."

Touched, I accepted the invitation.[31] It was a warm evening, with Lady Bird doing everything she could to relax her husband and saying some very complimentary things about me. LBJ loved sweets and she even had some candy for him (something she usually kept away because of his weight problem). At one point, knowing Lady Bird was indulging him, the President took a cigarette out from a crystal cylinder at his end of the table and put it between his lips. Since his heart attack in 1955, the President had religiously obeyed his doctor's orders to stay away from cigarettes, but he often spoke of how much he missed smoking. Mrs. Johnson rose from her end of the table, walked over to the President, and, with a broad smile, said, "Now, Lyndon, you know better," as she took the cigarette from between his lips. (Johnson told me there were two things he intended to do when he left the White House: one was to welcome back to the Johnson family Walter Jenkins, the devoted aide who resigned in the face of charges of making homosexual advances;[32] the other was to start smoking cigarettes again.)*

Pleasant as she'd tried to make the evening, Mrs. Johnson couldn't cloister us from events. During dinner, around 10:15 P.M., I handed Johnson an executive order and proclamation sending Army troops into yet another American city, Baltimore, in response to Maryland Governor Spiro Agnew's request. We feared the situation in Pittsburgh might also require troops; the President was prepared to send them, but fortunately the violence abated that evening and no soldiers were needed there.[33]

Even in times of great tragedy, the American political-ambition machine grinds away. Donald Kendall, president of PepsiCo and one of Nixon's closest supporters, called to suggest "in view of the President's desire for a show of national unity, that the President invite Nixon, Kennedy and McCarthy to ride down with him in the Presidential plane to the funeral of Martin Luther King. Therefore not one individual could play politics with this situation. I have discussed this with Nixon, who thinks it is a good idea and Nixon is agreeable, if the President agrees."[34] Robert Kennedy was walking the scorched streets of Washington with a large press contingent in tow. Senators, congressmen, administration appointees, and others jockeyed for position in the President's party at the King funeral, or to represent the President if he did not go.[35]

* He did both.

By Monday morning, April 8, the Secret Service and FBI reported several threats to assassinate the President; both agencies considered the likelihood of an attempt on Johnson's life at the King funeral quite high.[36] Reluctantly, the President agreed not to go to Atlanta. Instead, he sent Hubert Humphrey in a plane filled with top black administration appointees, including Thurgood Marshall, Robert Weaver, and Walter Washington. The King funeral was crowded with politicians and politics. Presidential candidates were there. Bobby Kennedy was cheered as mourners recalled his brother's call to King during the 1960 presidential campaign, Nixon was jeered with cries of "politicking," Eugene McCarthy was hardly noticed.

As the violence subsided, the President went to Camp David with Ellsworth Bunker, Ambassador to South Vietnam (although we were still sufficiently concerned to ship along with him copies of a proclamation and executive order with blanks to complete in case another American city needed troops).[37] Over the next few days, the President negotiated with Hanoi, accepted Larry O'Brien's resignation as Postmaster General so he could work in Kennedy's campaign, and announced Marvin Watson to succeed O'Brien and General Creighton Abrams to succeed Westmoreland in Vietnam.

Through it all, the President kept pressing the House to accept the Senate's fair-housing bill and send it to him for signature. On Wednesday April 10, the House did that and a solemn President praised the Congress. I wrote the President a memo urging him to appear before a joint session of Congress, come out swinging for an increase in social programs, and abandon his negotiations with Wilbur Mills, who wanted deep, across-the-board cuts in domestic programs in return for the tax bill. My memo infuriated Johnson, and he scribbled all over it:

JAC Memo	LBJ Pencil Notes
". . . I understand you are thinking about a TV statement from your office in lieu of a special message to a joint session of Congress."	"No!"
". . . You are publicly on record in promising a message."	"I promised nothing. I stated my intentions only. Since changed by riots!"
Instead of across-the-board reduction in social programs, I suggested cuts in:	

—the SST program

"You save very little."

—the highway program, noting "most Americans would rather ride a little bumpier road for a couple of years than sit at home under curfews or in such fear that they go out and buy guns. . . ."

"They don't & you can't save 100 mil in expen—"

—the space program: "It is more important for prestige purposes to show the world that a democratic society of different races can live together peacefully than it is to get to the moon on some experimental basis by 1970."

"I don't agree."

I urged spending $3 to $5 billion more on social programs on a list that one of my aides put together.

"Tell him to forget it—"

I urged abandonment of Treasury's across-the-board-cut strategy to get a tax bill—"Fowler is . . . emotionally involved."

"He is not really as emotional as most city advocates."

I urged rethinking balance of payments problems by McGeorge Bundy or Charles Murphy—"They are bright, tough minded and wise and have no preconceived views."

"Ha! Ha!"

"I consider it essential for you to go before a joint session of the Congress."

"Forget it."[38]

The following day, April 11, LBJ signed the fair-housing bill in the East Room of the White House, calling for the passage of his legislative and appropriations requests: "I urge the Congress to enact the measures for social justice that I have recommended in some twenty messages. . . . These measures provide more than $78 billion that I have urged the Congress to enact for major domestic programs. . . . We have come some of the way, not near all of it. There is much yet to do."

The President paused, looked directly at me—stared is how I felt—and concluded: "If the Congress sees fit to act upon these twenty messages and some fifteen appropriations bills, I assure you that what remains to be done will be recommended in ample time for you to do it after you have completed what is already before you."

That ending and that penetrating look were LBJ's way of expressing his exasperation to me; his whole demeanor said, "Do you understand, Goddamnit, do you understand now, finally, what my position is!"

The President's position! In the weeks ahead, the contest for the President's mind on domestic issues would be as intense as the struggle over Vietnam policy had been in February and March.[39]

The stature the President had gained as a leader willing to sacrifice his career and pride for the good of the people was invaluable as he sought to hold things together in the aftermath of King's assassination. It is frightening to contemplate what would have occurred had LBJ been required to assess each move after the murder in terms of his reelection and had ambitious partisan opponents, a skeptical press, angry blacks, and resentful whites measured his actions in that context.

Unfortunately, the President's withdrawal speech had no impact on House Ways and Means Committee Chairman Wilbur Mills,[40] who, in a House and Senate conference, held the tax bill hostage to his demands for deep spending cuts. By the end of April, the President's mind and energy were consumed with finding a way to pass the bill. He told me, "In hindsight, I never should have lowered taxes. My advice to my successor will be: never lower taxes." On April 26, at the inaugural meeting of the board of the Urban Institute, an independent think tank we created to assess our programs and develop sorely needed data for new approaches to social ills, Johnson entered the Cabinet Room with his prepared remarks, sat down, set them aside, and said: "I've got a set of remarks prepared by my intellectual, liberal advisers. But let me tell you what's on my mind. Your job is to worry about the future. Well, here's the number one problem for anyone that wants to help their country and the people in it. You've got to figure out how to raise the taxes to pay for these social programs our people need and to rebuild our cities and educate our children. I'm sure you're all smart enough to tell us which programs work and which don't. What we need is someone smart enough to tell us how to convince the American people that they should ante up. So look at that—figure out how to get the resources we need and you'll have done something special for the future of your country."[41]

I became convinced that Mills as Chairman of the House Ways and Means Committee was trying to torpedo both the tax bill and the Great Society. The White House was filled with rumors that the President was ready to capitulate to Mills at a press conference on May 3. The evening before, I wrote Johnson:

> . . . For the past month we have been moving with increased power and ability to get things done, as well as an increased sense of confidence because the American people believe you are doing whatever you do without any ax to grind and only because it is right. . . .
>
>   But this remarkable accretion of power in a lame duck status could deteriorate rapidly if Wilbur Mills rolls over us on the tax legislation. . . .
>
>   . . . if you get stuck either with no tax bill or with provisions of the kind Mills is now peddling, I think the ball game may well be over on the Hill for the rest of the year. Indeed, you may have an increasingly difficult time running the Executive Branch of the Government and leading the country. . . .
>
>   . . . I suggest that you give consideration to coming out fighting in your press conference tomorrow morning for [our] tax package. . . . I think we should turn loose everything we have to take the Ways and Means Committee away from Mills.[42]

The following morning I was in the rear of the East Room as the President entered for his press conference.[43] He announced that he had reached agreement with North Vietnam to meet in Paris. As reporters fired question after question on the peace talks and other subjects, I thought he'd never be asked about the tax bill. Then it came. Johnson paused and my heart skipped a beat. The President then lashed Congress publicly as he had never done before. He asked them to "stand up like men," accused them of "courting danger by this continued procrastination," and concluded, "I think the time has come for all of the Members of Congress to be responsible and, even in an election year, to bite the bullet and stand up and do what ought to be done for their country."

In a thinly veiled reference to Mills's constant demands for domestic spending cuts, Johnson said, "[Congress needs] to pass a tax bill without any 'ands,' 'buts,' or 'ors.' If they want to effect reductions, then as each appropriation bill comes up, they can offer their amendments like men out on the floor, and call the roll. But don't hold up a tax bill until you can blackmail someone into getting your own personal viewpoint over on reductions."

Johnson had not only slammed Mills, he had played shrewdly to the Appropriations Committee and its chairman, George Mahon (D-Texas), who was angry with Mills for stepping on his turf by insisting on specific spending reductions before supporting a tax bill. Later, on Air Force One going to Independence, Missouri, to wish Harry Truman happy birthday,[44] a reporter suggested to the President that he had been "rough" on Congressman Mills. Johnson replied teasingly, "I didn't think I was rough on anyone. . . . I am surprised that the press would ever detect anything that would lead into a controversy. . . . Now, the first thing they do after we get a site is try to start a war in Washington while we are trying to get peace in Paris." He also pointed out that the Congress itself was appropriating more money than he had asked for in some areas and was barely able to agree on possible cuts of only $4 billion, the figure Johnson preferred as part of a deal for his tax package.[45]

That evening, the President called me. He asked rather coyly what I thought of the press conference. I said it was "A-plus." He was in a great mood, chuckling and reveling in the wire-service stories. After all, he'd gotten the North Vietnamese to the negotiating table and he had vented his frustration about the Congress. He then told me one of his favorite stories, which ended with the statement, "Never tell a man to go to hell unless you're sure you can send him there," and added, "Well, I just told someone to go to hell. Now everybody's got to get off their ass and get that conference to report our tax bill."

On May 21, Arthur Okun, who had succeeded Gardner Ackley as CEA Chairman in March, sent LBJ a memo spelling out the world financial crisis that could result from failure to pass a tax bill. The memo was full of dire consequences, and he argued that "the first casualty might be the *Paris peace talks.*"

Okun had handwritten a cover note to the President: "The attached discussion is HIGHLY SENSITIVE. We can't make these arguments publicly because we will have to try as hard as we can to avoid these consequences if we don't get the tax bill!"[46] But the memo was too good for LBJ not to use. He privately called a number of members of Congress, reading them excerpts, and said, "That's the risk Wilbur Mills is taking with our country because his momma doesn't like the welfare program."

The President's fight to protect the Great Society from Wilbur Mills and the conservatives was not helped by the Poor People's Campaign that camped out in the nation's capital during the spring of 1968 as the struggle over the tax bill reached the critical stage. Martin Luther King had announced the campaign—to assemble the nation's poor in Washington to demand jobs, housing, education, health care, food, and social services—a few months before his assassination. "This will be a move," King explained at the time, "that will be consciously designed to develop massive dislocation [until Congress and the Administration act]." After King's assassination, his deputy, the Reverend Ralph David Abernathy, took it over.

From the beginning, Johnson thought the idea dangerous. It was asking for yet more when he hadn't been able to persuade Congress to pass what he had already requested. He feared, too, that the campaign might provoke new disturbances.

The campaign was poorly organized and financed. The first caravan arrived in Washington in mid-May 1968 and constructed a Resurrection City of shanties and tents in West Potomac Park, in sight of the Lincoln Memorial and Washington Monument. In a particularly rainy season, Resurrection City soon became a filthy mud swamp. Garbage cluttered the area. Poor sanitation threatened the health of its inhabitants. Gangs of black youths from northern and midwestern cities terrorized black southerners. Black and Mexican-American leaders clashed. Reports of excessive drinking and fighting arrived at the White House. Militants were urging violent demonstrations. Public-health officials feared outbreaks of serious illness. Johnson kept troops and National Guardsmen on alert.[47]

The President looked for a way to channel the participants' energies to some fruitful purpose. While the poor people camped out in West Potomac Park, a CBS special, "Hunger in America," and congressional hearings shocked Americans with reports of malnutrition and starvation among more than fourteen million of their fellow citizens. By late May the President began considering a major effort to deal with hunger in America.[48] Abernathy was calling on the government for unattainable action on all domestic fronts. Johnson thought a hunger program might be a way to get something done for the disadvantaged and, at the same time, give the demonstrators a graceful exit from Resurrection City. This way, Johnson thought, something could be salvaged from the failed campaign, which had offended most members of Congress and was jeopardizing his tax bill and social programs.

At the campaign's final rally of fifty thousand people at the Lincoln Memorial on June 19, as Johnson was getting his massive housing program out of the House Banking Committee and urging the House to pass his tax bill, Abernathy excoriated the administration and Congress and called the social and legislative advances of the prior five years a record of "broken promises." That did it for LBJ. Already wary of asking Congress for a major new program, he personally turned against doing anything that might be seen as a response to the campaign or Abernathy, and scrambled to get his tax bill.

Finally, grudgingly, Johnson had to agree to a $6 billion spending cut in fiscal 1969 as the price for passage of a 10 percent tax surcharge on corporations and individuals. Johnson signed the tax bill on June 28, but called the spending cuts unwise. Since he doubted that Congress would take that much out of the budget, and in any case he didn't want to, Johnson delayed making any reductions until he saw what action Congress itself took.

Johnson did indeed have the last laugh. Congress was unable even to cut $4 billion in spending, and Johnson declined to make any reductions above those passed on Capitol Hill. Fiscal 1969 ended with a $3.2 billion surplus—and the Great Society programs survived.

EIGHTEEN

Who Is LBJ's Candidate?

EVEN AFTER he'd withdrawn from the presidential race, Lyndon Johnson was determined to control the government right down to noon on January 20, 1969. He was possessed as never before by a need to be confident of the loyalty of his aides and cabinet secretaries. And he was ambivalent about the candidacy of Hubert Humphrey.

Johnson's mixed feelings about Humphrey stemmed in part from his admiration for Nelson Rockefeller. Ever since joining the White House staff, I had observed the close relationship between Johnson and the New York Governor. LBJ liked Rockefeller personally and considered him one of the nation's ablest and most dedicated public servants. When Rockefeller divorced his first wife, Mary Todhunter Clark, in 1962 and married Margaretta (Happy) Murphy in 1963, the New York Governor was widely criticized for adultery, divorce, and quick remarriage. Johnson felt "Nelson took a terrible beating in the press for marrying Happy" and repeatedly invited the couple to White House dinners to "put a stamp of approval on that marriage."[1]

The feeling, it seemed to me, was mutual. At the end of a letter thanking the President for his help during the 1966 New York City transit strike, Rockefeller wrote, "P.S. I just talked to Happy on the phone & told her you had asked after her. She sent her love!" After Johnson delivered his State of the Union message to Congress in January of that same year, Rockefeller called to tell the President that he and Happy had watched the address and "thought every bit of it magnificent."[2]

As soon as Rockefeller had been elected Governor in 1958, he was regarded as presidential material. He had stood no chance in 1960 and fared no better in 1964. By 1967, Rockefeller had tamed his presidential ambitions long enough to support another moderate Republican, Michigan Governor George Romney, until Romney self-destructed and pulled out of the race in late February 1968.

Following his own withdrawal, Johnson did everything he discreetly could to entice Rockefeller to run. On April 4, in their brief whispered exchange after Archbishop Cooke's installation at St. Patrick's Cathedral, Johnson had gently nudged Rockefeller to seek the Republican nomination. On April 5, J. Irwin Miller, chairman of Cummins Engine and a Republican who had supported LBJ in 1964, asked me to see if the President had any objection to his chairing a Rockefeller-for-President effort. The President told me to give Miller a full-speed go-ahead; Johnson made no attempt either to neutralize this very liberal Republican or tilt him toward Humphrey.[3] On April 10 Rockefeller announced he was "available" for his party's nomination.

On Tuesday evening, April 23, LBJ and Lady Bird had dinner at the White House alone with the New York Governor and his wife. Johnson had arranged the dinner so secretly that he had the Rockefellers come to the office of special counsel Larry Temple as though they had a meeting with the White House aide. Temple then quietly escorted them to the mansion for dinner.[4]

Johnson had already decided to be neutral among the Democratic candidates, a decision he communicated to Rockefeller at that dinner. While both Rockefeller and Humphrey would attempt to nourish the Great Society programs, Johnson seemed to believe that Rockefeller had a greater chance of success. That evening Johnson urged Rockefeller to seek the Republican nomination. As Happy Rockefeller later put it, "LBJ urged him to run. He did want Nelson to be president." As Lady Bird later said, "Lyndon thought Rockefeller was by far the best of the Republicans and wanted the best running for the American people to choose from. Lyndon thought Rockefeller was a good human being, a person who was for the disadvantaged, who was a man of compassion, with a capable and effective mind, and capable of being effective, getting things done. Lyndon urging Rockefeller to run was very much in line with what Lyndon thought of him."[5] Having Rockefeller as the Republican nominee was in line with another of LBJ's thoughts: if Kennedy turned out to be the Democratic candidate, Rockefeller was a good bet to beat him. On April 30, a week after the dinner with LBJ, Rockefeller announced his formal candidacy for the Republican presidential nomination.

Johnson despised Richard Nixon. If there was to be a Republican victor in the 1968 election, Nixon was the last man he wanted. As Vicky McCammon said, "He hated him. He said . . . he would like to have him for breakfast." But when he had been still holding open his option to run, Johnson had believed that Nixon would be the easiest Republican for him to defeat in a presidential campaign,[6] so he had deliberately helped make him the Republican front-runner.

Coming up to the 1966 midterm elections, Nixon had campaigned across the nation for Republican congressional candidates, attacking LBJ and his Great Society. Before a press conference on November 4, 1966, the President told me he was going to give "Ol' Nixon a little attention today."

A reporter asked about Nixon's comments that Johnson appeared too willing to get out of Southeast Asia "in a way that would leave South Vietnam to the mercy of the Vietcong." Johnson said he didn't want to debate foreign policy "with a chronic campaigner" who finds "fault with his country and his Government during a period of October every two years" and who "never did really recognize and realize what was going on when he had an official position in the Government."

When Johnson returned to his office and saw the wire-service tickers lead with his characterization of Nixon as a "chronic campaigner," he chortled, "That ought to put him out front!" But Johnson had outsmarted himself, as he later recognized in talking about whether he had any regrets about withdrawing. "My only regret is that . . . Richard Nixon is going to be the Republican nominee. I was never more sure of anything in my political career than of the fact that I could beat Richard Nixon. And I would very much like to do it."[7]

After Johnson withdrew, Hubert Humphrey scheduled the formal announcement of his candidacy for Saturday, April 27, and several cabinet officers planned to attend the Vice President's announcement luncheon. They assumed such action was par for the course as members of an administration Humphrey had loyally served and which two other Democratic candidates, Kennedy and McCarthy, had been kicking around for months. But they didn't understand what par was on Lyndon Johnson's political course.

The first of several harangues came over my telephone on April 23, as the President fumed about a wire-service report that Agriculture Secretary Orville Freeman had endorsed Hubert Humphrey. Johnson wanted Freeman and all other officials in the executive branch to stay out of the race: "I can't have the government torn apart by cabinet officers and presidential appointees fighting among themselves about Kennedy, McCarthy and Humphrey." The President directed me to call the cabinet and tell them to "stay out of the race or get out of the government." He didn't want any of them going to Humphrey's luncheon on Saturday.

When I called Freeman, he resisted. As a fellow Minnesotan, he felt he had to attend the lunch and wondered aloud whether he should resign. The next day Undersecretary of Agriculture John Schnittker announced his support of Robert Kennedy. LBJ told me to call every cabinet officer and the Vice President, and deliver this message in no uncertain terms: Cabinet officers should read to their presidential appointees the final paragraphs of the President's March 31 withdrawal speech (promising "not [to] permit the Presidency to become involved in the partisan divisions that are developing in this political year"); in order to maintain the sincerity of that speech, its letter and spirit had to be observed, and "this means no statements of support and no staff work and no activities of any kind for any candidate for President."[8]

Before I could complete the calls, late in the afternoon, one of the wire services carried a story that Assistant Secretary of Agriculture John Baker had declared for Humphrey. The story then breezily speculated about which candidate would get the most votes among the top Agriculture Department appointees. When Johnson read this wire on the machines in his office, he angrily hit the button to his secretary and shouted that he wanted "Freeman, Schnittker, and John Baker on the line at once and at the same time." He was so enraged that his secretaries and the White House operators couldn't understand his instructions.

As it turned out, Freeman and Schnittker were traveling in airplanes and the only one Johnson could get on the phone was Baker, a Kennedy holdover that Johnson had never before spoken to.[9] Johnson verbally whipped the skin off Baker's back for violating a presidential order and directed him to bring his resignation to the White House that evening and give it to me. As soon as I learned what had happened, I called Baker, a quiet man whom Johnson's tirade had turned into a basket case, and told him to forget about the President's instructions unless he heard from me in the morning. Baker kept repeating, "But I have a direct presidential order." I finally persuaded him to "go back to [his] job in the Agriculture Department." Johnson never mentioned Baker again.

On April 26 Theodore Sorensen, one of Robert Kennedy's campaign aides, complained about administration members favoring Humphrey. That made Johnson even angrier. He told me to call

Sorensen and inform him of his policy of neutrality, but to make it clear that "in no way does the President owe anything to Bobby Kennedy," that the President was determined "to stay as close to the national interest" as he could, out of partisan politics, away from "supporting, refraining from supporting or opposing anyone."[10]

Sorensen need not have been concerned. On April 29, Walter Reuther visited the President. I was present at the hour-long meeting. Most of the discussion centered on politics. Reuther favored Humphrey and urged the President, "Where possible [to] involve the Vice President publicly in big government decisions."

Johnson was uncharacteristically disengaged and distant. He said he wasn't "going to commit [to involve Humphrey], but I will try to." Johnson said he thought the "South [is] pretty well written off. . . . There are fifteen states in the U.S. that can't go with me. . . . I've spent my popularity." Johnson told the UAW president, "Do whatever you are going to do and put it on the line. I don't have the slightest doubt about where your best interest lies." The implication was that Reuther's best interest was with Humphrey, but never once did Johnson say to Reuther, "I think you should support my Vice President."[11]

NINETEEN

The Robert Kennedy
Assassination

LBJ WAS HAUNTED by the ghost of one Kennedy whose tragic assassination had elevated him to the presidency. But he had always admired Jack Kennedy, and he grieved for Jacqueline and did what he could to comfort her and to provide Secret Service protection. "My God, that poor woman," he said. "She never liked politics in the first place, and then to be left this way."[*][1]

Trying always to understand why John Kennedy was accorded such adulation while his own accomplishments were underappreciated, LBJ used to compare his record with his predecessor's. "Put together what we recommended to Congress and what we got," alongside "what Kennedy recommended to Congress and what he got," Johnson told me more than once.[3] There was, of course, no comparison. But even Johnson's lopsided margin of legislative achievement did not calm the storm of jealousy about the "Kennedy class" that threatened to drown him. As LBJ saw it, there was a poor kid working around the clock at Southwest Texas State Teachers College in San Marcos and there was a rich kid partying through the ivy halls of Harvard with plenty of time to acquire all the social graces in sophisticated Boston. Lyndon Johnson, who had achieved more in each year

---

[*] Though even here Johnson occasionally revealed how the Kennedy mystique obsessed him. In October 1968, when he read on the ticker that President Kennedy's widow was going to marry Greek playboy-tycoon Aristotle Onassis, he said to me, "Well, by God, that'll sure take its toll on the Camelot myth."[2]

of his presidency than most chief executives accomplish in all their White House years, was possessed by an internal class struggle with an icon, and tortured by an envy he could not exorcise. Remarkably, despite it all, Johnson often expressed privately his respect and affection for John Kennedy. He once told Robert Kennedy, "I've never thought of my administration as just the Johnson administration, but as a continuation of the Kennedy-Johnson administration." And he believed that he was acting as President Kennedy would have: "I feel that President Kennedy is looking down on what I've done and would approve."[4]

None of this respect and affection for John Kennedy spilled over to his brother Robert. LBJ saw Robert Kennedy as ruthless, ambitious, positioning himself as the heir apparent, feeding on any available discontent among the dismayed and baffled citizens who thought the country was coming apart at the seams, and horrified that Johnson was sitting in his brother's chair.

Johnson detested Senator Joseph McCarthy and had distrusted Robert Kennedy from the time he worked as assistant counsel to McCarthy's Permanent Subcommittee on Investigations. He had never forgiven the younger Kennedy for trying to keep him off the 1960 Democratic ticket by suggesting to him that he decline John Kennedy's invitation. Johnson suspected that as Attorney General Robert Kennedy had wiretapped his phones and bugged his offices.

After the Bay of Pigs fiasco, LBJ believed that it was Robert Kennedy who had spearheaded the Kennedy administration's policy to get rid of Fidel Castro, by assassination if necessary. He was convinced that the younger Kennedy's obsessive desire to eliminate the Cuban leader had something to do with JFK's murder in 1963. As he told me, "President Kennedy tried to get Castro, but Castro got Kennedy first."* Johnson never believed that one person could have accomplished President Kennedy's assassination. But in late 1966, when someone suggested that Johnson "convene a small (2–3) confidential task force" to reassess the Warren Commission findings, with particular attention to "alleged circumstantial evidence of the existence and continuance of a conspiracy" and "events since the assassination [suggesting] the continuance of a conspiracy,"[5] Johnson decided not to do so. He thought such action would serve no good at that time and would reopen all the wounds for the Kennedy family and for him as well.

---

* Soon after Johnson became President, he ordered a stop to all covert activity to eliminate or overthrow Castro.

Following President Kennedy's assassination, Johnson's suspicions about Robert Kennedy's ambition were confirmed when the younger brother's allies touted the Attorney General as the ideal vice-presidential nominee for 1964. Johnson was determined to win the presidency on his own, to amass an overwhelming majority without a Kennedy on the ticket. He had devised the cover that no cabinet member would be eligible to be his running mate in 1964. Johnson so distrusted Kennedy that when he told the then Attorney General of his decision, he used his speaker phone on his desk to record this conversation so he'd have it verbatim, should Kennedy try to distort what either of them said. It made matters worse that Kennedy was just as concerned about LBJ and didn't like or trust him. As Larry O'Brien, often pinched between the two, later said, "Both men were paranoid about each other."[6]

After Johnson's landslide election, the President proudly, almost gloatingly, and frequently, pointed out that he had carried New York State by 4.9 to 2.2 million votes, a 2.7 million vote spread, while Robert Kennedy had defeated Republican Senator Kenneth Keating by 3.8 to 3.1 million, a margin of only 700,000 votes. But from the moment Robert Kennedy entered the Senate, Johnson had had to watch as the media turned another Kennedy into a national hero, and as Robert moved himself into field position to succeed to the throne, making clear by his body language and words that he considered LBJ an interloper. On December 8, 1967, I reported to the President that Bill Moyers had called to say that "Shriver believed Bobby Kennedy was getting ready to run against you in 1968" (and that Shriver was interested in Goldberg's post of UN Ambassador, which would put him in the President's cabinet and neutralize him during the 1968 presidential contest).[7]

Reporters asked Senator Kennedy for comment on every program Johnson proposed. Far more often than not, Johnson had to bite his lip as the New York Senator found fault: the program did not go far enough to help the poor, provide enough low-cost housing units, train enough unemployed, or educate or assure health care for enough children. Johnson was furious in March 1967 when Kennedy split with him on the Vietnam War, convinced the New York Senator's overarching political ambition had led him to betray his own brother, whose cabinet Johnson had kept in place and whose policies Johnson believed he was carrying out. But the deepest personal hurt came as blacks, Mexican-Americans, and the poor began to adulate Kennedy, for it was Johnson, not Robert or even John Kennedy, who had put muscle and flesh on the dusty skeleton of the Emancipation Proclamation, and hammered into law the progressive Democratic legislative agenda that had accumulated for a generation. Johnson ached with hurt, jealousy, and rage as he saw these groups turn to RFK. LBJ knew that no one, including John, and certainly not Robert, could match his legislative achievements for the poor and the black, but knowing that only added salt to his wounds as he watched those to whom he offered his Great Society push and shove to touch the sleeve of another Kennedy.

Since he was well aware of his own psychological baggage, in no situation did Lyndon Johnson try harder to do the right thing—for the country, the Kennedy family, and himself—than in the hours and days following the shooting of Robert Kennedy at the celebration of his California primary victory over Eugene McCarthy at the Ambassador Hotel in Los Angeles.

"Too horrible for words," the shaken President blurted when national security adviser Walt Rostow phoned him with word of Kennedy's shooting at 3:31 A.M. on the morning of June 5, 1968.[8]

Though Kennedy was still hanging barely to life, LBJ knew this younger brother's martyrdom finished any opportunity he had to be acclaimed during his lifetime for his achievements for the disadvantaged. But he mustered his self-discipline to concentrate his effort and power to ease the burden for this tragic American family and to comfort the nation.

At the President's request, a few days after King's assassination, I had tried to secure congressional approval of Secret Service protection for presidential and vice-presidential candidates, but at the time of Robert Kennedy's shooting neither house had acted. This June morning, the President wasn't waiting for congressional action. Before dawn he simply ordered the protection provided, then telephoned bipartisan congressional leaders, told them what he had done, and asked them to pass legislation immediately.*[9]

Early that morning, Ramsey Clark called me at home: the President wanted me at the White House immediately. When I got there, Johnson had already issued a statement, had called Ted Kennedy and others close to Robert Kennedy,[10] and had put troops on alert for fear of trouble in Los Angeles and the nation's capital (which fortunately never materialized).

The President asked George Christian, Harry McPherson, and me to lunch.[11] Kennedy, and the violence and rancor that plagued our

* Congress acted the next day.

nation, dominated our conversation. The President was as concerned and thoughtful as I ever remember him. During lunch, Johnson was informed that Kennedy would almost certainly die, or if by some miracle he survived, would be a crippled vegetable. "God help the mother of those boys," he sighed. "Thank God He's given her such faith that she can withstand the tragedies the Good Lord has seen fit to subject her to."[12]

Even if final uncertainty over Kennedy's condition persisted through the night, we all agreed that the President should make some statement to the nation that evening, and he set McPherson to work on it. At the same time, he told me to start drafting a proclamation for a day of mourning to be issued immediately after Kennedy's death.[13]

LBJ then went to bed for his afternoon nap, but he couldn't sleep. He watched television reports on Kennedy's condition, as Frank Mankiewicz, the New York Senator's press aide, struggled in his grief to make hopeful announcements, and he called me once or twice to see if I had heard anything.[14] I, in turn, undertook with Larry Levinson the task of writing a proclamation and statement about a death that had not yet occurred.

That evening Johnson invited his Senate colleagues Everett Dirksen and Mike Mansfield to the Oval Office for a drink and some conversation.[15] For almost an hour, these old friends talked about the sour atmosphere in the country, trying to divine what was tearing it apart. Johnson also raised a more immediate concern: whether to launch an investigation into Robert Kennedy's death. Johnson had appointed the Warren Commission after President Kennedy's assassination. Now, he explained, he proposed to create a commission on violence, headed by Milton Eisenhower (President Eisenhower's brother and former president of Johns Hopkins University), not to investigate the circumstances of Kennedy's assassination, but to address "the whys" of violence in America. Johnson urged the senators not to mount congressional investigations, because he feared they would divide the nation and be devastating to the Kennedy family. Mansfield and Dirksen agreed.

Johnson then reviewed drafts of his remarks to the nation that evening and called prospective members of the commission. He struggled over each word of the speech, not only with McPherson and me, but with Fortas, Clifford, Ramsey Clark, Mansfield, and Dirksen, as we raced to meet television's ten-o'clock deadline.[16] LBJ wanted to reassure the people that "the Nation" had not shot Kennedy, but also to remind them that virulent extremism and demagogic calls for violence fostered a climate that encouraged such acts and threatened the fabric of American society.

By the time they got to the teleprompter, Johnson had written just about each of these words:

> We pray to God that He will spare Robert Kennedy and will restore him to full health and vigor. . . . The Kennedy family has endured sorrow enough, and we pray that this family may be spared more anguish.
>
> Tonight this Nation faces once again the consequences of lawlessness, hatred, and unreason in its midst. It would be wrong, it would be self-deceptive, to ignore the connection between that lawlessness and hatred and this act of violence. It would be just as wrong, and just as self-deceptive, to conclude from this act that our country itself is sick, that it has lost its balance, that it has lost its sense of direction, even its common decency. . . .
>
> Let us put an end to violence and to the preaching of violence.

As always, LBJ wanted to extract something out of tragedy. As he had taken the grim occasion of King's assassination to pass a fair-housing bill, so he seized this sad event to do something about gun control. Throughout his presidency, Johnson had proposed tough gun-control legislation and Congress had refused to act. Only three weeks earlier, the Senate, by an almost two-to-one margin, had defeated an administration provision to control rifles, shotguns, and pistols, substituting weak and inadequate restrictions on handguns. The gun lobby shrewdly worked behind the scenes to have the House pass this gutted Senate bill as a response to Kennedy's assassination. That cynical maneuver only made Johnson more determined to get effective gun-control legislation, which in his statement he asked Congress to enact.

At 1 A.M. (on June 6), Johnson walked from the Oval Office over to the mansion for dinner with Larry Temple, Christian, McPherson, and me.[17] His anguish was visible. His presidency had erupted out of the assassination of John Kennedy, a man who in death had assumed heroic proportions that LBJ would not achieve in life. Now, in the last months of his presidency, a murdered Robert Kennedy would likely leave a legacy of what-might-have-been that would rival his brother's. In life Robert Kennedy had been a political hammer; in death, he would be a haunting nightmare.

We were somber. The President would pick up the telephone attached under the table at his place to ask the Secret Serviceman on duty, "Is he dead yet?" On a number of occasions, he asked me, "Is he dead? Is he dead yet?" or signal me to the phone in the next room.

I knew what he wanted. I got up and called the Secret Service or Larry Levinson, "The President wants to know whether Bobby Kennedy has died." I couldn't tell, because Johnson didn't know, whether he hoped or feared the answer would be yes or no.

At 5:01 A.M. the next morning, the President received word that Robert Kennedy had died. That morning, Johnson read a brief statement and signed the proclamation declaring Sunday, June 9, a day of national mourning in honor of Robert Kennedy.[18]

The President wanted to know what kind of funeral Kennedy might have. He was apprehensive that the family might request a full state funeral, with the body lying in state in the Rotunda of the Capitol, but the family decided that Kennedy's body should lie in state in New York, with the funeral mass at St. Patrick's Cathedral, to be followed by a train trip to Washington for burial near his brother at Arlington National Cemetery. The family insisted that there be no military presence, honor guard, or salute at the gravesite. Johnson instructed me and others to provide whatever assistance Ethel Kennedy and the family wanted, and we used White House telephone operators to issue invitations for the funeral mass in New York. Johnson personally approved all government arrangements, including the burial site about one hundred feet from President Kennedy selected by Robert McNamara and the use of a military plane to return Senator Edward Kennedy's wife, Joan, to Washington.[19]

At 4 P.M., the President taped a television and radio statement on the need for gun-control legislation. When he later watched a replay of the tape with Tom Johnson, Christian, and me, he didn't like it: "Too many lines in my face and bad lighting." So he retaped the statement.[20] But even better makeup and lighting couldn't remove the lines from his face on this grim afternoon.

The President felt he should attend the funeral mass scheduled for June 8 in St. Patrick's Cathedral, both out of respect for the family and to avoid criticism for not being there. The President invited me to accompany him. Then, as reports of possible attempts on his life kept coming in, and the Secret Service urged him not to attend the funeral, Johnson said that I didn't have to go. I had two small children, he didn't want to endanger my life. I said I wanted to go with him.

Johnson stressed that he did not want to impose himself on the grieving family, and understandably he did not look forward to entering a church filled with grief-stricken Kennedy admirers who disliked him. He asked me to make certain that we walked in quietly (only Mrs. Johnson, Jim Jones, and I accompanied the President).[21] He wanted the "Mexican generals"—his fondly derisive name for the

Secret Service—to keep "out of sight." Turning to the signing table behind his desk, he then said, "I'm so tired this evening. I don't know whether I can finish all this paperwork."[22]

That night I called Archbishop Cooke, whom the President had named a member of his violence commission and who was arranging the services at St. Patrick's. I told him that the security people wanted the President to arrive as late as possible. Cooke assured me that he did "not anticipate a big procession . . . with all the bishops and cardinals." He said that the family would be seated about 9:30, and suggested the President arrive about 9:50 so the services could begin promptly at 10 A.M.[23]

The next morning when we landed in the helicopter in Central Park,[24] we were greeted with a report that a man had been stopped entering the church with a gun inside an attaché case. The President again offered to let me wait for him in the park.

It was a difficult entrance; the church was uneasily tense. Many in the church were taking out their anger and grief on the President. Lyndon Johnson and Robert Kennedy had been more than political rivals; they had been political enemies; they had both been ruthless political street fighters, and most of the congregation in St. Patrick's had been walking on Kennedy's side of the street. Worse, some there held society at large responsible for the violence that had tragically taken Robert Kennedy's life and they blamed LBJ for making society sick. A good number in these pews had expected to ride to power in the White House with Robert Kennedy and were bitterly disappointed as the assassination turned LBJ's Vice President Hubert Humphrey into the Democratic front-runner. Johnson knew all this. I could *feel* it as we walked down the aisle.

Archbishop Cooke proved sensitive to the situation when, in the course of his homily, he said, "President Johnson offered this nation wise counsel when he pointed out that two hundred million Americans did not fire the shot that ended Senator Kennedy's life. The act of one man must not demoralize and incapacitate two hundred million others."

Immediately after the services, driving back to the helicopter, the President spoke appreciatively of Cooke's words. As we boarded the helicopter, Johnson received an urgent message: Martin Luther King's assassin, James Earl Ray, had just been captured in London.[25]

That evening, the President, Mrs. Johnson, Jim Jones, and I went to meet the train that was carrying Kennedy's body to Washington's Union Station. We drove in the President's limousine through a light rain, reversing some of the route that the Kennedy casket and family would follow for the burial in Arlington Cemetery. The President's car arrived at the train loading area inside the station shortly before 9 P.M. House Speaker McCormack joined us inside the car as we waited. When the train pulled in, the President and Mrs. Johnson went to the rear of the hearse that would carry Kennedy's casket to the cemetery. LBJ spoke briefly with Ethel, Ted, and Robert Kennedy, Jr. Visibly moved, the President walked slowly back to his car, and we took our place in the motorcade procession to the cemetery, the fifteenth car, in line with the President's orders not to impose his office on the Kennedy family. The procession of cars stopped briefly at the Justice Department, as a gesture to Kennedy's work as Attorney General, and at the Lincoln Memorial, where some participants in the Poor People's Campaign stood by.[26]

In the car, Johnson spoke softly about Rose Kennedy, what she'd been through, what an extraordinarily difficult life she'd had, how much religion must have meant to her what with her husband's philandering, her son Joe's death in the war, Jack's and now Robert's assassination. "That woman has suffered more than anyone I know," he said. "Her religious faith is what brings her through these tragedies." Tears welled up in his eyes as he spoke, and Mrs. Johnson tenderly placed her hand on his arm.

The more LBJ talked about Rose Kennedy, the more I began to realize that he was also talking about what an increasingly important role religion had come to play in his own life. I began to understand what Lyndon Johnson was really saying: whatever I am suffering, it is nothing to what this mother and wife has been called upon to suffer in her lifetime, but I am better able to understand my own suffering by understanding hers and her faith in God.

At the cemetery, the Johnsons stood next to the Kennedy family, recited the Lord's Prayer, and knelt on the damp artificial grass mat with Ethel Kennedy as she prayed at the grave. At Ethel's thoughtful suggestion, the President left ahead of the family, quietly, and we drove to the White House.[27] Throughout the entire ride back, the President uncharacteristically did not say a word. He left the car silently, went up to the living quarters and retired with Lady Bird for the evening.[28]

On June 19th, Ethel Kennedy sent the President a handwritten note:

> You and Mrs. Johnson have done so much for my family and me in the past few days. You were both so kind and generous and I shall always remember with deep grat-

itude your warm and immediate assistance. . . . And the support we received from everyone in the federal government at your request, most particularly from Joe Califano and from Angie and Robin Duke . . . made such a difference. . . . Your kindnesses, both known and unknown, were many, but they were all surpassed by the feeling of personal human sympathy which you and Mrs. Johnson gave to my children and me and the entire Kennedy family. . . . We shall always be grateful to you, Mr. President, for honoring Bobby by attending his funeral, by meeting the train in Washington and by accompanying us to Arlington. I shall always remember the goodness of heart which prompted your thoughtfulness, your kindness and your help. . . . Love, Ethel.[29]

Johnson, genuinely touched, wrote back:

Practical assistance of the kind I could give is . . . never enough to assuage the loss. Only time and faith can do that, and the support of the people who love you. . . . Thank God you have so many who love you nearby, that you have been blessed with so many fine children, and with a strong affirmative spirit in yourself.[30]

Two days after the funeral, on June 10, LBJ met with the members of the National Commission on the Causes and Prevention of Violence.[31] His charge to the members was broad: "I ask you to undertake a penetrating search . . . into our national life, our past as well as our present, our traditions as well as our institutions, our culture, our customs, and our laws." In successive drafts of the statement, Johnson had insisted on more and more examples of violence to provide historical perspective.[32] As he finally delivered it, the statement noted that one in every five Presidents since 1865 had been assassinated and one in three had been the target of attempted assassination, and listed a series of killings over the prior five years of civil rights workers and extremists of the right and left. Finally, Johnson asked the commission to help with gun control.

The specific questions he put to the commission mirrored the fears of millions of Americans: "Is there something in the environment of American society or the structure of our American institutions that causes disrespect for the law . . . and incidents of violence? . . . Has permissiveness toward extreme behavior in our society encouraged an increase of violence? . . . Are the seeds of violence nurtured through the public's airwaves,* the screens of neighborhood theatres, the news media . . . ? Is violence a contagious phenomenon . . . ? What is the relationship between mass disruption of public order and the individual acts of violence?"†

The President hoped to make gun control a lasting legacy of the RFK assassination. He sought to ban all mail-order and out-of-state sales of handguns, shotguns, and rifles; stop the sale of guns to minors; and require national registration of guns and licensing of gun owners. Democratic Senator Joseph Tydings of Maryland, a member of the Judiciary Committee close to the Kennedy family, wanted somewhat different legislation than Johnson had proposed. LBJ thought at most we had only a couple of weeks, perhaps no more than ten days, to pass his bill. But he could not convince Tydings that the Senator's effort for his own bill would slow down the process and give the gun lobby time to organize and kill our bill. That's exactly what happened by a tie vote in the Senate Judiciary Committee, which LBJ's persuasive efforts could only partially turn around. The administration's proposals to license owners and register guns were defeated. In the gun-control battle, the President believed that liberals, like Tydings, had been their own worst enemies.

The President eventually signed a gun-control bill in the Cabinet Room on October 22, 1968. At least he got his provision to stop murder by mail order, sale of lethal weapons to the young, and importation of "$10 specials." But LBJ made no attempt to temper his anger with the gun lobby for defeating owner licensing and gun registration:

> The voices that blocked these safeguards were not the voices of an aroused nation. They were the voices of a powerful lobby, a gun lobby, that has prevailed for the moment in an election year. . . . We have been through a great deal of anguish these last few months and these last few years—too much anguish to forget so quickly. . . . So now we must complete the task which this long needed legislation begins.

* LBJ deliberately used the possessive here to remind network executives over whose airwaves they were broadcasting. "The airwaves belong to the people," he would say as he repeatedly put the " 's" after "public," "not to the network bosses."
† The commission reported to President Nixon in December 1969, suggesting a variety of measures to curb violence, but its central recommendation was that the federal government reorder its priorities away from defense toward domestic programs to tackle poverty and race discrimination.

The following evening, LBJ wrote this note to Alan Barth, for twenty-five years a *Washington Post* writer who since 1963 had anonymously authored hundreds of editorials calling for gun control:

Dear Alan:
Your editorials in the *Post* on gun control all hit the mark. They did not pass unnoticed, for I drew strength from them. And they helped to arouse the conscience of the Congress.
I deeply appreciated your tireless crusade, and I wanted you to have one of the pens I used in signing the Gun Control Act yesterday.

Sincerely,
Lyndon B. Johnson[33]

Two days after Robert Kennedy's assassination, Johnson's Safe Streets bill emerged from Congress vastly changed. The central provision to support local police forces survived, but congressional distaste for Ramsey Clark had so intensified—conservatives and even some moderate members viewed him as extreme on racial issues and soft on crime—that Congress established a three-man Law Enforcement Administration, independent of the Attorney General, to make grants to state governments. Over strenuous presidential objections, Congress authorized wiretapping and bugging in a number of situations, for local and state police officers as well as federal officials. And Congress took aim at Chief Justice Earl Warren and several Supreme Court decisions on criminal rights.

Johnson had to decide whether to sign or veto just as the Reverend Ralph David Abernathy was holding the final rally of the Poor People's Campaign. Dismay in the administration was widespread. McPherson wrote, "I recognize that you must sign this bill. . . . But it is the worst bill you will have signed since you took office." Ramsey Clark thought it was "clear that in the abstract the bill should be vetoed." But even Clark recognized, "From a practical standpoint, the result might be a worse bill. The mood of the country and the Congress indicate a crime bill will be passed this year. . . . The unconstitutional and the most harmful amendments proposed to the bill were defeated. If the Congress acted again it might . . . limit the jurisdiction and habeas corpus powers of the federal courts. This would be disastrous." Reluctantly, we all felt the lesser of two evils was for the President to sign the bill.[34]

I gave the President a draft signing statement that attacked several provisions of the legislation, and suggested that he send strong letters to the Speaker of the House and President of the Senate, attacking the limp gun-control section and invitation to promiscuous wiretapping and bugging. But presidents have many political fish to fry and LBJ did not want to anger conservative senators whose support or acquiescence he would soon need for a bruising Senate battle that was about to unfold. So Johnson wanted a signed statement less critical of Congress.[35] Abe Fortas, who reviewed my draft,[36] agreed with the moderating changes the President desired, and Johnson signed the bill on June 19.

TWENTY

The Fortas Fiasco

EVEN DURING Lyndon Johnson's White House years, political contests rarely came as brass-knuckled as the bout the President set off on June 26, 1968, when he nominated Justice Abe Fortas to succeed Earl Warren as Chief Justice.

Warren had advised the President of his intention to resign, "effective at your pleasure," in mid-June. With time running out on his administration, Johnson reached for the opportunity to guarantee a liberal Court, which could protect his Great Society against an increasingly conservative Congress and the possibility of a conservative executive.

Johnson saw the Court as a means of perpetuating his social reform, particularly racial justice. He also wanted the Court to uphold the compromise he had reached with Catholics on funds for parochial schools, as well as his consumer, health, and environmental legislation. Johnson saw changes in social policy as a protracted series of battles fought on many fronts. He realized that his Great Society legislation had stepped on many powerful economic and political interests that had the resources to continue to struggle in every available forum and for a long time. While the President had won most of these battles in Congress and the executive branch, the contest would inevitably play out in the courts long after he left the White House, and he intended to win them as well after he had gone.

Not surprisingly, immediately upon receiving Warren's resignation, Johnson concluded that Fortas would be the best man to take

Warren's place. By accepting Warren's "decision to retire effective at such time as a successor is qualified," Johnson figured that, if he could not get Fortas confirmed, at least Warren could stay in place.

While Fortas was the President's immediate choice, Johnson lingered awhile before selecting Homer Thornberry for the seat that Fortas's appointment as Chief Justice would vacate. Thornberry, whom LBJ had placed on the U.S. Court of Appeals in 1965, had turned out to be a good federal judge, but he was a close family friend. When White House special counsel Larry Temple pointed out that nominating Thornberry invited the charge of cronyism, Johnson rebuffed him, as he had on other occasions: "What political office did you ever get elected to? . . . don't come to me as any great knowledgeable political expert until you've run and gotten elected to a political office . . . then I'll listen to your political judgment." But at that point, Lady Bird interrupted, "Lyndon, he may be right about that, and that's what worries me about Homer—although I'd love to see him on the Supreme Court."[1]

Johnson took the temperature of key Senate colleagues, notably the leader of the southern Democrats, Richard Russell, and Minority Leader Everett Dirksen. When they committed to support Fortas and Thornberry, the President decided to send the nominations forward. But he never expected easy sailing. From the outset, he pushed for quick hearings and floor action. In the days immediately following his announcement, when we thought we had almost seventy votes (more than we needed to stop a filibuster), LBJ warned, "We've got to get this thing through . . . early, because if it drags out . . . Dirksen will leave us." When I pointed out that Dirksen was on the public record in support of Fortas and Thornberry, Johnson said, "Just take my word for it. I know him. I know that Senate. If they get this thing drug out very long, we're going to get beat. . . . Ev Dirksen will leave us."[2]

Even before it was announced, rumors of the Fortas nomination created plenty of political sound and fury to justify the President's concerns. Fortas was high on the right-wing hit list. An outspoken liberal, he had represented Owen Lattimore, the China expert Senator Joseph McCarthy had accused of being a "top Russian espionage agent," in 1950 Senate hearings, and he had defended Clarence Gideon, whom a Florida court had convicted of breaking and entering, in the Supreme Court case that established the right of an indigent defendant to counsel.

Michigan's freshman Senator Robert Griffin, a Republican maverick, announced his opposition to any Supreme Court nomination by a lame-duck president. Republican Senators John Tower of Texas and Strom Thurmond of South Carolina publicly agreed with Griffin. The day before Johnson announced the nomination, James Eastland, the Mississippi Democrat who chaired the Senate Judiciary Committee, which would consider the nomination, told White House aide Mike Manatos that "Abe Fortas cannot be confirmed as Chief Justice." John McClellan, the Arkansas Democrat and Judiciary Committee's second-ranking member, privately expressed the hope that the President would have "that S.O.B. [Fortas] formally submitted to the Senate so that [I can] fight his nomination."[3]

The issue that sends everyone to political battle stations is control of the Supreme Court. What Lyndon Johnson saw as an opportunity conservatives understood as a threat to hold the Court steady on a course of judicial activism—expanding rights of the accused beyond common sense, imposing desegregation and affirmative action on an unwilling majority, and opening the courthouse doors wide for attacks on established institutions.

Johnson sent the nominations forward to applause from Senate liberals and supporting statements from Dirksen and Mansfield. But even before the minority and majority leaders of the Senate had extolled Fortas and Thornberry, Griffin had begun his campaign to kill their nominations. By the end of the first day, Griffin had persuaded eighteen Republican senators to sign a statement opposing them. It was clear to us that he was prepared to mount a filibuster if necessary to defeat the nomination.

From the moment Griffin announced his opposition, there were charges of anti-Semitism, which Johnson encouraged. When Griffin began to feel the sting, he countered by saying that he would support Arthur Goldberg's return to the Court. Johnson told me to get someone to point up the inconsistency between this position and Griffin's previously asserted opposition to any appointment by a lame-duck president. Griffin argued that "Goldberg was on leave of absence" and had originally been nominated by Kennedy.[4]

By Saturday, June 29, the President, recognizing the fight on his hands, assumed personal direction of every detail of the effort to secure confirmation of his friend Fortas. That afternoon, in one of his rapid-fire telephone conversations, Johnson told me to "call Henry Ford and tell him to get" members of the National Alliance of Businessmen calling key senators for Fortas. "Tell him I didn't bring about the resignation. . . . Warren handed me his letter resigning. I had to look at the Court and the country . . . it wouldn't be a good thing for the country for the first Jewish Chief Justice to be turned down." Johnson thought Jewish businessmen should be concerned that Griffin's effort to defeat "the first Jew ever nominated for Chief Justice" would arouse anti-Semitic sentiments.[5]

In other phone conversations, Johnson told me to have lawyer William Coleman (a prominent black Republican) call Massachusetts Republican Senator Edward Brooke, also black, to nail down his support for Fortas. Johnson wanted New York lawyer Edwin Weisl to ask Samuel Newhouse, owner and publisher of a big newspaper chain, to print editorials supporting Fortas and to turn around his *New Orleans Times-Picayune*, which had run an editorial opposing confirmation. He wanted someone to talk to Albert Jenner, chairman of the American Bar Association committee that reviewed federal judicial nominations, and get him concerned because the Senate "might turn down Fortas because he was a Jew" and to have federal judge Leon Higginbotham line up "the Negro bar in Pennsylvania" to pressure its Republican Senator Hugh Scott to support Fortas. He told me to have White House aide Ernest Goldstein "get every Jew out there in Illinois to go up to Dirksen and thank him for his support." Johnson wanted me to enlist the aid of David Brody and Hyman Bookbinder, heads of Washington offices of the Anti-Defamation League and American Jewish Committee.[6]

Even in the circumstances, the President maintained some semblance of a sense of humor. Harry McPherson had found a photograph of Fortas and philanthropist David Lloyd Kreeger wearing yarmulkes as they played a violin duet at a benefit. He showed the picture to Johnson: "I'll circulate it and try to get the Jewish groups behind us." The President gazed at the photo. He turned to McPherson: "This doesn't mean a damn thing. I've had on more of those than Abe has."[7]

The President thought he might get Henry Ford to ask George Romney to issue a statement of support, and then get Coca-Cola president Paul Austin to contact the Georgia senators and others from the South. He had Clark Clifford call Crawford Greenewalt, chairman of the Finance Committee of Du Pont, which was headquartered in Delaware, to work on that state's senators. Johnson told me to be sure Rockefeller nailed down Republican Charles Goodell's vote (Rockefeller had appointed him to Kennedy's Senate seat). He wanted "John Harper [head of Alcoa] to call [Howard] Baker," the Tennessee Republican Senator and Dirksen son-in-law, who would take Robert Kennedy's slot on the Senate Judiciary Committee. Johnson had Paul Porter, Fortas's former partner and dear friend, write a speech (which Johnson himself reviewed) for Florida Democratic Senator George Smathers to deliver on the Senate floor.[8]

Still Griffin didn't budge. Henry Ford reported to me on June 31 that, despite the barrage of calls, Griffin "takes exception to anybody being appointed [by a lame duck president], and [he says] Abe Fortas is still the President's lawyer, [Johnson is engaged in] extreme cronyism and Griffin is going ahead with a filibuster."[9]

The President wanted two analyses of Fortas's opinions prepared: one for conservative senators and one for liberals.[10] When he asked me to edit these two versions, I said I was concerned that "the two different analyses might be exchanged and find themselves in the wrong hands. Fortas is essentially a liberal Justice and perhaps we should put our emphasis on that."

"We should put our emphasis on getting the votes to make him Chief Justice," Johnson barked, adding, "Remember the Texas schoolteacher during the Depression?"

I did, but I listened again as he told his story. An out-of-work high school teacher in Texas was desperate for a job during the Depression. He went to a rural Texas school board in the hopes of teaching in elementary school, even though he considered that a step down. Three members of the local school board interviewed him for several hours, during which they fired question after question at him. Finally, when the board seemed to have exhausted all its questions, the steely-eyed redneck chairman of the board bent over and looked down at this nervous and perspiring schoolteacher and asked, "Do you teach that the world is flat or do you teach that the world is round?" The Texas schoolteacher hesitated for a few seconds, wiping perspiration from his brow and behind his neck, and said, "I can teach it either way."

Johnson gave me one of his laser-beam stares. "The point is that the high school teacher wanted the job, just the way we want Fortas confirmed for Chief Justice. The teacher knew damn well that the world was round," he added, "and everyone knows damn well where Fortas stands. But we've got to give each senator ammunition to justify his vote."[11]

But early on Johnson made a serious misjudgment that cost him Richard Russell's support. Several months before, the patrician Senator from Georgia had recommended that Johnson nominate Alexander Lawrence, Jr., a close friend, to a federal district judgeship in southern Georgia. Senators from the President's party traditionally tell the President who to name to federal district court judgeships in their states. Shortly after it became public that Johnson intended to nominate Lawrence, allegations arose that he was a racist. Attorney General Clark resisted the nomination and Johnson wavered. He did not want to make the mistake he believed President Kennedy had, putting in segregationist judges to placate southern senators. Russell pressed and the evidence in Lawrence's favor mounted. The liberal *Atlanta Constitution* publisher Ralph McGill, a committed desegregationist, endorsed Lawrence. But Clark dragged his heels in opposition despite Johnson's pressure, and the Lawrence matter was still pending before the President as he worked to get Senate approval of Fortas.

Russell was bitter about the stalling. Now he wrote Johnson on July 1, accusing him of withholding the Lawrence nomination "until after you sent in the nominations of Fortas and Thornberry." Furious at "the long delay in handling and the juggling of this [Lawrence] nomination," Russell considered himself "released from any statements that I may have made to you with respect to your nominations."[12]

Johnson had damaged his friendship with Russell, and Russell was mistaken. Johnson was not holding up Lawrence to keep the Georgia Senator in line on Fortas and Thornberry. But in a rare miscalculation Johnson angered a Senate intimate beyond repair. The President knew that his misstep had placed Fortas's nomination in terminal jeopardy. Hurt and angry at himself, he told Russell that the Georgia Senator had no commitment to support Fortas and Thornberry, returned the letter to Russell, asked him to destroy all copies of it, and then quickly nominated Lawrence.*

All to no avail. Soon after he sent his letter, Russell promised Griffin his support. Now the Griffin campaign had become a bipartisan challenge. Though Johnson did not immediately discover the Russell-Griffin alliance, he recognized how much trouble the nomination was in. He ordered a staff secretary to destroy all papers reflecting Fortas's involvement with the White House since his appointment to the Court. (The President's chief secretary, Juanita Roberts, however, quietly and apparently on her own initiative, intercepted Johnson's order[13] and the papers ended up at the LBJ Library in Texas.)[14]

Fortas testified before the Senate Judiciary Committee from Tuesday, July 16, to Friday, July 19, the first time that either a nominee for Chief Justice or a confirmed sitting justice had made such an appearance. Some senators wished to challenge Fortas's liberal record on the Court, but Fortas was able to deflect this line of queries, pointing to separation of powers and the importance of the Court's independence.

---

* The Senate promptly confirmed, and Lawrence turned out to be a progressive pro–civil rights judge, who sought to desegregate Georgia's schools.

Several senators, however, did challenge the propriety of his relationship with Johnson. Fortas tried to minimize his role. He testified that the President expected him merely to "summarize" issues and that he had not advised Johnson on any cases pending before the Supreme Court. He denied writing the President's statement on sending troops into Detroit during the 1967 riots. Fortas's testimony was so misleading and deceptive that those of us who were aware of his relationship with Johnson winced with each news report of his appearance before the Senate committee. Cronyism was now the least of the charges some of us feared.

Even as the nomination had headed for the Senate, Johnson and Fortas had maintained their relationship, adding only a thin shield of discretion. In mid-June, for instance, Johnson asked me to have Fortas review a draft presidential signing statement for the recently passed but constitutionally controversial Safe Streets Act. When I called Fortas, he begged off coming to the meeting; he suggested "under the circumstances" that I get his views "privately." In mid-July, Fortas asked me whether he should attend a White House luncheon for potential contributors to the LBJ Library. I told him that I thought he should not and I wrote the President to confirm my judgment. On my memo to him, the President checked the Approve line, crossed out his check, started to write something, crossed that out, and finally wrote: "Call me. L." Fortas did not come to the lunch. On July 26, I sent the President a glossy pamphlet we had produced about his withdrawal speech, suggesting that he might want to delay its release because "it contains a picture of Abe Fortas" at one of the meetings to discuss the speech. The booklet was never distributed.[15]

Johnson and Fortas, each in his own way, believed they were exempt from many of the traditional rules. Fortas was unwilling to step away from the exhilaration of involvement in the most exciting and challenging matters his client ever faced. As so often happens in Washington, Fortas came to believe that he was above conventional standards of acceptable conduct. For his part, the President was convinced that, faced with the most demanding job in the free world, he was entitled to any advice and counsel he wished; given a mandate to revolutionize the social and economic structure of the nation, he had a right to any and all information and advice, independent of traditional standards of constitutional government—especially when the ends were so worthy (social and economic justice so long denied the black, the poor, and the old) and the means of his opponents were so nefarious (filibusters to block civil rights legislation, outright defiance of the law, character assassination).

Years later, Vicky McCammon captured the essence of the relationship when she recalled how Johnson would ask Fortas, "What is the Court going to do on [a particular bill]? . . . Which way do you think the Court will go on this? . . . I don't think [Johnson] really felt that just because Abe Fortas was on the Supreme Court that he and Abe Fortas should divorce themselves from each other. He really, legally didn't believe that that was necessary. He honestly didn't. He tried to be careful, because he didn't want to be criticized . . . he really tried not to ask Abe Fortas about a lot of things, but in the end result he really needed his judgment on it. I think it was hard for him to make huge, important decisions domestically without his counsel. It's sort of hard to get a new lawyer in the middle of your biggest trial."[16]

That was the molecule of the matter for LBJ: he refused to be denied access to his best attorney just because he had given him to the Supreme Court. It was not in LBJ to think there was any advice or information to which he was not entitled. If he was trying to get the first fair-housing bill in history passed, certainly the President was entitled to know whether a forthcoming Supreme Court decision might endanger the bill and, if necessary—though I don't believe it ever was—to get his friend Abe Fortas to delay its promulgation until after the vote on Capitol Hill. If he was contemplating the imposition of wage and price controls without congressional action, certainly the President had a right to know how the Court would react so as not to risk eroding presidential power. To LBJ it was incomprehensible that he would deny himself this man's advice and counsel simply because he was willing to share him with the Supreme Court. As for me, Fortas was so consistently present and Johnson so often directed me to consult him that the Supreme Court Justice became part of the staff and his involvement so routine that early shock and concern over time faded, like Fortas himself, into the woodwork of the White House.

As the Senate Judiciary Committee hearings wound down in late July, Johnson hoped to get the committee to report out his nominee before Congress adjourned in early August. Thurmond, however, launched a new attack, charging that Fortas's First Amendment interpretations had helped pornographers to peddle their smut. This new issue carried the hearings over into September. We began to fear that, even if we got the Fortas nomination out of committee, we might not have the votes to override a filibuster on the floor. Johnson lashed out at a meeting to review a head count with Temple, Sanders, me, and other staffers, "We're a bunch of dupes down here. They've got all the wisdom. All the sagacity is reposed up there. They're just smarter than we are. We're a bunch of ignorant, immature kids who don't know anything about this. . . . They're whipsawing us to death because they're dragging their feet. We've got to do something."[17]

When the Senate committee invited Fortas to return for more testimony in September, the President initially thought Fortas should accept. We breathed a sigh of relief as he and Fortas decided that the invitation should be declined.

The President now referred to the effort to block confirmation as a way for his enemies to attack him through Fortas. They couldn't bring down the President now, Johnson would say, they couldn't repeal his programs, his civil rights bills, but they could bring down Fortas. When we prompted the formation of a Lawyers Committee on Supreme Court Nominations to support Fortas, the fact that we couldn't get a single prominent lawyer from Mississippi to join until McPherson twisted an old friend's arm confirmed LBJ's view that the opposition to Fortas was rooted in bigotry and opposition to his civil rights programs.[18] So Johnson dug in, and we all tried harder.

The cronyism charge was sticking, and more questions were being raised about the propriety of Fortas's involvement in White House affairs. Even Johnson's allies on the committee were uneasy about the testimony—and none yet suspected just how vulnerable Fortas was. He had advised Johnson on the constitutionality of limits on the President's authority to close military bases and of the 1966 D.C. crime bill. He had helped assess the Supreme Court's likely response should the President unilaterally impose wage and price controls. He had been deeply engaged in shaping Vietnam and economic policies and in advising the President on a variety of crises, ranging from the Detroit riots to the 1967 railroad strike. Worst of all, he had advised the President on the Penn-Central case when it was pending before the Supreme Court and then written the Court's final opinion.

Republican presidential candidate Richard Nixon had finessed the bitter wrangling over Fortas by deferring to the Senate's prerogatives (a cover, Johnson thought, for Nixon's private assurances to wealthy conservatives that, if elected, he would serve up far more palatable nominees). Johnson felt that if he could get Nixon to at least oppose a filibuster, Fortas might have a chance. He had Arthur Krim, a close friend and Democratic party fundraiser, urge Urban League head Whitney Young and Walter Thayer, Republican president of the board of the *International Herald Tribune*, to speak to Nixon. Young said that he "spoke rather forcefully to Nixon" and Thayer claimed to have addressed him "pointedly," but Thayer reported that Nixon could not be turned around.[19] Finally, in mid-September, presidential candidate Hubert Humphrey put the heat on Nixon that Johnson needed. Humphrey charged that Nixon was "paying a political debt" to Thurmond by attacking the Court and thus undercutting the Fortas nomination. Nixon, who did not want to be identified with bigots and

the extreme right, came around. "I don't oppose Fortas. I don't support him," he told reporters. "I oppose a filibuster. I oppose any
filibuster."

By this time, however, it was too late. A new obstacle had arisen
to Fortas's confirmation, one neither the President nor his staff knew
about until just before its revelation in the Senate hearings.

Rumors began circulating on the Hill that Griffin and Thurmond
had something hot. We asked Fortas if he knew of any other vulner-
ability. He couldn't think of anything. I asked his best friend and
partner Paul Porter the same question. He had no idea. Nevertheless,
the rumors persisted.

Shortly before committee hearings resumed on September 13,
Paul Porter called and said he had to talk to me about something
regarding Fortas. When he came over early that evening, he showed
me a letter he had written[20] to several prominent businessmen.*
Some were clients of Fortas's old firm; all could be expected to have
matters in various federal courts, some likely to get to the Supreme
Court. The letter sought to raise money for Fortas to teach a summer
seminar at American University Law School.[21] Porter had raised
$30,000, of which $15,000 had already been paid to Fortas for semi-
nars he had been teaching the very summer in which we were fighting
for his nomination. Porter tried to justify the arrangement, saying it
wouldn't influence Fortas's behavior in the Court, but his eyes teared
as he talked to me. Senator Thurmond, Porter explained weakly, had
discovered the payments and planned to have the university's law
school dean, B. J. Tennery, testify about it before the committee on
September 13.†

After Porter left my office, I reported the matter to Larry Temple,[22] and talked to the President as soon as we could get to him later
that evening. When we informed him, Johnson nodded sadly. He was
silent for a long minute. Then, he said, "We won't withdraw the
nomination. I won't do that to Abe." Though we couldn't get the
two-thirds vote needed to shut off debate, Johnson said we could get
a majority, and that would be a majority for Fortas. "With a majority
on the floor for Abe, he'll be able to stay on the Court with his head

---

* Gustave Levy, investment banker at Goldman, Sachs and Company and chairman
of the New York Stock Exchange; Troy Post, president of Greatamerica Corporation;
Paul Smith, vice president and general counsel to Philip Morris; Maurice Lazarus,
vice chairman of Federated Department Stores; John Loeb, a banker with Carl M.
Loeb, Rhoades and Company; and publicist Benjamin Sonnenberg.
† What Porter did not tell me, and what I did not learn until years later, was that he
and Fortas were secretly working with Tennery on the latter's testimony before the
Senate committee.

up. We have to do that for him." Fortas also wanted the majority vote.[23]

After Tennery's testimony, as Johnson had predicted, Dirksen withdrew his support and announced he would not vote to shut off debate. On October 1, after a strenuous White House effort, a 45–43 majority of senators voted to end the filibuster, short of the 59 votes needed for cloture, but just barely the majority LBJ wanted to give Fortas. Later that day, Fortas asked the President to withdraw his nomination.

For a few days, Johnson thought about whether to try again. A week later, facing the reality of the calendar, LBJ indicated that he would not submit any further nominations for the Supreme Court.*

---

* In 1969, Fortas resigned amid a controversy arising from disclosure that he took a $20,000 fee from a foundation controlled by Louis Wolfson, a friend and former client, who at the time of the payment was under investigation for violating securities laws.

TWENTY-ONE

The Democratic Convention and Presidential Campaign

THE 1968 DEMOCRATIC National Convention was Lyndon Johnson's political crown of thorns. The convention had been set for the week of LBJ's sixtieth birthday, August 27, which was the day before the planned selection of the presidential candidate. As Johnson felt the warmth of the reaction to his withdrawal from the race, we all expected that he would address his party's convention.[1] With each new accolade more enthusiastic than the last, none anticipated a triumphant appearance more than Lyndon Johnson.

As the convention approached, Johnson pretended not to be involved in its preparation. In early July, when I sent him a memo about putting together a first draft of the platform, he wrote across the bottom, "Do nothing for God's sake on this."[2] Johnson wanted to present himself as aloof from the party's process and positions. Nevertheless, he sent McPherson and Levinson to Los Angeles to script a film about his presidency for presentation at the convention. And, because the President was still his party's leader, our people organized the convention and virtually dictated the platform. Johnson himself scuttled a compromise Vietnam plank calling for an immediate bombing halt. "This plank just undercuts our whole policy," Johnson told Humphrey, "and, by God, the Democratic party ought not to be doing that to me."

On July 30, Stephen Smith, a Kennedy brother-in-law, called to tell me that the family had a movie about Robert Kennedy, which they wanted to show at the convention.[3] Johnson responded with a reluctant "I've got no choice, so O.K." But because of his concern that this was a ploy to spark the nomination of thirty-six-year-old Massachusetts Senator Edward Kennedy, Johnson insisted that the film be screened on the night of Thursday, August 29, after the party's nominees had been chosen.

On August 10, George McGovern, the Democratic Senator from South Dakota, announced his candidacy for the presidential nomination as a peace candidate. He claimed some encouragement from the Kennedy family and expected to pick up the Robert Kennedy delegates who had not gone over to Eugene McCarthy. He said he hoped to capitalize on the antiwar feeling among many delegates, block Humphrey from winning the nomination, and then capture it for himself. Johnson suspected that McGovern was a stalking horse for Ted Kennedy.

Then Kennedy, on August 21, just five days before the convention opened, emerged from self-imposed seclusion following his brother's assassination. In a televised speech he urged an end of the war in Vietnam and promised to "pick up a fallen standard." Johnson in his own mind was now certain the Kennedys were planning a coup to wrest the nomination from Hubert Humphrey.

The threat of another Kennedy nomination stirred the President's juices for Humphrey. LBJ immediately got so involved in the convention that I was even clearing some planned speeches, suggesting inserts of specific items the President wanted mentioned.[4] Kennedy's operatives did scramble for delegate support, but (thanks to Johnson) found Humphrey in control and backed off.

That same week, Russian tanks pushed across Czechoslovakia's border to crush that nation's first move toward freedom. The brutal invasion dashed LBJ's plans for a final summit with Soviet Premier Alexei Kosygin, which he had hoped might pave the way to peace in Vietnam and a new era in Soviet-American relations. It also killed any chance for Senate ratification in 1968 of the nuclear nonproliferation treaty, which Johnson considered one of his most important achievements.[5] Finally, that week we also got a sense that serious trouble might await the Democrats in Chicago.

From late 1967, when the site of the convention was announced, antiwar demonstrators and hippies had been planning large demonstrations. Johnson wanted us to be ready for violence, but he didn't want to involve federal troops unless necessary. As concern about disturbances increased, Ramsey Clark, Clark Clifford, and I elicited the President's grudging approval to deploy "in absolute secrecy" six thousand Army troops to airfields near the city.[6] LBJ was annoyed when the press found out about the troop movements, but we thought the risk of discovery had been justified. We wanted to be ready because we felt the President was certain to celebrate his sixtieth birthday in Chicago and we were concerned about disruption during the convention.

Speechwriters Bob Hardesty and Harry Middleton had begun working on a convention speech. Their draft captured a little of what the President expected:

> (*After Welcoming Ovation*)
> For a moment there I closed my eyes and thought I was back in Atlantic City [the site of the 1964 convention that thunderously nominated Johnson for President in his own right].

Horace Busby did another draft, which I shipped to the President at the ranch on August 25. The next day, I sent LBJ what became the working draft, prepared by McPherson, Clifford, and me from the other drafts. The President began editing it immediately. But he never talked directly to me about his changes. Instead, Jones, Temple, and Levinson, who were with him at the ranch, called me with his revisions.[7] When I asked if these were the President's changes, Temple and Jones indicated they were—but that the President emphatically didn't want anyone to know that he was working on the speech.

Johnson also wished to gather intelligence on convention activities and still maintain his public pose of no involvement. So, instead of phoning Chicago himself, the President would have Temple or Jones place the call while he listened on another line. When LBJ had a question, he would put his hand over the receiver and tell Temple or Jones, "Ask John Connally" this or that, and Temple or Jones would repeat the question so the President could hear the answer.[8]

It became apparent to Temple at the ranch and me back at the West Wing of the White House that LBJ hoped, and probably anticipated, that the convention delegates in Chicago would offer to draft him to be their party's candidate, a draft he intended to turn down but one that would validate his presidency in the eyes of fellow Democrats.[9]

Johnson's hopes were not completely unfounded. Humphrey, who had the delegates for a first ballot nomination, did not look like a winner. He lagged far behind Nixon in the polls and many Democrats up for reelection worried that the Vice President would drag them down with him in November. Some Texas delegates threatened to bolt from Humphrey to Johnson. Governor Connally "was asked to go to meet with the governors of the southern delegations . . . to see if they would support President Johnson in a draft movement in

1968." Just before the convention began, Jake Jacobsen, a former White House staffer and a Texas convention delegate, called Jones to say that "this convention is going to draft the President if there is the slightest indication the draft will be accepted." Governor Connally, Marvin Watson, and Jake Jacobsen phoned Temple that Daley was saying, "If Lyndon Johnson wants this nomination, he has got our delegation."[10] When LBJ got these reports, he had to think that a party striving for unity could look for it in the President who had risen above partisanship.

Events smashed those hopes. Protests broke out on the convention's eve, leading to several arrests, and on the first day Chicago police waded into demonstrators, injuring 20 and arresting 140. As the convention got underway, the fight over the Vietnam plank increased tension among the delegates inside and outside the hall. The likelihood that Lyndon Johnson would be welcomed in Chicago steadily diminished. Reports mounted that he would be booed by antiwar protesters and that his appearance might incite greater disturbances and serious rioting. The Secret Service warned him of threats to his life. Nevertheless, throughout Tuesday, August 27, Johnson continued to work on his speech, as aides at the ranch telephoned his changes to me, and Liz Carpenter, Lady Bird Johnson's top aide and speechwriter, provided a menu of opening jokes for the President's selection.[11]

That afternoon, with Jones placing calls to Chicago and Johnson again using the charade of asking questions through his aide while listening on another line, the President talked to Mayor Richard Daley twice, and directly to Hubert Humphrey, Marvin Watson, and Democratic National Committee Treasurer John Criswell.[12]

Late that afternoon when the White House press corps visited the ranch to sing "Happy Birthday," the President held a brief press conference. Asked whether he was going to the convention, he gave a somewhat disingenuous answer:

> I have not decided yet. If there is anything I can do that might be helpful . . . I want to do it. . . . I would prefer to get the credentials problem settled and the platform settled and the candidate problems out of the way. Then I have the right and I might even have the duty to act as a citizen and exercise my prerogatives as a good American. . . . I am not talking to the Convention. I am not sending any emissaries. I don't have anyone reporting to me other than [CBS News anchor Walter] Cronkite. . . . If I conclude that it would be desirable to go there on the way back to Washington or for an evening—but I have not made any plans. The authorities

have urged me to come. They urged Mrs. Johnson to come and appear at the Convention, but I told them I have no plans to do so.

That evening, Johnson continued, as his press secretary George Christian later put it, "fantasiz[ing] that the convention would be such a mess that he would go in on a flying carpet and be acclaimed as the nominee." Johnson probably didn't want the nomination—by now he was becoming concerned about his health and fearful of another heart attack. But he certainly hoped it would be offered.[13]

No speech would be delivered by Lyndon Johnson and no acclaim accorded him, much less the offer of a draft he could decline. Temple called me late the evening of August 27 to say that the President was not going to Chicago. Instead, the next day LBJ sent a message, read by convention chairman Carl Albert, that his decision not to run was "irrevocable. . . . I ask therefore that my name not be considered by the Convention. I wish to express my deep appreciation to all those who might have wished me to continue. . . . During the remaining months of my term as President, and then for the rest of my life, I shall continue my efforts to reach and secure those enduring goals that have made America great—peace abroad and justice and opportunity at home."

Johnson was upset and frustrated by the violence in Chicago. He could not understand why such protests continued when he felt he was making progress toward peace in Vietnam. As Larry Temple later recalled, "After withdrawing from the race and getting the Paris peace talks with the North Vietnamese underway, he thought those people would find the situation more satisfying."[14] For a while Johnson skidded into self-pity, licking his wounds, feeling melancholy that he had been denied the draft he wanted the opportunity to turn down.

After Hubert Humphrey was nominated, Johnson even had to suffer the humiliation of making certain Humphrey's acceptance speech would recognize, as it did, that Johnson "rallied a grief-stricken nation when our leader was stricken by the assassin's bullet . . . and in the space of five years since that tragic moment, President Johnson has accomplished more of the unfinished business of America than any of his modern predecessors." LBJ appreciated the remarks, but by this time, after several days of watching the Democratic convention on television, he had begun to nurture serious misgivings about Humphrey—not just his ability to pull the party together during the campaign, but about what kind of a president he'd make.[15]

•

From the moment Hubert Humphrey had formally announced his candidacy in late April 1968, new tensions had sprouted between him and the President. The Vice President gulped hard and accepted Johnson's edict that administration appointees had either to stay out of the presidential nomination contest or get out of the administration because it made some sense and, in any case, he couldn't do anything about it. Nevertheless, Humphrey and his more ardent allies in the cabinet, like Freeman and Wirtz, couldn't understand why LBJ insisted on denying Humphrey even covert assistance against two other candidates, Kennedy and McCarthy, who had centered their campaigns on attacking the administration and the President personally.

When Kennedy was assassinated in early June, Humphrey expected a more genial and supportive attitude from the President. Instead, with Humphrey's nomination a foregone conclusion, Johnson sometimes privately ridiculed him. Once in July, Johnson looked at an evening newspaper with pictures of his Vice President and Senator Eugene McCarthy, each holding crying babies. "That's the way I feel when I look at the two candidates," Johnson cracked, "like crying."[16]

The President also kept a keen watch on Humphrey's words and music on Vietnam, the way a conservative Pope in Rome might monitor each sermon of a liberal American bishop he fears might stray from Vatican teaching. In Chicago, at least, despite his own misgivings, and despite the heckling in the convention and the violence outside, Humphrey had stayed glued to the President on Vietnam.

Once nominated, Humphrey recruited Larry O'Brien, who had begun helping the Vice President after Robert Kennedy's assassination, to be Chairman of the Democratic National Committee and campaign manager. Immediately after Labor Day, the Vice President asked if I would join his campaign. O'Brien would be in charge of the politics and I would be in charge of policy. He knew we worked well together, and he said he needed all the help he could get to defeat Nixon, who was well ahead in the polls.

I told Humphrey that I'd be delighted. We talked about the President's possible reaction. Johnson was acting like a man bleeding to death from a thousand small cuts; to him the departure of each administration official, however minor, was an act of betrayal. Humphrey was sensitive to the delicacy of the situation and the danger an angry reaction from this moody and hurt President held for his own campaign.

I offered to tell the President that I wanted to join Humphrey's campaign. The Vice President feared that LBJ might misread any such approach and accuse him of trying to steal me without first checking with "the highest authority." I recalled McNamara's sharp reaction when McGeorge Bundy and Bill Moyers had approached me in 1964 to join the White House staff without first talking to him. I agreed that Humphrey should make the initial approach, but I warned him that the President was beginning to act like the captain of a sinking ship who needed every able-bodied sailor to save the passengers. Humphrey said that, without mentioning our conversation, he would ask the President if he could seek to enlist me in his campaign.

Humphrey planned to talk to the President after the September 5 congressional leadership breakfast. The breakfast ended about 9:30 and, except for a brief photo session, Humphrey stayed alone with the President until a cabinet meeting began after 11.[17] I sat in the Cabinet Room trying to read their faces and looking forward to working in the campaign. I couldn't fathom from their expressions what had transpired.

After the cabinet meeting ended, the Vice President came by my office.[18] "What happened?" I asked.

Humphrey just shook his head. "Joe, you know he just seems so lonely and so concerned about people leaving him that I couldn't even bring myself to raise the issue with him. Maybe it's just as well for you either to raise it yourself at the right time or just stay with him."

Humphrey recounted Johnson's long discussion of how difficult it was now to run the government, pass legislation in Congress, confirm Fortas as Chief Justice, and induce the North Vietnamese to negotiate, and how much he needed everyone he could hold on to, specifically mentioning me among others. As Humphrey recounted the details, I was sure that LBJ had guessed what Humphrey wanted and had shrewdly preempted him. I knew there was no point in even thinking about joining the Vice President's campaign. My momentary disappointment quickly gave way to resignation that I would stay the course with Johnson, and to some uneasiness as to whether Humphrey was just too nice a guy to be President. If Humphrey couldn't do this, I thought, how could he take the much tougher actions demanded of presidents.[19]

Johnson made clear to Humphrey during that meeting his conviction that if the Vice President veered from the policies of the administration he could not defeat Nixon.[20] Then on September 9, Humphrey casually remarked to reporters in Philadelphia that he could just as easily run on the peace plank (which Johnson forces had defeated at the Democratic convention) and that, whatever happened at the Paris peace talks, he thought it might be possible to bring some American boys home from Vietnam in 1969. Steaming that his advice had been so quickly rejected, Johnson whacked Humphrey hard on the wrist the very next day by publicly warning the American Legion that "No man can predict" when any American troops could return from Vietnam.

The cooling relations between Johnson and Humphrey dropped into a deep freeze when the Vice President made his Vietnam speech on September 30. The administration had always insisted on some reciprocal action by Hanoi, such as ending the infiltration of troops into South Vietnam, as the quid pro quo for a complete bombing halt. In a well-prepared address taped in advance for nationwide television, Humphrey cautiously tried to separate himself from this position, just enough to comfort the liberal wing of the party, but not so much as to alienate or anger Johnson. Humphrey's carefully chosen words were:

> As President, I would stop the bombing of the North as an acceptable risk for peace because I believe it could lead to success in the negotiations and thereby shorten the war. . . . In weighing that risk—and before taking action—I would place key importance on evidence—direct or indirect—by deed or word—of Communist willingness to restore the demilitarized zone between North and South Vietnam.
>
> If the Government of North Vietnam were to show bad faith, I would reserve the right to resume the bombing.

Humphrey's words were just within the position Johnson had taken a year earlier in a widely reported speech. But Humphrey staffers let reporters know that the Vice President was in fact committing himself to a bombing halt without any qualifications. They also pointed reporters to another line in the speech in which Humphrey renewed his prediction that it would be possible to start withdrawing American troops from Vietnam in 1969, adding, "I do not say this lightly. I have studied this matter carefully."

Humphrey's aides emphasized to the press that their man had been introduced as the Democratic candidate for President, not as the Vice President, and that the paraphernalia of the office he held in the Johnson administration—the flag and seal—were deliberately absent during the televised address. Finally, Humphrey's staffers underscored that their candidate had not cleared his remarks with the President. Humphrey's speech turned the campaign into a horse race, though Johnson never forgave him for it.

A week later I came to appreciate how deep the rift had become. I told the President that I was giving Humphrey ideas for his campaign, since we wouldn't need them for a legislative program in January 1969. Johnson flushed and snapped that those are "my ideas from my staff and my task forces." He would decide whether to unfold them in January. There was no point in arguing. As Nixon heated the crime issue up, Larry O'Brien asked me to help draft a crime-fighting speech that Humphrey would deliver on national television. I quietly sneaked over to the Democratic National Committee for most of Saturday, October 12[21] and worked on the speech with Louis Martin and O'Brien, amazed at the guilt Johnson had roused in me for slipping a few ideas to his Vice President.

Ironically, Johnson's final push to end the fighting in Vietnam became the occasion for a lasting rift with Humphrey. Once Johnson had withdrawn from the race, he was determined to end the war before he left office. When the North Vietnamese had jockeyed for the month of April over where to meet, he had ingeniously used the Pope to get them to the negotiating table. He had me (as the designated White House Catholic) contact the Apostolic Delegate to the United States, Archbishop Luigi Raimondi, to suggest that Pope Paul VI offer the Vatican as a neutral place where the parties could sit down to decide when and where to negotiate.

On April 27, 1968, the Apostolic Delegate gave me a message for the President: His Holiness was ready to offer the Vatican as a site for the meeting and wished to know when and how he should make the offer.[22]

As soon as Johnson read Raimondi's memo, he phoned Rusk and then invited me into his office. Call Raimondi right now, Johnson said, and tell him: "As far as we're concerned, the sooner the Pope makes an announcement of his invitation the better." Johnson placed enormous importance on Raimondi's getting the Pope to issue the invitation. "Go visit Raimondi," Johnson told me. "Tell him that the sooner he makes the invitation the better, the more lives that may be saved, and tell him we think it's important that the Pope make it a public invitation without any prior notice [to the North Vietnamese]. If the Pope wants to be a peacemaker, doing it publicly and without prior notice will strengthen his hand and put more pressure on the North Vietnamese." Then the President told me to make sure Raimondi cabled that message to the Pope and to wait at the Delegate's house until the Vatican responded. I didn't wait there, but for three days, at Johnson's insistence, I pestered Raimondi.[23]

Finally, on April 30, the Apostolic Delegate delivered an invitation from the Pope offering the Vatican for confidential initial meetings of the North Vietnamese and U.S. governments. Raimondi told the President that "the Holy Father has decided to issue the invitation privately through diplomatic channels. The Holy Father thought the parties might be able to meet secretly without anyone's knowing about the meeting and that this would relieve external pressures on them." The Vatican was delivering the same message at this moment to Hanoi through European channels.[24]

Johnson accepted the Pope's invitation with a warm and conciliatory note.[25] He hoped this kind of pressure would bring Hanoi to the table somewhere, even if not at the Vatican. The North Vietnamese had to know that the offer from the Pope would not remain secret if they turned it down, and that would be costly to them in the psychological battle they were waging for world opinion.

On May 3, less than forty-eight hours after I had delivered the President's response to the Apostolic Delegate, Walt Rostow awakened LBJ at about 1 A.M., to report that "Hanoi has suggested we meet in Paris . . . on May 10 or a few days later."[26]

Unfortunately, the talks had dragged without making any progress toward the cease-fire Johnson yearned to achieve before he left office. To end the stalemate, in mid-October, LBJ began to set the stage for a total bombing halt, with the North Vietnamese implicitly committing themselves to exercise reciprocal military restraint and the U.S. and North Vietnam dropping their objections to negotiating directly with the Vietcong and South Vietnamese, respectively. Johnson thought he had South Vietnamese President Nguyen Van Thieu aboard.

Shortly before Johnson planned to announce the bombing halt, he was given an intercepted cable from the South Vietnamese embassy in Washington to Saigon. The cable urged Thieu to block the peace process until after the presidential election. Johnson already knew from intelligence sources that Anna Chennault, the Chinese-born widow of World War II hero General Claire Chennault, had been pressing Nixon to send word to the South Vietnamese that as President he would give them a much better deal, so Saigon should not go along with Johnson. LBJ now suspected that Nixon had acted on Chennault's advice and treasonously, to his thinking, subverted his own government in order to win the election.

At the last minute, Thieu began to raise objections to the imminent agreement. Johnson decided to go it alone, without Thieu. On October 31, the Thursday before the election, he placed a conference call to the three presidential candidates, Humphrey, Nixon, and Wallace, and warned them: "The fate of our country lies in your hands over the next few weeks. There would be serious trouble if anything anyone said were to interrupt or disrupt any progress we are trying to make to bring this war to a halt." That evening at eight, in a taped television appearance, Johnson announced a complete bombing halt. Later that evening Johnson wondered aloud "what [his sons-in-law] Chuck and Pat [who were in the armed services in Vietnam] would think" about his announcement. As for himself, the President said it was "the most important decision" he had ever made; "the times demanded this action. This is a step toward peace."[27]

The next day Thieu told his National Assembly that he would not join the peace talks if the Vietcong participated. Nixon had one of his campaign aides, Robert Finch, capitalize on Thieu's split by saying, "We had the impression that all the diplomatic ducks were in position. I think this will boomerang. It was hastily contrived." Now Johnson was certain in his own mind, whatever the evidence he could uncover to prove it, that Nixon had betrayed his country and enlisted Thieu to torpedo the arrangement. Nixon's denials, when Johnson phoned him, did nothing to undermine the President's conviction.

At last, now in the final hours, Johnson desperately wanted Humphrey to win the election. A Harris poll showed that Nixon and Humphrey were neck and neck. Instead of just getting mad, Johnson had a way to get even. He offered Humphrey the information on the activities (as he saw them) of Anna Chennault and Nixon, which included a wiretapped phone call from Chennault to the South Vietnamese embassy in Washington, to use in the final days of his campaign. Humphrey didn't want to do it. Johnson was furious, thinking it was "the dumbest thing in the world not to do it." Humphrey thought it would be "terrible to do that sort of thing," when he wasn't absolutely certain of the facts.[28] Johnson thought it would be worse to have as President a man so consumed with power that he would betray the country's national-security interests, undermine its foreign policy, and endanger the lives of its young soldiers to win the office.

Humphrey lost the election by a hair (43.2 to 42.7 percent of the vote; third-party candidate George Wallace carried 13.6 percent), and he never regained Johnson's respect or affection. Lady Bird remarked at the time how sad it was that, after all those years, the relationship between these two liberal warriors who had fought so hard for the same progressive causes had become so taut, distant, and strained.[29]

I thought my own relations with Humphrey had survived unscathed until May 2, 1976, when I read an excerpt in *Parade Magazine* from his book *The Education of a Public Man*. He described "sitting outside Joe Califano's office while he, an arrogant and pretentious young aide, went about his work inside at his own pace." I was hurt by the description and remembered no such occasion. After the 1968 election, Humphrey had thanked me as one of the few White

House aides who had helped him during the campaign, and at his request, as a private attorney, I had represented him in a politically inspired General Accounting Office investigation of his 1972 presidential-campaign finances. On May 3, 1976, I wrote Humphrey a sad letter. Months later, on October 4, from Bethesda Naval Hospital as he was about to undergo his first major surgery for the cancer that would take his life, Humphrey responded. He said the sentence had been written by an aide and that it did not reflect his view:

> . . . I apologize for any injustice or unhappiness that I may have inflicted upon you by anything that I have said or written in my book. . . .
>
> I know what a difficult assignment you had working with President Johnson. He was a remarkable man. I admired him greatly and owe him much, but all of us know there were times when he could be difficult to say the least. You put it well when you said "Lyndon Johnson was an extraordinarily complicated and aggressive President who made unusual demands on the time and energies of all who worked for him." That paragraph in your letter explains fully the difficult relationships that existed.
>
> Well, dear friend . . . I respect and admire you very much. . . . You were of great help to me in the campaign of '68 and you have been of help to me in recent months. . . .
>
> Somewhere it is written "to err is human" and I am afraid I am a very human person. But to have injured a friend brings me a feeling of sadness.[30]

TWENTY-TWO

Winding Down

THE FINAL MONTHS of 1968 were bleak. But, despite Johnson's hurt and disappointment, he got the North Koreans to release the crew members of the U.S. intelligence ship *Pueblo* and shoved a few more environmental measures through Congress. He had a respect for air, land, and water, rooted in his sense of the hill country's power. It had renewed his body after his heart attack in 1955, and regenerated his spirit in the most troubled days and darkest nights of his presidency.

Now, as his term was coming to an end, he seemed driven to pay nature back for all it had given him and make its powers of renewal available to all citizens. During these final days, he got Congress to enact his proposals to deal with noise pollution from aircraft, to create networks of scenic rivers and scenic trails, and to establish Redwood National Park in California, North Cascades National Park in Washington State, and several new wilderness areas, including Mount Jefferson in Oregon and Great Swamp, the last area of its kind in northern New Jersey.

LBJ's last budget and State of the Union message touched off one of my most contentious experiences with him. The 10 percent surcharge he had won in the summer of 1968 would give him a budget surplus for his final year in office. The key issue in the budget to be presented to Congress in January 1969 (for the first full fiscal year [1970] of Richard Nixon's administration) was whether to recommend continuation of the tax surcharge. Its extension for another year would permit realistic funding for Great Society programs and the war, and provide another surplus economists thought desirable. Without revenues from the surcharge, the President could offer a balanced budget only by resort to smoke-and-mirrors.[1] In late 1968, Johnson was leaning toward letting the surcharge expire. "Before the election, Nixon said, 'I will allow the ten percent surcharge to expire or at least will reduce it significantly,' " Johnson argued in one meeting. "Let's recognize the facts of life. People have selected Mr. Nixon. . . . He can elect his own economic course. Let him decide what to do."[2]

LBJ discussed the matter with the Democratic congressional leadership over breakfast on Monday morning, January 6, 1969. It was the first and only such breakfast that Ted Kennedy attended; the Friday before he had upset Russell Long of Louisiana for the post of Senate Majority Whip. LBJ set out his options. He slanted his presentation toward his predilection not to request extension of the tax surcharge.

Then Johnson canvassed each member of the leadership for his view. Conservative Senator Robert Byrd vigorously chimed in for no extension of the surcharge. Senate Majority Leader Mike Mansfield, Speaker John McCormack, House Majority Leader Carl Albert, and House Majority Whip Hale Boggs agreed that it would be better if the President could submit a budget without a recommendation to extend the surcharge. Mansfield, cagey through years of experience with LBJ, said he opposed extension based on what the President had just told them. "They're the only facts I have," he said.

Johnson then turned to Kennedy, the new Majority Whip. Johnson liked this youngest Kennedy brother and sensed in him a genuine and compatible populist streak and a respect for the Senate. He told me that he thought "Teddy has the potential to be the greatest of the three." The Massachusetts Senator replied that he wanted to think about it; he had no view to express at this time. Johnson's face darkened, but he went on to other matters.[3]

After the meeting as I rode down the East Wing elevator with Kennedy, he said he would "send the President a personal note on the surtax." I reported this to the President in a brief note.[4] Johnson immediately hit the hotline to me,[5] "Tell Kennedy I don't need any Goddamn memo from him on the surtax. Tell him you've already given me his views over and over again." Click.

I called Kennedy and told him it wasn't necessary to send a note. Kennedy said, "That's fine. But the more I think about it, Joe, the more I think the President should propose a surtax." I sent the President a brief note. At 12:50 P.M., the President called me on the hotline and told me to "tear up" both my notes to him on the "Kennedy thing."[6]

That afternoon, Johnson continued to prepare a balanced budget with no tax surcharge, while I worked furiously on a memo urging him to seek a one-year extension. I cited a few highly questionable expenditure cuts that he would have to resort to without a surtax: deferring federal pay raises, slashing space, crime, cities, and jobs programs, and a patently unrealistic assumption that Vietnam expenditures would decrease by more than $3 billion. On the revenue side, I ridiculed such ploys as pushing revenue up some $2 billion above Treasury Department estimates ("These technicians may traditionally underestimate, but they will be here on January 21 to talk about the pressure we placed on them to jack up revenues"), and a host of impossible-to-pass user charges and fees. I warned him that "the financial writers are sure to write stories about a 'phony budget' . . . (Imagine, for example, Joe Fowler's reaction at a Goldman Sachs board meeting when a budget like this is made public*)," and that he would "be attacked on two grounds: Gimmickry . . . [and] [f]ailure to maintain the momentum you have spent 5 years building in social programs."[7]

That memo earned me the President's first call of the following morning.[8] LBJ didn't need any "Goddamn memos" on the budget; if he'd wanted one, he would have "let Teddy send his." In any case, where had I gotten all those budget numbers? Finally, he had torn up my memo and he wanted me to destroy every copy I had. This order was later reinforced by Jim Jones, who checked with my secretaries to make sure they had destroyed it.

Later in the morning, Budget Director Charles Zwick and Art Okun called me. The President had told them I was not authorized to see any budget or economic figures; he didn't want them sending me any materials on the budget or the economy. Nor was I to attend any meetings on these subjects. I was disinvited to the bipartisan leadership meeting the President held that afternoon to discuss the budget.[9]

From his calls on the morning of January 7, until late afternoon on January 10, the President did not talk to me about his budget and economic messages to Congress.† Normally, I would have been deeply involved with his economic advisers and in almost constant commu-

---

* Treasury Secretary Fowler had left the administration in December 1968 to become a managing director of the investment banking firm.
† This was not my first condemnation to LBJ's deep freeze, but it was the longest. On other occasions when he was so annoyed he didn't want to talk to me, he would communicate his orders through my secretaries or another aide, usually Larry Levinson.

nication with him. On January 10 at midday he met with Zwick, Treasury Secretary Joseph Barr (who had succeeded Fowler), Okun, and McPherson to go over the budget, State of the Union, and economic messages.[10] It was the only such meeting I was not invited to in my years at the White House. That afternoon, the President had a picture taken with all the special assistants, but he ignored me at the photo session. Then at 6:22 P.M., the President had me come to his office with Levinson.[11] He talked about the messages and gave me copies of drafts of each. He told me to work with McPherson on the State of the Union and to put some life into the budget message. "Make it bleed," he told Levinson and me. "Only Italians and Jews know how to bleed, and God knows you all know how to bleed. So make this message bleed."

Levinson and I walked down the hall to my office. We had no stomach to render his phony budget more palatable to liberals. We sat down and started to read the draft message. The President was recommending extension of the full tax surcharge for all of fiscal 1970 and ample funding of the Great Society programs. We were elated. Later that evening I discovered that LBJ had talked to Nixon in the afternoon and persuaded the President-elect to support the extension publicly.[12]

The next day the President had me join him and Arthur Okun for almost an hour to edit the final Economic Report of the President as though nothing had transpired except the usual give-and-take of policy arguments. On January 13 he invited me and a number of others to go to New York for a final farewell dinner-dance hosted by his friends, including Henry Ford, Mrs. Vincent Astor, Arthur and Mathilde Krim, and the Laurance Rockefellers.[13]

On the 14th, he delivered his final State of the Union message. To a cheering joint session of Congress, an emotional, sentimental LBJ proudly reviewed his record of achievements—Medicare, voting rights, aid to elementary, secondary, and higher education, Head Start, millions of acres of land set aside (a burst of applause greeted his promise of more to come in the last few days of his term), eight and one-half million new jobs, five million Americans trained for work, and millions lifted out of poverty.

LBJ urged the new administration to advance the cause of civil rights and proposed legislation to guarantee medical care for every pregnant woman and child through the first year of life and to protect families against the cost of catastrophic illnesses. One of his great regrets was his failure to get a gun registration and licensing bill passed. He expressed his disappointment at not achieving peace in Southeast Asia and his hope for an early end to the war. In thanking

Democratic and Republican leaders, he included a special tribute to "the good commonsense counsel of" his old mentor, President pro-tempore of the Senate, Richard Russell, whose friendship he had shattered during the Fortas affair. LBJ closed movingly:

> Now, it is time to leave. I hope it may be said, a hundred years from now, that by working together we helped to make our country more just, more just for all of its people. . . .
>   That is what I hope. But I believe that at least it will be said that we tried.

He had entered to five minutes of waves of applause and he exited with a hundred handshakes and a chamber of wet-eyed political pros singing "Auld Lang Syne."

Lyndon Johnson's final full day in office was a quiet Sunday. After breakfasting with Mrs. Johnson, he went with Luci (who had converted to Catholicism on her eighteenth birthday in July 1965) to the White House solarium to attend Catholic mass offered by one of the priests who had celebrated his daughter's nuptial mass. Lady Bird walked the south grounds of the White House alone, a scarf over her hair, carrying an umbrella to protect her against the light rain. Later that morning, accompanied by Reverend Billy Graham, the President and Mrs. Johnson joined Sunday services at the National City Christian Church.[14]

During his years in the White House, Lyndon Johnson had grown increasingly religious. He attended services at the National City Christian Church in Washington or the First Christian Church in Johnson City. In mid-1966, when Johnson had authorized bombing of P.O.L. (petroleum, oil, and lubricant) pumping and storage facilities around North Vietnam's capital, Hanoi, and major port city, Haiphong, he was terribly distraught and restless. "I just know," he told me the afternoon of the mission, "that one of our Texas boys, probably from Johnson City, will drop one of those bombs down the smokestack of some hospital or on some school and kill a thousand civilians or children." That evening, his daughter Luci found her father in his bedroom and said, "Daddy, you look so awful and worried." The President explained why. Luci said that whenever she had a problem she went to see "my little monks" at St. Dominic's Catholic Church in Southwest Washington. So that evening, after dinner, the President, Mrs. Johnson, and Luci went over to St. Dominic's, which was opened just for them on that steamy Washington night.

They walked quietly to the front of the church, sat in the third pew and prayed silently for about ten minutes.[15]

In 1967, LBJ went to Roman Catholic mass fourteen times. In the last year in office, he went to mass more frequently, almost every other week, to the point where I wondered at times whether he would follow Luci into the church. Johnson especially enjoyed services at St. Dominic's in Washington and St. Francis Xavier Catholic Church in Stonewall, Texas, where he formed a close friendship with the pastor, Father Wunibald Schneider, who became a spiritual adviser. Over time, the President talked more often about seeking guidance from the Almighty and praying. I had a sense that he found comfort in his relationship with God, particularly during his final year in office.

Hubert Humphrey called early on that last afternoon: "Just thinking of you, and to thank you for all you've done for me, Mr. President." The Marine Corps band came by to serenade with the "Pedernales River March," as the President stood above them on the Truman balcony. LBJ, Lady Bird, Lynda, and Luci had a quiet lunch with Jack and Mary Margaret Valenti and their daughter Courtenay. Early that evening, Dean Rusk and Averell Harriman stopped by to say farewell, and the President called Nelson Rockefeller to thank him for his help and encourage him to stay in politics. The nation's first couple stopped by Henry Ford's party at the exclusive F Street Club, and then returned to the second floor of the mansion to host a buffet dinner for the immediate White House staff.[16]

The final evening party was a happy event. We shared a sense of relief that it was over and a sense of achievement, for despite the frightful cost of the Vietnam War in American lives and economic resources, these years had been by far the most prolific legislatively of any presidency. All of us knew we'd been part of a monumental social revolution. Personally, LBJ had drawn from most of us far more than we ever realized we had to give. For many of us, these would be our most productive years, when more was accomplished than would be the case for the rest of our lives.

The war had taken its political and personal toll on the President, the nation, and each of us. By the end of 1968, U.S. troop levels in South Vietnam had reached 535,000, and though peace negotiations had started, more Americans died in the war in that year than any before or after. Nevertheless, glorious efforts, like the tenacious battles for civil rights and Great Society legislation, had been exhilarating. But we were exhausted and we knew it was time to go.

The President was in good spirits, relieved, mingling happily with his staff, teasing many of us, recalling the good times, the funny gaffes, eating in his favorite chair near the dining-room entrance, chatting with his consumer-affairs assistant Betty Furness and a few other staffers gathered around him.[17]

I recalled the pleasant, personal moments, like the state dinner in honor of Italy's President Giuseppe Saragat on Tuesday, September 19, 1967.[18] The day before, the President had discovered that my mother and father were visiting me, and he invited them to the dinner. It was a black-tie affair, and my mother of course did not have an evening dress with her. No matter; the President arranged for a White House car to take her to Garfinckel's, a fashionable Washington department store, where he insisted she purchase an evening gown and all the trimmings at his expense.

The dinner was fully subscribed, so the President had Chief of Protocol James Symington and me eat in the kitchen to provide two seats for my parents. When they came up to shake hands with the President, he beckoned my mother (a retired New York City public school teacher) and father (a retired IBM office administrator) to stand in the receiving line with him, Lady Bird, and President Saragat as the rest of the guests passed through. After dinner and toasts and coffee in the parlor, the guests went to the East Room to hear excerpts from the hit musical *Man of La Mancha*.[19] The President made sure my parents had up-front seats. It was, of course, one of the most memorable evenings of their lives.

On another occasion when he had found out my father was in town, the President had said, "Bring him by, I want to see him." So my father came to the Oval Office, where Johnson saw him and had some pictures taken.[20] A few days later, LBJ gave me a color picture of the three of us, which he signed with this salutation: "To Joe Califano—The pride of both of us." As he handed it to me, he said, "You don't know how proud your father will be to have that picture. You can't understand until your children grow up."

For me, amid the reminiscences and jovial teasing that evening, the President had some rueful comments and personal advice. Playing his own Monday-morning quarterback, he talked about Foreign Relations Committee Chairman William Fulbright. The two men had split sharply and personally on two central administration policies: the Vietnam War and civil rights for black Americans. Privately, in conversations that must have gotten back to Fulbright, Johnson had never pulled punches. He ridiculed the Arkansas Democrat as "Senator Halfbright," a man who was "upset because he had not been named Secretary of State." Months after Fulbright had voted for the Gulf of Tonkin resolution, the Senator claimed he hadn't fully understood what it meant. Recounting this assertion, Johnson would recite all the questions Fulbright had asked during the bill's drafting and the Senate debate, and conclude, "For a Rhodes scholar to say that he didn't know what was in that resolution is more than this hillbilly will ever believe."[21] Johnson had often mimicked Fulbright when he would recite how the Arkansas Senator opposed the minimum wage when it was forty cents an hour and how he opposed three of Johnson's civil rights bills.* Johnson believed much of Fulbright's opposition to the Vietnam War emanated from his prejudice. "All he thinks about is England, the Marshall Plan, or Europe. He doesn't give a damn about Asians because they're brown."[23]

On one occasion, Johnson had called Fulbright a "revolving son of a bitch" and then turned to me to ask, "You know what a revolving son of a bitch is, don't you?" I didn't. "That," Johnson said, "is someone who's a son of a bitch any way you look at him!"[24]

On this final evening in the White House, though, Johnson appeared to have second thoughts about such personal barbs and how he sometimes treated people. "Perhaps it would have been different with Fulbright," he mused, "if we had only talked to him more, had him over here more, found some things to agree with him on. We never should have let the fight become so personal."

Later that evening, Johnson had me in the corner of the living room near the elevator, his face looking down inches above mine, his right forefinger poking just below my left shoulder. He teased me about the hundreds of memos I'd written to start new federal programs. "It's too late to get them back," he chided. "Nixon's going to accuse you of being the socialist in the White House."

Then LBJ began to talk seriously about Nixon during the McCarthy years, reminiscing as he occasionally did about Helen Gahagan Douglas, the wife of actor Melvyn Douglas and congresswoman whom Nixon defeated for the Senate in 1950 by falsely implying that she was a Communist. Johnson had advised her during that campaign. "She was a fine person," Johnson said sadly of this woman with whom he'd had an affair years before,[25] "and he destroyed her."

Then Johnson looked at me, leaning down, almost eyeball to eyeball, and, speaking just above a whisper, offered me some advice. "You're going to make some money now for the first time in your life. First, invest it in land. This Nixon knows nothing about the economy and it's going to go to hell. Second, when you pay your income taxes, after you figure them out, pay an additional five hundred dollars. It's not enough for Nixon to win. He's going to have to

---

* Johnson had a marvelous talent for mimicking people. In addition to Fulbright, he enjoyed imitating Dirksen's voice and laugh, David Brinkley, Valenti, McNamara, and J. Edgar Hoover's bulldog expression.[22]

put some people in jail. Third, the more you succeed, watch out for jealous people. Jealousy and sex drive people to do more damn mean and crazy things than anything else."

Later in the evening, we sang "Auld Lang Syne" and "For He's a Jolly Good Fellow," and McPherson made some gracious remarks about how proud we all were to have been a part of Johnson's impact on his country.[26]

The President offered some impromptu remarks of his own,[27] mentioning that he intended to take only one more action as President—he was going to add lots more land to the National Park system, on top of the 1.3 million acres that he had added to the National Wildlife Refuge System in December.* He then bade farewell to everybody, and went into his bedroom shortly before 11 P.M..[29]

I stayed awake most of the night thinking about this consumed and complex man, his extraordinary intelligence and deep flaws, his achievements and failures, the love-hate relationship he sparked in so many who came close to him. And I've spent many hours since then reflecting on these years.

In a nation of unprecedented wealth, Lyndon Johnson simply refused to accept poverty. There was no child he could not feed; no adult he could not put to work; no disease he could not cure; no toy, food, or medical device he could not make safer; no air or water he could not clean; no discriminatory barrier he could not topple—just as there was no war he could not win and no cease-fire or peace he could not negotiate. For sure he made overpromises, but they were based on high hopes and great expectations and on his ability to move the system.

At times he lost sight of the fact that laws were not an end in themselves. Perpetually trying to get everyone—business, labor, churches, schools, cities, and states—working on every problem, at moments Johnson failed to accept that he couldn't do it all. His own singular capacity to enact so many laws and programs led him to overestimate the capacity of the government to administer and the nation to absorb so much so fast.

* Johnson particularly prided himself on two achievements: For the first time in generations, in his last two years in office a President had preserved more land for conservation than the nation had bulldozed and paved over for industrial and urban development; and of the 35 National Park areas he pushed through Congress, 32 were within easy driving distance of large cities. At the end of his administration, few accolades gave him more pleasure than the one he received when Dr. Melville Grosvenor, National Geographic's chairman, called him "our greatest conservation President."[28]

It was a reflection of his immense ego. But it was also a measure of his ability to see the difference between his duty as president and his responsibilities as a legislator. And it sprang from his roots in the harsh, dry hill country of poor farmers and Mexican-Americans, in the South where he saw blacks endure degrading humiliation, and in two decades of cold war with the Communists, which influenced his thinking on Vietnam. He saw an America with the economic wealth to wage both wars. His failing, as he sensed it, was that he could not inspire the people to stay both courses.

The Vietnam War took a frightful toll on the nation and the President. Its bloody battles sapped the American spirit, took thousands of young lives, and stunted the development of the Great Society. No matter how Lyndon Johnson mustered his persuasive powers, he could not communicate to the American people why he was convinced we had to be in Vietnam; and, if there, why it made sense to walk his line between all-out war and surrender so that the nation could deal with its domestic problems. Perhaps it was because Johnson himself, contrary to the popular caricature of his day, was so reluctant to be in Vietnam and so frustrated that the war against poverty, ignorance, and disease, which he wanted to wage, was being subverted by the war in Southeast Asia, which he felt he had to wage.

The war in Vietnam ended four years after he left office. Much of the Great Society has survived. Its impact remains in health care for the old and millions of the needy; in land preserved, water cleaned, and a born-again respect for the environment still gaining momentum in the 1990s; in Head Start and in the miracles of the National Institutes of Health and regional medical centers; in food stamps for the poor and scholarships for graduate students; in mass transportation and auto safety; in thousands of black elected officials across the nation and the rise of a black middle class.

Of course LBJ's Great Society did not solve all the problems it set out to correct. Social programs failed to achieve their goals for much of the black underclass. The specters of racial prejudice and poverty amidst affluence still haunt the American attic. The fruits of successful efforts, like the increase in life expectancy prompted by Medicare, Medicaid, and the investment in medical research, carried their own new challenges, like the aging of America and rising health-care costs. New ills, like rampant drug addiction, plague the nation. Despite LBJ's warnings and his programs, scores of thousands of black families continue to disintegrate.

At his best, Lyndon Johnson put the thumb of government forcefully on the scale for the vulnerable among us and brought talented people into public service. Almost to the point of nagging, he reminded the American people that God and history would judge them not just on how much the gross national product grew, but on how they spent it; not simply on how many millionaires the nation's booming economy produced, but on how many millions of people it lifted out of poverty; not simply on how many miles of highway and how many bridges they built, but on how many acres of land they preserved and restored.

At his worst, Lyndon Johnson destroyed his own credibility. He hid the true cost of the military buildup in Vietnam as he first unfolded it. He heard what he wanted and hoped to hear from the military about the war and passed their optimistic reports on to the American people as his own. He lied about little things like appointments to office and his schedule. He learned too late that the manipulative and devious behavior commonplace in the back alleys of legislative politics appalled the American people when exposed in their President. He paid a fearful price as first the press corps in Washington and Saigon and then millions of Americans came to doubt his word. He never seemed able to accept what the war did to the American spirit.

Astonishingly, this President of powerful personal presence, remarkable intelligence, penetrating psychological insights, and enormous political talent was insecure. He longed to be recognized for his achievements. He wanted to be loved for them. His envy for the glamour that surrounded the Kennedys in life and the adulation that attended them in death was Shakespearean. He yearned for appreciation from the Ivy League intellectuals whose ideas he had turned into law, from the young to whom he opened the doors of higher education, from the poor and the black. But the policies to which he devoted his presidency and his complex personality denied him the affection of the people who elected him their President.

Lyndon Johnson had the courage to accept the inevitable risks of his policies. But that didn't ease the pain when he was attacked for doing too much for blacks or as being a cavalier gunslinger who didn't care enough about the lives at risk in South Vietnam. He knew, as he said at the time, that his pursuit of racial justice carried a high price. He chose consciously to keep his appointment in Samara, mindful of the cost to his party and himself. At bottom, in the White House, he was on many matters a true believer, using the street smarts, skills, and cunning of pragmatic politics, which he had honed as representative, senator, and senate majority leader, to promote the domestic agenda of his presidency. He was prepared to land on his sword, if that's what it took, to advance the cause of the poor and the black, resist the Communist aggression he saw in Southeast Asia, and heal the divisions in our nation he had come to symbolize.

Consumed and driven, Lyndon Johnson had his moments of frustration to the cusp of despair. Much of the years in retirement was spent wondering how he might have moved the ball a little further down the field. In the last public speech of his life, when his civil rights papers were opened to the public, Lyndon Johnson said, "Well, this cry of 'never' I've heard since I was a little boy, all my life. And what we commemorate this great day is some of the work which has helped . . . to make 'never' now."

Through it all—the war, the hurt, the devious and crude behavior, the ghosts of the Kennedys, the ambition for his country and himself, during what LBJ called "the most serious" times "confronted by the nation . . . in the course of my lifetime"[30]—he never lost his concentration on trying "to make 'never' now." He left plenty of achievements to build on and plenty of mistakes to learn from. However history measures those successes and failures, it must recognize that Lyndon Johnson cared and that he tried.

Epilogue

On January 22, 1973, almost to the day four years after he left the White House, Lyndon Baines Johnson, who for nearly two decades had been terrified of suffering a heart attack alone in bed, died as he was taking an afternoon rest at his Texas ranch. His heart gave out just as he picked up the phone to call for help. He was alone.

LBJ finally came to rest on his ranch in the hill country of Texas, in a family gravesite near the Pedernales River, where he had gone so often to regenerate his body and spirit.

Acknowledgments

This book stems from three and one-half years of intensive work for Lyndon Johnson, almost twenty-five years of reflection on the man and his work, and four years of research and writing.

Several colleagues read all or parts of various drafts of the manuscript: Frederick Bohen, Ervin Duggan, Michael Gillette, Lawrence Levinson, Gerald Rosberg, and Susan Tammen. Their insights and suggestions have been of great help, as have those of my wife, Hilary, who also read a draft of the manuscript.

Karen O'Connell, Carol Massetti, and Lynn Soltis managed the various drafts through word processors and maintained the backup files. Their administrative skills, meticulous attention to detail, common sense, patience, and good humor deserve a special commendation. Maxine Walker kept my schedule going through the final months of work. The word-processing staff at Dewey Ballantine's Washington office, led by Martha Myricks, were responsive, careful, and helpful. My law partners and Sue Brown were understanding and patient.

In Marcel Bryar I was blessed with an extraordinary research assistant. He worked with me for almost three years, putting my files in order, assembling papers from them and the LBJ Library, checking and double-checking facts and figures. He is a young man of high intellect, dedication, and self-discipline. He raised many of the hard questions and helped keep me on course. He has a great future ahead of him as a lawyer and, I hope, public servant.

Harry Middleton, director of the LBJ Library, and the library staff, particularly those working on the oral history project, were unfailingly responsive.

I could not have written this book without the special love and understanding of my wife. She is a woman of extraordinary insight and tenderness. In less than a decade, Hilary has given more love than most men receive in a lifetime. She made many personal sacrifices because she knew how important this task was to me.

Alice Mayhew, ever overworked and dedicated, was the editor I wanted for this enterprise, and her insights and suggestions have made this a better book, as have those of George Hodgman. Sterling Lord, as always, provided support and encouragement.

All these and many others helped. But what is said on these pages is my responsibility alone.

JOSEPH A. CALIFANO, JR.
Washington, D.C.
August 1991

Source Notes

To refresh my memory, I have relied on primary sources available in my personal files and at the Lyndon B. Johnson Library in Austin, Texas. My own files contain hundreds of pages of contemporaneous notes and copies of almost every memo and letter that I wrote and received during the Kennedy and Johnson years. I supplemented these files with papers from the LBJ Library and public sources. With the publication of this book, I am giving all of my personal papers for this period to the LBJ Library. I am also turning over to the Library files related to this book, including papers assembled chapter by chapter to provide convenient access for scholars and historians. Where available, I have cited the primary sources in these notes.

In addition to primary sources, I have used numerous secondary sources, notably including *The Washington Post, The New York Times, Time, Newsweek, U.S. News and World Report, Congressional Quarterly* and its almanacs and volumes of *Congress and the Nation*, Lyndon B. Johnson's *Public Papers, The New York Times's* version of *The Pentagon Papers*, and scores of books and magazine articles. I have not cited these sources or other publicly available materials such as transcripts of press conferences and speeches, although in most cases copies of such materials are in the files I am turning over to the LBJ Library.

Primary sources include my daily telephone logs and Day-at-a-Glance daily calendar, steno pads, presidential daily diaries, 1969 notes, author interviews, and oral histories. The telephone logs and Day-at-a-Glances are records secretaries kept of many of the phone calls I placed and received and of the meetings I held and attended. The steno pads are contemporaneous notes I took of meetings and conversations, on the phone and in person, with the President and others during my years in the White House. The steno pads are mostly notebooks I carried around with me almost everywhere I went, but sometimes I took notes on the nearest piece of paper, and those notes are also cited as steno pads. The presidential daily diaries provide a schedule of what the President did each day with an indication of many of the people he talked to; they are familiar to Johnson scholars. The 1969 notes are recollections of President Johnson that I dictated in 1969 when they were still fresh in my mind so they would be available when I could write this book. The author interviews are interviews my research assistant and I conducted with various individuals to check my memory of events. Finally, the oral histories are interviews that LBJ Library oral historians conducted with people associated with Johnson (including my own in 1969, 1970, and 1973).

In the Source Notes, I refer to these primary sources with the following abbreviations:

Telephone Logs	TL
Day-at-a-Glance	DG
Steno Pads	SP
Presidential Daily Diary	PDD
1969 Notes	69N
Author Interviews	AI
Oral Histories	OH

PROLOGUE

1. The above is based in part on 69N.
2. JAC memo to Cyrus Vance, November 24, 1963, LBJ Library. "Order" setting aside land for John F. Kennedy's burial, signed by Cyrus Vance and Robert McNamara, LBJ Library.

1. THE BEGINNING

1. DG, November 4, 1964.
2. PDD, August 21, 1964. DG, August 21, 1964.
3. DG, November 4, 1964.
4. PDD, November 9–10, 1964.
5. PDD, July 8, 1965. DG, July 8, 1965.
6. PDD, October 14, 1964. "Statement of Mrs. Lyndon B. Johnson," October 15, 1964, LBJ Library.
7. DG, July 9, 1965.
8. Rebekah Johnson letter to LBJ and Lady Bird, November 30, 1934, LBJ Library.
9. Rebekah Johnson letter to LBJ, April 1937, LBJ Library.
10. For events of this weekend, see PDD, July 10–12, 1965.
11. See 69N and OH, JAC, April 14, 1969, Interview I, pp. 11–13.
12. John Connor, Speech, University of Virginia, October 13, 1986, p. 15.
13. PDD, November 27, 1967.
14. Johnson's day is based in part on 69N.
15. For this dinner, see: PDD, October 5, 1965. AI, Henry Fowler.
16. PDD, October 5, 1965. AI, Hugh O'Brian.
17. SP, December 8–17, 1967.

18. OH, Victoria McCammon, June 6, 1975, tape 1 of 5, p. 33. OH, Victoria McCammon, June 9, 1975, tape 4 of 5, pp. 49–50.

2. THE DECISION

1. Chronology of Events Tuesday, August 4, and Wednesday, August 5, 1964, Tonkin Gulf Strike, Third Draft, August 25, 1964, LBJ Library. Tonkin Chronology, undated draft, LBJ Library.
2. Clark M. Clifford letter to LBJ, May 17, 1965, LBJ Library.
3. McGeorge Bundy memo to Robert McNamara, June 30, 1965, LBJ Library. Dean Rusk memo to LBJ, July 1, 1965, LBJ Library.
4. McGeorge Bundy memo to LBJ, June 30, 1965, LBJ Library.
5. Cyrus Vance cable to Robert McNamara, July 17, 1965, LBJ Library.
6. Robert McNamara memo to LBJ, July 20, 1965, LBJ Library.
7. McGeorge Bundy memo to Robert McNamara, June 30, 1965, LBJ Library.
8. For this meeting, see: Chester Cooper, "Memorandum for the Record," July 21, 1965, meeting on Vietnam, July 22, 1965, LBJ Library. PDD, July 21, 1965.
9. PDD, July 21, 1965.
10. McGeorge Bundy memo to LBJ, July 21, 1965, 8 P.M., LBJ Library.
11. PDD, July 22, 1965.
12. Ibid.
13. Ibid.
14. Ibid.
15. Ibid.
16. Robert McNamara plans, three of them, no titles, except Plan I, Plan II, and Plan III, and dated "7/23/65," "7/23/65," and "7/24/65—Rev #1," respectively.
17. PDD, July 23, 1965.
18. Talk with President Johnson, August 12, 1969, William Jorden, p. 20, LBJ Library.
19. PDD, July 23, 1965. Paul Popple memo to LBJ, July 23, 1965, 3:40 P.M., LBJ Library. JAC memo to LBJ, August 11, 1965, Personal Papers.
20. PDD, July 23, 25, 1965.
21. PDD, July 25, 1965. Arthur Goldberg memo to LBJ, July 23, 1965 (Attachment: handwritten, "Draft Resolution on Viet Nam"), LBJ Library. Transcript of LBJ, Goldberg, McNamara, Clifford, Busby, and Valenti Camp David meeting in Aspen Lodge, July 25, 1965, LBJ Library.
22. PDD, July 25, 1965.
23. PDD, July 26, 1965.
24. Ibid. McGeorge Bundy memo to LBJ, July 26, 1965, 11:30 A.M. (Attachment: "Agenda. Meeting at 12:00, Monday, July 26, 1965"), LBJ Library.

25. PDD, July 27, 1965.
26. PDD, July 27, 1965. Lawrence O'Brien memo to LBJ, July 27, 1965, LBJ Library.
27. PDD, July 27, 1965.
28. Ibid. Bromley Smith, "Summary Notes of 553rd NSC Meeting, July 27, 1965, 5:40 P.M.–6:20 P.M.," LBJ Library.
29. Johnson made similar remarks in his National Security Council meeting earlier in the day: Bromley Smith, "Summary Notes of 553rd NSC Meeting, July 27, 1965, 5:40 P.M.–6:20 P.M.," LBJ Library.
30. Talk with President Johnson, August 12, 1969, William Jorden, p. 1, LBJ Library.
31. My extensive notes of this meeting are in SP, July 27, 1965, "Leadership meeting on Vietnam." See also: "Memorandum, prepared in December 1968, of a meeting with the Joint Leadership on July 27, 1965, at 6:30 P.M.," LBJ Library. "Congressional Leadership Meeting, Tuesday, July 27, 1965," LBJ Library.
32. PDD, July 27, 1965.
33. Mike Mansfield memo to LBJ, July 27, 1965, LBJ Library.
34. Ibid. JAC memo to Robert McNamara, July 28, 1965, LBJ Library. LBJ letter to Mike Mansfield, July 28, 1965, LBJ Library.
35. PDD, July 28, 1965.
36. Ibid.
37. PDD, July 29, 1965. DG, July 29, 1965.
38. PDD, July 28, 1965.
39. Ibid.
40. Ibid.
41. 69N.
42. PDD, July 28, 1965.
43. Abe Fortas letter to LBJ, July 19, 1965, LBJ Library. Abe Fortas letter to LBJ, July 29, 1965, LBJ Library.
44. PDD, July 29, 1965.
45. In mentioning this incident in *Governing America*, I mistakenly placed it in the Oval Office.
46. PDD, July 30, 1965.
47. PDD, July 31, 1965. DG, July 31, 1965.
48. For this conversation, see 69N.
49. JAC memo to LBJ, August 11, 1965, Personal Papers.

3. Racing Against High Expectations

1. PDD, October 7, 1966.
2. AI, Howard Shuman. See unpublished paper of Howard Shuman, "Lyndon B. Johnson: The Senate Democratic Leader."
3. AI, Bill Moyers.

4. PDD, February 9, 1965. See Lee White, "Points that Dr. King Might Make Upon Leaving the White House," LBJ Library.
5. OH, Victoria McCammon, June 9, 1975, tape 4 of 5, p. 19.
6. PDD, August 4–5, 1965.
7. PDD, August 6, 1965. SP, #1, to August 13, 1965. JAC memo to LBJ, August 5, 1965, Personal Papers. JAC memo to LBJ, August 6, 1965, Personal Papers.
8. AI, Berl Bernhard.
9. PDD, August 11, 1965. OH, JAC, April 14, 1969, Interview I, pp. 15–16. OH, JAC, July 18, 1969, Interview III, pp. 1–8.
10. PDD, August 12, 1965.
11. TL, August 13, 1965. PDD, August 13, 1965.
12. TL, August 14, 1965. PDD, August 14, 1965.
13. SP, #2, August 14–21, 1965. SP, from loose, undated pages with steno pads. TL, August 14, 1965. *Military Support of Law Enforcement During Civil Disturbances: A Report Concerning the California National Guard's Part in Suppressing the Los Angeles Riot—August 1965*, p. 28.
14. TL, August 14, 1965. PDD, August 14, 1965. SP, from loose, undated pages with steno pads. SP, #2, August 14–21, 1965. JAC memo to Jack Valenti, August 14, 1965, 11:52 P.M., LBJ Library.
15. TL, August 14, 1965. SP, from loose, undated pages with steno pads. SP, #2, August 14–21, 1965.
16. Jack Valenti memo to LBJ, August 14, 1965, 6:25 P.M., LBJ Library. PDD, August 14, 1965.
17. For the above conversation, see: PDD, August 15, 1965. SP, #2, August 14–21, 1965.
18. Eugene P. Foley memo to JAC, August 22, 1965, LBJ Library. Jackson Graham memo to JAC, August 23, 1965, LBJ Library. Lawrence McQuade memo to JAC, August 23, 1965, LBJ Library. John Schnittker memo to JAC, August 23, 1965, LBJ Library. Franklin Dryden memo to JAC, August 23, 1965, LBJ Library. Calvin Kytle memo to JAC, August 23, 1965, LBJ Library. Lisle Carter memo to JAC, August 23, 1965, LBJ Library. SP, #2, August 14–21, 1965.
19. JAC and Lee White memo to LBJ, August 24, 1965, LBJ Library.
20. LeRoy Collins memo to JAC, undated (Attachments: LeRoy Collins letter to LBJ, undated, and LeRoy Collins memo to LBJ, undated), LBJ Library. My account of the Watts riots is based in part on OH, JAC, August 21, 1969, Interview IV, pp. 18–29.
21. OH, Victoria McCammon, June 6, 1975, tape 1 of 5, pp. 6–8 and 20; June 8, 1975, tape 2, of 5, p. 11.
22. JAC memo to Nicholas Katzenbach, September 8, 1965 (Attachment: Berl Bernhard memo to Bill Moyers, Lee White, and Harry McPherson, August 24, 1965), Personal Papers.
23. Hubert Humphrey memo to LBJ, September 17, 1965, 2 P.M., LBJ Library.
24. PDD, September 18, 1965.

25. PDD, September 17, 1965.
26. See JAC memo to LBJ, September 16, 1965, 7:55 P.M., LBJ Library.
27. TL, September 20, 1965.
28. Marvin Watson memo to LBJ, September 20, 1965, 8:45 P.M. (Attachments: Nicholas Katzenbach memo to LBJ, September 20, 1965, and "Suggested Summary of Re-organization of Civil Rights Responsibilities"), LBJ Library. PDD, September 22, 1965.
29. For this meeting, see: 69N. AI, Lee White.
30. PDD, September 23, 1965.
31. Ibid.
32. TL, September 23, 1965. DG, September 23, 1965.
33. JAC and Lee White memo to LBJ, September 24, 1965, 1:20 A.M. (Attachment: Hubert Humphrey memo to LBJ, September 24, 1965, 10 A.M.), LBJ Library.
34. JAC and Lee White Memo to LBJ, September 24, 1965, 1:20 A.M., LBJ Library. AI, Lee White.
35. JAC and Lee White memo to LBJ, September 24, 1965, 1:20 A.M. (Attachment: Hubert Humphrey memo to LBJ, September 24, 1965, 10 A.M.), LBJ Library.
36. The civil rights reorganization is based in part on 69N. OH, JAC, September 12, 1969, Interview V, pp. 16–19.
37. JAC memo to LBJ, August 24, 1965, 10:55 P.M., Personal Papers. Francis Keppel memo to Douglass Cater, undated (Attachment: Francis Keppel memo to JAC, August 29, 1965), LBJ Library. Francis Keppel memo to JAC, September 2, 1965, LBJ Library. JAC memo to LBJ, September 8, 1965, 7:55 P.M., LBJ Library.
38. DG, August 26 and 31 and September 9 and 17. JAC memo to LBJ, September 10, 1965, 8 P.M., LBJ Library. JAC memo to LBJ, September 14, 1965, 5:45 P.M., Personal Papers. Jake Jacobsen memo to LBJ, September 17, 1965, 5:30 P.M., LBJ Library. Transcript of JAC office meeting, September 10, 1965, LBJ Library.
39. JAC memo to LBJ, August 30, 1965, 1:10 P.M. (Attachment: "As of Close of Business, August 30, 1965, Status of Desegregation Plans under Title VI, Civil Rights Act of 1964"), LBJ Library. Carol Herzman memo to Marvin Watson, August 30, 1965, "copy sent to Connally spec. del., 8/31," LBJ Library. FS memo to LBJ, September 3, 1965, 11:45 A.M., LBJ Library. JAC memo to LBJ, September 10, 1965, 9:30 A.M., LBJ Library. JAC memo to LBJ, September 10, 1965, 8 P.M., LBJ Library. JAC memo to LBJ, September 14, 1965, 5:45 P.M., Personal Papers. Jake Jacobsen memo to LBJ, September 17, 1965, 5:30 P.M., LBJ Library.
40. PDD, October 3–4, 1965.
41. PDD, October 4, 1965. OH, Douglass Cater, April 29, 1969, tape 1, pp. 21–22.
42. For this meeting, see: 69N. AI, Paul Marcinkus. PDD, October 4, 1965.
43. TL, October 4, 1965. The Daley desegregation incident is based in part on 69N.

44. Marvin Watson memo to LBJ, December 15, 1965, 6:30 P.M., LBJ Library.

4. THE WAR AGAINST POVERTY AND THE BATTLE FOR BEAUTY

1. R. Eugene Livesay memo, April 2, 1964, Personal Papers.
2. PDD, Aug. 7, 1964. AI, Sargent Shriver.
3. See OH, Victoria McCammon, June 9, 1975, tape 4 of 5, pp. 5–7.
4. Sargent Shriver memo to LBJ, October 20, 1965, LBJ Library.
5. Charles Schultze memo to LBJ, September 18, 1965, LBJ Library. Hubert Humphrey memo to Marvin Watson, September 22, 1965 (Attachment: Donald Stinnett memo to Hubert Humphrey, September 20, 1965), LBJ Library. Hubert Humphrey memo to LBJ, December 2, 1965, 6 P.M., LBJ Library.
6. Hayes Redmon memo to Bill Moyers, November 5, 1965, LBJ Library. Charles Schultze memo to LBJ, November 6, 1965, LBJ Library. Sargent Shriver memo to LBJ, November 6, 1965, LBJ Library.
7. JAC memo to LBJ, December 18, 1965, 6:40 P.M., LBJ Library.
8. PDD, June 14, 1967.
9. SP, #1, to August 13, 1965.
10. For this meeting, see: PDD, September 11, 1965. SP, #5, September 8–17, 1965. JAC memo to LBJ, Mrs. Lyndon B. Johnson, and White House staff, September 11, 1965, 5:30 P.M. (Attachment: JAC memo re "Beautification Bill," September 11, 1965), LBJ Library. JAC memo to LBJ, September 12, 1965, 5:15 P.M. (Attachment: Sheldon Cohen memo re "Outdoor Advertising Signs—Tax Depreciation and Investment Credit," undated), LBJ Library. Tina Lawson typed notes of September 11, 1965, staff meeting, July 17, 1972, LBJ Library.
11. SP, #8, October 1–11, 1965.
12. 69N on the men around Johnson, pp. 59–61. AI, Alan Boyd.
13. JAC memo to LBJ, September 12, 1965, 5:15 P.M. (Attachment: Sheldon Cohen memo re "Outdoor Advertising Signs—Tax Depreciation and Investment Credit," undated), LBJ Library. Lawrence O'Brien memo to LBJ, September 18, 1965, LBJ Library.
14. PDD, October 7, 1965.

5. SCRAMBLING

1. PDD, August 17, 1965. Union position paper, July 29, 1965, LBJ Library.
2. For Johnson's story, see 69N.
3. JAC memo to Otto Eckstein, August 18, 1965. Personal Papers. JAC memo to LBJ, August 19, 1965, 8:40 P.M., LBJ Library.
4. JAC memo to LBJ, August 19, 1965, 8:40 P.M. (Attachment: Otto Eck-

stein memo to LBJ, August 19, 1965), LBJ Library. PDD, August 19, 1965.

5. JAC memo to LBJ, August 23, 1965, 8:45 P.M., LBJ Library. W. Willard Wirtz memo to LBJ, August 24, 1965, LBJ Library.

6. JAC memo to LBJ, August 25, 1965, 4 P.M. (Attachment: John Connor memo to LBJ, August 25, 1965), LBJ Library. JAC memo to LBJ, August 25, 1965, 9 P.M., LBJ Library.

7. JAC memo to LBJ, August 26, 1965, 5:45 P.M. (Attachment: Connor memo to LBJ, August 26, 1965, LBJ Library), Personal Papers.

8. For the above meeting, see PDD, August 26, 1965, and SP, #3, August 23–30, 1965.

9. PDD, August 27, 1965. JAC memo to LBJ, August 27, 1965, 8:55 P.M., LBJ Library.

10. PDD, August 28, 1965.

11. LBJ letter to Wayne Morse, August 25, 1967, Personal Papers.

12. PDD, August 28, 1965.

13. DG, August 28, 1965. 69N on the President and the economy—jawboning, p. 23.

14. JAC memo to LBJ, August 30, 1965, 2:45 A.M., LBJ Library.

15. PDD, August 30, 1965. SP, #4, August 30–September 8, 1965.

16. PDD, August 30, 1965.

17. Gardner Ackley memo to LBJ, August 30, 1965, LBJ Library.

18. Note on White House stationery saying where negotiators located, LBJ Library. JAC memo to Bill Moyers, September 3, 1965, LBJ Library.

19. PDD, August 30, 1965.

20. PDD, August 31 and September 2, 1965.

21. SP, #4, August 30–September 8, 1965.

22. PDD, September 2, 1965. JAC memo to LBJ, September 2, 1965, 10:35 A.M. (Attachment: "Points for Visit to Steel Negotiators"), Personal Papers.

23. JAC memo to LBJ, September 2, 1965, 8:25 A.M., LBJ Library. PDD, September 2–3, 1965. JAC memo to Bill Moyers, September 3, 1965, LBJ Library.

24. JAC memo to Bill Moyers, September 3, 1965, LBJ Library.

25. PDD, September 3, 1965.

26. JAC memo to Bill Moyers, September 3, 1965, LBJ Library. DG, September 3, 1965. PDD, September 3, 1965.

27. PDD, September 3, 1965.

28. Ibid.

29. Ibid.

30. R. Conrad Cooper letter to LBJ, September 9, 1965, LBJ Library. I. W. Abel letter to LBJ, September 9, 1965, LBJ Library. For the steel labor negotiations, see: 69N on the President and the economy—jawboning, pp. 18–35. OH, JAC, April 14, 1969, Interview I, pp. 16–17, and July 18, 1969, Interview III, pp. 8–22.

31. PDD, November 9, 1964.

32. For the military base closure, see: OH, JAC, October 17, 1969, Interview VI, pp. 20–25.
33. JAC memo to Robert McNamara, August 20, 1965, Personal Papers. DG, August 21, 1965.
34. PDD, August 21, 1965. DG, August 21, 1965.
35. Ibid.
36. JAC memo to LBJ, November 16, 1965 (Attachment: Chronology of events relating to disposal of aluminum stockpile surplus), Personal Papers. JAC memo to LBJ, August 28, 1965, 5:50 P.M. (Attachment: Elmer B. Staats memo to LBJ, August 27, 1965), LBJ Library.
37. JAC memo to LBJ, September 8, 1965, 7:45 P.M., LBJ Library.
38. JAC memo to LBJ, September 8, 1965, 7:45 P.M. (Attachment: Lawson Knott memo to JAC, September 2, 1965), LBJ Library. JAC memo to LBJ, November 16, 1965 (Attachment: Chronology of events relating to disposal of aluminum stockpile surplus), Personal Papers.
39. PDD, October 29, 1965. Otto Eckstein cable to LBJ, October 29, 1965, LBJ Library.
40. PDD, October 30, 1965.
41. PDD, September 11, 13–16, 18, and 23, December 3 and 14, 1965.
42. John Connor, Speech, University of Virginia, October 13, 1986, pp. 23–24.
43. JAC memo to LBJ, October 30, 1965, LBJ Library. JAC memo to LBJ, November 16, 1965 (Attachment: Chronology of events relating to disposal of aluminum stockpile surplus), Personal Papers.
44. PDD, October 29–30, 1965. AI, Lady Bird Johnson.
45. PDD, November 1, 1965.
46. Otto Eckstein memo to JAC, October 31, 1965 (Attachment: "Background Material on Vietnam"), Personal Papers.
47. JAC, "Draft Memorandum for the Record," November 1, 1965, Personal Papers. JAC memo to LBJ, November 16, 1965 (Attachment: Chronology of events relating to disposal of aluminum stockpile surplus), Personal Papers.
48. Robert McNamara Special Press Briefing, November 10, 1965, 9:45 to 10:06 P.M., at the Pentagon, Personal Papers.
49. For the aluminum price fight, see: OH, JAC, September 12, 1969, Interview V, pp. 29–30. 69N on the President and the economy, pp. 1–41.
50. Gardner Ackley cable to LBJ, November 8, 1965, LBJ Library.
51. DG, November 12, 1965.
52. Ibid.
53. DG, November 16, 1965. PDD, November 16, 1965.
54. For the copper price fight, see: 69N on the President and the economy, pp. 42–47.
55. JAC memo to LBJ, December 31, 1965, LBJ Library.
56. SP, from loose notes on New Year's Eve, 1965, price increase.
57. White House press release, "Statement by the President," December 31, 1965, LBJ Library.

58. DG, January 1, 1966.
59. SP, from loose notes on New Year's Eve, 1965, price increase. JAC memo to LBJ, January 2, 1966, 10 P.M., LBJ Library.
60. LBJ cable to steel executives, January 2, 1966, Personal Papers. JAC memo to LBJ, January 2, 1966, 10 P.M., LBJ Library.
61. For the above conversation, see: SP, from loose notes on New Year's Eve, 1965, price increase.
62. JAC and Gardner Ackley backgrounder, January 2, 1966, 2:15 P.M., p. 6, LBJ Library.
63. For the steel price fight, see: 69N on the President and the economy, pp. 47–55.

6. Guns and Butter

1. Gardner Ackley memo to LBJ, June 3, 1965, LBJ Library. Gardner Ackley memo to LBJ, September 16, 1965, LBJ Library. Gardner Ackley memo to LBJ, October 5, 1965, LBJ Library. Charles Schultze memo to LBJ, October 4, 1965, LBJ Library. Henry Fowler memo to LBJ, October 6, 1965, LBJ Library. PDD, October 6, 1965.
2. For this meeting, see: SP, October 1–11, 1965.
3. Gardner Ackley memo to LBJ, October 11, 1965, LBJ Library.
4. JAC memo to LBJ, November 29, 1965, LBJ Library.
5. JAC memo to LBJ, December 3, 1965, LBJ Library.
6. DG, December 6, 1965. PDD, December 6, 1965. The discount-rate increase is based in part on 69N on the new economics Johnson style, pp. 11–14; OH, JAC, September 12, 1969, Interview V, pp. 12–14.
7. PDD, February 1, 1966. William Martin letter to LBJ, February 2, 1966, LBJ Library.
8. William Martin letter to LBJ, February 2, 1966, LBJ Library.
9. 69N.
10. AI, Russell Long.
11. PDD, March 9, 1966.
12. DG, August 20, 1965. PDD, August 20, 1965. JAC memo to LBJ, August 16, 1965, LBJ Library. Marvin Watson memo to LBJ, August 19, 1965, 10:15 P.M., LBJ Library. Notes "From Cab Rm meet 8-20-65, 6:20/9:30 P.M.," LBJ Library. JAC memo to LBJ, December 18, 1965, 12:25 P.M., Personal Papers. JAC memo to LBJ, December 23, 1965, Personal Papers.
13. JAC memo to LBJ, December 23, 1965, LBJ Library.
14. Ibid.
15. Charles Schultze memo to LBJ, December 17, 1965, LBJ Library. JAC memo to LBJ, December 17, 1965, 6:15 P.M. (Attachment: Gardner Ackley memo to LBJ, December 17, 1965), LBJ Library.
16. Lawrence Levinson memo to LBJ, December 29, 1965 (Attachment: Henry Fowler memo to LBJ, December 29, 1965 [Attachment: "Mem-

orandum of Meeting, December 22, 1965, between Chairman Mills, Secretary Fowler, and Assistant Secretary Surrey"]), LBJ Library.

17. Henry Wilson memo to LBJ, March 15, 1966, 4:10 P.M., LBJ Library.

18. JAC memo to LBJ, August 11, 1965, LBJ Library. JAC memo to LBJ, October 12, 1965, LBJ Library. JAC letter to John Kenneth Galbraith, November 12, 1965, Personal Papers. JAC letter to Dean Acheson, November 12, 1965, Personal Papers.

19. Harry McPherson memo to JAC, December 10, 1965, LBJ Library. See OH, Victoria McCammon, June 8, 1975, tape 2 of 5, pp. 13–14.

20. David Bunn memo to JAC, December 14, 1965 (Attachment: "Special Assistance Lunch Programs for Elementary And Secondary Poor Schools"), LBJ Library. JAC memo to Harry McPherson, December 18, 1965 (Attachment: Hubert Humphrey memo to LBJ, December 14, 1965), LBJ Library. JAC memo to LBJ, March 22, 1966, 6:15 P.M., Personal Papers.

21. For the 1966 legislative program presentation, see: DG, December 29, 1965. PDD, December 29, 1965. JAC memo to LBJ, December 28, 1965 (Attachment: JAC memo to LBJ, December 28, 1965, 11:05 A.M. [Attachment: " 'The Great Society'—A Second Year Legislative Program"]), LBJ Library.

22. LBJ memo to "Heads Of Departments and Agencies," November 15, 1965, LBJ Library. Jack Valenti memo to LBJ, November 27, 1965, 8:45 P.M., LBJ Library.

23. Jack Valenti memo to LBJ, November 27, 1965, 8:45 P.M., LBJ Library. Lawrence Levinson memo to JAC, December 7, 1965, 6:40 P.M. (Attachment: Jack Valenti memo to JAC, December 7, 1965), LBJ Library.

24. Jack Valenti memo to LBJ, December 26, 1965, 3:15 P.M., LBJ Library. Gardner Ackley memo to JAC, January 2, 1966, forwarded to Richard Goodwin, LBJ Library. Wayne Morse letter to JAC, January 10, 1966, LBJ Library. Jake Jacobsen memo to LBJ, January 11, 1966, LBJ Library. Henry Fowler memo to JAC, January 5, 1966, LBJ Library. Henry Fowler memo to JAC, January 7, 1966, LBJ Library. Henry Fowler memo to LBJ, January 10, 1966, LBJ Library.

25. PDD, January 12, 1966.

26. DG, January 12, 1966.

27. PDD, January 12, 1966.

28. Ibid.

29. The 1966 legislative program and State of the Union Message are based in part on 69N on the new economics Johnson style, pp. 14–20.

30. PDD, January 29, 1966. SP, January 18–29, 1966. Notes of January 29, 1966, NSC meeting, LBJ Library.

31. JAC memo to LBJ, January 29, 1966, Personal Papers.

32. AI, Lady Bird Johnson.

7. Going for the Great Society

1. JAC and Lee White memo to LBJ, January 28, 1966, 11:30 A.M., Personal Papers. 69N on the men around Johnson, pp. 61–62.
2. Lee White memo for the files, December 14, 1965, LBJ Library. Lee White memo for the files, December 16, 1965, LBJ Library. Lee White memo for the files, December 23, 1965, LBJ Library.
3. For a sense of LBJ's early legislative concerns, see: JAC memo to LBJ, February 7, 1966, 1 P.M., Personal Papers. JAC memo to LBJ, February 13, 1966, 9:15 P.M., LBJ Library. JAC memo to LBJ, February 14, 1966, 7:45 P.M. (Attachment: Henry Wilson memo to LBJ, February 14, 1966, 7:30 P.M. [Attachment: Mike Manatos memo to JAC, February 14, 1966]), LBJ Library. Lee White and JAC memo to LBJ, February 17, 1966, 7:45 P.M., LBJ Library. JAC memo to LBJ, February 18, 1966, 7:55 P.M., Personal Papers. JAC memo to LBJ, February 22, 1966, LBJ Library. JAC memo to LBJ, February 25, 1966, 7:05 P.M., Personal Papers. JAC memo to LBJ, March 1, 1966, 9:05 P.M. (Attachment: "Congressional Contacts, Summary of the Transportation Message"), LBJ Library.
4. JAC memo to LBJ, August 31, 1966, 6 P.M. (Attachment: "The Transportation Department and the Maritime Administration, Chronology of the Negotiations at the White House"), Personal Papers.
5. JAC and Harold Barefoot Sanders memo to LBJ, undated, Personal Papers. JAC memo to LBJ, June 9, 1966, 5 P.M., Personal Papers. JAC memo to LBJ, July 13, 1966, 10:25 A.M., Personal Papers. JAC memo for the record, June 21, 1966, Personal Papers. JAC memo to Lawrence O'Brien, May 12, 1966, Personal Papers. JAC memo to LBJ, June 10, 1966, 1:15 P.M., Personal Papers.
6. JAC memo to LBJ, May 24, 1966, 8:30 P.M., Personal Papers.
7. 69N.
8. JAC memo to LBJ, October 13, 1966, 8:05 P.M., Personal Papers. JAC memo to LBJ, August 30, 1966, 11:45 P.M., Personal Papers. PDD, October 15, 1966.
9. DG, October 27, 1965.
10. JAC memo to LBJ, October 31, 1965, Personal Papers.
11. SP, #9, October 11–27, 1965. JAC memo to LBJ, October 18, 1965, 11:50 A.M., Personal Papers. JAC memo to LBJ, October 19, 1965, Personal Papers. JAC memo to LBJ, November 17, 1965 (Attachment: Draft Robert Weaver letter to James Harvey, undated), Personal Papers. JAC memo to LBJ, February 1, 1966, 6:55 P.M. (Attachment: Robert Weaver memo to LBJ, February 1, 1966), Personal Papers.
12. SP, #10, October 27–November 9, 1965.
13. JAC memo to LBJ, November 4, 1965, 8:11 P.M, LBJ Library.
14. DG, November 2, 1965.
15. PDD, November 2, 1965.
16. PDD, November 3, 1965. TL, November 3, 1965.

17. SP, #10, October 27–November 9, 1965.
18. DG, November 3, 1965.
19. PDD, November 3, 1965.
20. Ibid.
21. SP, #10, October 27–November 9, 1965. Marvin Watson memo to LBJ, November 18, 1965, 7:30 P.M. (Attachment: Clifton Carter memo to Marvin Watson, November 18, 1965 [Attachment: Frank Horne letter to "Special Key People," November 8, 1965]), Personal Papers.
22. For Weaver's appointment, see: OH, JAC, September 12, 1969, Interview V, pp. 1–12. 69N on the men around Johnson, pp. 24–35.
23. PDD, September 17, 1965. JAC memo to LBJ, September 16, 1965, 7:55 P.M., LBJ Library.
24. JAC memo to LBJ, October 9, 1965, 6 P.M., LBJ Library. JAC memo to LBJ, October 13, 1965, Personal Papers. "Summary Non-Task Force Meeting: October 15, 1965," LBJ Library. Robert Wood letter to LBJ, December 21, 1965 (Attachment: 1965 Urban Problems Task Force Report), LBJ Library.
25. JAC memo to Charles Schultze, May 23, 1966 (Attachment: Robert Weaver memo to LBJ, May 22, 1966), LBJ Library.
26. JAC memo to Lawrence O'Brien, Henry Wilson, and Mike Manatos, May 24, 1966 (Attachment: "Weaver Proposal," May 21, 1966), LBJ Library. Robert Weaver memo to JAC, May 24, 1966 (Attachment: "Summary Statement on Proposed Amendments to Demonstration Cities Bill," May 24, 1966), LBJ Library. Milton Semer memo to LBJ, May 25, 1966, 5 P.M., LBJ Library. Henry Wilson memo to LBJ, May 30, 1966, 6:25 P.M., LBJ Library. Milton Semer memo to LBJ, May 31, 1966, 3:15 P.M., LBJ Library.
27. PDD, May 31, 1966.
28. PDD, June 7, 1966. SP, #19, June 3–20, 1966. JAC memo to LBJ, June 6, 1966, LBJ Library.
29. DG, June 22, 1966.
30. DG, June 23, 1966. JAC memo to LBJ, June 23, 1966, 11:35 A.M., Personal Papers.
31. DG, July 6, 1966. Lawrence Levinson memo to Lawrence O'Brien, July 5, 1966, Personal Papers.
32. PDD, July 19, 1966. JAC memo to LBJ, July 18, 1966, 10:30 A.M., Personal Papers.
33. PDD, July 26, 1966. JAC memo to LBJ, July 26, 1966, 11:15, P.M., LBJ Library.
34. SP, #24, August 13–26, 1966. SP, December 6–16, 1966. JAC memo to LBJ, December 7, 1966, 5:45 P.M. (Attachment: Louis Martin memo to JAC, December 7, 1966), Personal Papers. JAC memo to LBJ, August 10, 1966, 4:30 P.M., Personal Papers. JAC memo to LBJ, August 17, 1966, 5:55 P.M., Personal Papers. JAC memo to LBJ, August 18, 1966, 11:30 P.M., Personal Papers.
35. JAC memo to LBJ, September 30, 1966, 10 P.M., Personal Papers.

36. DG, October 6, 1966. JAC memo to LBJ, October 6, 1966, 1 P.M., Personal Papers.

37. Model Cities is based in part on "Demonstration Cities Act, A Chronology," LBJ Library.

38. JAC memo to LBJ, May 13, 1966, 9:15 A.M., Personal Papers. JAC memo to LBJ, May 20, 1966, 8:30 P.M., Personal Papers. JAC memo to LBJ, May 23, 1966, 8:45 P.M., Personal Papers. JAC memo to Bill Moyers, May 25, 1966, Personal Papers.

39. For this meeting, see: PDD, May 26, 1966.

40. JAC memo to LBJ, February 11, 1966, 11:30 P.M., LBJ Library. JAC memo to LBJ, January 26, 1966, 3:30 P.M., Personal Papers. JAC memo to LBJ, February 28, 1966, 9:45 P.M., Personal Papers. Lawrence Levinson memo to JAC, April 2, 1966, LBJ Library. JAC memo to LBJ, November 7, 1966, 9:30 P.M., Personal Papers. SP, March 7–15, 1966. SP, November 15–23, 1966.

41. JAC memo to LBJ, January 18, 1966, 11:30 P.M., Personal Papers. JAC memo to John Connor, January 9, 1966, Personal Papers. JAC memo to John Connor and Robert McNamara, February 4, 1966 (Attachment: Gardner Ackley memo to JAC, February 3, 1966), Personal Papers. JAC memo to LBJ, April 13, 1966 (Attachment: Gardner Ackley memo to LBJ, April 13, 1966), Personal Papers. JAC memo to LBJ, April 26, 1966, 7 P.M., Personal Papers. JAC memo to LBJ, April 27, 1966 (Attachment: JAC memo for the record, April 27, 1966), Personal Papers. JAC memo to LBJ, March 16, 1966, 10:30 P.M., LBJ Library. JAC memo to LBJ, March 18, 1966, 6:45 P.M. (Attachment: Cyrus Vance memo to LBJ, March 18, 1966), LBJ Library. Lawrence Levinson memo to LBJ, March 21, 1967, Personal Papers.

42. JAC memo to John Robson, September 1, 1966, 11:35 P.M. (Attachment: John Robson memo to JAC, September 1, 1966 [Attachment: Esther Peterson letter to Paul Ignatius, September 1, 1966]), LBJ Library. John Robson memo to Gardner Ackley, September 30, 1966, LBJ Library.

43. JAC memo to LBJ, June 18, 1966, 6:05 P.M. (Attachment: Gardner Ackley memo to JAC, June 16, 1966), LBJ Library.

44. JAC memo to LBJ, December 20, 1965, 3:15 P.M., Personal Papers.

45. Ibid.

46. John Robson memo to JAC, December 14, 1966, LBJ Library.

47. John Robson memo to JAC, December 28, 1966, LBJ Library.

48. JAC memo to John Macy, May 2, 1966, Personal Papers. JAC memo to Marvin Watson, June 27, 1966, Personal Papers. PDD, July 14, 1966.

49. This section and some of this jawboning chapter are based in part on John Robson, "Anti-Inflation Efforts, July 1966–February 1967," Personal Papers, and 69N.

50. SP, #14, February 17–March 5, 1966.

51. SP, March 7–15, 1966.

52. For the Fowler-Patman episode, see: SP, March 7–15, 1966. JAC memo to LBJ, March 7, 1966, 3:50 P.M. (Attachment: Economic Statistics),

Personal Papers. PDD, March 7, 1966. Wright Patman letter to Henry Fowler, March 8, 1966, *Congressional Record*, March 9, 1966. JAC memo to LBJ, March 16, 1966, 10:30 P.M., LBJ Library. John Douglas memo to JAC, March 24, 1966, LBJ Library.

53. PDD, March 12, 1966. PDD, March 30, 1966. JAC memo to LBJ, March 16, 1966, 10:30 P.M., LBJ Library. John Douglas memo to JAC, March 24, 1966, LBJ Library. JAC memo to LBJ, April 16, 1966 (Attachment: Charles Schultze memo to LBJ, April 15, 1966), LBJ Library.

54. See: JAC memo to LBJ, April 5, 1966, 9:15 P.M., Personal Papers. JAC memo to LBJ, April 9, 1966, 6:30 P.M., LBJ Library. JAC memo to LBJ, April 11, 1966, Personal Papers. JAC memo to LBJ, April 15, 1966, 8:40 P.M., LBJ Library. JAC memo to LBJ, May 9, 1966, 7 P.M. (Attachment: Frederick Donner letter to LBJ, May 4, 1966), LBJ Library.

55. John Robson, "Anti-Inflation Efforts, July 1966–February 1967," p. 36. JAC memo to LBJ, September 10, 1966, 5:15 P.M., Personal Papers. JAC memo to LBJ, September 15, 1966, 8:30 P.M. (Attachment: Henry Fowler memo to LBJ, September 14, 1966 [Attachment: Frederick Deming memo on "Federal Credit Programs"]), Personal Papers. JAC memo to LBJ, September 16, 1966, 5:45 P.M. (Attachments: Gardner Ackley memo to LBJ, September 16, 1966, and Joseph Barr memo to LBJ, September 15, 1966), Personal Papers. JAC memo to LBJ, January 24, 1967, 7:15 P.M. (Attachments: Henry Fowler memo to LBJ, January 18, 1967, and James Duesenberry memo to JAC, January 23, 1967), Personal Papers. JAC memo to LBJ, June 10, 1967 (Attachment: Henry Fowler memo to LBJ, June 10, 1967), Personal Papers.

56. SP, March 7–15, 1966.

57. SP, #11, December 11–21, 1965.

58. 69N.

59. Marvin Watson to LBJ, August 17, 1965, 7:48 P.M., LBJ Library.

60. JAC memo to Marvin Watson, July 31, 1965, Personal Papers.

61. JAC memo to LBJ, April 20, 1966, 9:20 A.M., Personal Papers.

62. PDD, April 21, 1966.

63. JAC memo to LBJ, April 20, 1966, 11:15 P.M. (Attachment: W. Willard Wirtz memo to JAC, April 20, 1966), LBJ Library.

64. JAC memo to LBJ, July 23, 1966, 9:30 P.M. (Attachment: JAC memo to LBJ, July 23, 1966, 8:30 P.M.), LBJ Library.

65. PDD, July 29, 1966. "Talking Points for President's Joint Meeting with Airlines And Union," LBJ Library. Marvin Watson memo to LBJ, July 29, 1966, 9:07 A.M., LBJ Library.

66. PDD, July 29–30, 1966.

67. PDD, July 31, 1966.

68. JAC memo to Bill Moyers, August 20, 1966, LBJ Library.

69. Gardner Ackley memo to LBJ, August 2, 1966, Personal Papers.

70. JAC memo to LBJ, October 5, 1966, 8:45 P.M. (Attachments: John Robson memo to JAC, October 5, 1966, and Department of Justice memo, re "Legal authority to control prices and wages under § 5(b) of the Trading

with the Enemy Act"), LBJ Library.
71. Wage and price controls, based in part on 69N and John Robson, "Anti-Inflation Efforts, July 1966–February 1967," pp. 39–43.
72. JAC memo to LBJ, July 18, 1966, 9 P.M. (Attachment: Charles Schultze memo to LBJ, July 18, 1966), LBJ Library. JAC memo to LBJ, August 20, 1966. JAC memo to LBJ, August 16, 1966, 12:45 A.M., LBJ Library. DG, August 22, 1966. JAC memo to LBJ, August 23, 1966, 8:10 P.M. (Attachment: Otto Eckstein memo to JAC, August 23, 1966), LBJ Library. PDD, August 23, 1966. JAC memo to LBJ, August 29, 1966, 9:30 P.M. (Attachments: Gardner Ackley memo, "A Program to Insure Stable Prosperity," Henry Fowler memo, "On September 1966 Program"; Henry Fowler memo, "On General Economic and Financial Program"), LBJ Library. JAC memo to LBJ, September 1, 1966, 2:35 P.M., Personal Papers. Gardner Ackley memo to JAC, September 7, 1966, LBJ Library.
73. PDD, August 8, 1966. SP, August 1–8, 1966.
74. Gardner Ackley memo to LBJ, August 26, 1966, LBJ Library.
75. DG, September 2, 1966. Henry Fowler, Robert McNamara, Nicholas Katzenbach, Lawrence O'Brien, Charles Schultze, Gardner Ackley, David Ginsburg, and JAC memo to LBJ, September 2, 1966, 2:20 P.M., LBJ Library.

8. THE GREAT 89TH

1. PDD, October 17, 1966.
2. PDD, November 2, 1966.
3. 69N. JAC memo to LBJ, October 14, 1966, 12:30 P.M., Personal Papers. JAC memo to LBJ, October 26, 1966, Personal Papers. Charles Maguire memo to Robert Kintner, October 27, 1966, 6:30 P.M., Personal Papers. Robert Kintner memo to Marvin Watson, October 28, 1966, 8:05 P.M., LBJ Library. JAC memo to LBJ, October 29, 1966, 6:05 P.M., LBJ Library.
4. Charles Maguire memo to Robert Kintner, October 27, 1966, 6:30 P.M., LBJ Library. JAC memo to LBJ, October 29, 1966, 6:05 P.M., LBJ Library.
5. PDD, November 2, 1966.
6. Harry McPherson and JAC memo to LBJ, November 8, 1966, 9 P.M., Personal Papers. Harry McPherson and JAC memo to LBJ, November 10, 1966, 8:10 P.M. (Attachment: Clark Clifford memo, November 10, 1966), Personal Papers.
7. JAC memo to LBJ, November 12, 1966, Personal Papers.
8. Lawrence Levinson memo to James Jones, December 27, 1967, Personal Papers.
9. JAC memo to LBJ, February 3, 1966, 1:30 P.M., LBJ Library.
10. PDD, March 30, 1966.

11. JAC memo to LBJ, November 14, 1966, 10 P.M. (Attachment: National Catholic Welfare Conference, "Statement on the Government and Birth Control," November 14, 1966), LBJ Library.
12. Ibid.
13. Ibid. SP, November 15, 1966. SP, October 25–November 11, 1966.
14. This conversation is based in part on: TL, November 15, 1966. JAC memo to LBJ, November 15, 1966, 1:30 P.M., Personal Papers.
15. My conversation with the President is based in part on JAC memo to LBJ, November 15, 1966, 8 P.M. (Attachment: John Dearden letter to LBJ, November 15, 1966), Personal Papers.
16. Ibid. PDD, November 15, 1966. DG, November 15, 1966.
17. JAC memo to LBJ, November 15, 1966, 8 P.M., Personal Papers. 69N.
18. JAC memo to LBJ, November 15, 1966, 8 P.M., Personal Papers. JAC memo to LBJ, November 15, 1966, 1:30 P.M., Personal Papers.
19. JAC memo to LBJ, October 12, 1967, 2:30 P.M., Personal Papers.
20. JAC letter to Francis Hurley, October 14, 1967, Personal Papers.
21. JAC memo to LBJ, November 21, 1966, 7 P.M., LBJ Library.
22. Harold Reis memo to Ramsey Clark, November 25, 1966, LBJ Library.
23. JAC memo to LBJ, November 21, 1966, 7 P.M. (Attachment: Nicholas Katzenbach letter to Stewart [sic] Saunders, September 4, 1964 [Attachment: Robert Kennedy memo for the files, September 3, 1964]), LBJ Library.
24. Ibid. Diary Cards for Stuart Saunders, January 9, 1964; March 31, September 30, and October 4, 1965; March 30, May 3–5, August 18, September 8, and November 3, 1966. Stuart Saunders letter to LBJ, July 14, 1964, LBJ Library.
25. Ramsey Clark memo to JAC, November 21, 1966 (Attachment: Department of Justice memo on the Penn-Central merger case, undated), LBJ Library. JAC memo to LBJ, November 21, 1966, 7 P.M. (Attachment: Nicholas Katzenbach letter to Stewart [sic] Saunders, September 4, 1964 [Attachment: Robert Kennedy memo for the files, September 3, 1964]), LBJ Library.
26. PDD, November 19–27. JAC memo to LBJ, November 21, 1966, 7 P.M., LBJ Library.
27. TL, November 23, 1966. SP, November 16–28, 1966.
28. DG, November 23, 1966. Ramsey Clark memo to JAC, November 21, 1966 (Attachment: Department of Justice memo on the Penn-Central merger), LBJ Library.
29. PDD, November 23, 1966. Alan Boyd memo to Ramsey Clark, November 21, 1966, LBJ Library.
30. DG, November 24, 1966.
31. PDD, November 24, 1966.
32. Ibid.
33. See Thurgood Marshall memo to Ramsey Clark, November 22, 1966, LBJ Library.
34. Gardner Ackley memo to Thurgood Marshall, November 25, 1966, LBJ

Library. Gardner Ackley memo to JAC, November 26, 1966, LBJ Library.

35. Draft United States brief to the Supreme Court, Baltimore and Ohio Railroad Company et al., Appellants v. United States of America et al. (642), October Term, 1966, Personal Papers.

36. TL, November 28, 1966.

9. THE PRESS AND THE CREDIBILITY GAP

1. OH, Victoria McCammon, June 8, 1975, tape 3 of 5, pp. 20–21.
2. Cf. OH, Victoria McCammon, June 8, 1975, tape 3 of 5, pp. 22–23. PDD, May 30, 1967.
3. AI, Lee White.
4. JAC memo to Jack Valenti, July 14, 1965, Personal Papers. JAC memo to Marvin Watson, July 15, 1965, Personal Papers.
5. JAC memo to LBJ, December 20, 1966, 11:45 A.M. (Attachment: "Estimated Federal Funds (NOA) for Programs Assisting the Poor, Fiscal Years 1960–1968"), Personal Papers.
6. JAC memo to LBJ, February 20, 1967, 3:45 P.M., Personal Papers. JAC memo to LBJ, April 17, 1967, Personal Papers.
7. Cf. OH, Victoria McCammon, June 8, 1975, tape 3 of 5, pp. 28–29.
8. AI, Harry McPherson.
9. Ibid.
10. James Gaither memo to JAC, May 26, 1967, Personal Papers. AI, James Gaither.
11. PDD, January 17, 1967.
12. PDD, May 12, 1967.
13. JAC memo to LBJ, May 19, 1967, 7:45 P.M. (Attachment: "Members of the Task Force on Education"), Personal Papers. JAC memo to LBJ, July 24, 1967, 11 A.M., Personal Papers.
14. PDD, August 21, 1967.
15. Will Sparks memo to Dorothy Territo, December 6, 1966 (Attachment: Hayes Redmon memo to Bill Moyers, December 2, 1966), LBJ Library.
16. PDD, October 2, 1966. Cf. OH, Victoria McCammon, June 8, 1975, tape 3 of 5, pp. 21–23. SP, October 10–17, 1967.
17. PDD, February 11, 1967.

10. STATE OF THE UNION 1967

1. JAC memo to LBJ, May 14, 1966, 6:15 P.M., Personal Papers. JAC memo to LBJ, August 9, 1966, 5:25 P.M., LBJ Library. JAC memo to LBJ, August 16, 1966, 1 P.M., Personal Papers.
2. JAC memo to LBJ, November 7, 1966, 9:40 P.M., Personal Papers. Henry Wilson memo to LBJ, November 22, 1966, 4:45 P.M., LBJ Library.

3. Ibid.
4. Henry Wilson memo to JAC, April 5, 1966, LBJ Library.
5. PDD, December 21, 1966. AI, John Gardner. AI, Ramsey Clark.
6. PDD, December 21, 1966. AI, Robert McNair. AI, James Jones.
7. DG, December 22, 1966. PDD, December 22, 1966. 69N.
8. PDD, October 4, 1966. JAC memo to LBJ, October 5, 1966, 10:15 P.M. (Attachment: Charles Schultze memo to LBJ, October 5, 1966), Personal Papers. JAC memo to LBJ, October 11, 1966, 1 P.M., Personal Papers. JAC memo to Philip Lee, October 15, 1966, Personal Papers.
9. For this meeting, see: PDD, November 4, 1966. JAC memo to LBJ, October 11, 1966, 1 P.M., Personal Papers. JAC memo to Charles Haar, November 19, 1966 (Attachment: Lewis Davis letter to JAC, November 8, 1966), Personal Papers. AI, Lewis Davis. 69N. "Report of the [1966] Task Force on Nursing Homes and Other Institutions for the Care of the Elderly," Personal Papers.
10. For my briefing on the 1967 legislative program, see: DG, December 22, 1966. PDD, December 22, 1966. 1967 Legislative program book, " 'The Great Society,' A Third Year Legislative Program," Personal Papers.
11. This anecdote is based in part on 69N.
12. PDD, December 31, 1966.
13. JAC memo to LBJ, November 21, 1966, 7:15 P.M., Personal Papers. JAC memo to LBJ, December 8, 1966, 7:25 P.M., Personal Papers. JAC memo to LBJ, December 31, 1966, 5 P.M., Personal Papers.
14. Ibid. JAC memo to LBJ, January 2, 1967, 4:25 P.M. (Attachment: Henry Fowler, Charles Schultze, and Gardner Ackley memo to LBJ, December 31, 1966), Personal Papers.
15. Robert McNamara, Henry Fowler, W. Willard Wirtz, John Connor, Charles Schultze, Gardner Ackley, Clark Clifford, and JAC memo to LBJ, January 9, 1967, 5:30 P.M., LBJ Library. DG, January 9, 1967.
16. JAC memo to LBJ, January 7, 1967, 1:45 P.M., Personal Papers. JAC memo to LBJ, January 8, 1967, 5:30 P.M., LBJ Library.
17. PDD, January 9, 1967. Henry Wilson memo to LBJ, November 22, 1966, 4:45 P.M., LBJ Library.
18. PDD, January 9, 1967. Robert McNamara, Henry Fowler, W. Willard Wirtz, John Connor, Charles Schultze, Gardner Ackley, Clark Clifford, and JAC memo to LBJ, January 9, 1967, 5:30 P.M., LBJ Library.
19. Marvin Watson memo to LBJ, January 6, 1967, 4:45 P.M., LBJ Library. Robert Kintner memo to LBJ, January 9, 1967, 10:30 A.M., LBJ Library. Robert Kintner memo to LBJ, January 10, 1967, 11 A.M., LBJ Library.
20. PDD, January 10, 1967.
21. Clifford Alexander memo to LBJ, January 11, 1967, 5:12 P.M., LBJ Library. Lawrence Levinson memo to LBJ, January 11, 1967, LBJ Library.
22. SP, January 11–February 8, 1967.
23. Ibid. JAC memo to LBJ, January 11, 1966 [sic], 12:30 P.M., Personal Papers.

24. PDD, January 11, 1967. PDD, January 5, 1967. JAC memo to LBJ, January 5, 1967, 1:45 P.M., Personal Papers. JAC and Lawrence Levinson memo to LBJ, January 11, 1967, Personal Papers. JAC memo to LBJ, January 19, 1967, 9:55 P.M. (Attachment: W. Willard Wirtz memo to LBJ, January 19, 1967), Personal Papers. JAC memo to LBJ, January 24, 1967, 8:45 P.M., Personal Papers. JAC memo to LBJ, February 6, 1967, 11:45 P.M., Personal Papers. DG, February 21, 1967. JAC memo to LBJ, February 24, 1967, 8:45 P.M., Personal Papers. JAC memo to LBJ, March 7, 1967, 6:30 P.M., Personal Papers. JAC memo to LBJ, March 8, 1967, 11:45 P.M., Personal Papers. PDD, March 9, 1967.

25. The Labor-Commerce merger is based in part on OH, JAC, September 12, 1969, Interview V, pp. 21–23.

26. JAC memo to Harry McPherson, January 20, 1967, Personal Papers. JAC memo to LBJ, February 5, 1967, 8:30 P.M., Personal Papers.

27. 69N.

28. OH, Victoria McCammon, June 9, 1975, tape 4 of 5, pp. 41–42.

29. LBJ memo to heads of executive departments and agencies, June 30, 1965, LBJ Library. JAC and Lee White memo to LBJ, February 9, 1966, 6:45 P.M., Personal Papers.

30. Marvin Watson memo to LBJ, May 28, 1966, 3:35 P.M. (Attachment: Sheldon Cohen memo to Marvin Watson, May 27, 1966), LBJ Library.

31. OH, Victoria McCammon, June 9, 1975, tape 4 of 5, pp. 39–40. OH, Victoria McCammon, June 8, 1975, tape 2 of 5, pp. 40–41.

32. SP, December 21, 1966.

33. Ibid.

34. JAC memo to LBJ, April 7, 1967, 3:15 P.M. (Attachment: W. Willard Wirtz memo to LBJ, April 7, 1967), Personal Papers.

35. For this meeting, see: PDD, April 9, 1967. SP, April 6–10, 1967. JAC memo to Juanita Roberts, April 11, 1967 (Attachment: Lawrence Levinson memo for the record, April 10, 1967), Personal Papers. JAC memo to LBJ, April 10, 1967, 2 A.M. (Attachments: "Draft Statement" and "Message on the Impending Nation-Wide Rail Strike"), LBJ Library.

36. For this meeting, see: SP, April 6–10, 1967. PDD, April 10, 1967.

37. For this meeting, see: ibid.

38. James Jones memo to Marvin Watson, undated (received April 19, 1967, in Central Files), LBJ Library.

39. PDD, April 23, 1967.

40. SP, April 21–May 2, 1967. PDD, April 24, 1967.

41. DG, April 24, 1967.

42. JAC memo to LBJ, April 24, 1967, 9:45 P.M., LBJ Library.

43. Ibid.

44. PDD, April 26, 1967. JAC memo to LBJ, April 26, 1967, LBJ Library.

45. JAC memo to LBJ, April 27, 1967, 7 P.M. (Attachments: "Basic Alternatives in the Rail Dispute," "Major Elements of Railroad Emergency Legislation," and "Major Elements of Emergency Legislation for Shopcraft Rail Dispute"), LBJ Library. SP, April 21–May 2, 1967.

46. JAC memo to LBJ, April 26, 1967, 9:05 P.M., LBJ Library.
47. For this meeting, see: SP, April 26–May 5, 1967. PDD, May 3, 1967.
48. PDD, May 3, 1967. SP, April 26–May 5, 1967.
49. DG, June 14, 1967. AI, Warren Christopher.
50. For Wirtz and the letter, see: PDD, June 14, 1967. DG, June 14, 1967.
    JAC memo to LBJ, June 15, 1967, 1:30 P.M. (Attachment: W. Willard
    Wirtz letter to Carl Albert, June 15, 1967), Personal Papers. OH, JAC,
    June 17, 1970, Interview VII, pp. 13–15.
51. W. Thomas Johnson memo to LBJ, July 16, 1967, 8 P.M. (Attachment:
    "Notes of the President's Emergency Meeting With the Bipartisan Con-
    gressional Leadership and the Chairmen and Ranking Minority Mem-
    bers of Appropriate Congressional Committees"), LBJ Library. PDD,
    July 16, 1967.
52. Lawrence Levinson memo to LBJ, September 15, 1967, 4:35 P.M., Per-
    sonal Papers.

11. Who Shall Serve in Vietnam When Not All Serve

1. JAC memo to LBJ, June 25, 1966, 6:45 P.M., Personal Papers.
2. JAC memo to Mildred Stegall, July 23, 1966, Personal Papers. JAC
   memo to LBJ, July 28, 1966, 11:25 A.M., Personal Papers. JAC memo to
   Bill Moyers, July 29, 1966, Personal Papers. JAC memo to LBJ, August
   26, 1966, 10:45 P.M., Personal Papers.
3. JAC memo to LBJ, February 28, 1967, 4:10 P.M. (Attachment: "The
   Commission's Major Recommendations"), Personal Papers. JAC memo
   to LBJ, February 23, 1967, Personal Papers.
4. JAC memo to LBJ, January 12, 1967, 6:40 P.M. (Attachment: Cyrus
   Vance memo to JAC, January 11, 1967), Personal Papers. JAC memo to
   LBJ, February 26, 1967, 6:25 P.M., Personal Papers. DG, February 27,
   1967.
5. SP, February 16–March 2, 1967. JAC memo to LBJ, June 29, 1967, Personal Papers. Lawrence Levinson memo to LBJ, September 1, 1967, 4 P.M.
   (Attachment: Lewis Hershey letter to LBJ, August 31, 1967), Personal
   Papers. Lawrence Levinson memo to LBJ, September 9, 1967, Personal
   Papers.
6. JAC memo to LBJ, June 12, 1967, 8 P.M., Personal Papers.
7. SP, October 18–November 3, 1967. PDD, October 20, 1967. LBJ memo
   to Ramsey Clark, Lewis Hershey, J. Edgar Hoover, October 20, 1967,
   Personal Papers.
8. PDD, October 20, 1967. SP, October 18–November 3, 1967.
9. JAC memo to LBJ, October 5, 1967, 3 P.M. (Attachment: Warren Christopher memo to JAC, Paul Nitze, Lawson Knott, David McGiffert,
   Stephen Pollak, and Harry Van Cleve, October 4, 1967 [Attachment: J.
   Walter Yeagley information memo #1, October 3, 1967]), Personal
   Papers. JAC memo to LBJ, October 7, 1967, 4 P.M. (Attachment: Warren

Christopher memo to JAC, Paul Nitze, Lawson Knott, David McGiffert, Stephen Pollak, and Harry Van Cleve, October 5, 1967 [Attachment: J. Walter Yeagley information memo #2, October 5, 1967]), Personal Papers. JAC memo to LBJ, October 11, 1967, 4:30 P.M. (Attachment: Warren Christopher memo to JAC, October 11, 1967 [Attachment: J. Walter Yeagley information memo #5, October 10, 1967]), Personal Papers. JAC memo to LBJ, October 12, 1967, 6:30 P.M. (Attachment: Ramsey Clark memo to LBJ, October 12, 1967 [Attachment: "Recent Developments—October 21 Pentagon Demonstration," October 12, 1967]), Personal Papers. JAC memo to LBJ, October 19, 1967 (Attachment: Ramsey Clark memo to LBJ, October 19, 1967 [Attachment: "Recent Developments—October 21 Pentagon Demonstration," October 19, 1967]), Personal Papers. JAC memo to LBJ, October 19, 1967 (Attachment: Ramsey Clark memo to LBJ, October 19, 1967 [Attachment: List of some people on the administrative committee coordinating the October 21 demonstration]), Personal Papers. JAC memo to LBJ, October 16, 1967, 9 P.M., Personal Papers. JAC memo to LBJ, October 17, 1967, 9 P.M. (Attachment: Matthew Nimetz memo to JAC, October 17, 1967), Personal Papers. Memo, "Forces Available in the Area," October 19, 1967, Personal Papers. JAC memo to LBJ, October 21, 1967, 11:20 A.M., Personal Papers. JAC memo to LBJ, October 21, 1967, 3 P.M., Personal Papers. W. Thomas Johnson memo for George Christian, October 21, 1967, Personal Papers. Lawrence Levinson memo to JAC, October 20, 1967, 9:45 P.M., Personal Papers.

10. PDD, October 22, 1967.

11. JAC memo to LBJ, October 26, 1967, 8:35 P.M. (Attachment: Obscene report), Personal Papers. JAC memo to LBJ, November 15, 1967, 8:05 P.M., Personal Papers. JAC memo to LBJ, October 24, 1967, 9:30 P.M., Personal Papers.

12. Lewis Hershey letter to "All Members of the Selective Service System," October 26, 1967 (Attachment: Lewis Hershey, "Local Board Memorandum No. 85," October 24, 1967), LBJ Library. Lewis Hershey letter to Charles Schultze, October 27, 1967 (Attachment: "Executive Order: Amending the Selective Service Regulations"), LBJ Library.

13. JAC memo to LBJ, November 18, 1967, 11:30 P.M. (Attachment: Larry Temple memo to LBJ, November 16, 1967), Personal Papers.

14. JAC memo to LBJ, November 18, 1967, 11:30 P.M., Personal Papers. SP, November 14–27, 1967. PDD, November 18, 1967. JAC memo to LBJ, November 18, 1967, 11:30 P.M., Personal Papers. JAC memo to LBJ, November 29, 1967, 12:45 P.M. (Attachment: Lewis Hershey letter to JAC, November 20, 1967), Personal Papers.

15. JAC memo to LBJ, November 15, 1967, 8 P.M., Personal Papers. JAC memo to LBJ, November 17, 1967, 9 P.M. (Attachment: Matthew Nimetz memo to JAC, November 17, 1967), Personal Papers. LBJ memo to Ramsey Clark, November 18, 1967, Personal Papers.

16. JAC memo to LBJ, December 7, 1967, 9:30 P.M., Personal Papers. JAC

memo to LBJ, December 9, 1967 (Attachment: "Joint Statement of Attorney General Ramsey Clark and Director of Selective Service Lewis B. Hershey"), 1:15 P.M., Personal Papers.

17. JAC memo to LBJ, December 11, 1967, Personal Papers.
18. Kingman Brewster letter to LBJ, December 21, 1967, Personal Papers.
19. PDD, December 24–26, 1967. JAC letter to Kingman Brewster, December 26, 1967, Personal Papers.
20. JAC memo to LBJ, December 14, 1967, 10:30 A.M., Personal Papers. PDD, December 14, 1967.

12. Six-Day War

1. OH, Harry McPherson, January 16, 1969, Interview III, pp. 36–38.
2. JAC memo to LBJ, June 5, 1967, 11:05 A.M., Personal Papers. JAC memo to LBJ, June 5, 1967, 5:25 P.M., Personal Papers. JAC memo to LBJ, June 7, 1967, 10:15 A.M., Personal Papers.
3. SP, May 31–June 5, 1967. TL, June 5, 1967.
4. Lawrence Levinson and Ben Wattenberg memo to LBJ, June 7, 1967, 7:45 P.M., Personal Papers.
5. PDD, June 7, 1967. AI, Lawrence Levinson.
6. Notes of National Security Council Special Committee meeting, June 9, 1967, LBJ Library.

13. Burn, Baby, Burn!

1. OH, Ramsey Clark, October 30, 1968, Interview I, pp. 24–25. PDD, September 28, 1966.
2. In recounting this exchange in *Governing America*, I mistakenly related it to Nicholas Katzenbach.
3. PDD, July 14, 1967. James Jones memo to Marvin Watson, July 14, 1967 (Attachment: Transcript of July 14, 1967, LBJ phone conversation with Richard Hughes), LBJ Library.
4. Lawrence Levinson memo to LBJ, July 15, 1965, 6:30 P.M. (Attachment: UPI ticker 231A, July 15, 1967), LBJ Library. Hubert Humphrey memo to LBJ, July 17, 1967, 8:30 P.M., LBJ Library.
5. Hubert Humphrey memo to LBJ, July 17, 1967, 8:30 P.M., LBJ Library.
6. Ibid.
7. Marvin Watson memo to LBJ, July 19, 1967, 3 P.M., LBJ Library. "Notes of the President's Meeting with the Cabinet, in the Cabinet Room, July 19, 1967," Personal Papers. PDD, July 19, 1967. See Hubert Humphrey memo to LBJ, July 27, 1967, 12 P.M., LBJ Library.
8. For this meeting, see: SP, July 19, 1967. Cf. PDD, July 19, 1967. Cf. PDD, March 10, 1966.
9. JAC memo to LBJ, July 19, 1967, 7 P.M., Personal Papers.

10. PDD, July 23, 1967. JAC memo to LBJ, July 23, 1967, Personal Papers. Lawrence Levinson memo to LBJ, July 29, 1967, 9:15 P.M. (Attachment: "The Detroit Riots: Chronology"), LBJ Library. Lawrence Levinson memo to LBJ, July 23, 1967, 10:45 P.M., LBJ Library.

11. Lawrence Levinson memo to LBJ, July, 29, 1967, 9:15 P.M. (Attachment: "The Detroit Riots: Chronology"), LBJ Library.

12. "Telephone Calls of Attorney General, July 24," 1967, LBJ Library. "Final Report of Cyrus R. Vance, Special Assistant to the Secretary of Defense, Concerning the Detroit Riots, July 23 through August 2, 1967," LBJ Library.

13. PDD, July 24, 1967.

14. Lawrence Levinson memo to LBJ, July 29, 1967, 9:15 P.M. (Attachment: "The Detroit Riots: Chronology"), LBJ Library. "Final Report of Cyrus R. Vance, Special Assistant to the Secretary of Defense, Concerning the Detroit Riots, July 23 through August 2, 1967," LBJ Library. "The Events of the Early Morning of July 24th (As taken from the wires)," LBJ Library.

15. JAC memo to LBJ, July 24, 1967, 10:50 A.M. (Attachment: George Romney telegram to LBJ, July 24, 1967), Personal Papers.

16. LBJ telegram to George Romney, July 24, 1967, LBJ Library. Draft LBJ telegram to George Romney, July 24, 1967, LBJ Library.

17. JAC memo to LBJ, July 24, 1967, 3 P.M. (Attachment: George Romney wire to Ramsey Clark, July 24, 1967), LBJ Library.

18. For this meeting, see: PDD, July 24, 1967. W. Thomas Johnson memo to LBJ, July 24, 1967, 9 P.M. (Attachment: "Notes from the President's Meeting with the Congressional Leadership, July 24, 1967, in the Cabinet Room"), LBJ Library.

19. SP, July 22–27, 1967. SP, July 27–August 8, 1967.

20. DG, July 24, 1967. PDD, July 24, 1967. Lawrence Levinson memo to LBJ, July 29, 1967, 9:15 P.M. (Attachment: "The Detroit Riots: Chronology"), LBJ Library.

21. Ramsey Clark memo to LBJ, July 21, 1967, LBJ Library.

22. AI, Harry McPherson.

23. For the events and conversations after dinner until the President addressed the nation, see: PDD, July 24, 1967. SP, July 22–27, 1967. W. Thomas Johnson memo to LBJ, July 25, 1967, 1:30 P.M. (Attachment: "Notes of the President's Activities During the Detroit Crisis, July 24, 1967"), LBJ Library. Lawrence Levinson memo to LBJ, July 29, 1967, 9:15 P.M. (Attachment: "The Detroit Riots: Chronology"), LBJ Library.

24. SP, July 22–27, 1967.

25. Martin Luther King telegram to LBJ, July 25, 1967, LBJ Library.

26. E.g., Federal Bureau of Investigation, "Prevention and Control of Major Disturbances," May 29, 1967, LBJ Library; Federal Bureau of Investigation, "Racial Violence Potential in the United States This Summer," May 23, 1967, LBJ Library.

27. PDD, July 27, 1967.

28. W. Thomas Johnson memo to LBJ, July 29, 1967 (Attachment: "The President's Meeting with the National Advisory Commission on Civil Disorders, July, 29, 1967"), LBJ Library.
29. JAC memo to LBJ, July 31, 1967, 8:30 P.M., LBJ Library. George Romney, July 31, 1967, 12 P.M., press conference, LBJ Library. Marianne Means, August 2, 1967, column from Washington, LBJ Library.
30. JAC memo to LBJ, September 12, 1967, 9:30 P.M. (Attachment: "Statement by Attorney General Ramsey Clark," September 12, 1967), LBJ Library.
31. For this meeting, see: PDD, August 2, 1967. W. Thomas Johnson memo to LBJ, August 2, 1967, 6:30 P.M. (Attachment: "Notes of the President's Meeting with the Cabinet, in the Cabinet Room, August 2, 1967"), LBJ Library. Cf. OH, Victoria McCammon, June 9, 1975, tape 4 of 5, p. 20.
32. PDD., September 7–8, 1967.
33. JAC memo to LBJ, September 12, 1967, 9:35 P.M. (Attachments: Alan Boyd memo to LBJ, September 9, 1967, and W. Willard Wirtz memo to LBJ, September 12, 1967), Personal Papers. Also see: JAC memo to LBJ, February 3, 1968, 8 P.M. (Attachment: Sargent Shriver memo to LBJ, February 2, 1968), Personal Papers. Sargent Shriver memo to LBJ, October, 2,0, 1965, LBJ Library.
34. JAC memo to LBJ, November 11, 1967, 6 P.M., Personal Papers.
35. JAC memo to LBJ, December 4, 1967, 10:30 A.M., Personal Papers.
36. JAC memo to LBJ, January 18, 1968, 9:30 P.M., Personal Papers. PDD, January 22, 1968. TL, January 22, 1968.
37. PDD, January 22, 1968.
38. Ibid.
39. For this meeting, see: PDD, January 27, 1968. AI, Leo Beebe.
40. JAC memo to LBJ, May 30, 1968, 7 P.M., Personal Papers.

14. ARM TWISTING FOR THE NATION'S CAPITAL

1. Marvin Watson memo to LBJ, August 16, 1965, 6:45 P.M. (Attachment: JAC memo to Marvin Watson, August 13, 1965), LBJ Library. JAC memo to LBJ, September 9, 1965, 10:05 A.M. (Attachment: "Summary of Grants Awarded to Southwest Texas State College"), Personal Papers.
2. Marvin Watson memo to LBJ, August 30, 1965, 7 P.M., LBJ Library. Lawrence O'Brien memo to LBJ, September 2, 1965, LBJ Library. Jack Valenti letter to Albert Thomas, September 2, 1965, LBJ Library. Lawrence O'Brien memo to LBJ, September 2, 1965, LBJ Library. White House Usher memo to LBJ, September 3, 1965, 7:45 A.M., LBJ Library.
3. Marvin Watson memo to LBJ, September 14, 1965, 9:16 P.M., LBJ Library. JAC memo to Lawrence O'Brien, September 27, 1965, LBJ Li-

brary. JAC memo to Lawrence O'Brien, September 27, 1965, 4:30 P.M., LBJ Library.

4. JAC memo to LBJ, May 13, 1966, 8:20 P.M., Personal Papers.

5. JAC memo to LBJ, May 28, 1966, 7:50 P.M. (Attachment: James Rowe letter to JAC, May 23, 1966), LBJ Library.

6. JAC memo to LBJ, June 18, 1966, 7:30 P.M., Personal Papers. JAC memo to LBJ, June 23, 1966, 4 P.M., Personal Papers. PDD, June 27, 1966. JAC memo to LBJ, June 27, 1966, 10:20 P.M., Personal Papers. AI, Walter Washington.

7. JAC memo to LBJ, October 13, 1966, 8:55 P.M., Personal Papers. DG,October 3, 1966.

8. JAC memo to LBJ, March 2, 1967, 4 P.M., Personal Papers. JAC memo to LBJ, April 20, 1967, 3 P.M. (Attachments: Stephen Pollak memo to LBJ, April 15, 1967, and Stephen Pollak memo to LBJ, April 19, 1967, 7 P.M.), Personal Papers. JAC memo to LBJ, May 17, 1967, 8:05 P.M., Personal Papers. JAC memo to LBJ, May 30, 1967, 5:45 P.M., Personal Papers. JAC memo to LBJ, May 31, 1967, 10:30 P.M., Personal Papers.

9. JAC memo to LBJ, April 20, 1967, 3 P.M. (Attachment: Stephen Pollak memo to LBJ, April 15, 1967), Personal Papers. JAC memo to LBJ, May 30, 1967, 5:45 P.M., Personal Papers. JAC memo to LBJ, May 31, 1967, 10:30 P.M., Personal Papers. JAC memo to LBJ, June 23, 1967, 11:50 A.M. (Attachment: *The Washington Post*, June 23, 1967, p. A20), Personal Papers.

10. JAC memo to LBJ, August 9, 1967, 9:20 P.M., Personal Papers. JAC memo to LBJ, August 9, 1967, 9:50 P.M., Personal Papers. JAC memo to LBJ, August 14, 1967, 8:30 P.M., Personal Papers. JAC memo to LBJ, August 16, 1967, 2:45 P.M., Personal Papers. JAC memo to LBJ, August 18, 1967, 1:45 P.M., Personal Papers.

11. SP, August 1967.

12. PDD, August 22, 1967.

13. Ibid.

14. Walter Washington letter to LBJ, August 23, 1967, Personal Papers.

15. For Johnson's recruitment of Washington until the evening of August 23, 1967, see: Draft JAC memo to LBJ, August 24, 1967, Personal Papers.

16. Draft JAC memo to LBJ, August 24, 1967, Personal Papers.

17. PDD, August 24, 1967.

18. DG, August 24, 1967.

19. PDD, August 24, 1967.

20. JAC memo to LBJ, September 11, 1967, 7 P.M., Personal Papers. Lawrence Levinson memo to LBJ, September 14, 1967, 6:30 P.M., Personal Papers.

21. JAC memo to LBJ, October 6, 1967, 1:05 P.M., Personal Papers. JAC memo to LBJ, October 13, 1967, 8:30 P.M. (Attachment: Hubert Humphrey memo to JAC, October 12, 1967 [Attachment: "Testimony of

Max M. Kampelman Before the United States Senate Committee on the District of Columbia," draft, October 6, 1967]), Personal Papers.

22. JAC memo to LBJ, October 13, 1967, 8:30 P.M. (Attachment: Hubert Humphrey memo to JAC, October 12, 1967 [Attachment: "Testimony of Max M. Kampelman Before the United States Senate Committee on the District of Columbia," draft, October 6, 1967]), Personal Papers.

23. PDD, October 10, 1967.

24. Lawrence Levinson letter to John Hechinger, October 12, 1967 (Attachment: John Steadman memo to Lawrence Levinson, October 12, 1967 [Attachment: Air Force files record of John Hechinger's military service]), Personal Papers. Lawrence Levinson letter to John Hechinger, October 18, 1967 (Attachment: "Military Biography: John Walter Hechinger, Washington, D.C."), Personal Papers.

25. PDD, October 11, 1967.

26. DG, October 11, 1967.

27. PDD, October 11, 1967. TL, October 11, 1967.

28. DG, October 11, 1967.

29. PDD, October 13, 1967. JAC memo to LBJ, October 13, 1967, 4:30 P.M. (Attachment: "Meeting with District of Columbia Mayor and City Council," October 13, 1967), Personal Papers. For the D.C. reorganization and the appointment of its new government, particularly Hechinger's appointment, see: 69N; Hechinger, John, "Story of J. W. Hechinger Appointment to Chairman of the City Council, October 12 [sic], 1967," Personal Papers.

15. THE GOING GETS TOUGHER

1. For this meeting, see: SP, June 6–10, 1967. JAC memo for the files, June 9, 1967, Personal Papers. PDD, June 7, 1967. DG, June 7, 1967. JAC memo to LBJ, June 7, 1967, 3:10 P.M., Personal Papers.

2. JAC memo to Bromley Smith, April 25, 1967 (Attachment: Robert Eisner letter to JAC, April 21, 1967), Personal Papers. JAC memo to LBJ, April 26, 1967, 10:30 P.M., Personal Papers. PDD, April 26, 1967. JAC memo to LBJ, April 27, 1967, 3:15 P.M. (Attachment: Walter Heller memo to LBJ, April 27, 1967, 10:50 A.M.), Personal Papers. JAC letter to Benjamin Ward, May 11, 1967, Personal Papers.

3. JAC memo to LBJ, June 12, 1967, 8 P.M., Personal Papers. JAC memo to LBJ, June 17, 1967, 5:30 P.M., Personal Papers. JAC memo to Henry Fowler, June 23, 1967 (Attachment: Gardner Ackley memo to JAC, June 23, 1967), Personal Papers. JAC memo to LBJ, July 10, 1967, 10:30 A.M. (Attachments: JAC memo to Robert McNamara, July 7, 1967, and Robert McNamara memo to JAC, July 10, 1967), LBJ Library.

4. JAC memo to LBJ, July 14, 1967, 8:30 P.M., Personal Papers.

5. Henry Fowler, W. Willard Wirtz, Alexander Trowbridge, Robert Mc-

Namara, Charles Schultze, Gardner Ackley, and JAC memo to LBJ, July 22, 1967, 3:30 P.M., Personal Papers.

6. PDD, July 26, 1967. SP, July 22–27, 1967.

7. JAC memo to LBJ, October 7, 1967, 6:30 P.M., Personal Papers. SP, September 27–October 3, 1967. JAC memo to LBJ, October 10, 1967, 12:45 P.M. (Attachment: Alan Boyd news release, October 9, 1967), LBJ Library.

8. For this meeting, see: PDD, December 13, 1967. SP, December 8–17, 1967.

9. JAC memo to LBJ, November 18, 1967, 12:30 P.M., Personal Papers.

10. SP, December 8–17, 1967. JAC memo to LBJ, December 14, 1967, 8:30 P.M., Personal Papers.

11. JAC memo to LBJ, December 22, 1967, Personal Papers. JAC memo to LBJ, December 20, 1967, Personal Papers. JAC memo to LBJ, December 22, 1967, LBJ Library. JAC memo to LBJ, December 23, 1967 (Attachment: Gardner Ackley memo to LBJ, December 23, 1967), LBJ Library. JAC memo to LBJ, December 23, 1967, 7:25 P.M. (Attachments: Gardner Ackley memo to LBJ, December 23, 1967, and Henry Fowler memo to LBJ, December 23, 1967), LBJ Library.

12. PDD, December 23–24, 1967.

13. SP, December 29, 1967–January 9, 1968. PDD, December 30, 1967. JAC memo to LBJ, December 30, 1967, Personal Papers. JAC memo to LBJ, December 31, 1967, 2:40 P.M., Personal Papers. JAC memo to LBJ, December 31, 1967, 7:10 P.M., Personal Papers. DG, December 30, 1967–January 1, 1968. PDD, January 1, 1968.

14. PDD, September 27, 1967.

15. Ibid.

16. 69N. PDD, August 23, 1967. See JAC memo to LBJ, November 30, 1967 (Attachment: Press Conference by George Woods, November 30, 1967, in which Woods said he had spoken to McNamara in April 1967, and the Defense Secretary had indicated he was interested in the World Bank job), Personal Papers.

17. SP, August 18–30, 1966. William Jorden talk with President Johnson, August 12, 1969, p. 21. AI, Robert McNamara.

18. AI, James Jones.

19. William Jorden talk with President Johnson, August 12, 1969, p. 21.

16. "I Shall Not Seek and Will Not Accept . . ."

1. JAC memo to LBJ, March 27, 1967, 9:20 P.M., Personal Papers. JAC memo to LBJ, August 2, 1967, 2:30 P.M., Personal Papers.

2. JAC memo to LBJ, August 2, 1967, 2:30 P.M., Personal Papers.

3. JAC memo to LBJ, December 4, 1967, 7:30 P.M., Personal Papers.

4. DG, December 28, 1967. PDD, December 28, 1967.

5. JAC memo to LBJ, February 3, 1968, 8:05 P.M., Personal Papers.

6. For my briefing on the 1968 legislative program, see: "A Fourth Year Legislative Program: 1968," Personal Papers.

7. JAC memo to LBJ, December 6, 1967, 3:50 P.M. (Attachments: Matthew Nimetz, "Summary of State of the Union Messages [Truman]," Fred Panzer memo to Hayes Redmon, December 3, 1966, and "Word Count of State of the Union Messages Since 1934"), Personal Papers. Marvin Watson memo to LBJ, January 14, 1967, Personal Papers. JAC and Harry McPherson memo to LBJ, January 15, 1968, 5:45 P.M., Personal Papers. JAC memo to LBJ, January 17, 1968, 2 A.M., Personal Papers. JAC memo to LBJ, January 17, 1968, 3:05 P.M., Personal Papers.

8. JAC memo to LBJ, January 17, 1968, 3:05 P.M., Personal Papers.

9. DG, January 16, 1968. JAC memo to LBJ, January 15, 1968, 10:35 A.M., Personal Papers.

10. JAC memo to LBJ, January 16, 1968, 1:10 P.M. (Attachment: new crime section for State of the Union message), Personal Papers.

11. PDD, January 17, 1968.

12. 69N on the men around Johnson, pp. 45–49. AI, John Gardner.

13. William Westmoreland memo to Earle Wheeler, April 12, 1968, LBJ Library.

14. 69N, chapter I, p. 2. JAC memo for the record, April 3, 1968, Personal Papers.

15. JAC memo to LBJ, October 7, 1967, 4 P.M. (Attachment: David Ginsburg memo to LBJ, October 7, 1967), Personal Papers.

16. DG, February 27, 1968. JAC memo to LBJ, February 28, 1968, 9:20 P.M., Personal Papers.

17. JAC memo to LBJ, February 28, 1968, 9:20 P.M., Personal Papers. See also JAC memo to LBJ, March 2, 1968 (Attachment: Harry McPherson memo to JAC, March 1, 1968), Personal Papers.

18. PDD, February 29, 1968. SP, March 1–6, 1968.

19. Will Sparks memo for the record, February 29, 1968, LBJ Library.

20. Ibid.

21. TL, February 29, 1968. JAC memo to LBJ, February 29, 1968, 7:15 P.M., Personal Papers.

22. DG, October 15, 1968.

23. For the Kerner Commission, see: OH, JAC, August 21, 1969, Interview IV, pp. 38–43.

24. For this meeting, see: DG, February 27, 1968. 69N. Harry McPherson notes of February 27, 1968, meeting, LBJ Library. AI, Harry McPherson. See also Earle Wheeler memo to LBJ, February 27, 1968, LBJ Library.

25. PDD, February 28, 1968.

26. AI, Lawrence O'Brien.

27. For this meeting, see: PDD, March 28, 1968. JAC memo for the record, April 3, 1968, Personal Papers. 69N, chapter I, pp. 3–7. AI, Harry McPherson.

28. For this meeting, see: PDD, March 29, 1968. 69N, chapter I, pp. 7–8.
29. JAC memo to LBJ, March 8, 1968, 8:10 P.M., Personal Papers. JAC memo to LBJ, March 14, 1968, 7:30 P.M., Personal Papers. JAC memo on LBJ, March 25, 1968, 9 P.M., Personal Papers. AI, James Gaither.
30. Emphasis added. Marie Fehmer memo for the record, undated (Attachment: LBJ final draft of peroration to March 31, 1968, speech), LBJ Library. AI, Horace Busby and Harry McPherson.
31. PDD, April 1, 1968.
32. For this meeting, see: PDD, April 2, 1968. James Jones memo for the record, "Congressional Leadership Breakfast, Tuesday, April 2, 1968," undated, LBJ Library.
33. Ibid.
34. PDD, April 4, 1968.
35. Ibid.
36. Ibid. See Fred Panzer memo to LBJ, April 5, 1968, 11:05 A.M., LBJ Library.

17. The King Assassination

1. PDD, April 4, 1968.
2. Ibid.
3. Ibid.
4. SP, loose, undated pages.
5. PDD, April 4, 1968.
6. TL, April 4, 1968.
7. SP, April 5, 1968. SP, loose, undated pages. TL, April 4, 1968. JAC and Harry McPherson memo to LBJ, April 5, 1968, 3:30 A.M., Personal Papers. JAC memo to LBJ, April 5, 1968, 10:40 A.M., Personal Papers. JAC memo to LBJ, re John Gardner, undated, Personal Papers. Harry McPherson memo to James Jones, April 5, 1968, 4 A.M., Personal Papers. JAC memo to LBJ, April 5, 1968, 10:30 A.M., Personal Papers. JAC and Nicholas Katzenbach "Agenda for Meeting," April 5, 1968, 11:10 A.M., LBJ Library.
8. JAC and Harry McPherson memo to LBJ, April 5, 1968, 3:30 A.M., Personal Papers. PDD, April 5, 1968. James Gaither memo to LBJ, April 5, 1968, 8:35 A.M., LBJ Library.
9. JAC memo to LBJ, April 5, 1968, 11:22 A.M., LBJ Library. James Gaither memo to LBJ, April 5, 1968, 4:50 A.M., LBJ Library. PDD, April 5, 1968.
10. For this meeting, see: JAC memo to LBJ, April 5, 1968, 10:55 A.M. (Attachment: "Talking Points/Civil Rights Meeting—Friday"), Personal Papers. W. Thomas Johnson memo to LBJ, April 7, 1968 (Attachment: "Notes of the President's Meeting With Negro Leaders," April 5, 1968), LBJ Library.
11. PDD, April 5, 1968.
12. SP, March 25–April 12, 1968.

13. JAC memo to LBJ, April 5, 1968, 7:55 P.M. (Attachment: LBJ letter to Gerald Ford, April 5, 1968), Personal Papers.
14. OH, Victoria McCammon, June 8, 1975, tape 2 of 5, p. 46.
15. SP, April 21–May 2, 1968.
16. PDD, April 5, 1968.
17. SP, March 25–April 12, 1968.
18. Ibid. PDD, April 5, 1968.
19. See: Situation Room reports, King assassination disturbances, Personal Papers.
20. JAC memo to LBJ, April 5, 1968, 6 P.M., Personal Papers. JAC memo to LBJ, April 6, 1968, 3 P.M., Personal Papers. Matthew Nimetz memo to JAC, April 6, 1968, 5:40 P.M., Personal Papers. Cf. OH, Victoria McCammon, June 9, 1975, tape 4 of 5, pp. 14–15.
21. PDD, April 5, 1968.
22. Ibid.
23. Transcript of phone conversation between JAC and Cyrus Vance, undated, Personal Papers.
24. 69N.
25. PDD, April 5, 1968.
26. JAC memo to LBJ, April 6, 1968, 11:05 A.M., Personal Papers. JAC memo to LBJ, April 6, 1968, 11:50 A.M., Personal Papers.
27. JAC memo to LBJ, April 6, 1968, 2 P.M., Personal Papers.
28. Larry Temple memo to LBJ, April 6, 1968, 11:05 A.M., Personal Papers.
29. PDD, April 7, 1968.
30. Ibid.
31. For my conversation with Mrs. Johnson, see 69N. PDD, April 7, 1968.
32. Cf. OH, Victoria McCammon, June 8, 1975, tape 2 of 5, p. 38.
33. PDD, April 7, 1968. SP, March 25–April 12, 1968. JAC memo to LBJ, April 7, 1968, 4 P.M., Personal Papers. JAC memo to LBJ, April 8, 1968, 12:10 P.M., Personal Papers.
34. Carol memo to Marvin Watson, April 5, 1968, 5:45 P.M., Personal Papers.
35. JAC memo to LBJ, April 8, 1968, 1:50 P.M., Personal Papers. Marvin Watson memo to LBJ, April 8, 1968, Personal Papers. JAC memo to LBJ, April 8, 1968, 3:10 P.M., Personal Papers. Mike Manatos memo to LBJ, April 5, 1968, 3:30 P.M., Personal Papers. Marvin Watson memo to James Jones, April 5, 1968, 7:25 P.M., Personal Papers. Marie Fehmer memo to LBJ, April 5, 1968, 3:02 P.M., Personal Papers.
36. Marvin Watson memo to LBJ, April 8, 1968, Personal Papers. James Rowley memo to LBJ, April 8, 1968, Personal Papers.
37. SP, April 6–11, 1968. JAC memo to James Jones, April 12, 1968, Personal Papers. PDD, April 8, 1968.
38. JAC memo to LBJ, April 10, 1968, 12:20 P.M., Personal Papers.
39. For the King assassination, see: OH, JAC, October 17, 1969, pp. 25–36.
40. PDD, April 2, 1968. JAC memo to LBJ, April 3, 1968, 6:50 P.M., Personal Papers.

41. PDD, April 26, 1968. 69N.
42. JAC memo to LBJ, May 2, 1968, 8:30 P.M., Personal Papers.
43. PDD, May 3, 1968.
44. Ibid.
45. Off-the record press briefing by LBJ, aboard Air Force One, 11:58 A.M., May 3, 1968, Personal Papers.
46. Arthur Okun memo to LBJ, undated (Attachment: Arthur Okun memo to LBJ, May 21, 1968), Personal Papers.
47. JAC memo to LBJ, April 27, 1968, 6:55 P.M., Personal Papers. JAC memo to LBJ, May 16, 1968, 8:30 P.M., Personal Papers. Robert Taylor memo to James Jones, May 17, 1968, Personal Papers. JAC memo to LBJ, May 17, 1968, 7:30 P.M., Personal Papers. Robert Taylor memo to James Jones and JAC, May 20, 1968, 5 P.M., Personal Papers. Matthew Nimetz memo to JAC, May 23, 1968, Personal Papers. Matthew Nimetz memo to JAC, May 24, 1968, Personal Papers. Matthew Nimetz memo to JAC, May 28, 1968, Personal Papers. Matthew Nimetz memo to JAC, May 29, 1968, Personal Papers. Robert Taylor memo to James Jones and JAC, May 29, 1968, 3 P.M., Personal Papers. See also: Matthew Nimetz memo to JAC, June 8, 1968, Personal Papers. Lawrence Levinson memo to LBJ, June 18, 1968, 8:30 P.M., Personal Papers. Matthew Nimetz memo to JAC, June 20, 1968, Personal Papers. JAC memo to LBJ, June 21, 1968, 2:05 P.M., Personal Papers.
48. JAC memo to LBJ, May 22, 1968, 3:45 P.M., Personal Papers. JAC memo to LBJ, May 22, 1968, 4:05 P.M., Personal Papers. JAC memo to LBJ, May 22, 1968, 8:15 P.M., Personal Papers. JAC memo to LBJ, May 22, 1968, 8:30 P.M., Personal Papers. JAC memo to LBJ, May 23, 1968, 5 P.M., Personal Papers.

18. Who Is LBJ's Candidate?

1. 69N. AI, Mrs. Lyndon B. Johnson. AI, Robert Douglass. AI, Mrs. Nelson (Happy) Rockefeller.
2. Nelson Rockefeller letter to LBJ, January 7, 1966, LBJ Library. JAC memo to LBJ, January 14, 1966, 11:20 A.M., LBJ Library.
3. PDD, April 4, 1968. AI, Robert Douglass. JAC memo to LBJ, April 7, 1968, 1 A.M. (Attachment: Fred Bohen memo to JAC, April 5, 1968), Personal Papers.
4. PDD, April 23, 1968. OH, Larry Temple, June 26, 1970, tape 3, pp. 15–16.
5. AI, Mrs. Nelson (Happy) Rockefeller. AI, Mrs. Lyndon B. Johnson. AI, Robert Douglass.
6. OH, Victoria McCammon, June 8, 1975, tape 3 of 5, pp. 1 and 3.
7. OH, Victoria McCammon, June 8, 1975, tape 3 of 5, p. 1.
8. JAC memo to LBJ, April 24, 1968, 9:45 P.M., Personal Papers. JAC

memo to LBJ, April 25, 1968, 9 P.M., Personal Papers. SP, April 15–29, 1968.

9. PDD, April 25, 1968.

10. "Summary of Califano's telephone discussion with Ted Sorensen at 8:20 P.M., April 26," 1968, Personal Papers. SP, April 15–29, 1968.

11. For this meeting, see: PDD, April 29, 1968. SP, April 15–29, 1968.

19. THE ROBERT KENNEDY ASSASSINATION

1. OH, Victoria McCammon, June 8, 1975, tape 2 of 5, p. 9.

2. 69N.

3. SP, #24, August 13–26, 1966.

4. Charles Murphy, "Notes on Meeting of the President with Senator Robert Kennedy, April 3, 1968," draft, April 4, 1968, LBJ Library. Walt Rostow, "Memorandum of Conversation: The President, Senator Robert F. Kennedy, Theodore Sorensen, Charles Murphy, and W. W. Rostow, 10 A.M., April 3, 1968," LBJ Library.

5. JAC memo to Bill Moyers, December 10, 1966 (Attachment: "Reassessment of the Warren Commission Findings"), Personal Papers. Presidential counsel Lee White has no recollection of preparing the Attachment. It may be that he is not the person who sent me the attachment, despite what my memo to Moyers indicates.

6. OH, Victoria McCammon, June 8, 1975, tape 2 of 5, p. 10. AI, Victoria McCammon. AI, Lawrence O'Brien. OH, Round Table Discussion, May 4, 1990, pp. 165–67.

7. JAC memo to LBJ, December 8, 1967, 3:15 P.M., Personal Papers.

8. PDD, June 5, 1968.

9. JAC memo to LBJ, April 8, 1968, 12:20 P.M., Personal Papers. PDD, June 5, 1968.

10. PDD, June 5, 1965.

11. Ibid.

12. 69N.

13. JAC memo to LBJ, June 5, 1968, 2:45 P.M., Personal Papers. JAC memo to LBJ, June 6, 1968, 12:30 A.M., Personal Papers.

14. PDD, June 5, 1968.

15. Ibid.

16. Ibid.

17. PDD, June 6, 1968.

18. Ibid.

19. James Gaither memo to LBJ, June 6, 1968, 8:55 A.M., Personal Papers. James Gaither memo to LBJ, June 6, 1968, 9 A.M., Personal Papers. JAC memo to LBJ, June 6, 1968, 10:25 A.M., Personal Papers. JAC memo to LBJ, June 7, 1968, 10:45 A.M., Personal Papers. Ethel Kennedy letter to LBJ, June 19, 1968, Personal Papers.

20. PDD, June 6, 1968.

21. PDD, June 8, 1968.
22. PDD, June 7, 1968.
23. "Archbishop Cooke returning Mr. Califano's call re when President Johnson should arrive for funeral services," June 7, 1968, 10:45 P.M., Personal Papers.
24. PDD, June 8, 1968.
25. Ibid.
26. Ibid.
27. Ibid.
28. Ibid.
29. Ethel Kennedy letter to LBJ, June 19, 1968, Personal Papers.
30. LBJ Letter to Ethel Kennedy, June 19, 1968, Personal Papers.
31. PDD, June 10, 1968.
32. JAC memo to LBJ, June 9, 1968, 2:30 P.M. (Attachment: "Statement by President to the Commission Investigating Violence," June 9, 1968, draft), Personal Papers. JAC memo to LBJ, June 10, 1968, 10:05 A.M. (Attachment: "Statement by President to the Commission Investigating Violence"), Personal Papers.
33. AI, Mrs. Alan (Adrian) Barth. For Robert Kennedy's assassination, see: 69N. OH, JAC Interview I, April 14, 1969, pp. 30–31. JAC interview with Jean vanden Heuvel, September 21, 1968, pp. 7–15, Personal Papers.
34. Harry McPherson memo to LBJ, June 14, 1968, 6:50 P.M., Personal Papers. Ramsey Clark memo to LBJ, June 14, 1968, Personal Papers. Charles Zwick memo to LBJ, June 13, 1968, Personal Papers. JAC memo to LBJ, June 19, 1968, 2 P.M., Personal Papers. JAC memo to LBJ, June 19, 1968, 4:15 P.M., Personal Papers.
35. JAC memo to LBJ, June 17, 1968 (Attachment: "Safe Streets Act Signing Statement, June 17, 1968"), Personal Papers. Lawrence Levinson memo to JAC, June 18, 1968, Personal Papers. JAC memo to LBJ, June 19, 1968, 2 P.M. (Attachment: "Safe Streets Act Signing Statement, June 19, 1968"), Personal Papers. JAC memo to LBJ, June 19, 1968, 4:15 P.M. (Attachment: "Safe Streets Act Signing Statement, June 19, 1968"), Personal Papers.
36. JAC memo to LBJ, June 17, 1968, Personal Papers.

20. THE FORTAS FIASCO

1. OH, Larry Temple, August 11, 1970, tape 6, pp. 4–8.
2. OH, Larry Temple, August 11, 1970, tape 5, pp. 41–43.
3. Mike Manatos memo to LBJ, June 25, 1968, 3 P.M., LBJ Library.
4. JAC memo to LBJ, June 29, 1968, 5:50 P.M. (Attachment: *Chicago Tribune*, June 29, 1968, no page number), LBJ Library. Chronology of events relating to Fortas-Thornberry nominations, compiled by Jack Hushen, Press Secretary to Senator Griffin, LBJ Library.

5. SP, June 28–July 16, 1968.
6. Ibid. JAC memo to LBJ, June 29, 1968, 7:30 P.M., LBJ Library.
7. OH, Harry McPherson, September 19, 1985, Interview VII, pp. 4–5.
8. SP, June 28–July 16, 1968. JAC memo to LBJ, June 29, 1968, 7:30 P.M. (Attachment: First draft, Statement by Senator George Smathers, Confirmation of Justice Fortas), LBJ Library. JAC memo to LBJ, July 1, 1968, 3:25 P.M. (Attachment: Final version, Statement by Senator Smathers, Confirmation of Justice Fortas and Judge Thornberry), LBJ Library. Mike Manatos memo to LBJ, September 10, 1968, 6:30 P.M., LBJ Library.
9. SP, June 28–July 16, 1968.
10. AI, Larry Temple.
11. For Johnson's story, see: 69N.
12. Richard Russell letter to LBJ, July 1, 1968, LBJ Library.
13. Norma Arata memo to Dorothy Territo, July 2, 1968, 4 P.M., LBJ Library. Norma Arata memo to Dorothy Territo, July 29, 1968, LBJ Library.
14. For the Lawrence affair, see OH, Larry Temple, August 11, 1970, tape 5, pp. 12–40.
15. JAC memo to LBJ, June 17, 1968, Personal Papers. JAC memo to LBJ, July 23, 1968, 7 P.M., LBJ Library. PDD, July 25, 1968. Fortas's name appeared on the list of the attendees of this meeting, but it was crossed out. JAC memo to LBJ, July 26, 1968, 7 P.M. (Attachment: pamphlet, "I Want to Speak to You Tonight of Peace . . ."), LBJ Library. Charles Maguire memo to LBJ, July 27, 1968, LBJ Library.
16. OH, Victoria McCammon, June 9, 1975, tape 4 of 5, pp. 31–32.
17. OH, Larry Temple, August 11, 1970, tape 5, pp. 42–43.
18. James Gaither memo to JAC, August 19, 1968, LBJ Library. James Gaither memo to Larry Temple, August 29, 1968, Personal Papers. JAC memo to LBJ, September 11, 1968, 9:30 P.M., LBJ Library. JAC memo to LBJ, September 12, 1968, 7 P.M., LBJ Library. JAC memo to LBJ, September 13, 1968, 11:30 A.M., Personal Papers. AI, Harry McPherson.
19. James Jones memo to LBJ, September 6, 1968, 7:20 P.M., LBJ Library.
20. Paul Porter letter, February 1, 1968, Personal Papers.
21. Ibid.
22. JAC memo to Larry Temple, September 12, 1968 (Attachments: Dean Tennery letter, February 15, 1968, and Paul Porter letter, February 1, 1968), LBJ Library. AI, Larry Temple.
23. AI, Larry Temple.

21. Democratic National Convention and Presidential Campaign

1. OH, Larry Temple, August 13, 1970, tape 7, pp. 31–32. OH, George Christian, June 30, 1970, tape 4, p. 34.

2. JAC memo to LBJ, July 11, 1968, 6:30 P.M., Personal Papers. JAC memo to LBJ, July 15, 1968, 9:30 P.M., Personal Papers.
3. JAC memo to LBJ, July 30, 1968, 4 P.M., Personal Papers.
4. See, e.g., JAC memo to Robert Weaver, August 24, 1968, Personal Papers.
5. SP, April 15–29, 1968.
6. Daniel Walker, *Rights in Conflict: The Violent Confrontation of Demonstrators and Police in the Parks and Streets of Chicago During the Week of the Democratic National Convention of 1968*, November 1968, pp. 69–72.
7. Robert Hardesty and Harry Middleton memo for LBJ, August 23, 1968, Personal Papers. JAC memo to LBJ, August 25, 1968, 4:45 P.M., LBJ Library. JAC memo to LBJ, August 26, 1968, LBJ Library. AI, James Jones. PDD, August 26–27, 1968.
8. AI, James Jones. AI, Larry Temple.
9. OH, Round Table Discussion, April 17, 1984, pp. 68–69. AI, Larry Temple.
10. James Jones memo to LBJ, August 24, 1968, 1:10 P.M., LBJ Library. OH, Larry Temple, August 13, 1970, tape 7, p. 33. OH, Round Table Discussion, May 4, 1990, pp. 262–64.
11. OH, Larry Temple, August 13, 1970, tape 7, pp. 34–35. "Possible Opening Chicago," Liz Carpenter.
12. PDD, August 27, 1968.
13. OH, Round Table Discussion, April 17, 1984, p. 69. AI, Larry Temple.
14. AI, Larry Temple. AI, James Jones.
15. OH, Round Table Discussion, April 17, 1984, pp. 65–66 and p. 71.
16. PDD, July 31, 1968.
17. PDD, September 5, 1968.
18. DG, September 5, 1968.
19. For Humphrey's effort to recruit me, see 69N.
20. OH, Victoria McCammon, June 8, 1975, tape 3 of 5, p. 6.
21. DG, October 12, 1968.
22. DG, April 27, 1968. JAC memo to LBJ, April 27, 1968, 3:30 P.M. (Attachment: Memorandum, April 27, 1968, re Vietnam), Personal Papers.
23. PDD, April 27, 1968. JAC memo to LBJ, April 29, 1968, 5:20 P.M., Personal Papers. SP, April 15–29, 1968. TL, April 27, 1968. JAC memo to LBJ, April 29, 1968, Personal Papers.
24. For this meting, see: DG, April 30, 1968. PDD, April 30, 1968. SP, April 29–May 2, 1968. JAC memo for the record, May 1, 1968 (Attachment: Message from Pope Paul VI to LBJ), Personal Papers.
25. JAC memo for the record, May 1, 1968 (Attachment: LBJ letter to Pope Paul VI, May 1, 1968), Personal Papers.
26. PDD, May 3, 1968. For these contacts with the Pope, see 69N.
27. PDD, October 31, 1968. AI, Harry McPherson.
28. OH, Victoria McCammon, June 8, 1975, tape 3 of 5, p. 8.

29. OH, Victoria McCammon, June 8, 1975, tape 3 of 5, p. 9.
30. JAC letter to Hubert Humphrey, May 3, 1976, Personal Papers. Hubert Humphrey letter to JAC, October 4, 1976, Personal Papers.

22. WINDING DOWN

1. Arthur Okun memo to LBJ, December 27, 1968 (Attachments: budget tables), Personal Papers. JAC memo to LBJ, January 6, 1969, 5:20 P.M., Personal Papers.
2. SP, October 31–December 4, 1968.
3. For this meeting, see: PDD, January 6, 1969. SP, December 1968–January 1969.
4. JAC memo to LBJ, January 6, 1969, 10:05 P.M., Personal Papers.
5. JAC memo to LBJ, January 6, 1969, 11:25 A.M., Personal Papers. PDD, January 6, 1969. SP, January 1969.
6. PDD, January 6, 1969.
7. SP, January 1969. JAC memo to LBJ, January 6, 1969, 5:20 P.M., Personal Papers.
8. PDD, January 7, 1969.
9. Ibid.
10. PDD, January 10, 1969.
11. Ibid.
12. Ibid. For Kennedy and the tax surcharge, see 69N.
13. PDD, January 11 and 13, 1969.
14. PDD, January 19, 1969.
15. 69N. PDD, June 28–29, 1966. PDD, September 18, 1966. 69N.
16. PDD, January 19, 1969. AI, Robert Douglass.
17. PDD, January 19, 1969.
18. PDD, September 19, 1967.
19. Ibid.
20. DG, June 20, 1967. PDD, June 20, 1967.
21. SP, December 11–21, 1965. OH, Round Table Discussion, April 17, 1984, pp. 5–6.
22. OH, Victoria McCammon, June 8, 1975, tape 2 of 5, p. 44. OH, Victoria McCammon, June 8, 1975, tape 3 of 5, pp. 24–29.
23. 69N. OH, Round Table Discussion, April 17, 1984, p. 26.
24. Cf. OH, Round Table Discussion, April 17, 1984, p. 75.
25. AI, Harry McPherson and Horace Busby.
26. PDD, January 19, 1969.
27. Ibid.
28. Melville Grosvenor letter to LBJ, October 16, 1968, LBJ Library.
29. PDD, January 19, 1969.
30. W. Walt Rostow, "Memorandum of Conversation: The President, Senator Robert F. Kennedy, Theodore Sorensen, Charles Murphy, and W. W. Rostow, 10 A.M., April 3, 1968," LBJ Library.

Index

About the Author

JOSEPH A. CALIFANO, JR., was born on May 15, 1931, in Brooklyn, New York, where he grew up. He received his Bachelor of Arts degree from the College of the Holy Cross in 1952 and his LL.B. from Harvard Law School in 1955. Mr. Califano then served for three years as a commissioned officer in the office of the Judge Advocate General of the Navy in Washington, D.C. After three years with Governor Thomas Dewey's Wall Street law firm, he joined the Kennedy administration, first as special assistant to Defense Department General Counsel Cyrus Vance, and then successively as special assistant to the Secretary of the Army, general counsel of the Army, and Secretary of Defense Robert McNamara's special assistant and top troubleshooter. President Lyndon Johnson named Mr. Califano his special assistant for domestic affairs in 1965, a position he held until the President left office on January 20, 1969. During his service in that post, *The New York Times* called Mr. Califano "Deputy President for Domestic Affairs." In accepting his resignation, the President wrote, "You were the captain I wanted and you steered the course well." From 1969 to 1977, Mr. Califano practiced law in Washington, D.C., and served as attorney for *The Washington Post*, *Newsweek*, and others during the Watergate years, and as counsel to the Democratic National Committee from 1969 to 1972. From 1977 to 1979, he was Secretary of Health, Education, and Welfare. Since then he has been practicing law in Washington, D.C., and New York City most recently with Dewey Ballantine. In 1982 and 1983, he served as special counsel to the House Committee on Standards of Official Conduct, to head the committee's investigation of allegations of drug use and sexual misconduct involving members of Congress and pages. Mr. Califano is the author of seven previous books (two with Howard Simons, former managing editor of *The Washington Post*) and has written articles for *The New York Times*, *The Washington Post*, *Reader's Digest*, *The New Republic*, and other publications. Mr. Califano serves on several corporate and nonprofit boards and is recognized as an expert on health-care costs and the health-care industry, subjects on which he consults and lectures.